SYMBOLIC COMPUTATION

Computer Graphics – Systems and Applications

Springer Series
SYMBOLIC COMPUTATION
Computer Graphics – Systems and Applications

J. Encarnação, E. G. Schlechtendahl:
Computer Aided Design. Fundamentals and System Architectures. IX, 346 pages, 183 figs., 1983

G. Enderle, K. Kansy, G. Pfaff:
Computer Graphics Programming. GKS – The Graphics Standard. Second, revised and enlarged edition, XXII, 651 pages, 100 figs., 1987

J. Encarnação, R. Schuster, E. Vöge (eds.):
Product Data Interfaces in CAD/CAM Applications. Design, Implementation and Experiences. IX, 270 pages, 147 figs., 1986

U. Rembold, R. Dillmann (eds.): Computer-Aided Design and Manufacturing. Methods and Tools. Second, revised and enlarged edition, XIV, 458 pages, 304 figs., 1986

Y. Shirai: Three-Dimensional Computer Vision. XII, 296 pages, 313 figs., 1987

Yoshiaki Shirai

Three-Dimensional Computer Vision

With 313 Figures

Springer-Verlag
Berlin Heidelberg New York
London Paris Tokyo

Yoshiaki Shirai
Computer Vision Section, Computer Science Division
Electrotechnical Laboratory
1-1-4, Umezono, Sakuramura, Niiharigun
Ibaraki, 305 Japan

ISBN-13: 978-3-642-82431-9 e-ISBN-13: 978-3-642-82429-6
DOI: 10.1007/978-3-642-82429-6

Library of Congress Cataloging in Publication Data. Shirai, Yoshiaki. Three-dimensional computer vision. (Symbolic computation. Computer graphics) Bibliography: p. 1. Computer vision. 2. Three-dimensional display systems. I. Title. II. Series. TA1632.S55 1986 006.4'2 86-25996

2145/3140-543210

Preface

The purpose of computer vision is to make computers capable of understanding environments from visual information. Computer vision has been an interesting theme in the field of artificial intelligence. It involves a variety of intelligent information processing: both pattern processing for extraction of meaningful symbols from visual information and symbol processing for determining what the symbols represent. The term "3D computer vision" is used if visual information has to be interpreted as three-dimensional scenes. 3D computer vision is more challenging because objects are seen from limited directions and some objects are occluded by others.

In 1980, the author wrote a book "Computer Vision" in Japanese to introduce an interesting new approach to visual information processing developed so far. Since then computer vision has made remarkable progress: various rangefinders have become available, new methods have been developed to obtain 3D information, knowledge representation frameworks have been proposed, geometric models which were developed in CAD/CAM have been used for computer vision, and so on. The progress in computer vision technology has made it possible to understand more complex 3D scenes.

There is an increasing demand for 3D computer vision. In factories, for example, automatic assembly and inspection can be realized with fewer constraints than conventional ones which employ two-dimensional computer vision. 3D vision is being developed for mobile robots capable of passing through corridors and stairs, avoiding obstacles. Those robots are useful not only for carrying objects in factories but also for work in hazardous conditions such as in nuclear plants.

This book describes the fundamental technology of 3D computer vision for various demands. The first four chapters are devoted to basic methods of computer vision. Chapter 5 deals with the interpretation of two-dimensional line drawings as 3D objects. In Chapter 6, a gradient space method and a new algebraic method are introduced for determining whether a given line drawing really corresponds to an actual scene or not. Chapter 7 describes approaches to stereo vision, which is now attracting great interest as a next generation robot vision. Chapter 8 introduces methods of obtaining 3D shape information from monocular images making use of various constraints on scenes. The last six chapters deal with the processing of 3D information and the construction of explicit descriptions of scenes using knowledge about objects.

I hope that this book will provide readers with an insight into the current status of 3D computer vision technology and a firm basis for developing or applying this technology.

Ibaraki, January 1987 Y. Shirai

Table of Contents

1 Introduction

1.1 Three-Dimensional Computer Vision

The purpose of computer vision is to enable a computer to understand its environment from visual information. Visual information processing holds an important position in the intelligent activities of humans. Computer vision, therefore, has been of interest as a research theme in artificial intelligence (AI), and has been studied from the early stages of AI research.

Objects of computer vision may be outdoor scenes, indoor scenes, machine parts, characters, and so on. Practical systems have been developed for some particular purposes such as reading characters, i.e., optical character recognition (OCR), automatic bonding of integrated circuits (ICs), inspection of printed circuit boards, and so on. Most practical systems deal with two-dimensional (2D) objects. Computer vision addresses difficult fields in which basic techniques have not yet been established. Since a method of understanding three-dimensional (3D) scenes is not yet established, such scenes have been the most popular objects of research into computer vision. The term '3D computer vision' is used to specify explicitly the objects of this type of computer vision. In the early years of AI research, however, the term 'scene analysis' was used to accentuate the distinction between 3D computer vision and the processing of two-dimensional images.

3D computer vision processes comprise many components which perform particular functions in coordination with other components. Figure 1.1 is a block diagram of the main components and types of information involved in such a process. First, visual information must be taken from a 3D scene. Input may be light intensity images, color images, or range data (directly or derived from multiple images).

The rest of the processing sequence depends on tasks, objects, and/or *a priori* information. A typical process for a light intensity image of a simple scene with a block and a triangular prism is as follows. Edges are extracted from the input image as those points where the light intensity changes abruptly (illustrated in Fig. 1.2(a)). Note that these edges are image features and therefore need not correspond to edges of surfaces of real objects. Series of edges are obtained by connecting edges; those with open ends are removed, and line equations are fitted to the series. The result is a line drawing as shown in Fig. 1.2(b). The line drawing is still an image feature. Processing up to the stage of obtaining image features is called low level processing.

The line drawing is interpreted as a 3D scene by assigning physical meanings to the lines. The result is illustrated in Fig. 1.2(c), where labels attached to lines denote the meanings. The interpreted line drawing is a scene description because lines with labels represent features (edges of surfaces) of the scene. Now the line drawing is segmented into two parts (by following arrows in Fig. 1.2(c)). Each part is

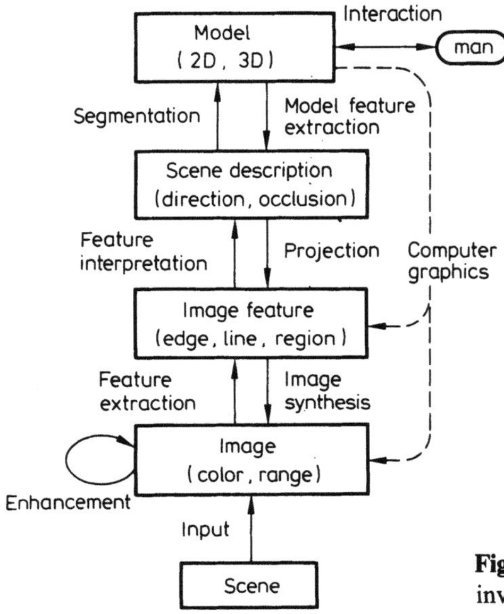

Fig. 1.1. Main components and information types involved in computer vision

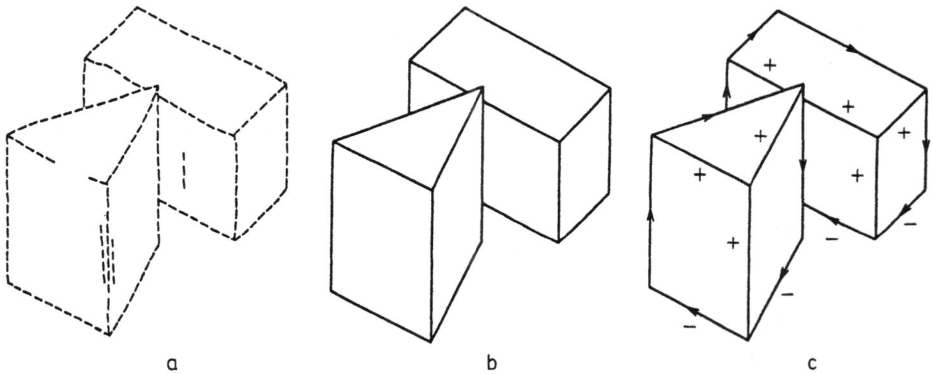

Fig. 1.2a–c. Example of image understanding process: **(a)** edges extracted from input image; **(b)** line drawing; **(c)** interpreted line drawing

recognized by being matched to object models which are stored in the computer system by humans. Processing after the extraction of image features is called high level processing.

This example is called a 'bottom-up' process because it proceeds from the bottom to the top in Fig. 1.1. The bottom-up process is not always effective. If enough constraints are imposed on the object class and the orientation of objects, the image can be directly matched to object models (expected images of objects). The top-down process is very efficient because it can obtain the result with the minimum of computation. This top-down process is often employed in industrial applications such as locating IC chips for bonding. It is seen that recognition of objects requires matching of information derived from the scene to object models at some level. Object models at various levels may be prepared by humans or transformed automatically from those at other levels.

The top-down process is impractical if too few constraints are available, because a great number of object models is required. In that case, matching must be performed at a higher level. Recognition of blocks of various sizes, for example, may be achieved by matching at the level of image features. In order to understand complex scenes, however, a simple bottom-up or top-down process is insufficient. The result of a bottom-up process may be used in higher level processing, and the result of higher level processing may be used in lower level processing.

Several of the many techniques used in 3D computer vision were originally developed in other fields. Examples are noise removal, feature extraction, and pattern matching. This book does not deal with all of those techniques, but concentrates on the subjects most closely related to the main stream of research in 3D computer vision.

One of the most important problems in 3D computer vision is the recognition of 3D objects from their partial view. Objects may be occluded by other objects or even by themselves. It is, in principle, impossible to see occluded parts. However, if something is known *a priori* about the scene or, in other words, if models of objects are given, occluded parts can be inferred and objects recognized.

Another important problem is the interpretation of 2D images as 3D scenes. For example, humans can guess convex and concave edges from a photograph of blocks. This problem has been intensively dealt with in the field of AI.

Use of range data is also an interesting problem. It was not much studied until range data recently became easily obtainable by various methods. Range data provide more reliable information about geometries of scenes than light intensity, facilitating the solution of higher level problems such as matching 3D models to range data of a scene with multiple objects occluding one another.

1.2 Related Fields

There are many fields which share common techniques of visual image processing. Examples are image processing, pattern classification, pattern recognition, image understanding, and computer graphics. Among these, image understanding is taken to have a similar meaning to computer vision. Although the other fields were originally different from 3D computer vision, the distinction is diminishing. In particular, image processing and pattern recognition are no longer distinguished from computer vision. Brief descriptions of the fields related to computer vision are given in the following subsections.

1.2.1 Image Processing

The purpose of image processing or picture processing in the narrow sense is to improve an input image for the benefit of human viewers. For example, defocused images are sharpened, or the contrast is changed so that important parts may be

Table 1.1. Feature set of five characters

Character	Number of holes	Number of end points
A	1	2
B	2	0
C	0	2
D	1	0
E	0	3

enhanced. As well as digital processors, analog signal processors or even optical equipment can provide fast image processing.

Since image processing is performed for human inspection, details (or parameters) of processing are specified by humans. The processing system, therefore, is not concerned with what the image represents.

1.2.2 Pattern Classification and Pattern Recognition

The purpose of pattern classification is to classify a given pattern into predetermined categories. A typical example is character recognition. Each input character is discrete, and categories of characters are fixed. Pattern classification can be regarded as a special case of computer vision in that the output is only the name of an object.

Patterns are usually classified according to a set of features extracted from the input image. The feature set is compared with that predetermined for each category, and a decision is made based on some criterion. Since the purpose is to discriminate a category from others, the classifying system need not be concerned with what the image represents. A best feature set may be selected on the basis of statistical theories. In a simple case, features may be used which are easy to extract. For example, if given categories of characters are 'A', 'B', 'C', 'D', and 'E', then the number of holes and the number of end points may be a feature set for classification as shown in Table 1.1. The selected feature set, therefore, need not describe the image.

The decision is simple if a set of reliable features is extracted, and the set coincides with one of the model categories. In practice, however, a set of extracted features is not identical to any of the models. The decision must be made to which model it is the most similar. In such a case, statistical decision theories are often employed.

In the early days, pattern classification was the only research field that can be regarded as pattern recognition. For this historical reason, the term 'pattern recognition' is, in the narrow sense, equivalent to pattern classification.

1.2.3 Computer Graphics

The purpose of computer graphics is to generate images by means of a computer. It is just the opposite of computer vision. The input to computer graphics is often the description of images. Real images may be taken as an input to graphics. They are edited by a human operator for use in the generation of new images. Computer graphics is important in computer aided design (CAD) for the display of designed objects to a designer. In order to display images some kind of image processing is necessary. This is sometimes called 'image processing' in the field of CAD, although the term is not proper.

Techniques of computer graphics are used to transform higher level models into lower level models as shown in Fig. 1.1. Many lower level models can be generated from a single 3D model.

Realistic images have recently been generated from the 3D description of a scene. The problem of representing the 3D description is also important in 3D computer vision. The development of methods for describing moving objects is a common problem requiring future solution.

1.3 Mainstream of 3D Computer Vision Research

The history of computer vision research is reviewed in this section. It is easy to trace the main streams of research in the early stages of the field's development because there were few research groups in the world. Now, however, computer vision is studied in universities, institutes, and companies in many countries. It is, therefore, difficult to decide which are the current main streams. Representative areas of work up to a few years ago are described briefly below. Most of these areas will be examined in greater detail in the succeeding chapters.

1.3.1 Pioneering Work

Prior to the development of computer vision, work was carried out on image processing and pattern recognition. Typical examples are character recognition and chromosome analysis. Most of them concerned classification of 2D patterns of isolated (or segmented) objects.

The pioneering work in 3D computer vision was that of Roberts in the early 1960s at MIT Lincoln Laboratory. His program understood scenes with polyhedra from their photographs. Edge points were first detected from the input image and then linked into series of points. Line equations were fitted to them, and the resultant line drawing was the description of the image.

Roberts' program had 3D models to recognize each polyhedron. The representation of the model resembled that for computer graphics. It was represented by the coordinates of the vertices. A set of vertices was selected in the line drawing and matched to models. When the match succeeded, the object was completely recognized in that the 3D structure was known even in the occluded parts. This was the greatest difference from conventional 2D image processing.

Roberts' work included many useful components of 3D computer vision: edge detection, edge linking, line drawings, 3D models, and matching. However, the program was just a serial combination of those components from low level to higher level processing. This bottom-up approach had a limitation because a component can use only the result of the previous component. Therefore, input images must be simple and clean enough for every component to process correctly.

1.3.2 First Generation Robot Vision

In the late 1960s, projects on intelligent robots were undertaken by a few research centers: Massachusetts Institute of Technology (MIT), Stanford University (Nilsson, 1969), Stanford Research Institute (SRI) (Feldman et al., 1969), and Edinburgh University. They may be called the first generation intelligent robots. The task of a vision system for such a robot was to recognize blocks on a controlled background. The level of the task was not higher than that of Roberts' work. The main emphasis was on testing the feasibility of computer vision and on demonstrating the possibility of integrated robots.

Through these experiments, it was learned that real visual data are so different from what we might expect that the series of detected edge points include spurious edges and exclude real edges.

Fig. 1.3. Assembly by visual feedback (Shirai and Inoue, 1973)

Stimulated by those demonstrations, intelligent robot projects started in Japan around 1968 at the Electrotechnical Laboratory (ETL) and Hitachi Company. The results of these projects were demonstrated in 1970. Hitachi's robot constructed an assembly of blocks as specified by a drawing (Ejiri et al., 1972). The ETL showed many fundamental techniques (ETL, 1971) including an assembly task by visual feedback (Fig. 1.3).

Although the first generation intelligent robot had a limited capability, it had much influence on later work. Many research themes were born and developed during the project, and many important problems, whose solutions were required if the limitations of robot vision were to be overcome, were revealed.

1.3.3 Interpretation of Line Drawings

Interpretation of line drawings of polyhedra was first studied by Guzman at MIT in the late 1960s. In contrast to Roberts' work, his program, SEE, tried to segment a line drawing into bodies without using object models. Guzman paid attention to the shape of junctions that appear in line drawings and made many heuristic rules for grouping regions in line drawings. While SEE demonstrated a remarkable performance for some complex line drawings, it failed for other drawings. The reason for failure was not clear because the decision was based on heuristics.

In 1971 Huffman at the University of California at Santa Cruz and Clowes at Sussex University independently proposed a theory of line drawings. Lines in a drawing may correspond to convex edges, concave edges, or discontinuous (occluding) edges in the 3D scene. Interpretation of line drawings is reduced to asigning these line types to all the lines. For a given class of objects, shapes of junctions are classified, and types of lines involved in each junction are enumerated. Then the interpretation problem is to determine line types that are consistent with the allowable junction types.

In 1972 Waltz at MIT extended this theory to a larger set of line types, including shadow edges. Interpretation of polyhedral line drawings was almost completed. However, these methods work only for correct line drawings. The work of line drawing interpretation was extended in a few different directions: interpretation of imperfect line drawings, that of curved objects, and determination of realizability of line drawings.

In 1972 Falk at Stanford University developed a program, INTERPRET, for interpreting line drawings with missing lines. INTERPRET segmented lines and inserted lines according to heuristic rules and 3D models of polyhedra. The interpretation was verified by matching the modified drawing to the original one.

1.3.4 Feature Extraction

In the 1960s most vision projects extracted line drawings from gray images in ways similar to Roberts' method: detect edge points, link them into sequences, and fit line equations to the sequences. In Roberts' method, edge detection was performed by a 2×2 filter. Later various 3×3 filters were proposed and became more popular.

In 1970 Brice and Fennema at SRI proposed a region method. It detected uniform regions by merging similar small regions. The method was extended and applied to recognition of curved objects by Popplestone et al. at Edinburgh University. Later, region splitting methods and split-and-merge methods were developed. Most color image analysis projects have used region methods.

1.3.5 Range Data Processing

Realizing that extraction of line drawings from gray images is difficult, a few research groups developed rangefinders to directly obtain geometries of scenes. The rangefinders project a sheet of light on objects and observe the image with a TV camera. In 1971, the author presented the results of a study of the recognition of polyhedra using range data. Later a group at Stanford University (Agin and Binford, 1973) represented range data of curved objects by general cylinders.

It is easy to obtain the types of edges or 3D surface equations directly from range data. Taking advantage of this facility, ETL developed in the 1970s a method for describing scenes with polyhedra and simple curved objects in terms of edges guided by a junction dictionary, and a method for recognizing objects occluding one another. Since the development of rangefinders took much effort, there has, until recently, been little work on range data processing. Recently, however, commercial rangefinders have become available. Not only research institutes but industrial companies are trying to apply range data processing techniques to the sensor data of industrial robots.

1.3.6 Realizability of Line Drawings

When the method of interpreting perfect line drawings was developed, a problem of realizability was raised by Huffman in 1971. It was not known whether interpreted line drawings really exist or not. He proposed 'dual space' to test the realizability. The dual space was also called 'gradient space' because it represents the direction of surface normals. Some impossible line drawings were detected by transforming the line drawing into the gradient space. An acceptable result of a test by this method, however, was not a sufficient condition for a line drawing to be realizable.

On the other hand, Falk proposed, for interpretation of line drawings, the use of plane equations for the determination of the 3D geometry of polyhedra. The method was further extended to an algebraic theory for the determination of the realizability of any interpreted line drawings.

Although gradient space was not adequate to provide a complete solution, it did provide 3D computer vision with a useful representation of objects. For example, recovery (or reconstruction) of a three-dimensional surface has been explained conveniently in terms of gradient space.

1.3.7 Use of Knowledge About Scenes

Use of range data is one way to obtain reliable descriptions of scenes. Another way is to use knowledge about scenes to compensate for imperfect descriptions. If we regard a line drawing as representing edges of objects, the complete line drawing is not always obtained. If we admit lines corresponding to boundaries of uniform brightness, then the line drawing may include spurious edges or exclude real edges.

Humans usually interpret the same image, or even the same imperfect line drawing, correctly because they have knowledge about objects in a scene. Instead of the bottom-up approach, a heterarchical approach was proposed by Minsky and Papert (Winston, 1972). In 1972 the author implemented at MIT a heterarchical program for semantic finding. The program guessed where lines would be found and what type of lines they might be, based on semantics of polyhedra and lines obtained previously.

At Stanford University, Yakimovsky and Feldman (1973) developed a semantics-based region analyzer which started from an incomplete result of a region method and obtained better regions with the interpretations based on a statistical decision theory. In 1976, a method of interpretation-guided segmentation was proposed by an SRI vision group. It also merged imperfect regions obtained by a region method based on a model of the scene. The model represented the geometrical relationship among regions. Those two were typical works which interpreted color images of real outdoor scenes and indoor scenes.

1.3.8 Use of Physics of Imaging

By formulating the relation between the geometry of a scene and the observed image(s), 3D surfaces may be recovered completely or partially. At the end of the 1960s, Horn proposed, in his thesis at MIT, a method of recovering shape from shading. The method used the relation between the light intensity of an image and the surface normal of 3D bodies. The shape was recovered by solving differential equations derived from the relation.

If the reflectance of a surface is known, the light intensity of a point in the image constrains the surface normal to a one-dimensional locus in the gradient space. In the mid-1970s, Horn developed the so-called 'photometric stereo' method: recovering surface normals from multiple images illuminated from different directions.

Barrow and Tenenbaum (1978) at SRI discussed the problem of recovering characteristics of a scene from the image. The characteristics of a scene were discriminated from that of the image, and were called 'intrinsic characteristics'. They argued that the intrinsic characteristics are obtainable by a nonpurposive process (without semantics) exploiting constraints derived from assumptions about the nature of the scene and the physics of the imaging process.

Constraints on the 3D geometry were also exploited for shape recovery. At the end of the 1970s, Kender at Carnegie-Mellon University (CMU) recovered the surface normal of a plane from regularly planed textures, and Kanade at CMU proposed a method of shape recovery exploiting a symmetry assumption.

1.3.9 Marr's Theory of Human Vision and Computer Vision

In the late 1970s, Marr's work on the theory of human vision greatly influenced thinking on computer vision. He argued that the vision process transforms original images into three levels of representation: primal sketch, $2\frac{1}{2}$D sketch, and 3D representation. The primal sketch is a collection of image features: various light intensity changes. The $2\frac{1}{2}$D sketch stores information about surfaces. Finally, 3D representation of each object is expressed with an object-centered coordinate.

His group at MIT implemented the theory as computer programs. Observations in human vision systems or empirical psychology were modeled in feature extraction, feature aggregation (like edge linking), and stereopsis. Many research projects followed those ideas: use of the zero-crossing as the image feature, feature-based stereo, and hierarchical models.

2 Image Input

Human eyes capture visual information which includes light intensity, color, and range. Unfortunately, no such powerful input device is currently available for computer vision.

In the early stage of 3D computer vision research, even obtaining light intensity images was a difficult problem. Roberts (1963), for example, took a photograph of a scene and converted it to a video signal by a facsimile device. Later, television (TV) cameras were employed for directly obtaining light intensity images from scenes. Only direct data capturing methods are described in this chapter. Color images are similarly obtained by a color TV camera or a combination of filters and a monochromatic TV camera. Range data acquisition is still a difficult problem. Direct range data input methods are described in this chapter; other methods which require sophisticated calculation (stereo vision) or knowledge of surface reflectance (photometric stereo) are described later.

2.1 Imaging Geometry

Most imaging devices employ a set of lenses to produce an image of a scene in a specified plane (image plane or focal plane). The imaging geometry can be

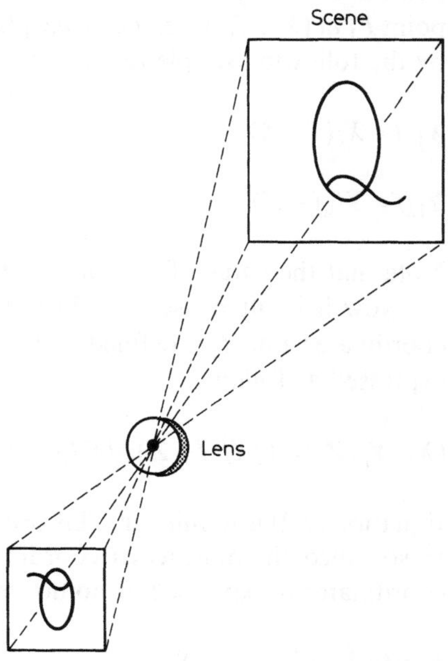

Fig. 2.1. Camera model

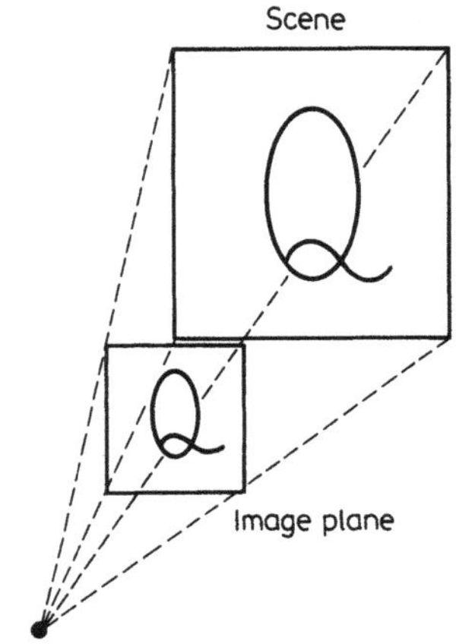

Fig. 2.2. Revised camera model

represented by a camera model such as that shown in Fig. 2.1, in which a single lens replaces the set of lenses used for a typical optical system. The rectangular image plane is behind the lens and the image is reversed. It is more convenient to rearrange the geometry so that the image plane is placed at the symmetrical position with respect to the lens center (see Fig. 2.2). Now the same image is obtained except that it is not reversed.

The coordinate system X–Y–Z is set so that the X–Y plane coincides with the image plane, with the origin at its centre (see Fig. 2.3). The view point (lens center) is on the Z axis at $Z=f$ (f is the focal length of the lens) and looking in the negative direction of the Z axis.

Let us formulate the relation between a point in a scene and the corresponding point in the image plane. Suppose a point P at (X, Y, Z) in a scene is mapped to a point P_1 at $(X_1, Y_1, 0)$ in the image plane as shown in Fig. 2.3. X_1 and Y_1 are derived by the following simple relations:

$$X_1/f=X/(f-Z)$$
$$Y_1/f=Y/(f-Z) \tag{2.1}$$

Note that the value of Z is always negative.

Now it is often useful to introduce the depth of the projected point, whose coordinate value Z_1 is defined in the same way as in Eq. (2.1). Thus the new point is expressed as follows:

$$(X_1, Y_1, Z_1)=(fX/(f-Z), fY/(f-Z), fZ/(f-Z)) \ . \tag{2.2}$$

Equation (2.2) is nonlinear. This projection is expressed as a linear transformation in so-called 'homogeneous coordinates'. The vector $V=(X, Y, Z)$ in Cartesian coordinates is expressed in homogeneous coordinates as:

$$V_h=(wX, wY, wZ, w)^t \tag{2.3}$$

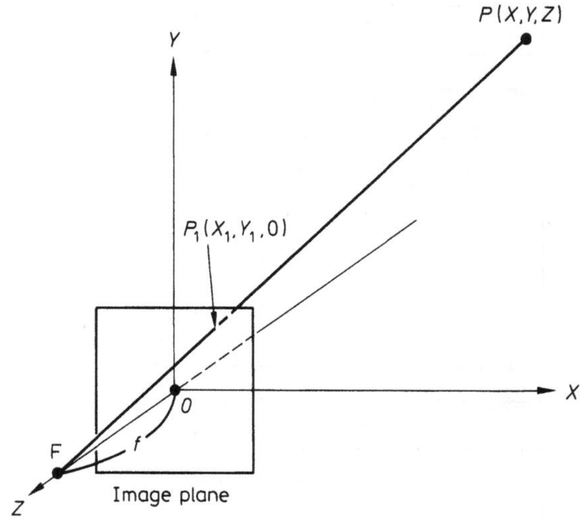

Fig. 2.3. Relation between scene and image

where w is an arbitrary constant. Note that $(wX, wY, wZ, w)^t$ is equivalent to $(X, Y, Z, 1)^t$.

The projection defined by Eq. (2.2) is expressed in homogeneous coordinates as a linear matrix operation:

$$(X_{h1}, Y_{h1}, Z_{h1}, w_1)^t = \begin{pmatrix} 1 & 0 & 0 & 0 \\ 0 & 1 & 0 & 0 \\ 0 & 0 & 1 & 0 \\ 0 & 0 & -1/f & 1 \end{pmatrix} (wX, wY, wZ, w)^t . \tag{2.4}$$

In fact, by letting arbitrary w be 1, we obtain the homogeneous coordinates vector $(X, Y, Z, (f-Z)/f)^t$, which is equivalent to Eq. (2.2).

This projection is called perspective projection. The projected size of an object decreases with increasing distance of the object from the image plane. Thus the projection of parallel lines may be distorted such that two lines come together. If the lens center is placed infinitely far from the image plane (i.e., f is infinity), the projection is orthographic. In orthographic projection, $X = X_1$, and $Y = Y_1$. If the distance of a camera from objects is large compared with their sizes, perspective projection can be approximated by orthographic projection. This facilitates calculation because orthographic projection is much simpler.

2.2 Image Input Devices

There are many methods for directly obtaining a digital image of light intensity in a computer. In any method, a video signal is first obtained, and then the analog signal is converted to a digital image. This section describes typical imaging devices for obtaining video signals.

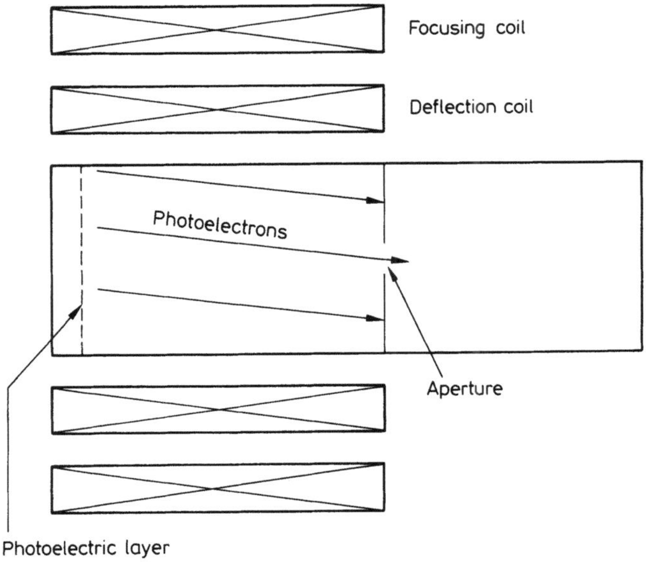

Fig. 2.4. Image dissector

2.2.1 Image Dissector

The image dissector was used at an early stage of computer vision. The principle of its operation is shown schematically in Fig. 2.4. An image is projected by an optical system on a cathode which is coated with a photoelectric layer. Photoelectrons are emitted by the cathode in proportion to the light intensity, and an electron image is produced on the aperture plane. A small part of the electron image is allowed to pass through the aperture and is detected by a photomultiplier. The detected part of the image is called a pixel or a picture element. By controlling the current in the deflection coil, a computer can access any part of the image.

One of the advantages of the image dissector is that the scanning speed is determined by a computer. Thus even a slow computer can input an image directly to the memory. Another advantage is the ability of random scanning. A computer can use the image dissector as an image memory which provides any pixel data on demand. These advantages were attractive to users of early computers with low memory capacity.

On the other hand, a disadvantage of the image dissector is that it takes a long time to take one pixel data. Detection of light intensity starts when the deflection is fixed. A certain number of electrons must be detected in order to obtain a high signal-to-noise (S/N) ratio. The image dissector is now used only for special purposes.

2.2.2 Vidicon

The vidicon is most widely used for computer vision as a conventional TV camera. An image is projected on a transparent electrode surface attached to a photoconductive layer (Fig. 2.5). The photoconductor is regarded as an array of pixels, each

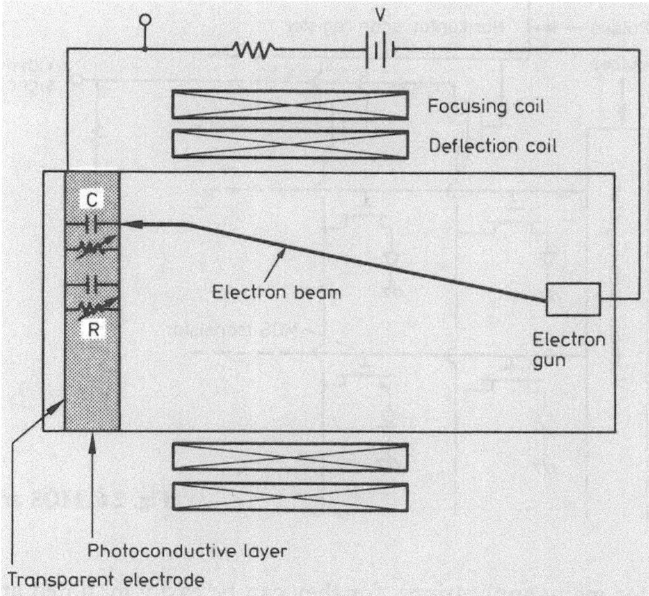

Fig. 2.5. Vidicon

of which consists of a resistor and a capacitor. An electron beam is emitted from the electron gun, deflected, and focused at the photoconductive layer. When a portion of the photoconductor is struck by the electron beam, the capacitor is charged. While the beam is scanning other parts of the photoconductor, the capacitor is discharged. The discharge rate depends on the resistance of the photoconductor, which decreases with increasing intensity of light incident upon it. When this part is again scanned by the beam, the amount of discharge is detected as the modulation of the electron beam current as it recharges the capacitor. The scanning rate must be fixed; it is usually 60 frames/s, or 30 frames/s in the case of interlace.

One of the advantages of the vidicon is that an entire image is input rapidly with a high S/N ratio, because the charge on each pixel is the integral of light intensity during a scanning cycle. It is interesting that an instantaneous image is obtained by use of strobe-light illumination, for discharge occurs at all pixels only during the flash. A better image of moving objects is obtained by this method. Another advantage is that the vidicon tube is small, light and cheap, compared with other image tubes.

The disadvantage is that the scanning rate is fixed and a random scan is impossible. This is no longer a serious limitation, however, owing to the development of high speed A/D converters and cheap, fast memories.

2.2.3 Solid Devices

The solid camera device is principally an array of photosensitive elements integrated in a chip. Thus it can be made much smaller than camera tubes and has no geometrical distortions. Solid devices have recently come to replace camera tubes

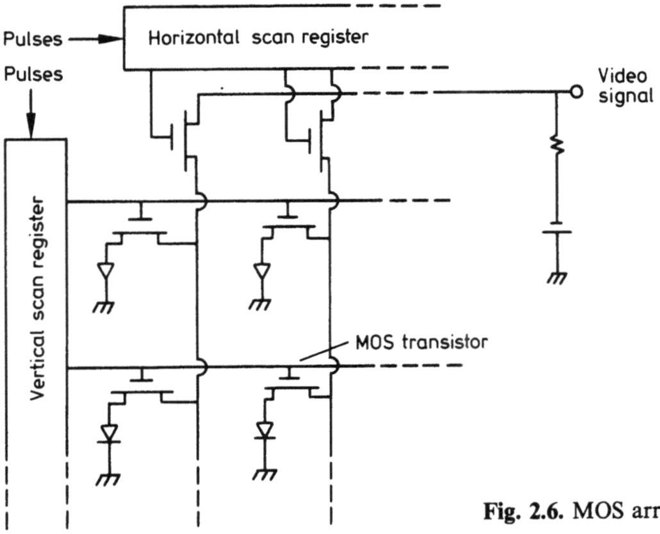

Fig. 2.6. MOS array

for many applications, for they can be easily mounted at a variety of places. The scanning mode of the solid camera device is similar to that of the vidicon camera in that the amount of the charge integrated during a fixed time (usually 1/60 s or 1/30 s) is transferred to the output. Solid cameras are categorized according to the charge transfer method into two types.

One type consists of an array of MOS transistors or MOS capacitors. The charges induced by light are read by an X–Y addressing technique (Fig. 2.6 shows an example of an MOS type device). This type was the first to be developed and is now used in practice.

Another type transfers charges like shift registers. The typical device is a charge-coupled device (CCD) which consists of an array of closely spaced MOS capacitors. Charges are transferred to neighboring elements by applying a series of clocking pulses to the electrodes. Figure 2.7 shows a frame transfer CCD. The charges are

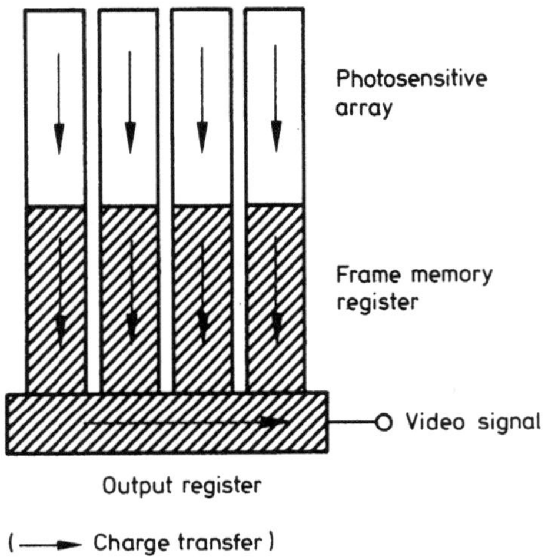

Fig. 2.7. CCD array (frame transfer type)

transferred to a frame memory register during a blanking period (between the end and beginning of a scanning), and read while MOS capacitors are storing charges. Another method transfers charges to neighboring shift registers and then transfers through the shift registers line by line. The CCD device can be integrated more efficiently and is thus expected to be used widely.

2.3 Color

Color plays an important role in human visual perception. Computer vision also needs color information, especially for recognition of natural scenes such as those including the sky, water, trees, etc. There are three factors in human color sensation: hue, saturation, and brightness. Hue mainly determines the name of each color such as red or yellow. Saturation represents 'purity' of color. For example, the saturation of red is higher than that of pink. Brightness (intensity) determines the strength of color in the same manner as in monochromatic images.

2.3.1 Color Representation

When we see light of a single wavelength, we have a certain color sensation. However, natural scenes do not usually emit single-wavelength light. In spite of that, we have a single color sensation. We cannot, for example, discriminate yellow which is made by adding red and green from that of a single wavelength. It is well known that almost all colors can be synthesized with a weighted sum of three principal colors. Usually red, green, and blue are selected as the principal colors. Let ***R***, ***G***, and ***B*** denote unit vectors corresponding to three principal colors; then every color is represented by components of these vectors ***R***, ***G***, and ***B***. These three values are called tristimulus values. Note that tristimulus values are psychological values which depend on each individual. Now any color can be represented by a

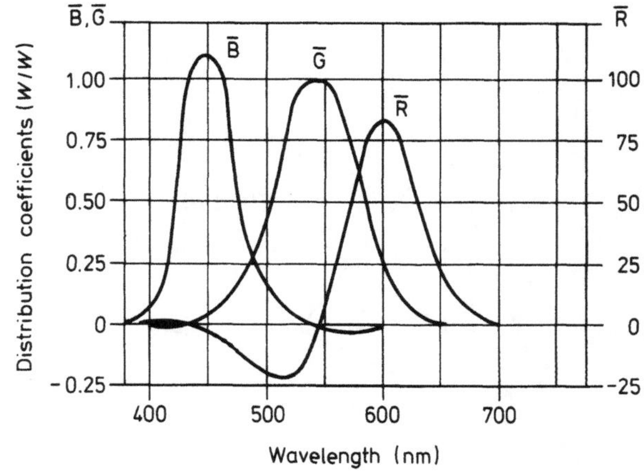

Fig. 2.8. Distribution coefficient curves (powers of (***R***), (***G***), and (***B***) equivalent to 1 W single-wavelength color)

vector (R, G, B). Some colors, however, cannot be made by mixing light of $\boldsymbol{R}$, $\boldsymbol{G}$, and $\boldsymbol{B}$. Such color has a minus component. For example, if a color $\boldsymbol{F}=(R, G, B)$ has a minus component B, it means that mixture of $\boldsymbol{F}$ and $(0, 0, -\boldsymbol{B})$ becomes a color $(R, G, 0)$.

The tristimulus values have been obtained for all wavelengths (within the visible wavelength range 380–780 nm) by experiments with many persons. The CIE (International Commission of Illumination, or Commission International de l'Eclairage) selected as principal colors, single wavelength colors of 780 nm, 546.1 nm, and 435.8 nm, and determined tristimulus values (called distribution coefficients). The three principal colors are denoted by $(\boldsymbol{R})$, $(\boldsymbol{G})$, and $(\boldsymbol{B})$, and the distribution coefficients by $(\bar{R}, \bar{G}, \bar{B})$, respectively. Figure 2.8 shows distribution coefficient curves. According to Fig. 2.8, the mixture of 1 W (watt) single wavelength of 500 nm and 17.4 W of $\boldsymbol{R}$ is equivalent to that of 0.4 W of $\boldsymbol{G}$ and 0.16 W of $\boldsymbol{B}$.

Suppose the spectral composition of a certain color is represented by $E(\lambda)$; then the distribution coefficients are calculated by the following equations:

$$
\begin{aligned}
R &= \int E(\lambda)\bar{R}(\lambda)\,\mathrm{d}\lambda \\
G &= \int E(\lambda)\bar{G}(\lambda)\,\mathrm{d}\lambda \\
B &= \int E(\lambda)\bar{B}(\lambda)\,\mathrm{d}\lambda
\end{aligned}
\tag{2.5}
$$

The interval of the integrations is within the visible wavelength range. The coefficients for white are derived by letting $E(\lambda)$ equal 1 in Eq. (2.5).

It is convenient to use a new unit for distribution coefficients so that white is made from the same amount of coefficients. The new unit is called a trichromatic unit. The curve of new distribution coefficients in the new unit is derived from the distribution curves in Fig. 2.8 by normalizing them with corresponding distribution coefficients of white. The new coefficients are denoted by r, g, and b. The color specification using these curves is called the RGB color specification of the CIE. The

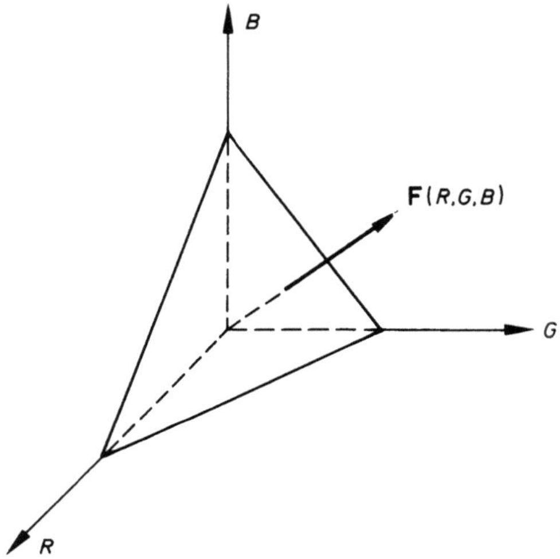

Fig. 2.9. Color representation in RGB space

distribution coefficients of a color with $E(\lambda)$ are calculated by the following equations:

$$R=\int E(\lambda)\bar{r}(\lambda)\,d\lambda$$
$$G=\int E(\lambda)\bar{g}(\lambda)\,d\lambda \tag{2.6}$$
$$B=\int E(\lambda)\bar{b}(\lambda)\,d\lambda$$

These R, G, and B are widely used in computer vision because $R=G=B$ corresponds to white.

Now let $\boldsymbol{F}$ denote a color vector (R, G, B) in the three-dimensional color space shown in Fig. 2.9. The length of $\boldsymbol{F}$ represents the brightness, and the direction represents the chromaticity (hue and saturation). The chromaticity can also be represented by the crosspoint P of the vector $\boldsymbol{F}$ and the plane defined by $R+G+B=1$. The coordinate of the crosspoint (r, g, b) is called the chromaticity coordinate. Let $T=R+G+B$; then the chromaticity coordinate is given by $r=R/T$, $g=G/T$, and $b=B/T$. It is sometimes convenient to use the triangle on the plane $R+G+B=1$ cut by the three coordinate planes (see Fig. 2.9). If the triangle is shrunk such that its height is 1, the lengths of lines from P to the edges are r, g, and b as shown in Fig. 2.10. This figure is a chromaticity diagram. The center of gravity represents white, and corresponds to $r=g=b=1/3$. A point close to the edge of the triangle represents a color with high saturation.

In computer vision, hue and saturation are often defined by using such a triangle. The hue of a point P in Fig. 2.11 is defined as the angle θ between WR and WQ, where W (White) is the center of the triangle. The saturation is defined as WP/WQ, where Q is the crosspoint of WP and the nearest edge. Let P be represented by (r, g, b); then the hue θ is formulated by using θ_1 as follows:

$$\theta_1=\cos^{-1}\left[(2r-g-b)/\sqrt{6\{(r-1/3)+(g-1/3)+(b-1/3)\}}\right] \tag{2.7}$$

where $0<\theta_1<\pi$

$$\theta=\begin{cases}\theta_1 & g\geq b\\ 2\pi-\theta_1 & g<b\end{cases} \tag{2.8}$$

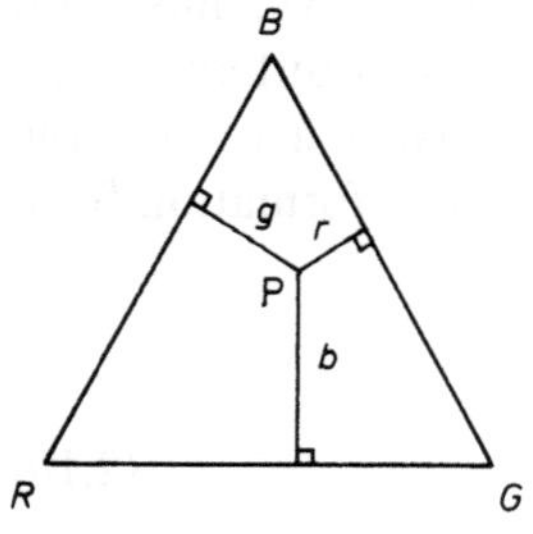

Fig. 2.10. Chromaticity diagram

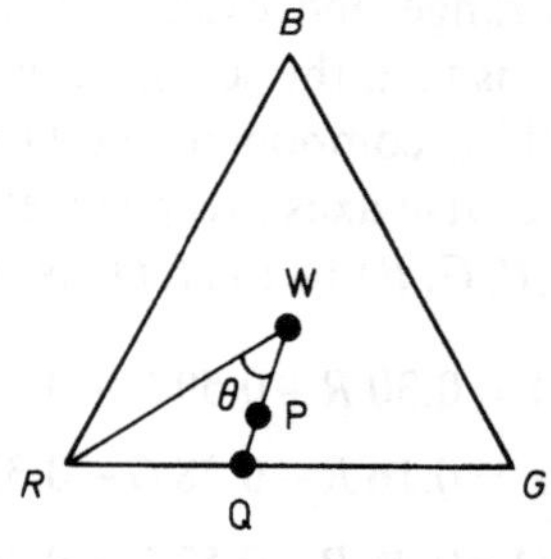

Fig. 2.11. Hue and saturation

The saturation S is given as follows:

$$S = 1 - 3 \min(r, g, b) \tag{2.9}$$

Thus color is represented by both (R, G, B) and (T, θ, S). Although the correspondence of the latter to (brightness, hue, saturation) is not precise, it is useful for its simplicity.

2.4 Color Input

The principle of color image input is to observe light intensity through color filters. We can use a conventional monochromatic TV camera to take three images through three color filters, or use a color TV camera in which filters are inserted in the optical system.

If spectral transmission characteristics of filters are the same as those of the distribution coefficient curves, R, G, and B are immediately derived. In practice, however, it is difficult to obtain such filters. Therefore, three filters of known characteristics (see Fig. 2.12, for example) are used, and observed intensities are normalized with characteristics of filters and a camera. Note that filters must be selected so that any wavelength is transmitted through at least one filter.

2.4.1 TV Signals

In the United States of America, the NTSC (National Television System Committee) determined a standard format for TV signals. The image consists of 480 lines, which are divided into two fields of equal lines (240). The fields are interlaced, i.e., one field contains the odd-numbered lines, the other, even-numbered lines, and they are displayed alternately. Scanning one field takes 1/60 s, so a complete image takes 1/30 s. The blanking period (between each field) is equivalent to scanning 22.5 lines. Thus the total number of horizontal scan-line periods per image is 525.

In the NTSC system, color TV signals are divided into three components, which correspond to human color sensations. The first component corresponds to brightness, which alone can be used for monochromatic TV. It is called the luminance signal, and denoted by Y. The rest represent chromaticity. They must be zero for monochromatic light. This constraint alone is not enough to determine the two components. Human vision is sensitive to the difference in color between orange and cyan, less sensitive between yellowish green and purple. Based on this fact, the second component is assigned to represent the former difference, the third component the latter. They are called the 'fine chrominance axes' and the 'coarse axes', respectively, and represented by I and Q. The transformation from (R, G, B) to (Y, I, Q) is defined as follows:

$$\begin{aligned} Y &= 0.30\,R + 0.59\,G + 0.11\,B \\ I &= 0.16\,R - 0.28\,G - 0.32\,B \\ Q &= 0.21\,R - 0.52\,G + 0.31\,B \end{aligned} \tag{2.10}$$

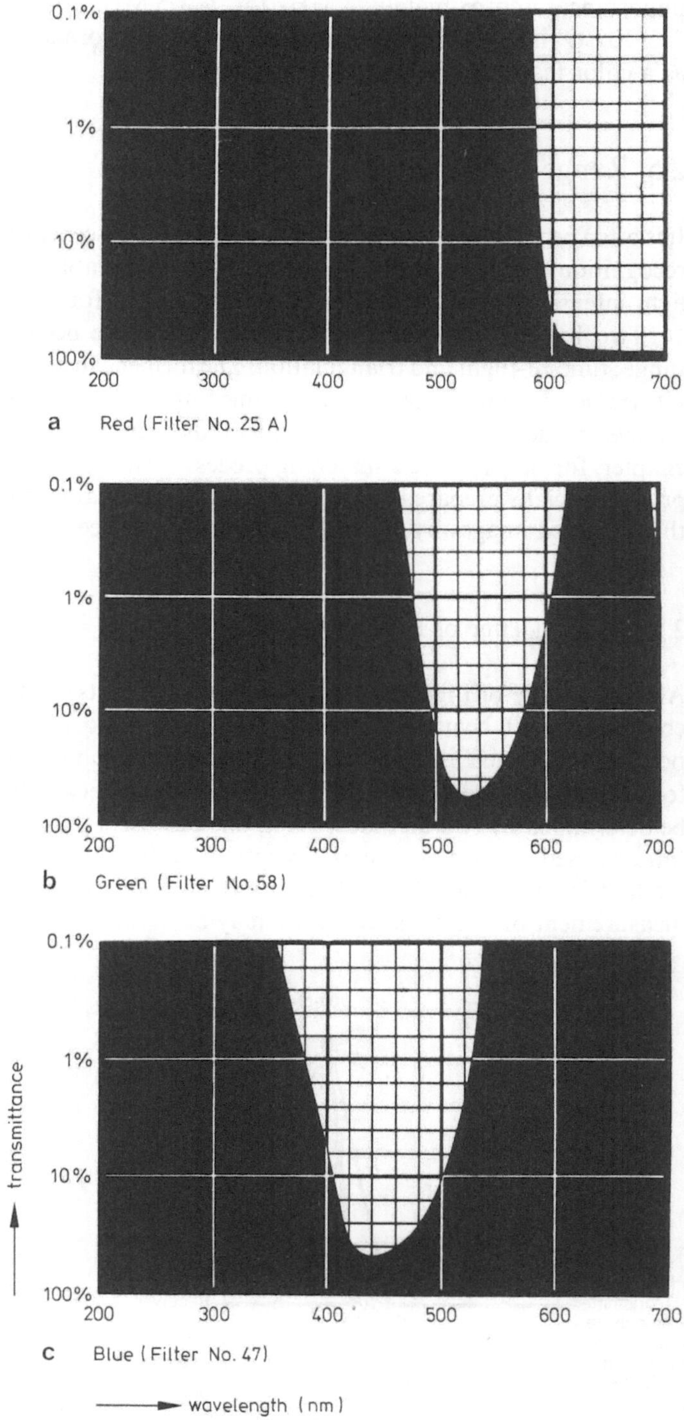

Fig. 2.12. Transmission characteristics of wratten gelatine filters (*horizontal axis* represents wavelength in nm)

In order to send color TV signals, they are allocated a bandwidth according to their importance: approximately, 4 MHz for Y, 1.5 MHz for I, and 0.5 MHz for Q.

(Y, I, Q) is easily obtained by simple linear transformation. It is sometimes used as a color feature as well as (R, G, B) and (T, θ, S).

2.5 Range

It is often necessary to capture directly range data of scenes for representation or for recognition. While various sensory systems are available for obtaining an array of light intensities, we have no such standard system for range data.

Two basically different optical techniques have been developed to measure range: time-of-flight and triangulation. The former can be subdivided into light and ultrasonic ranging according to the medium. Triangulation is subdivided into passive and active methods. Passive methods (stereo vision) are excluded from this chapter, for they involve a matching process between two images. Active methods project specially prepared light (in this case, a light beam through a slit) and observe the projected images by conventional imaging devices.

2.5.1 Optical Time of Flight

An optical time-of-flight rangefinder typically consists of a transmitter that emits a collimated light beam, a scanning mechanism, and a receiver that detects the portion of reflected light on the target. The range is obtained from the time needed for the light to travel from the transmitter to the target and back. Time of flight can be determined by two methods. First, one can use a pulsed laser and measure the time elapsed from emission to reception, rather like a radar. (Sometimes this method is called 'lidar', which comes from light radar.) This requires accurate measurement of time; a sharp pulse may be deformed when it is reflected, and a

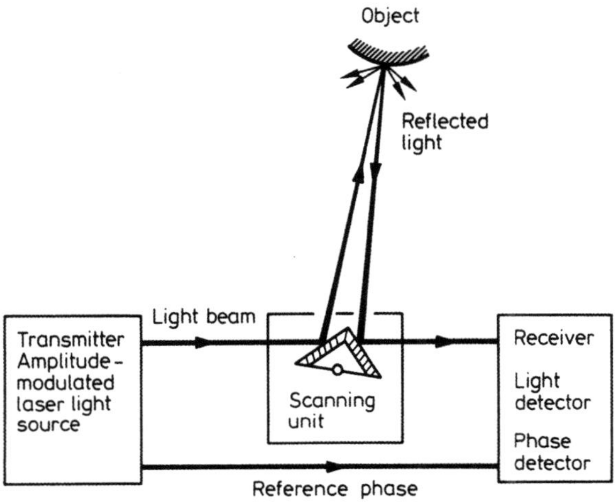

Fig. 2.13. Schematic diagram of optical time-of-flight rangefinder

difficult problem is how to determine the time at which the deformed pulse is received.

The second method is to modulate a laser beam im amplitude and measure the phase shift of reflected light. A typical rangefinder is illustrated in Fig. 2.13 (Nitzan, Brain and Duda, 1977). The instrument emits a laser beam that is amplitude-modulated with a sinusoidal wave form. The beam is deflected by the mirror in the scanning unit. When the beam strikes an object, a portion of the light is reflected back to the scanning unit, and deflected into the photomultiplier of the receiver. The phase of the signal, relative to the reference phase, is proportional to the time of flight. The amplitude of the signal is proportional to the reflectance of the object. Thus the instrument obtains both light intensity and range data. It obtains a 128×128 depth map with a range of 1–5 m and a depth resolution of 1 cm.

A disadvantage of this method is that it requires a two-dimensional scanning mechanism which is usually realized by rotating mirrors. Another problem is that the system is large because it involves three units that cannot be made compact.

2.5.2 Ultrasonic Ranging

Ultrasound has been used for ranging in water, and recently for automatic focusing of cameras. The measurement of the time of flight is easier because the velocity of ultrasound is much slower than that of light. Another advantage is that it can be used under natural illumination.

The ultrasonic rangefinder also needs a scanning mechanism. Another difficulty is that a narrow beam of ultrasound cannot be produced, and thus a high resolution range map cannot be obtained. Ultrasonic rangefinders are used for obstacle detection rather than for object recognition.

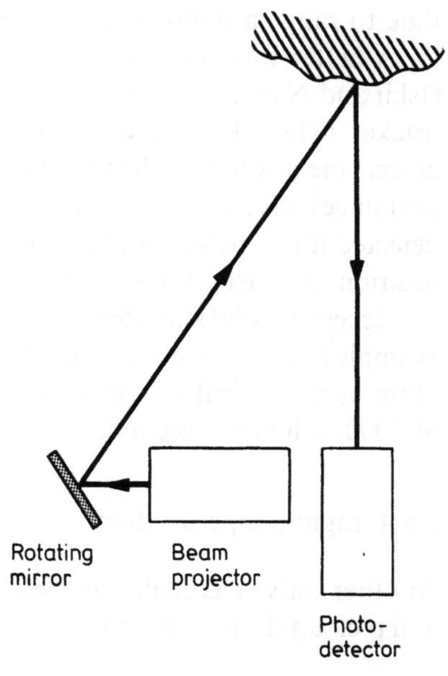

Fig. 2.14. Simple spot projection rangefinder

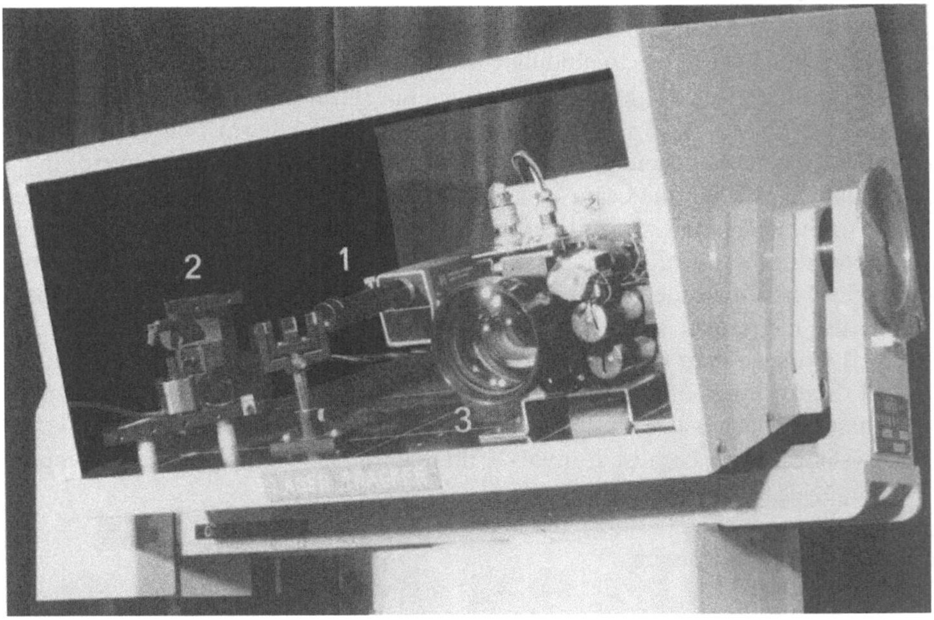

Fig. 2.15. Laser tracker

2.5.3 Spot Projection

One of the simplest triangulation methods is to project a spot beam and detect the reflected beam. An old mobile robot developed at SRI International (Forsen, 1968) employed a rangefinder as shown in Fig. 2.14. A light beam is deflected by the rotating mirror and the reflected beam is detected by the photomultiplier. The rotation angle determines the range by triangulation. The instrument takes much time to range a point because it requires a rotation of the mirror.

A better way is to detect a spot by a camera. An early system was developed (Ishii and Nagata, 1976) for tracking object boundaries. The system, called 'laser tracker' (Fig. 2.15), projects a laser beam, deflects it with the rotating mirrors, and detects the position of the projected spot on the object by the image dissector. Since the image dissector can scan at any part of an image, the spot position can quickly be detected if it is predicted. Special hardware was attached for detection of the spot position in order to realize online tracking.

Recently, solid state devices have been developed for spot position detection. An example is a PIN diode position-sensitive chip that directly outputs the x–y position of the spot. Typical systems detect spot positions with 1/1000 resolution at a speed of 1000 points per second.

2.5.4 Light-Stripe Method

Another active triangulation method is to project a sheet of light (instead of a spot) and pick up the image with a TV camera. One of the earliest systems was developed

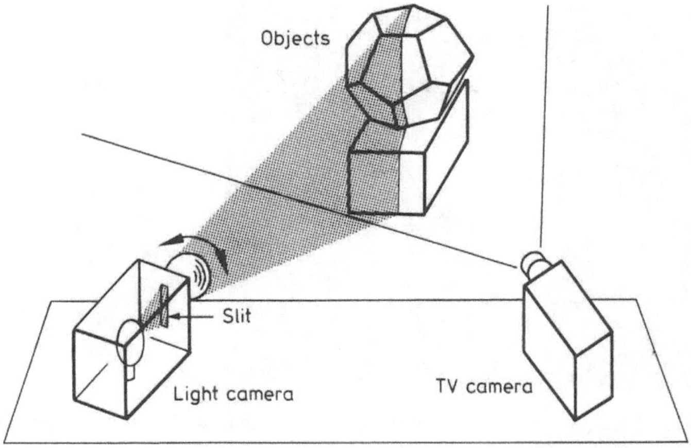

Fig. 2.16. Principle of stripe projection rangefinder

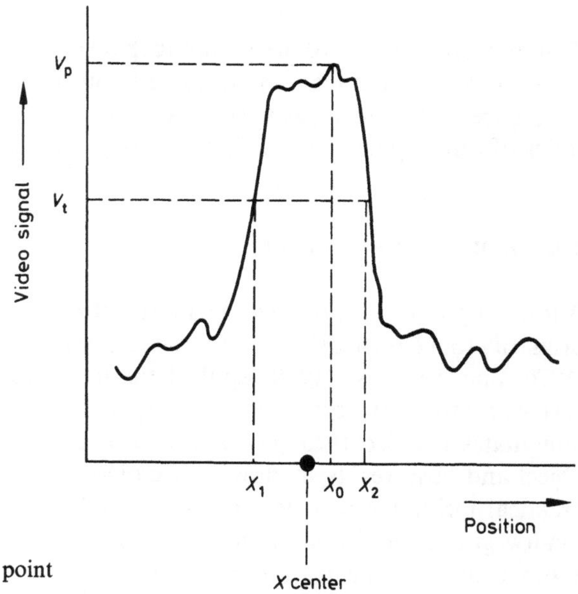

Fig. 2.17. Determination of center point

at the Electrotechnical Laboratory (Shirai and Suwa, 1971). Figure 2.16 depicts the principle of the system. A light-stripe is scanned by rotating a mirror (instead of the projector itself) with a computer-controlled stepping motor, and the image is taken for every direction of the light. Special hardware (Oshima and Takano, 1973) was developed to determine the center position of the stripe image. This hardware accepts digitized video signals as its input, and obtains the peak V_p and the position x_0 in real time (see Fig. 2.17). During the horizontal blanking time, it determines the left side and the right side of the peak using a threshold V_t as shown, and obtains the center point as the midpoint. V_t is determined by the following equation with two parameters c_1 and c_2.

$$V_t = V_p - 2^{-c_1} V_p - c_2 \tag{2.11}$$

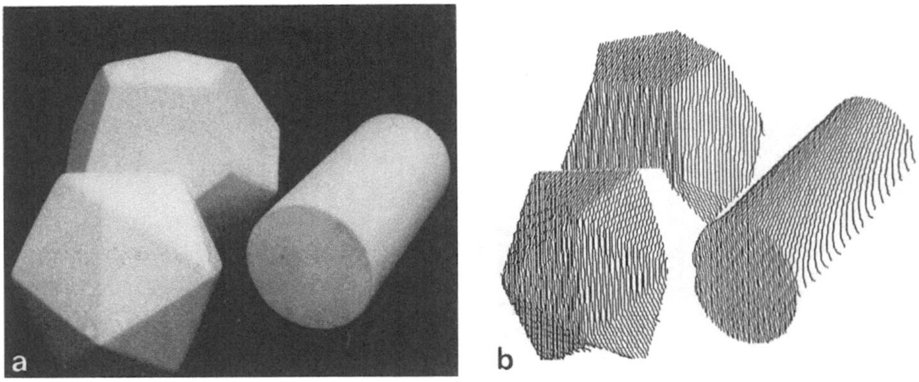

Fig. 2.18a, b. Example of input data: (**a**) scene with a light beam; (**b**) center points of stripes are superposed

Thus the time required for determining the center position of a strip image is exactly the same as that for scanning a frame (1/60 s).

Figure 2.18 shows an example of a scene and input data (each stripe consists of a series of center points; usually, more stripes are obtained).

2.6 Moiré Topography

Another approach is provided by moiré pattern techniques, which have been used primarily to measure deformation in stress analysis. Meadows, Johnson and Allen (1970) and Takasaki (1970) applied the moiré topography method to visualize surface contours of large objects like airplane models or mannequins. Their method illuminates an object through a large equispaced plane grating placed in front of the object and observes its shadow on the object through the grating. Later, another practical technique was developed that did not use a large grating; instead, a shadow grating produced by projecting a grating onto an object is observed through another grating, as shown in Fig. 2.19.

The 3D shape of a known object is found by the contour lines in the moiré image (see Fig. 2.20 for example). Generally, however, it is not possible to determine whether a contour line is lower or higher than the adjacent contour line; that is, the moiré fringe order is ambiguous. Fortunately, this difficulty is solved by moving the grating in the observation system. The direction of the position change caused by moving the grating determines the relative fringe order. The same result can be obtained without actually moving the grating. A new method (Idesawa, Yatagai and Soma, 1976) eliminates a grating in the observation system and directly inputs an image with a shadow of a grating. When the image is scanned, the effect of the grating is simulated by an appropriate sampling controlled by computer. Since the position of the simulated grating is arbitrarily controlled, the fringe number can be easily determined. The problem is that a very high resolution image is necessary to apply the above method.

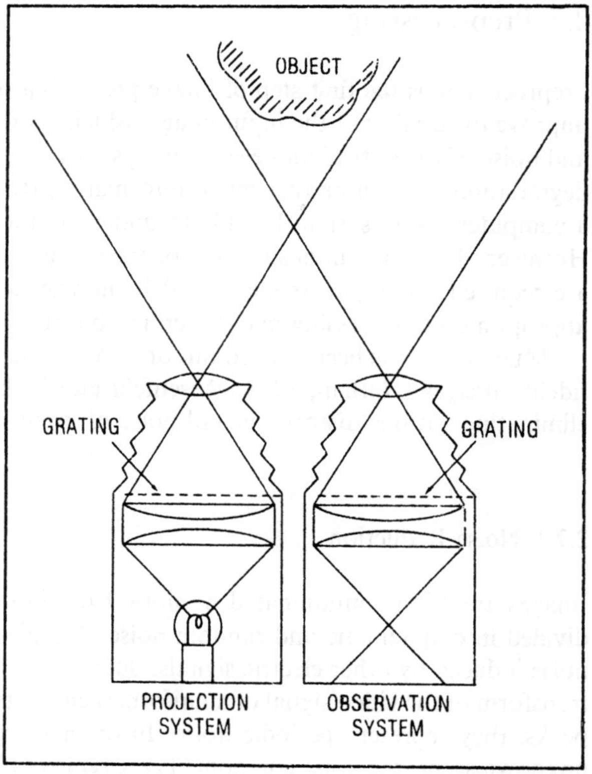

Fig. 2.19. Schematic arrangement of projection type moiré topography

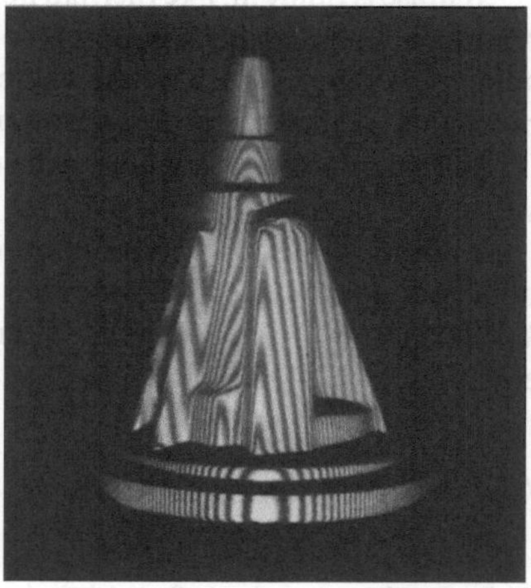

Fig. 2.20. Example of moiré image

Another difficulty is the determination of the center position of moiré fringes, which are blurred and wide on the planes nearly perpendicular to the viewing direction. A possible solution is to find ridges of the moiré image, but this not easy for certain classes of image. A semiautomatic ridge detector has been developed for an interactive fringe analysis system (Idesawa and Yatagai, 1980) and is currently used in medicine for measurement of the deformation of the human spinal column.

2.7 Preprocessing

Preprocessing is the first step of image processing by computer. Its purpose is to improve the quality of the input image, which is often degraded by the distortion and noise of the optical and electronic systems of the input device. In spite of the degradation, we can extract much information from images. It is desirable that a computer vision system be able to understand a scene without preprocessing. However, if the light intensity itself or the precise shapes and positions of objects are required, the input image should be improved by preprocessing. Moreover, appropriate preprocessing may lessen the burden of the later image processing.

Much work has been carried out on enhancement in order to reconstruct high fidelity images (Nathan, 1968; Rosenfeld and Kak, 1976). Typical methods for eliminating various distortions and noise of input devices are described below.

2.7.1 Noise Reduction

Images are often contaminated by noise from input devices. Noise of images is divided into systematic and random noise. A typical systematic noise is periodic noise induced by other electric signals. Such periodic noise is detected by Fourier transform of the video signal of a uniform scene. If the Fourier transform has high peaks, they represent periodic noise. In order to reduce periodic noise from an unknown scene, the noise components are removed from the Fourier transform of the video signal, and then the inverse Fourier transformation is applied to the result.

If noise is random, like thermal noise, it cannot be detected on the basis of spatial relations. One possible solution is to discriminate it on the basis of light intensity value. The simplest case is that where noise corresponds to the brightest or darkest pixel (this is called salt and pepper noise). Once a noise pixel is detected, its intensity is replaced by some reasonable value (e.g., one interpolated from neighboring pixel values).

Another way is to apply a smoothing operation. If multiple images of a scene are obtained, noise is effectively reduced by ensemble averaging. Let $g_k(i,j)$ denote the kth image ($k=1,2,\ldots n$). The ensemble average is calculated by the following equation:

$$f(i,j)=(1/n)\sum_{k=1}^{n} g_k(i,j) \tag{2.12}$$

This simple averaging of multiple images reduces noise by a factor of $(1/n)$ in the variance without loss of detail.

A simple method of smoothing is to take an average over a local region, called a 'window'. A conventional way is to replace a pixel $g(i,j)$ by an average of pixels in the 3×3 window around the pixel.

$$f(i,j)=(1/9)\sum_{k=-1}^{1}\sum_{l=-1}^{1} f(i-k,j-l) \tag{2.13}$$

Generally this local averaging is formulated as follows:

$$f(i,j)=\left\{\sum_{(k,l)\in\text{neighbor}} w(k,l)f(i-k,j-l)\right\}\Bigg/\left\{\sum_{(k,l)\in\text{neighbor}} w(k,l)\right\} \tag{2.14}$$

2.7.2 Geometrical Correction

Geometrical distortion is caused by optical and electronic imaging systems. Camera tubes especially cause considerable electronic imaging distortion. A typical distortion pattern is shown in Fig. 2.21. The distortion pattern can be measured by showing many known points (e.g., grid points) in the field of sight. The positions of other points are corrected by interpolation based on a few known points in the neighboring region around it.

Another correction method is based on the distortion model. Geometrical distortion is defined by a set of transformation equations from an ideal position (x, y) to the distorted position (x', y'):

$$\begin{aligned} x' &= h_x(x,y) \\ y' &= h_y(x,y) \end{aligned} \tag{2.15}$$

These equations are usually linear (for perspective distortion) or quadratic (for camera tube distortion as shown in Fig. 2.21).

Now positions of image points are corrected, and thus lengths or areas can be precisely calculated. Sometimes correction of an original image is necessary so that image processing may be applied to a better image. This is called resampling and usually takes much computation. Let $f(x, y)$ and $g(x, y)$ denote the ideal and distorted image respectively. It seems that $f(x, y)$ can be recovered by the following equation:

$$f(x,y)=g(x',y') \tag{2.16}$$

where x' and y' are defined by Eq. (2.15). However, x' and y' in the above equation may not be integers. The simplest way to solve this problem is to copy the value of the nearest neighbor of (x', y') into $f(x, y)$.

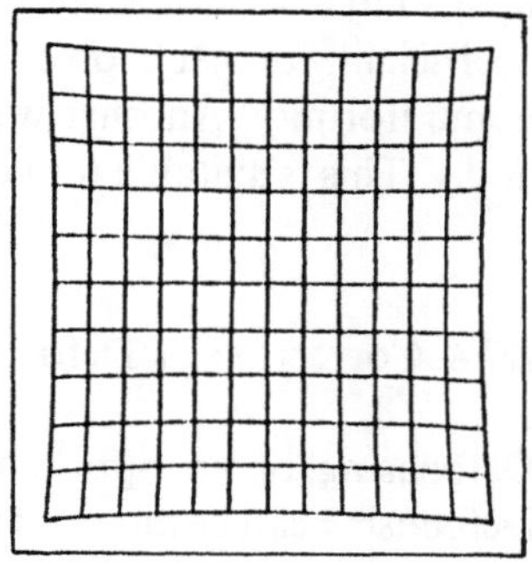

Fig. 2.21. Distorted image of grid pattern

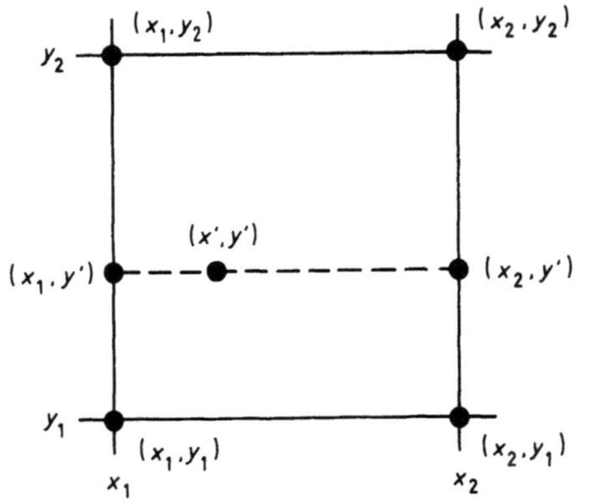

Fig. 2.22. Interpolation of $g(x', y')$ based on the neighbor values

A better way is to interpolate a value based on the values of pixels around (x', y'). Suppose the nearest pixels to (x', y') are four crosspoints of four lines as shown in Fig. 2.22, where x_1 and y_1 are integers, and $x_2 = x_1 + 1$ and $y_2 = y_1 + 1$. First the $f(x_1, y')$ and $f(x_2, y')$ are interpolated, and then $f(x', y')$ is interpolated as follows:

$$
\begin{aligned}
f(x_1, y') &= (y_2 - y')\, g(x_1, y_1) + (y' - y_1)\, g(x_1, y_2) \\
f(x_2, y') &= (y_2 - y')\, g(x_2, y_1) + (y' - y_1)\, g(x_2, y_2) \\
f(x', y') &= (x_2 - x') f(x_1, y') + (x' - x_1) f(x_2, y')
\end{aligned}
\tag{2.17}
$$

This method is also used to correct distorted aerial images so that they may match corresponding maps.

2.7.3 Gray-Level Correction

Gray-level correction compensates for the nonuniformity of the input device. The vidicon camera has high sensitivity at the center of the image, and lower sensitivity in the peripheral region. This nonuniformity is called 'shading'. On the other hand, the solid camera may have random nonuniformity depending on the sensitivity of each element of the photosensitive array.

The sensitivity of pixels can be calibrated by illuminating the input device with a light source of uniform brightness. One way of correcting gray level is to use a scale coefficient for each pixel. This method is effective for correction of random nonuniformity. Another way is to use transform functions of the two variables x and y. This is suitable for correction of systematic nonuniformity such as shading.

2.7.4 Correction of Defocusing

Defocusing of an optical or electronic system may result in a blurred image. Defocusing can be modeled as follows. Let an ideal image be denoted by $f(x, y)$. The actual image is formulated by the following equation:

$$g(x,y)=\iint_{-\infty}^{\infty} h(x,y,u,v)f(u,v)\,\mathrm{d}u\mathrm{d}v \tag{2.18}$$

Sometimes we can regard $h(x,y,u,v)$ as a function of $(x-u)$ and $(y-v)$, which means that it does not depend on the position (x,y). Then Eq. (2.18) is simplified as

$$g(x,y)=\iint_{-\infty}^{\infty} h(x-u,y-v)f(u,v)\,\mathrm{d}u\mathrm{d}v \tag{2.19}$$

where h is called a point spread function. An efficient way of calculating Eq. (2.19) is to apply Fourier transformation to both sides of the equation. Then the following equation is derived:

$$G(a,b)=H(a,b)\,F(a,b) \tag{2.20}$$

where G, H, and F are results of Fourier transform of g, h, and f, respectively. $F(a,b)$ is derived from the equation above as:

$$F(a,b)=G(a,b)/H(a,b) \tag{2.21}$$

The ideal image $f(x,y)$ is obtained by applying inverse Fourier transformation to $F(a,b)$.

The point spread function is often approximated by the following normal distribution function.

$$h(x,y)=\frac{1}{2\pi}\,\mathrm{e}^{-(x+y)/2\sigma^2} \tag{2.22}$$

The Fourier transform is:

$$H(a,b)=\frac{1}{2\pi}\iint_{-\infty}^{\infty} h(x,y)\,\mathrm{e}^{-\mathrm{j}(ax+by)}\,\mathrm{d}x\mathrm{d}y \tag{2.23}$$

where $\mathrm{j}=\sqrt{-1}$. In this case F is obtained by the following equation.

$$\begin{aligned}F(a,b)&=H^{-1}(a,b)\,F(a,b)\\&=2\,\mathrm{e}^{\sigma^2(a^2+b^2)/2}F(a,b)\end{aligned} \tag{2.24}$$

Equation (2.24) reinforces high frequencies which have been lost by defocusing. Note that $F(a,b)$ cannot be calculated for high frequencies (for large a and b) because $f(x,y)$ is only defined for integer x and y.

Generally, gray-level correction with Fourier transformation may reinforce a certain bandwith. In the above example, high frequency noise is also reinforced. It is, therefore, desirable to reduce such noise before applying the correction.

3 Image Feature Extraction

This chapter deals with the problem of extracting features from two-dimensional image data. Extraction of three-dimensional features from range data is described in Chap. 10.

One of the most important image features in 3D computer vision is the 'edge' or the boundary line of a uniform region. Edges are useful clues to ways of segmenting an image into meaningful regions. The edge is defined as a series of edge points where the pixel values (light intensity, color, or range) change abruptly. One way to extract edges from an image is to detect edge points and then link them into edges. Such a method is called an 'edge method'. The edge method is divided into two main classes: a parallel method, by which processing of a part of the image does not depend on the results of processing of other parts, and a sequential method, by which processing does depend on the results of the previous processing of other parts.

Another way to extract edges is to segment an image into uniform regions and then to obtain the boundary lines of those regions. Such a method is called a 'region method'. The region method can extract edges with open ends because all edges are extracted as boundary lines. The region method is not only used for edge extraction but also for the extraction of regions themselves.

On the other hand, edges extracted by the edge method do not always constitute closed boundaries. In order to obtain many regions, therefore, a greater number of edges must be extracted.

Edges and regions are basic image features, and many other features may be derived from these basic features.

3.1 Edge Point Detection

Edge points are detected in two steps: an edge operator is applied to every pixel to evaluate its likelihood as an edge point, then edge points are determined on the basis of output values of the operator. The exact method used depends on the type of edges to be detected.

3.1.1 Edge Types for a Polyhedral Image

In this subsection, a description is given of types of edges which appear in an image of a scene including only polyhedra. First let us consider types of lines in line drawings of polyhedra. Figure 3.1 shows an example of a line drawing containing four types of line as follows:

1. Contour line: a line separating a body from the background (in Fig. 3.1, lines AB, BC, ..., HI, IA).

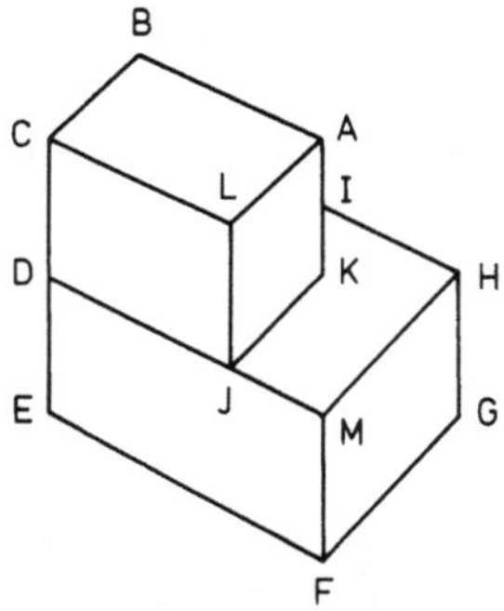

Fig. 3.1. Types of line in a line drawing

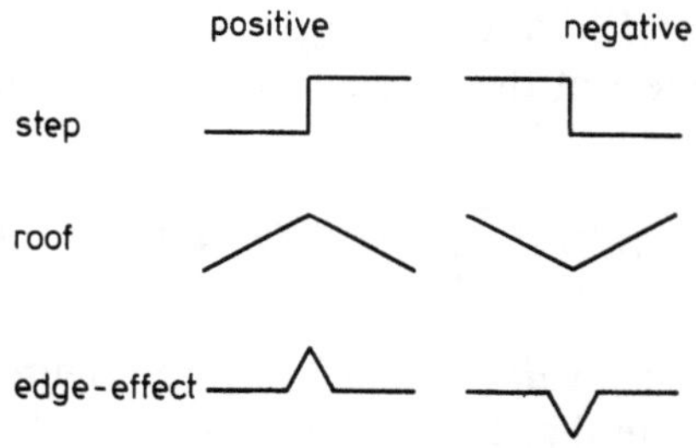

Fig. 3.2. Types of intensity profile across an edge

2. Boundary line: a line separating bodies. Note that a contour line is also a boundary line. (In Fig. 3.1, lines DJ, JK, KI and the contour lines are boundary lines.)
3. Internal line: a line appearing inside a body (CL, LA, ..., MF).
4. Crack: a line where the edges of two bodies coincide (DJ).

Edge points which correspond to each type of line must be detected in order to build up a complete line drawing.

Let us consider light intensity change across an edge. It varies with the illumination condition and the orientations of planes at the edge. Typical experimentally-obtained light intensity profiles are shown in Fig. 3.2. Illuminated from far away, a typical edge may produce a step type profile. If the light source is near, a roof type profile is observed. At a crack, a negative edge-effect may appear. A positive edge-effect is produced at an internal line where specular rays are reflected.

The six types of profile in Fig. 3.2 are abstracted from experiments. Actual profiles, however, are not so simple, because multiple types are superposed and surfaces of objects are not uniform. Edge detection methods must, therefore, be robust against such disturbances.

3.1.2 One-Dimensional Edge Operators

One-dimensional edge operators are useful for finding edge points at an edge whose direction is predicted. Let us consider, first, operators for step type edges. These operators must be sensitive to the difference in light intensity from one side to the other.

Let i denote a position of a pixel along a line perpendicular to an edge, and $f(i)$ denote the light intensity at i. The simplest operator is the difference in light intensity, calculated by the following equation:

$$D_d(i)=f(i+d)-f(i-d) \tag{3.1}$$

If $D_d(i)$ is positive, the edge is a positive step type, and vice versa. Figure 3.3 shows the output of the operator with $d=1$ for typical profiles. Note that even an ideal step edge may be observed in a digital image as shown in Fig. 3.3(b) if the edge is at the center of a pixel.

The difference $D_d(i)$ may become large for a noisy image. In order to reduce the effect of the noise, we can use the difference of averages:

$$D_{d_1,d_2}(i) = \sum_{k=d_1}^{d_2} \{f(i+k) - f(i-k)\}/(d_2 - d_1 + 1) \tag{3.2}$$

Usually $d_1 = 1$, and $2 < d_2 < 5$. Figure 3.3 shows an example with $d_1 = 1$ and $d_2 = 2$. Note that this difference is equivalent to the average of $D_d(i)$. For example,

$$D_{1,3}(i) = \sum_{k=-1}^{1} D_2(i+k)/3 \tag{3.3}$$

If we must apply the operator to all pixels in an image (except peripheral pixels), we can calculate more effectively by using the smoothed image. Instead of applying $D_{1,3}(i)$, for example, we may first obtain the smoothed image $f_1(i)$ defined by:

$$f_1(i) = \sum_{k=-1}^{1} f(i+k) \tag{3.4}$$

and then apply $D_2(i)$ to $f_1(1)$.

The smoothed difference operator can be further generalized to a two-dimensional averaging. Let the j-axis be defined in the predicted direction of an edge, and the i-axis perpendicular to the j-axis as shown in Fig. 3.4. The output of the operator at a point (i,j) is the difference between certain regions on either 'side' of the point. Let A and B denote these regions as shown in Fig. 3.4. The operator is defined by the following equation:

$$DD(i,j) = \sum_{(k,l)\in B} f(k,l)/|B| - \sum_{(k,l)\in A} f(k,l)/|A| \tag{3.5}$$

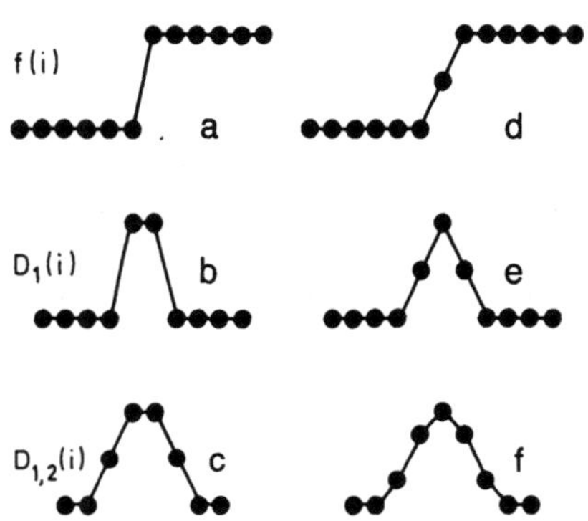

Fig. 3.3. Intensity profiles and outputs of operators

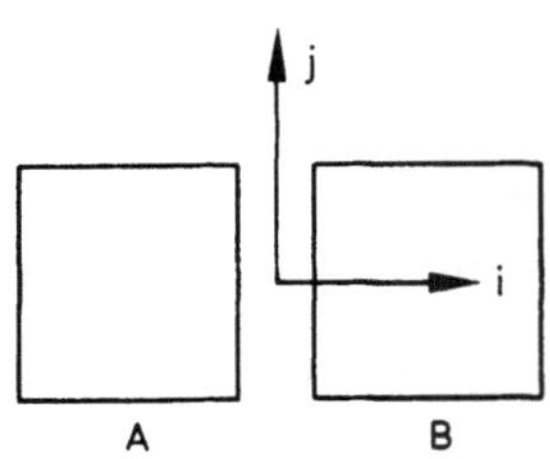

Fig. 3.4. Averaging regions for difference operator

where $|A|$ is the area of region A. We can also obtain the same result by first calculating the smoothed image with two-dimensional averaging, and then applying a simple difference operator defined by Eq. (3.1).

For other types of edge we must modify the operators for step type edges. Roof type edges are detected by comparing the slope of the profile on the two sides. The slope at i can be represented by $D_d(i)/2d$. A roof edge operator is defined as follows:

$$L_{d,d'}(i)=\{D_d(i+d')-D_d(i-d')\}/2d \tag{3.6}$$

If the output of the operator is positive, the edge is a negative roof type, and vice versa. Because the parameter d is constant, Eq. (3.6) can be simplified:

$$L_{d,d'}(i)=\{D_d(i+d')-D_d(i-d')\} \tag{3.7}$$

Equation (3.7) represents the second-order difference. Usually the two parameters d and d' are given the same value. Letting $L_d(i)$ denote $L_{d,d}(i)$, we have:

$$\begin{aligned} L_d(i)&=\{D_d(i+d)-D_d(i-d)\}\\ &=f(i+2d)+f(i-2d)-2f(i) \end{aligned} \tag{3.8}$$

The operator can also be modified to reduce the effect of noise in the same way as for step type edge operators.

Edge-effect types are detected by comparing the intensity value with that on each side. A simple way is to use $L_d(i)$ of Eq. (3.8), where the value of the parameter d should be small ($d=1$, or even $d=1/2$) in this case. If the output value is positive, the edge is a negative edge-effect type, and vice versa. For edge-effect type edge operators, we can also use averaged values to reduce noise. For example,

$$L_{d,m}(i)=\sum_{k=-m}^{m} L_d(i+k)/(2m+1) \tag{3.9}$$

It has been shown that operators for roof type and edge-effect type edges are represented by combinations of operators for step type edges. Therefore, step type edge operators will mainly be described below.

Since all the various operators described above are linear functions of $f(i)$, they can be represented by a convolution of an image and a weighting function. For example, $D_{d_1,d_2}(i)$ in Eq. (3.2) can be rewritten as:

$$D_{d_1,d_2}(i)=\sum_{k=-d_2}^{d_2} \{f(i+k)w(k)\}/(d_2-d_1+1) \tag{3.10}$$

where

$$w(k)=\begin{cases} -1 & -d_2\le k\le -d_1\\ 0 & -d_1<k<d_1\\ 1 & d_1\le k\le d_2 \end{cases} \tag{3.11}$$

Note that the weighting function $w(k)$ resembles a step profile. The convolution operation, therefore, can also be regarded as calculating the correlation between the weighting function and a light intensity profile.

3.1.3 Two-Dimensional Edge Operators

If the directions of edges are not predicted, two-dimensional edge operators are used for finding the edge points of all directions. In order to determine whether a pixel is an edge point or not, the neighboring pixels must be taken into consideration. The definition of the neighbor ('window') depends on the operators. Generally, small windows are sensitive to details of the image and are easily calculated.

When Roberts (1963) developed the first program for recognition of polyhedra, he used a 2×2 window for the edge operator (for step type edges). This is a kind of two-dimensional difference:

$$D_2(i,j)=\sqrt{\{f(i,j)-f(i+1,j+1)\}^2+\{f(i+1,j)-f(i,j+1)\}^2} \tag{3.12}$$

Equation (3.12) is equivalent to the gradient value of $f(i,j)$. Figure 3.5 shows an example of the result of Roberts' operator (in fact the input image was first transformed by taking square roots of all pixels and then Roberts' operator was applied). Instead of calculating the square root of the sum of squares in Eq. (3.12), the sum of absolute values can be used to save computing time (Forsen, 1968).

Most operators use 3×3 windows, because they contain all the neighbors of the center pixel. Let light intensities in the 3×3 window be denoted as shown in Fig. 3.6. The gradient $\boldsymbol{G}$ at a pixel can be obtained by calculating the components G_x and G_y using the neighboring pixel values as follows:

$$\begin{aligned} G_x &= (C+2F+I)-(A+2D+G) \\ G_y &= (A+2B+C)-(G+2H+I) \\ \boldsymbol{G} &= (G_x, G_y) \end{aligned} \tag{3.13}$$

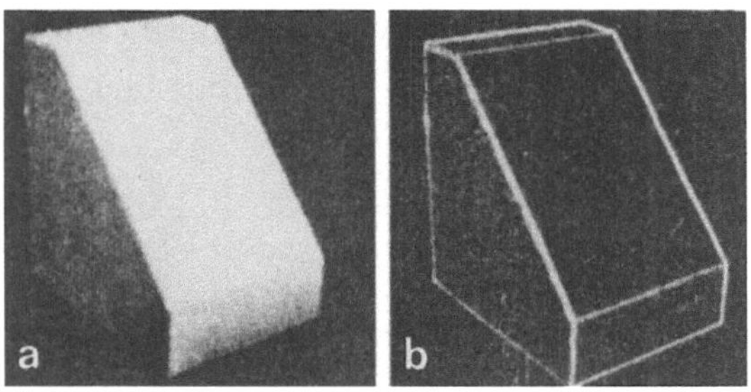

Fig. 3.5a, b. Example of filtered image by Roberts' operator (Roberts 1963): (**a**) original image; (**b**) filtered image

A	B	C
D	E	F
G	H	I

Fig. 3.6. Light intensity values in 3×3 window

If the gradient magnitude $|\boldsymbol{G}|$ is large, the steepest direction and the edge direction are defined as:

$$\begin{aligned}\alpha &= \tan\,(G_y/G_x)\\ \theta &= \alpha + \pi/2\end{aligned} \tag{3.14}$$

The gradient can be approximated by the following simple equations (Rosenfeld and Kak, 1976):

$$\begin{aligned}G_x &= (C+F+I)-(A+D+G)\\ G_y &= (A+B+C)-(G+H+I)\\ |\boldsymbol{G}| &= |G_x|+|G_y|\end{aligned} \tag{3.15}$$

In order to detect roof type or edge-effect type edge points, Laplacian operators are used. The Laplacian is defined for a continuous function $f(x,y)$ as follows:

$$\nabla^2 f(x,y) = \partial^2 f(x,y)/\partial x^2 + \partial^2 f(x,y)/\partial y^2 \tag{3.16}$$

For a digital image, the Laplacian can be defined by using the 3×3 window. The Laplacian operator with four neighbors is:

$$DD_2 = (B+D+F+H-4E)/4 \tag{3.17}$$

and with eight neighbors is:

$$DD_2 = (A+B+C+D+F+G+H+I-8E)/8 \tag{3.18}$$

Besides the basic two-dimensional operators described above, those which are modified versions of the basic ones are used for specific purposes, or those with larger windows are sometimes used to reduce the effect of noise.

3.1.4 Pattern Matching Operations

It is shown in Subsection 3.1.2 that the weighting function of an operator is similar to the intensity profile to be detected. This observation can be extended to pattern matching methods.

Griffith (1973) classified one-dimensional profile patterns across edges into six model patterns as shown in Fig. 3.7. Each model consists of 15 sample points, and is normalized so that the average of sample values is 0. In order to examine a profile pattern in an image, 15 pixels are similarly sampled. They are normalized so that the average is 0, and then the profile is matched to six models. The matching of profile $f(i)$ to the jth model $g_j(i)$ is given by the following convolution:

$$s_j = \sum_{i=1}^{15} f(i)\,g_j(i) \tag{3.19}$$

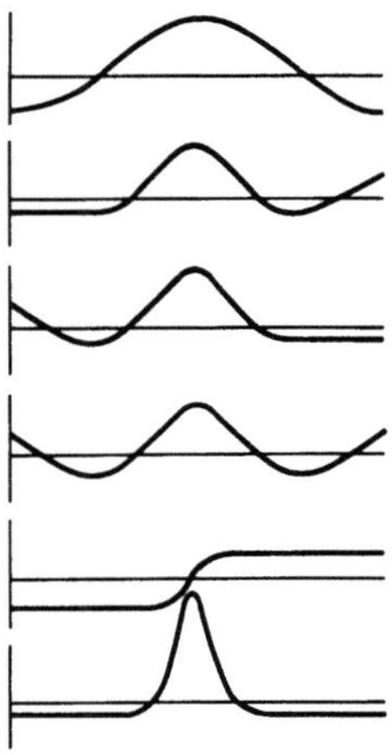

Fig. 3.7. Model patterns at edges (Griffith, 1973)

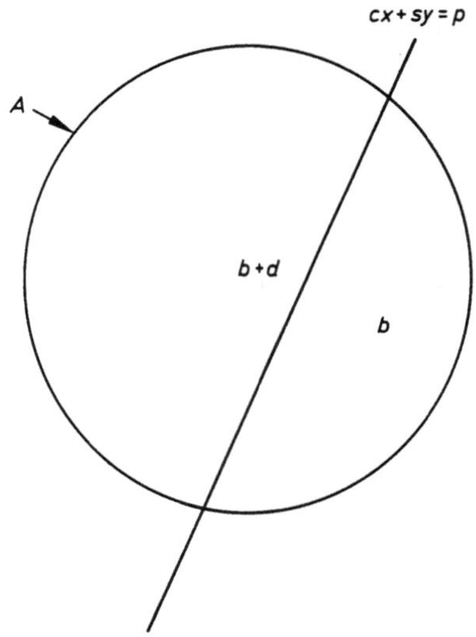

Fig. 3.8. Hueckel's model of edge

The value of s_j represents goodness of fit to the jth model. This operator was applied to polyhedral scenes (Griffith, 1973).

The pattern matching technique can be applied to two-dimensional cases, where the direction of an edge is not predicted. It is, however, inefficient to prepare many models of edge patterns for all directions.

A two-dimensional pattern matching operation that has been applied to real images involves the Hueckel operator (Hueckel, 1971). The model of the edge is confined to a step type, and the window is a circular region as shown in Fig. 3.8 (actually a digital region that is approximately circular). An edge is assumed to be linear, and on each side of the edge, light intensity is constant. Let the straight line be denoted by $cs+sy=p$ (where $c+s=1$), the light intensity on one side be denoted by b, and that on the other side by $b+d$. The model pattern of the edge is formulated by the following equation:

$$g(x,y,c,s,p,b,d)=\begin{cases} b & cx+sy<p \\ b+d & \text{otherwise} \end{cases} \tag{3.20}$$

The matching of a part of image $f(x,y)$ to the model is realized by determining parameters c, s, p, b, and d so that they minimize the following evaluation function:

$$E(c,s,p,b,d)=\int_A \{f(x,y)-g(x,y,c,s,p,b,d)\}\,\mathrm{d}x\,\mathrm{d}y \tag{3.21}$$

where A is the circular window.

It is inefficient to minimize directly Eq. (3.21). Instead, functions f and g are transformed to a frequency space, and the distance in the space is measured. This is accomplished with polar-coordinate Fourier transformation. Let $\{H_i(x,y), i=1,2,\ldots\}$ be a set of the basis functions by which f and g are expanded.

Coefficients of f and g are defined by:

$$u_i=\int_A H_i(x,y)f(x,y)\,dx\,dy$$
$$v_i(c,s,p,b)=\int_A H_i(x,y)g(x,y,c,s,p,b,d)\,dx\,dy \tag{3.22}$$

Now the problem is reduced to minimizing the error E given as:

$$E(c,s,p,b,d)=\sum_{i=0}^{\infty}\{u_i-v_i(c,s,p,b,d)\}^2 \tag{3.23}$$

For a digital image, however, this sum need only be carried out for the first few (eight in this case) terms, because of real limitations of resolution and size of the window. Thus Hueckel's operator returns, for each window, the best parameters of an edge and goodness of fit. If E is small and d is large, c, s, and p indicate the position of the edge. The operator was applied to natural images such as those of human faces (Hueckel, 1971). Although the operator can detect step type edges precisely, the amount of computation required is much more than that for conventional two-dimensional operators.

3.1.5 Color Edge Operators

Since color has three independent features, edge detection methods may depend on what features are taken into account. Brightness, which is one of the color features, can be treated in the same way as in the case of monochromatic images. Edge detection operators based on chromaticity are described in this subsection.

Let the chromaticity be represented by (r,g,b) in the chromaticity diagram as shown in Fig. 2.10. The difference of two colors $c_1=(r_1,g_1,b_1)$ and $c_2=(r_2,g_2,b_2)$ can be defined as follows:

$$D_1(c_1,c_2)=\{(r_1-r_2)^2+(g_1-g_2)^2+(b_1-b_2)^2\}^{\frac{1}{2}} \tag{3.24}$$

$$D_2(c_1,c_2)=|r_1-r_2|+|g_1-g_2|+|b_1-b_2| \tag{3.25}$$

$$D_3(c_1,c_2)=\max\{|r_1-r_2|,\ |g_1-g_2|,\ |b_1-b_2|\} \tag{3.26}$$

The value of D_1 reflects the angle between two color vectors $\boldsymbol{F}_1$ and $\boldsymbol{F}_2$ in the (R,G,B) space. D_2 and D_3 are approximations of D_1. Strictly speaking, none of them corresponds to human visual characteristics. However, they are often used to constitute an objective color edge operator because they are easily computed.

Once the difference of colors is defined, edge operators can be defined in the same way as described in Subsections 3.1.2 and 3.1.3. For example Eq. (3.2) can be extended to the following equation for a color edge operator:

$$D'_{d_1,d_2}(i)=\sum_{k=d_1}^{d_2}\{D_1(c(i+k),\ c(i-k))\}/(d_2-d_1+1) \tag{3.27}$$

where $c(j)$ denotes the color at j.

3.1.6 Determination of Edge Points

In the previous two subsections operators for edge point detection have been discussed. This subsection provides a description of the problem of determining, on the basis of outputs of these operators, whether edge points exist or not, and where they are if they exist.

The simplest way of determining edge points is to threshold the output of an operator. Suppose, for example, the output of the operator $D_{1,2}(i)$ is thresholded (see Fig. 3.3), then edge points are determined as those pixels with high contrast. If the threshold is low compared with the contrast, many pixels are regarded as edge points; that is, the result is a binary image of wide lines. One way to obtain thin edge lines is to apply a thinning operation to the binary image (Rosenfeld and Kak, 1976). This approach is not always effective, because thinning often produces extra branches and, moreover, it takes much computation.

Another way is to detect the local maxima. If the intensity profile at an edge is smooth, and operator $D_{1,2}$ is applied to it as in Fig. 3.3, the local maximum corresponds to the center of the edge. This method is usually applied to smoothed images or outputs of edge operators with a smoothing effect (such as $D_{d_1,d_2}(i)$ or $DD(i,j)$), because noisy profiles may have fluctuating positions of the maxima. The local maxima can also be detected by the zero-crossing method (Marr, 1982) described in the following subsection.

If the output of an edge operator is not smooth, we must employ a method of determining the edge position that is insensitive to small fluctuations of the output profile. Suppose that, based on the output of operator $D_d(i)$ shown in Fig. 3.9, the existence of a step edge and its position are to be determined in the interval $[L, R]$.

If a step edge exists in the interval, the $D_d(i)$ must satisfy the following conditions (Shirai, 1975a):

1. There must exist a maximum of $D_d(i)$ at i_m where i_m is other than at L or R.
2. It must be the case that $D_d(i_m) > T_a$ where T_a is a threshold on absolute height.
3. There must exist a minimum of $D_d(i)$ at $i = i_l$ between L and i_m and a minimum of $D_d(i)$ at $i = i_r$ between i_m and R such that

$$\begin{aligned} &D_d(i_m) - D_d(i_l) > T_r \\ &D_d(i_m) - D_d(i_r) > T_r \end{aligned} \tag{3.28}$$

where T_r is a threshold on relative height.

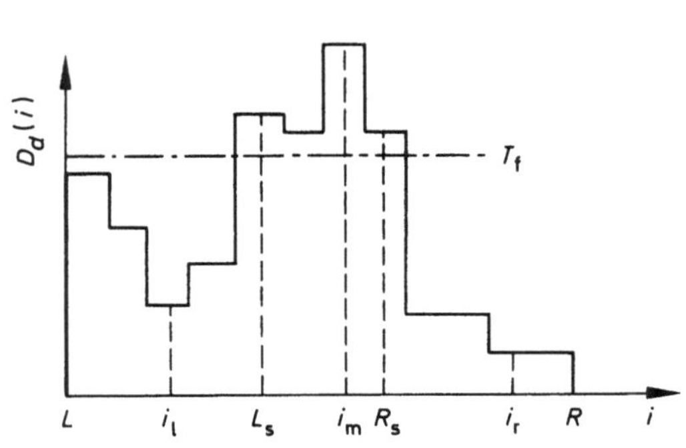

Fig. 3.9. Determination of existence of edge and its position based on output of edge operator

Note that T_a is usually determined by properties of the total image, and that T_r depends on local properties of the image, e.g., on the value $D_d(i_m)$.

If the three conditions are satisfied, then the existence of the edge is established. A peak that passes these tests often has a broad, flat top. Small amounts of noise can therefore move the maximum point widely between the peak's shoulders. Consequently, the location of the edge is not recorded as the peak but rather as the midpoint between the sharply defined shoulders. The left shoulder L_s and the right shoulder R_s are determined as the nearest intersection of $D_d(i)$ with the horizontal line at T_f as shown in Fig. 3.9. The threshold T_f can be determined by the following equation:

$$T_f = C_1 D_d(i_m) + C_0 \tag{3.29}$$

where $C_0(>0)$ and $C_1(0<C_1<1)$ are constants.

In the discussion above, it is assumed that the direction of an edge is predicted. This assumption is reasonable, because the direction can be predicted from the output of edge operators, even if it is not known before operators are applied.

3.1.7 Zero-Crossing Method

The principle of the zero-crossing method is, instead of finding maxima of a profile, to find zero-crossings of the differentiated profile (see Fig. 3.10). The method was proposed by Marr and Hildreth (1980) for feature extraction in the initial image processing. They argued that the best operation was to apply the Gaussian operator to the original image for smoothing, and then apply the Laplacian operator.

The two-dimensional Gaussian distribution is represented by:

$$G(x,y) = \frac{1}{2\pi\sigma^2} \exp\left(-\frac{x^2+y^2}{2\pi\sigma^2}\right) \tag{3.30}$$

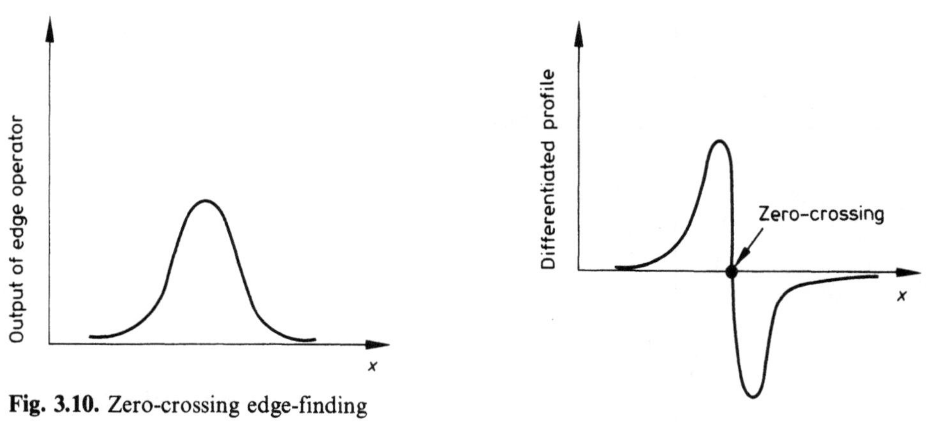

Fig. 3.10. Zero-crossing edge-finding

where σ is the standard deviation. The total operation applied to the original image $f(x, y)$ is formulated as:

$$\nabla^2 G(x,y) * f(x,y) = \left(\frac{\partial^2}{\partial x^2} + \frac{\partial^2}{\partial y^2}\right) \iint_{-\infty}^{\infty} G(x-\xi,\ y-\eta) f(\xi,\eta)\, d\xi\, d\eta$$
$$= \left\{\left(\frac{\partial^2}{\partial x^2} + \frac{\partial^2}{\partial y^2}\right) G(x,y)\right\} * f(x,y) \qquad (3.31)$$

The total operator $\nabla^2 G$ is represented by:

$$\nabla^2 G(r) = \left(\frac{r^2 - 2\sigma^2}{2\pi\sigma^6}\right) \exp\left(\frac{-r^2}{2\sigma^2}\right) \qquad (3.32)$$

where $r = (x^2 + y^2)^{\frac{1}{2}}$.

This operator is a rotationally symmetric function whose cross-section is shown in Fig. 3.11. Note that the diameter of its negative circle in the figure is given by:

$$w = 2\sqrt{2}\sigma \qquad (3.33)$$

The size of the operator may be specified by the value of w as well as σ.

An example of this type of processing is shown in Fig. 3.12. The result of applying this operator at various sizes is called the raw primal sketch (Marr, 1982).

The characteristics of the operator in the frequency domain are analyzed by applying the two-dimensional Fourier transformation to Eq. (3.31):

$$F\{[\nabla^2 G(x,y)] * f(x,y)\} = F\{\nabla^2 G(x,y)\}\, F\{f(x,y)\} \qquad (3.34)$$

The first term of the right hand side is given as:

$$F\{\nabla^2 G(x,y)\} = Q(u,v) = -(u^2+v^2) \exp(-\sigma^2(u^2+v^2)/2)$$
$$= -\omega^2 \exp(-\sigma^2\omega^2/2) \qquad (3.35)$$

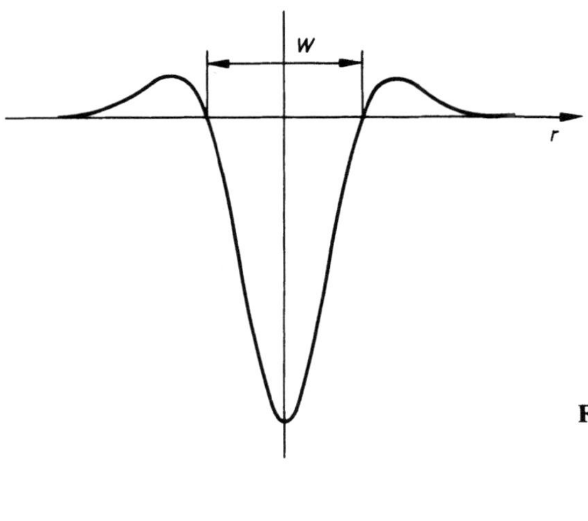

Fig. 3.11. Cross-section of $\nabla^2 G(r)$

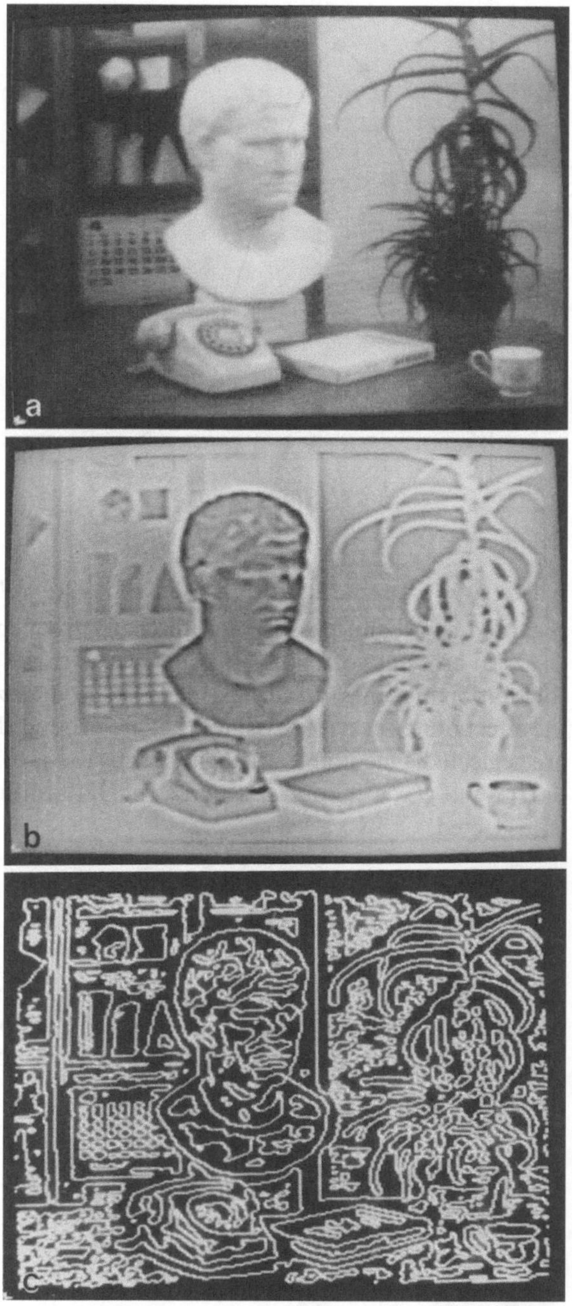

Fig. 3.12a–c. Example of zero-crossing method: (**a**) sample image; (**b**) the convolution of the image with the $\nabla^2 G$ operator ($\sigma = 1.5$ pixel); (**c**) the zero-crossing of (**b**)

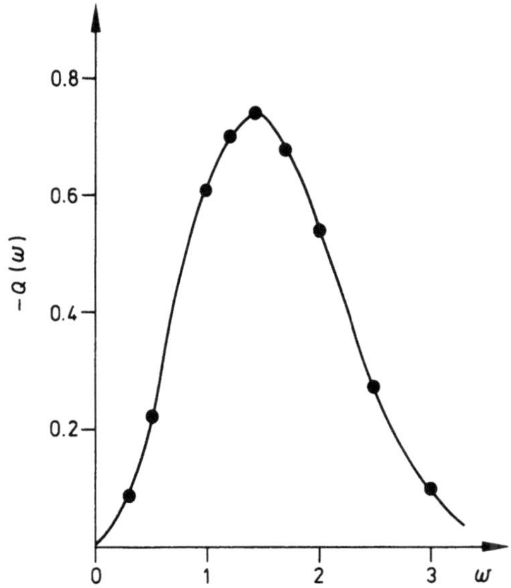

Fig. 3.13. The Fourier transform of $\nabla^2 G$

where $\omega^2 = u^2 + v^2$. Figure 3.13 shows $-Q(\omega)$. Note that the operator can be regarded as a band-pass filter with center frequency $\omega = \sqrt{2}/\sigma$.

Zero-crossings of a noise-free image may correspond to edges. However, a small fluctuation in a uniform surface may also produce zero-crossings. In order to avoid the effect of noise, zero-crossings that are produced by small light intensity changes are neglected. One simple way of achieving this is to examine the difference of $f(x, y)$ or $G(x, y) * f(x, y)$ across a zero-crossing. If the difference is small, the zero-crossing is neglected.

3.1.8 Edge of a Curved Surface

At an edge of a curved surface, the light intensity profile is different from that of a polyhedron. Suppose that in Fig. 3.14, for example, the background is dark, the brightness of a curved surface increases from left to right, and a front surface is the

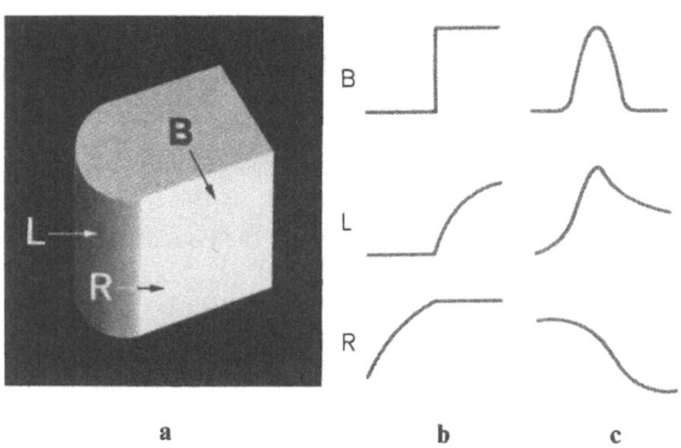

Fig. 3.14. Intensity profiles of edges

brightest. Light intensity profiles and the gradients across three typical edges are illustrated in Fig. 3.14. They are classified into type B, R, L, respectively. The last two profiles are not symmetric. A simple zero-crossing method may not be able to detect these edges correctly. A better method is necessary to detect edges of both planar and curved surfaces.

Since the gradient is large in any case, a two-dimensional edge operator described earlier is able to detect edge candidates and their directions. However, if the direction of the edge is predicted, as is the case in edge following, a one-dimensional operator is adequate. Once the direction of an edge candidate is known, an edge point is determined using a one-dimensional edge operator as described below (Shirai, 1978).

Imagine Cartesian coordinates $U-V$ such that V is the direction of the edge (the direction is decided so that the right side of the edge is brighter). Let $D(u,v)$ denote the difference of light intensity at (u,v) computed according to Eq. (3.5). Usually the area over which the averaging is done in Eq. (3.5) is small (e.g., 3×3 square). Point (u,v) is determined to be an edge if it satisfies the following conditions:

(C1) $D(u,v)>D_t$

(C2) $\exists_i\{D(u+i,v)<f(D(u,v))\wedge -w<i<w\}$

(C3) $\nabla_i\{2D(u,v)<D(u-i,v)+D(u+i,v)\wedge 1<|i|<w\}$

where D_t is a threshold, w is usually less than 4, and $f(x)=c_0+c_1x\,(c_1>0)$.

The condition (C1) means that the light intensity must change at an edge. The condition (C2) means that at least one neighboring point must have a smaller difference value. The condition (C3) ensures concavity of the gradient profile and rejects the points near the true edge.

Edges are classified when the condition (C2) is examined. If there exist both positive i and negative i, then the point is classified as type B; if there is no negative i, it is classified as type L; and otherwise as type R. The value of $D(u,v)$ represents a measure of confidence in the edge point.

3.2 Local Edge Linking

This section introduces two methods for linking edge points which are extracted by edge operators described in the previous section.

3.2.1 Roberts' Edge-Linking Method

The edge-linking method developed by Roberts (1963) accepts as an input a differentiated image obtained by Roberts' edge operator (see Subsection 3.1.3).

The first step in the process chooses edge points which seem to be on an edge line. The point with the maximum differential value in each 4×4 square point is considered as a candidate if the value exceeds a small threshold. For each candidate, the direction of the edge is determined by correlations of light intensities in the

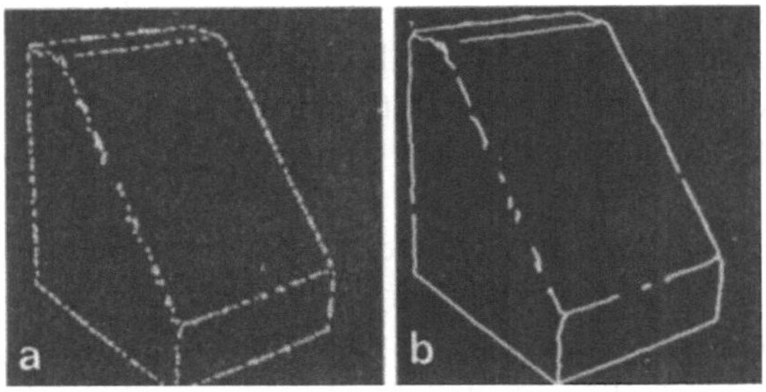

Fig. 3.15a,b. Roberts' edge-linking method (Roberts 1963): (**a**) candidate edge points; (**b**) result of edge linking

neighboring region. If a point has no prominent edge direction, it is removed from the candidates. Figure 3.15(a) shows candidate points obtained from Fig. 3.5(b). A problem with this step is that important edges may be removed if they are on a line with some fluctuations.

The next step links neighboring candidate points on the basis of directions of the points. Specifically, a pair of points is connected if the points are in contiguous 4×4 squares and if the difference of their directions is within a threshold. Any points left unconnected are eliminated. Figure 3.15(b) shows the result of this step.

Each step of this process can be executed in parallel, because the processing for an edge point depends only on the local neighbor and does not depend on the results of processing for other points.

3.2.2 Edge Linking by Relaxation

The purpose of edge linking is to find a set of edges which have enough contrast and are consistent with one another. This process can be modeled by the probabilistic relaxation method proposed by Zucker, Hummel, and Rosenfeld (1977).

In the formulation of Zucker et al., each pixel has $m+1$ labels. Each of m labels corresponds to the direction of the edge at the pixel, and the last one corresponds to the case in which no edge is present. For each pixel i, the probability of label λ is defined (denoted by $p_i(\lambda)$). The initial value of this probability $p_i(\lambda)$ is calculated by applying an edge operator to the pixel. Each probability is updated iteratively according to neighbors' probabilities.

For each pair of neighboring pixels i, j and each pair of labels λ, λ', the compatibility function $r_{i,j}(\lambda, \lambda')$ is defined, denoting a measure of compatibility between λ at i and λ' at j. Let us assume that the compatibility function has values between -1 and 1, where 1 denotes complete compatibility, -1 denotes complete incompatibility, and 0 means no relations. The compatibilities between line labels are shown in Fig. 3.16 (Zucker, Hummel, and Rosenfeld, 1977).

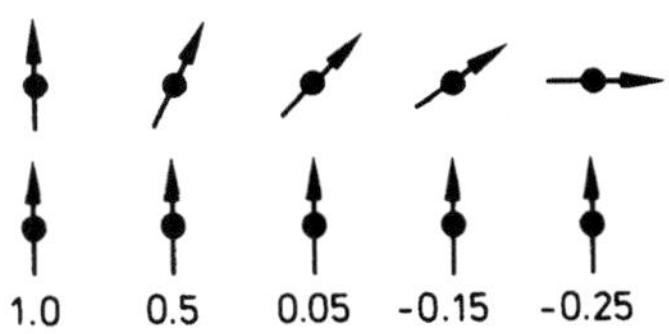

Fig. 3.16. Compatibility between edge labels (Zucker et al., 1977)

The probability $p_i(\lambda)$ is strengthened by λ' of a neighboring pixel j if $r_{i,j}(\lambda, \lambda')$ is positive and vice versa. The effect of λ' at j is proportional to both $r_{i,j}(\lambda, \lambda')$ and $p_j(\lambda')$. Thus the total effect of the pixel j is represented by:

$$\sum_{\lambda'} r_{i,j}(\lambda, \lambda') p_j(\lambda') \tag{3.36}$$

The pixel i is affected by neighboring pixels. Let $d_{i,j}$ denote the strength of the effect of the pixel j, which depends on the geometrical relation between points i and j. The effect of all other pixels is represented by the following equation:

$$q_i(\lambda) = \sum_j d_{i,j} \sum_{\lambda'} [r_{i,j}(\lambda, \lambda') p_j(\lambda')] \tag{3.37}$$

Suppose that the $k+1$th value of the probability $p_i^{k+1}(\lambda)$ is calculated from $p_i^k(\lambda)$ and other probabilities of labels at neighboring pixels. An updating rule is defined by:

$$p_i^{k+1}(\lambda) = \frac{p_i^k(\lambda)[1 + q_i^k(\lambda)]}{\sum_{\lambda'} p_i^k(\lambda')[1 + q_i^k(\lambda')]} \tag{3.38}$$

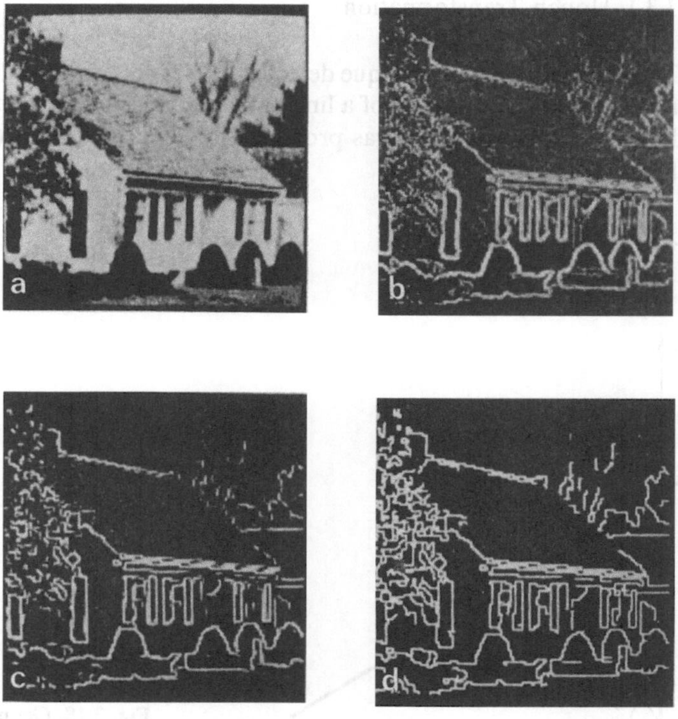

Fig. 3.17. Edge linking by relaxation (Hanson and Riseman, 1978)

Note that the denominator of the right hand side normalizes $p_i^{k+1}(\lambda)$ such that the following condition holds:

$$\sum_{\lambda} p_i^{k+1}(\lambda)=1$$

Usually the relaxation process links edges, suppressing noisy edges and enhancing long smooth edge lines, after several iterations. Figure 3.17 shows an example of the results of the relaxation process (Hanson and Riseman, 1978).

Relaxation methods can also be applied to corner detection, template matching, and clustering.

3.3 Edge Point Clustering in Parameter Space

Given edge points in an image plane, the problem here is to find a set of edge points on each edge line, the equation of which is represented by parameters. If edge points in the image space are appropriately transformed to another space (parameter space), they form clusters corresponding to edge lines. Since this method was first proposed by Hough (as a patent) for the detection of straight lines, it is called the Hough method. Later it was extended to the generalized Hough method of detecting various features such as curves or specific shapes.

3.3.1 Hough Transformation

The original Hough technique detected lines from edge points whose direction was not known. The equation of a line in this technique was represented by $y=ax+b$. Later, a better equation was proposed by Duda and Hart (1972) as follows (see Fig. 3.18):

$$x \cos \theta+y \sin \theta=p \tag{3.39}$$

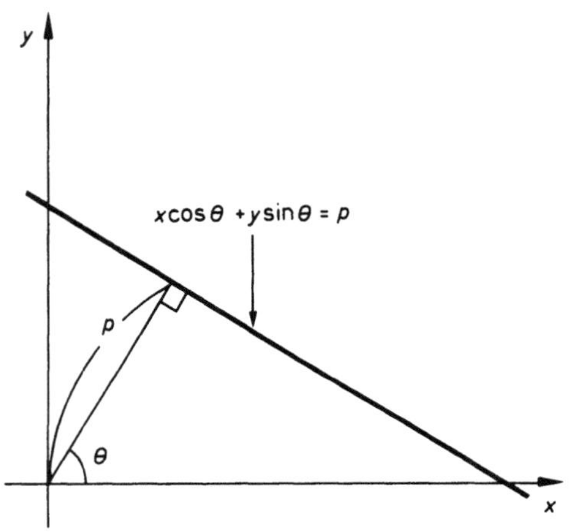

Fig. 3.18. Geometrical meaning of line equation

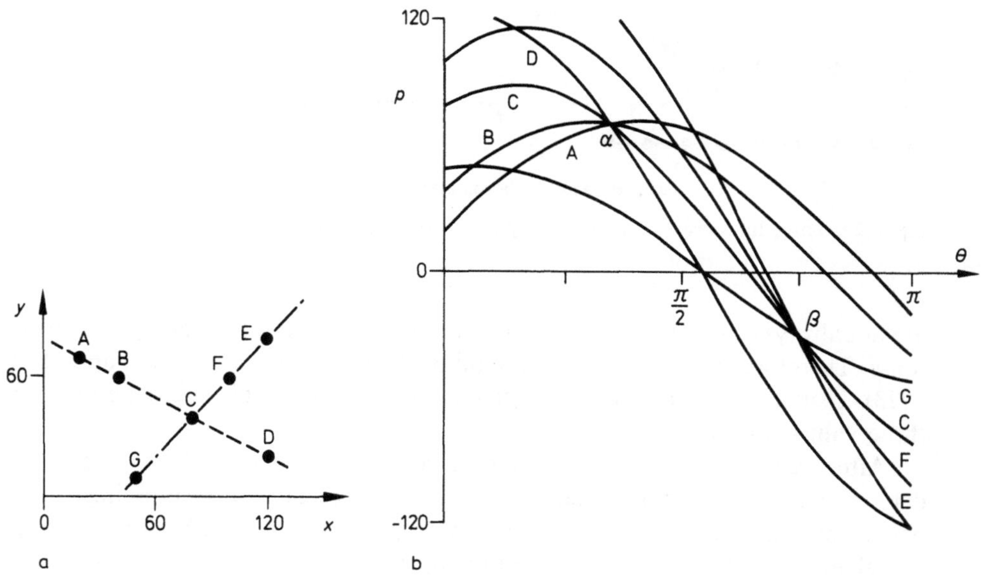

Fig. 3.19a,b. Line detection by Hough transformation: (**a**) edge points in x–y plane; (**b**) trajectories in parameter space

The parameters of this equation, θ and p, are uniformly sensitive to change in the line direction. If p is allowed to be negative in Eq. (3.39), every line is represented by p and $\theta\,(0<\theta<\pi)$.

Suppose an edge point A is given in the image plane. All lines passing through point A are represented by:

$$x_A \cos\theta + y_A \sin\theta = p \tag{3.40}$$

where (x_A, y_A) denotes the position of A.

Now consider a two-dimensional parameter space with θ and p axes as shown in Fig. 3.19(b). A line in the image plane is represented by a point in the parameter space. All lines passing through point A lie on the sinusoidal curve defined by Eq. (3.40).

Suppose that points A, B, C, and D lie on a straight line in the image as shown in Fig. 3.19(a). All lines passing through those points are transformed to similar curves in the parameter space. Note that all curves in the parameter space pass through a point ('α' in Fig. 3.19(b)) which denotes the line in the image plane. In Fig. 3.19(b), another point β also represents a set of points on a line in the image (see Fig. 3.19(a)).

In order to execute this process on a computer, the parameter space must be digitized into square regions. Let (i,j) denote the square defined as the intersection of the ith interval of θ and the jth interval of p, and $H(i,j)$ denote the two-dimensional histogram matrix (initially every element is 0). For each curve in the parameter space, $H(i,j)$ is increased by one if the curve passes through the region (i,j). After H is calculated for all curves, peaks of H are located. Edge points in a line

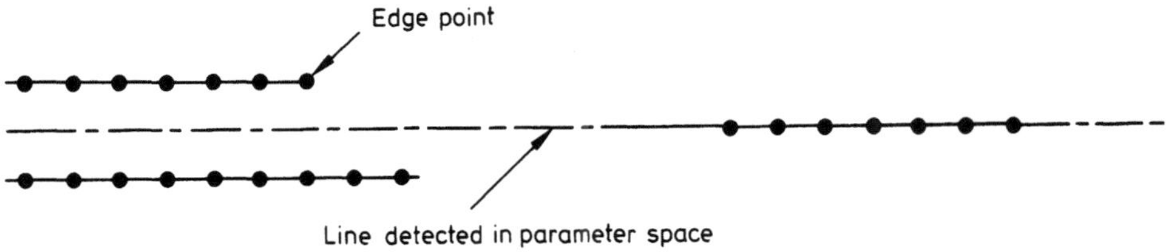

Fig. 3.20. Three lines corresponding to a point in parameter space

are not always transformed to a single point because of the effect of digitization or noise. Therefore, peak detection is a kind of clustering problem (Duda and Hart, 1973). Usually, histogram H is first smoothed, and then peaks are determined as those values higher than a threshold.

After peaks are obtained, a pair of parameters of each line equation is determined as center points. The next problem is to find lines corresponding to each pair of parameters. Since the line equation represents a line with infinite length, actual lines must be determined by examining edge points in the image. Note that if edge points are given as shown in Fig. 3.20, only one peak may be detected in the parameter space. Then the line corresponding to the peak is projected into the original plane, edge points near the line are examined, and finally three lines might be obtained as in Fig. 3.20 (O'Gorman and Clowes, 1973).

3.3.2 Extension of Hough Transformation

One extension of the Hough transformation is the use of edge direction. The direction of edge points can be detected by edge operators as described in the previous section. If the direction is available, the dimension of the trajectory in a parameter space is reduced.

Suppose the direction of edge A is known (to be θ_A). Then the equation of the line passing through the point is uniquely determined as:

$$x \cos \theta_A + y \sin \theta_A = x_A \cos \theta_A + y_A \sin \theta_A$$

The line is transformed to a point $a(\theta_A, x \cos \theta_A + y \sin \theta_A)$ in the parameter space (see Fig. 3.21). The calculation of the histogram $H(i,j)$ in this case is very simple, and the clustering problem becomes easier.

Another extension of the Hough transformation is the detection of curves with known parameters. Suppose the equation of curves is represented by:

$$y = ax^2 + c \tag{3.41}$$

A new parameter space with coordinates a and c is defined. For each edge point, the curve is obtained in the parameter space. The rest of the processing is the same as that described in the previous subsection.

If the direction of edges is known, curves in the parameter space also degenerate to points. The direction of an edge θ represents dy/dx of the equation of the curve.

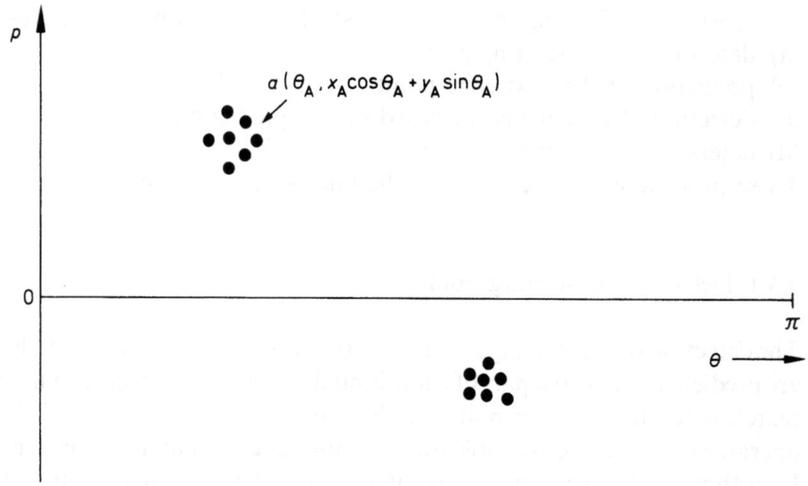

Fig. 3.21. Hough transformation of edges with known directions

For example, if a curve is represented by Eq. (3.41), the following equation is derived by differentiating Eq. (3.41) and substituting $\tan\theta$ for dy/dx:

$$\tan\theta = 2ax \qquad (3.42)$$

For an edge point, a pair of parameters (a, c) is obtained by solving the simultaneous Eqs. (3.41) and (3.42).

If curves are represented by many parameters, the dimension of the parameter space increases. For example, arcs are represented by the equation of the circle with three parameters, $(x-a)^2+(y-b)^2=r^2$. Calculation of the histogram in three-dimensional space requires much computation and memory. Detection of curves with more than two parameters is not practicable. If the radius of circles is known, or the direction of edges is known, then the dimension of the parameter space is reduced to two, and the method can be applied.

Edge point clustering in a parameter space is not sensitive to local noises because it uses global information of an image. The process is suitable for parallel processing. One difficulty is that it cannot detect curves with many parameters or those which are not represented by equations.

3.4 Edge-Following Methods

Edge-following methods try to trace edge points on a straight line or a curve. Edge points are usually detected during the edge-following process, although edge points in the entire image may be detected earlier. The main advantages of edge-following methods are that they can find arbitrary curves and that they can make use of the information previously obtained.

Most edge-following methods consist of the following procedures:
(a) detection of the starting point,
(b) prediction of the next edge point,
(c) detection of an edge point based on the prediction,
(d) determination of the next step.
These procedures are described in the following subsections.

3.4.1 Detection of Starting Point

The detection of the starting point for edge following depends on whether edge lines are predicted or not. If a part of a line is predicted to be in a region, only the region is searched for the starting point. If the direction of a line is predicted, the edge operator which is most suitable for detecting edges in that direction can be selected. If nothing is known, the entire image must be searched by two-dimensional operators until a reliable starting point is found.

The threshold for determining edge points should be high enough that only reliable edge points are selected. The starting point should also be on a smooth line, i.e., should not be near the corner or the end of the line. A better way is to check after an edge is found, whether there are enough edge points with similar edge directions in the neighboring region. If such an edge is found, the initial position and the direction of the edge must be determined on the basis of those of the edge points in the neighbor.

3.4.2 Prediction of Next Edge Point

Prediction of the next edge point generally depends on those points already obtained. If only straight lines are followed, the prediction is very simple. Usually the line equation is fitted to known points by the least-square method, and the next point is predicted to be on the line beyond the last-found point (see Fig. 3.22). The predicted region is centered on the predicted point, and the region is searched for the next edge point.

The increment (distance between the last point and the predicted point) is often the smallest resolution of the image, i.e., one pixel. The increment can be set larger in

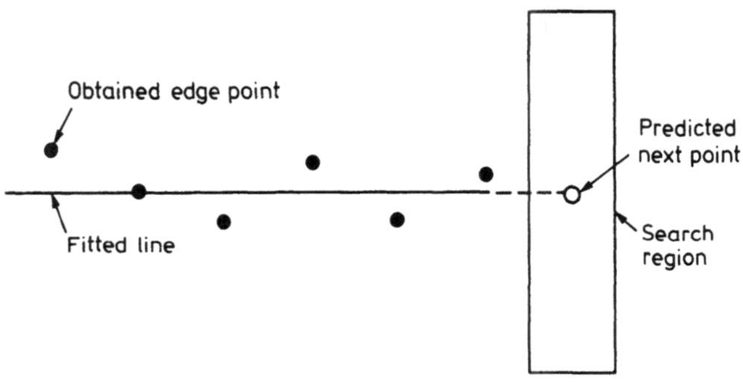

Fig. 3.22. Prediction of the next point for line following

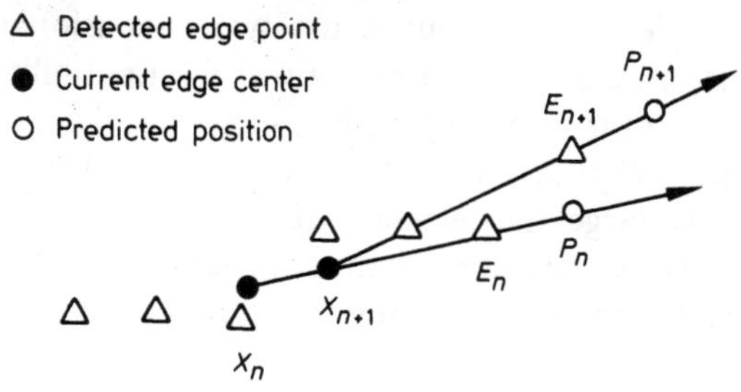

Fig. 3.23. Prediction of the next point for curve following

order to follow obvious edges quickly, and set smaller when no obvious edge is found.

The prediction of the next point is more difficult for curve following, because a linear equation cannot be used. Generally, the next point is predicted on the basis of several points found recently rather than on all points. The prediction of the next point on a smooth curve is based on the fact that a short segment of the curve is approximately linear.

An example of the prediction method is shown in Fig. 3.23 (Shirai, 1978). The prediction is based on the current position and the direction of the curve segment. The initial position and the direction are determined by several edge points which are obtained during detection of the starting point as described above. The current position and the direction are updated as edges are followed.

Let X_n denote the current position of the curve segment after the nth edge point is detected, and E_n denote the edge point as in Fig. 3.23. The next point P_n is predicted to be on the extension of the line $X_n E_n$. The neighbor of P_n is searched for the next edge point. Suppose E_{n+1} is detected as the next point. The current position X_{n+1} is moved by one unit along the line $X_n E_n$, and then the current direction is updated to be the vector from the current position X_{n+1} to the new edge E_{n+1} (see Fig. 3.23). The predicted next point P_{n+1} is similarly on the extension of the vector $X_{n+1} E_{n+1}$.

The distance between the current position of the curve segment and the predicted position of the next point is determined *a priori*. If it is long, the curve-following process is less sensitive to noise and does not easily follow curve segments with large curvatures.

3.4.3 Detection of Edge Point on Basis of Prediction

Detection of the next edge point is easier if the position and the direction of the edge is predicted. A one-dimensional edge operator, which is sensitive to edges in the predicted direction, can be used. A suitable edge operator can be chosen, because the type of the edge is known to be the same as that of edges previously obtained.

Thresholds for edge detection may be fixed, or adjusted according to the properties of edge points already followed. For example, the threshold of the contrast for detection of a step type edge is adjusted to be a linear relation with the average contrast of the last few edge points. Thus a curve can be followed if the contrast changes smoothly along it. If more than one edge point is found, the best one is chosen on the basis of their positions and the edge values.

We may, of course, use two-dimensional edge operators, in which case the direction of the edge is obtained. Compatibility of edge directions can be taken into account in selecting the best edge. Let θ denote the direction of the previous edge and $\theta'(i,j)$ denote that of the detected edge at (i,j). If the difference between these two is large, the detected edge is not regarded as the extension of the previous edge. One way of combining the edge value and the difference of the directions is to define the following evaluating function:

$$g(i,j)=|D(i,j)| \cos(\theta'(i,j)-\theta) \tag{3.43}$$

3.4.4 Determination of Next Step

The result of edge detection may be classified into the following five cases:
1. An edge point is at the predicted position.
2. There is no edge point.
3. An edge point is not at the predicted position.
4. It is undecided whether an edge point is at the predicted position or not.
5. It is undecided whether there is an edge point or not.

According to the cases listed above, the decision is made whether the edge following is to be continued or stopped, and how it is to be continued in the former case. The decision must satisfy the following two requirements: (a) edge following should terminate at the end of the curve, and (b) it should not be disturbed by other lines or noise. These two requirements are contradictory, since edge following which is insensitive to noise may also be insensitive to the end of the curve. In order to satisfy these requirements the following strategy can be adopted.

In case (1), the detected edge point is added to the sequence of edges obtained previously, and parameters such as the current position and the direction of the curve (which may be a straight line) are updated. For extraction of curved edges, thresholds of edge detection are also modified so that edges with smoothly changing contrast may be followed. Finally, the edge-following process is continued. In case (2), the decision depends on the past history of the edge-following process. For example, if results of the last m iterations are cases other than (1), then the process is stopped (m is a threshold). Otherwise, it is established that an edge is not found because of disturbances such as noise or other lines (see Fig. 3.24(a) for example), and the process is continued. Parameters are not updated in this case. The threshold m is determined on the basis of the resolution of the image and the characteristic of noise. Case (3) is dealt with in a similar way to case (2). It may correspond to the case of detecting P_1 in Fig. 3.24(c) or P_1 in Fig. 3.24(d).

It is important in low level computer vision to deal with ambiguous cases such as those of (4) and (5). In case (4), the detected point may be on the end of another curve (see Fig. 3.24(b)) or may be on the same curve where the edge position is displaced by some disturbance (see Fig. 3.24(d)). In case (5), the properties of the edge point (the edge value or the direction) are different from those of the previous edges. This case may also correspond to Fig. 3.24(b) or (d). It is important to see that Fig. 3.24(b), (c) and (d) are not discriminated locally (near point P). The correct decision should be based on further information about a region beyond the

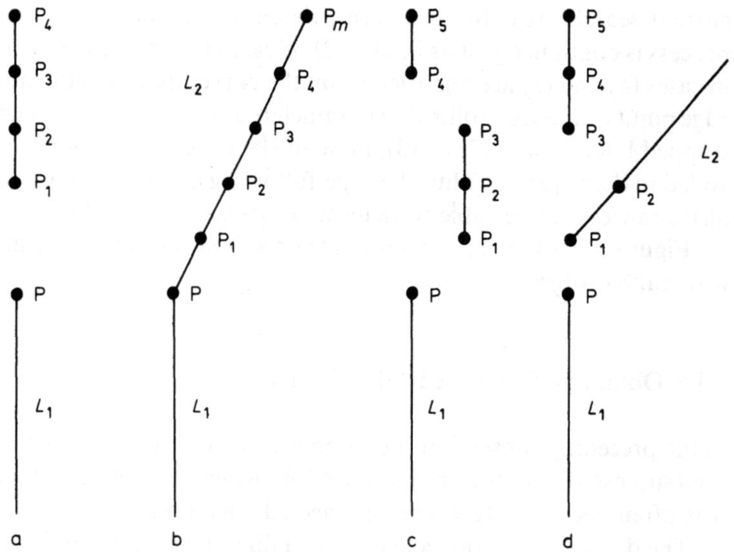

Fig. 3.24a–d. Results of edge detection: (**a**) no edge; (**b**) disturbed; (**c**) junction; (**d**) same line

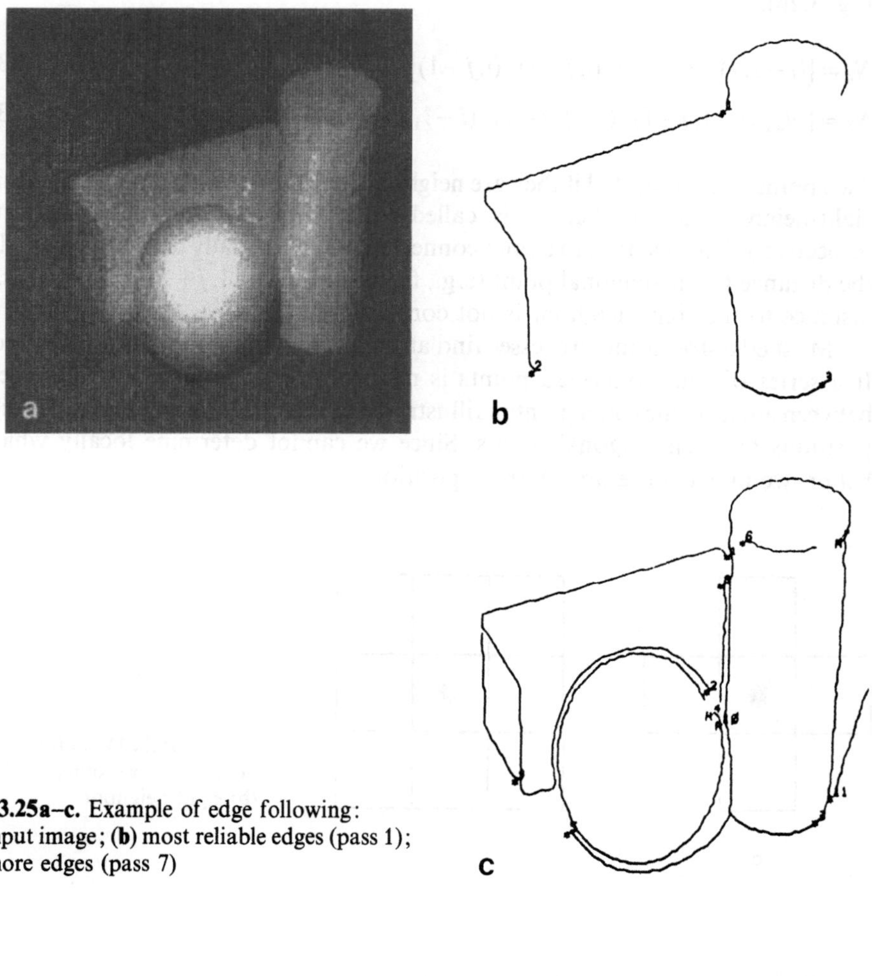

Fig. 3.25a–c. Example of edge following: (**a**) input image; (**b**) most reliable edges (pass 1); (**c**) more edges (pass 7)

current search area. In both cases, therefore, the decision is postponed and the process is continued just as in case (2). If case (1) occurs later, all edge points found in cases (4) and (5) are regarded as on the curve, they are added to the sequence of edge points, and edge-following parameters are updated using them. If the process is stopped later in case (2) or (3), none of the edge points found in case (4) or (5) is added to the sequence. Thus the edge-following process is robust against small noise disturbances and yet able to determine precisely the end of the curve.

Figure 3.25 shows an example of the result of edge following applied to an image with curved objects.

3.4.5 Obtaining Connected Edge Points

In the preceding subsections no attention is paid to the connection of edge points. Two successive points found by edge following may not be connected in the image. It is often necessary to obtain connected edge points.

The definition of connectedness in a digital image depends on the definition of neighbors. There are two definitions of neighbors: four-neighbor and eight-neighbor. Let a point at (i,j) in an image be denoted here by (i,j). Four-neighbors, N_4, and eight-neighbors, N_8, of a point (i,j) are the following points (see also Fig. 3.26).

$$N_4=\{(i-1,j),\ (i+1,j),\ (i,j-1),\ (i,j+1)\} \tag{3.44}$$

$$N_8=\{N_4,\ (i-1,j-1),\ (i+1,j-1),\ (i-1,j+1),\ (i+1,j+1)\} \tag{3.45}$$

Two points are connected if they are neighbors of each other. If a point is a four- or eight-neighbor of another, it is called 'four-connected' or 'eight-connected', respectively. The distance to a four-connected point is usually defined to be 1. Then the distance to the diagonal point (e.g., from (i,j) to $(i+1,j+1)$) is 2. That is, the distance to the eight-neighbor is not constant.

Most edge-following processes find an eight-connected point as the next point. If a series of four-connected points is necessary, extra points must be inserted between adjacent diagonal points as illustrated in Fig. 3.27. There are two candidate positions between diagonal points. Since we cannot determine locally which is better, we may choose an arbitrary position.

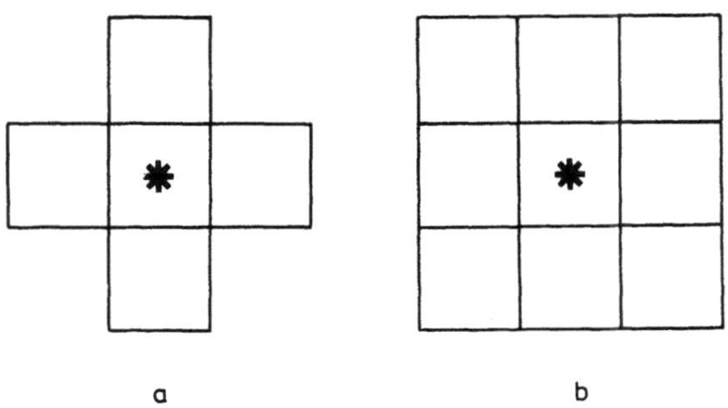

Fig. 3.26a, b. Definitions of neighbors: **(a)** four-neighbors; **(b)** eight-neighbors

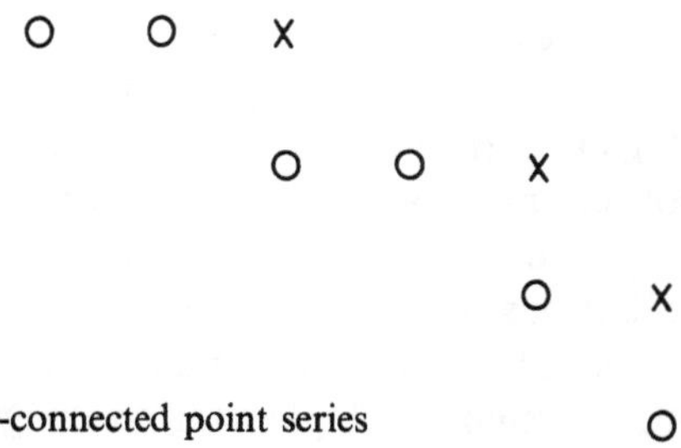

Fig. 3.27. Extra points (x) inserted to obtain a four-connected point series

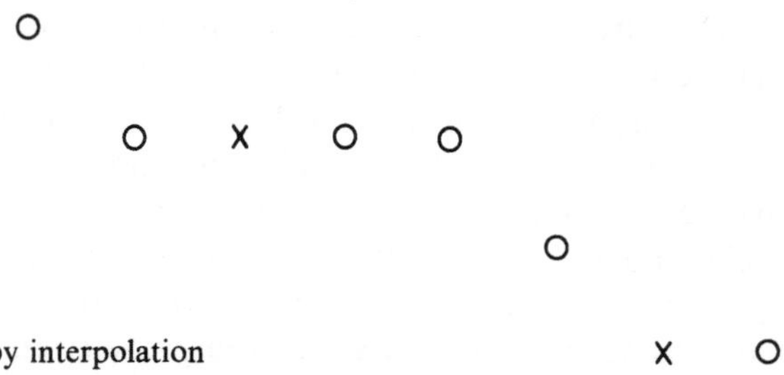

Fig. 3.28. Extra points (x) inserted by interpolation

Two adjacent points may not be connected when the increment of the edge-following process is greater than 1 or the next edge point is extracted at a larger distance in edge following. In such cases, extra points are also inserted. We can easily insert points by interpolation. Figure 3.28 illustrates the interpolation used to obtain an eight-connected point series.

3.5 Region Methods

While previous sections describe methods of extracting edge lines where two different regions meet, this section introduces region methods which try to extract regions of similar properties such as brightness, color, or texture. Region methods are categorized according to the processing strategy into the following classes:

1. Region merging. Starting with tiny uniform regions, such as individual pixels, merge similar regions until no further merging is possible.
2. Region splitting. Starting with a large region such as the entire image, split it into multiple regions. Continue the splitting process until no further splitting is possible.
3. Split and merge. Starting with medium-sized regions, such as squares of a fixed size, merge similar regions, and then split regions which are not merged (Pavlidis and Horowitz, 1974).

The following subsections describe typical region merging methods and region splitting methods commonly used in three-dimensional computer vision.

3.5.1 Region Merging

Region merging starts with many tiny atomic regions: individual pixels or collections of adjacent pixels with similar properties such as gray level, color, texture, or the like. One of the earliest works (Brice and Fennema, 1970) started with collections of adjacent pixels with the same gray level. An example of the atomic regions obtained from an image with 16 levels is shown in Fig. 3.29. The number of atomic regions is higher for an image with a greater number of levels.

In later work (Barrow and Popplestone, 1971), atomic regions consisted of pixels that have a gray level within a certain range (3 levels for an image with 16 levels). Extraction of these atomic regions is not trivial because the result depends on the order of processing (e.g., if the level of a sequence of pixels is 1, 2, 3, 4, and 5, possible segmentations are $\{(1,2,3), (4,5)\}$, $\{(1,2), (3,4,5)\}$, and so on). In their work, kernels of the atomic region are spread over the image, one at every 4×4 pixels. Starting from each kernel, an atomic region is expanded pixel by pixel. If the level of a pixel is outside the range of ± 1 from the level of the kernel, the pixel is regarded as outside of the atomic region. Note that atomic regions thus obtained may overlap because they start from predetermined kernels.

This method works well if the size of regions is within a certain range. Otherwise, it is not known how many kernels should be spread at first.

A better way to extract atomic regions is to use edges. Edges are extracted by edge methods. In order to obtain many atomic regions, the threshold for edge extraction must be low enough so that edges with low contrast may be detected. After edges are extracted in the image, atomic regions are determined as those enclosed by edges (i.e., edges with open ends are neglected).

In the region merging process, adjacent similar regions are merged until no two adjacent regions are sufficiently similar to be merged. The typical region merging algorithm repeats calculation of the criterion of merging for each pair of adjacent regions, and merging of the best pair. The criterion is based on the similarity of regions. The two principal criteria of similarity of two adjacent regions are: the

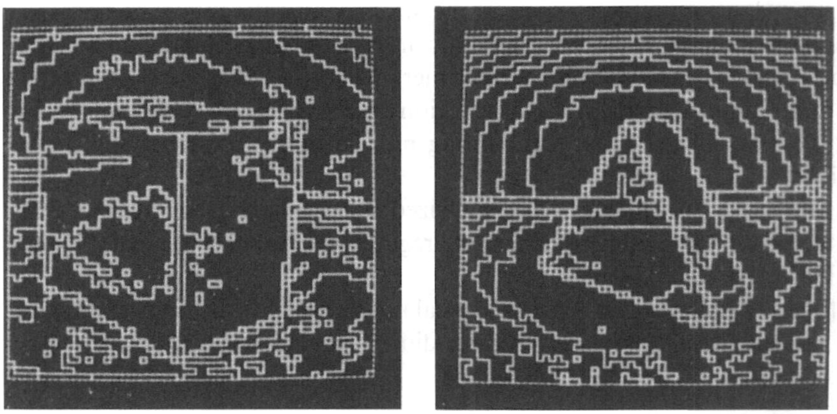

Fig. 3.29. Examples of atomic regions (60×60 resolution) (Brice and Fennema, 1970)

difference of the levels along the border, and the difference of the average levels. The criterion sometimes involves object-dependent heuristics.

Brice and Fennema (1970) developed a region method based on two heuristics called phagocyte heuristic and weakness heuristic (the latter is actually equivalent to the similarity of regions). The phagocyte heuristic depends on shapes of regions and gray level difference along the border. Let regions R_i and R_j have border B whose length is I, and have perimeters whose lengths are P_i and P_j respectively. A boundary interval is called a weak boundary if the difference of gray levels of two adjacent pixels is within a certain threshold. Let W denote the sum of lengths of weak boundaries in B. If W is large, boundary B is not clear. The phagocyte heuristic merges R_i and R_j in the following case:

$$W/\min\{P_i, P_j\} > p_t \tag{3.46}$$

where p_t is a threshold. According to the heuristic, a pair of regions having the same W value may or may not be merged depending on their shapes. Suppose in Fig. 3.30 that the boundary of regions R_i and R_j is weak everywhere (i.e., $W=I$). It is easily seen that the shorter the perimeter of the merged region, the larger is the value of the criterion. That is, the phagocyte heuristic is effective for scenes with convex polyhedra. Results of applying the phagocyte heuristic are shown in Fig. 3.31.

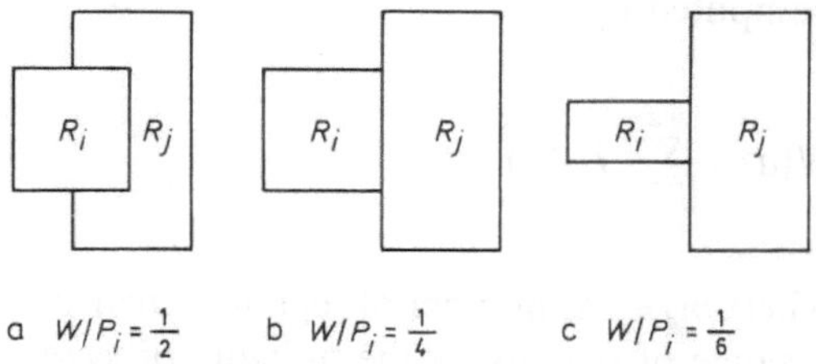

Fig. 3.30. The criterion of the phagocyte heuristic

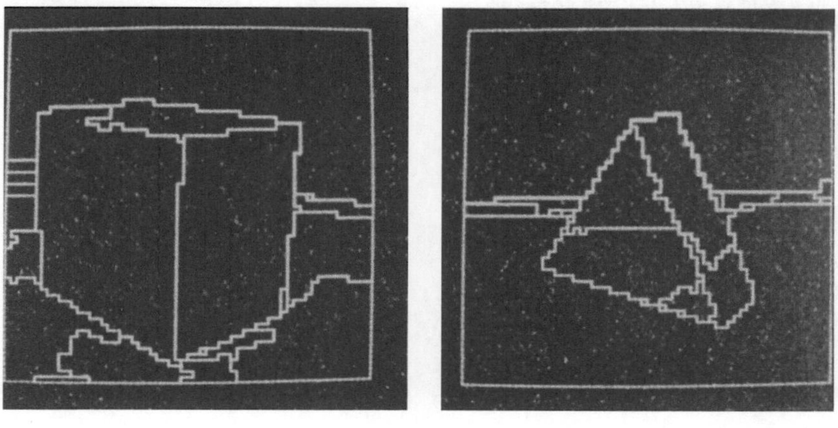

Fig. 3.31. Results of phagocyte heuristic applied to Fig. 3.29 (Brice and Fennema, 1970)

The weakness heuristic simply merges R_i and R_j if the boundary includes long, weak boundary segments. The criterion is given by:

$$W/I > w_t \tag{3.47}$$

where w_t is a threshold. Results of this heuristic are shown in Fig. 3.32.

If objects in scenes are not constrained, an object-dependent heuristic cannot be used. In the work of Barrow and Popplestone (1971), the criterion is the difference of the average levels of the adjacent regions. If the difference is less than a threshold (about 2.1), regions are merged. In the merging process an available region is taken and tested against all adjacent regions. Those which may be merged with it are merged simultaneously and a new region is created. These two processes are repeated. A curved surface with continuously changing brightness can be obtained as one region because the difference of the average levels in overlapping atomic regions may be small, and they are merged simultaneously. This method therefore works effectively for overlapping atomic regions.

Most atomic regions, however, are disjoint to one another. In such a case another method has been proposed (Tomita, Shirai, and Tsuji, 1982). It starts with atomic regions obtained from edges as described above. If the difference of the average levels in two adjacent regions is less than or equal to a threshold d (initially, $d=1$), the regions are merged. Whenever a new region is created, the average is computed. After the entire image is processed, the total change in the level is computed by:

$$N(d) = \sum_{k=1}^{m_d} |D_d(k)| \tag{3.48}$$

where m_d is the number of regions which are merged and $D_d(k)$ is the change in the average of regions by the merging process with threshold d.

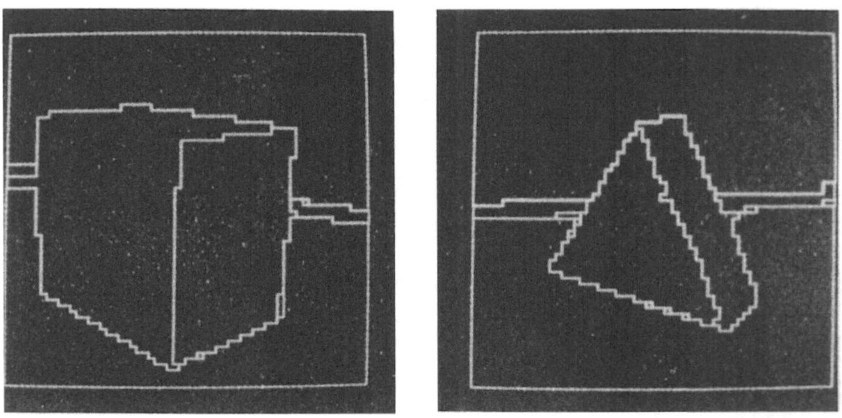

Fig. 3.32. Results of weakness heuristic applied to Fig. 3.29 (Brice and Fennema, 1970)

Next, d is increased by one ($d \leftarrow d+1$), and the merging process is repeated at least n times ($n=4$ for images with 64 levels) until one of the following conditions is satisfied:

(a) $N(d) > c \min_{4<d'<d} \{N(d')\}$

(b) $N(d) > t_1$

(c) $N(d) < t_2$

where c, t_1, and t_2 are constants (experimentally determined values for images of 64×64 pixels are $c=1.5$, $t_1=5000$, $t_2=1000$). Conditions (a) and (b) imply that d is large enough to merge nonuniform regions. Condition (c) implies that the

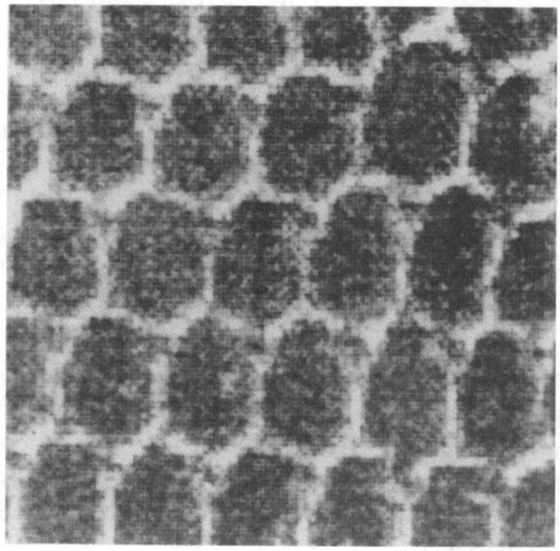

Fig. 3.33. Input image for region merging (reptile skin)

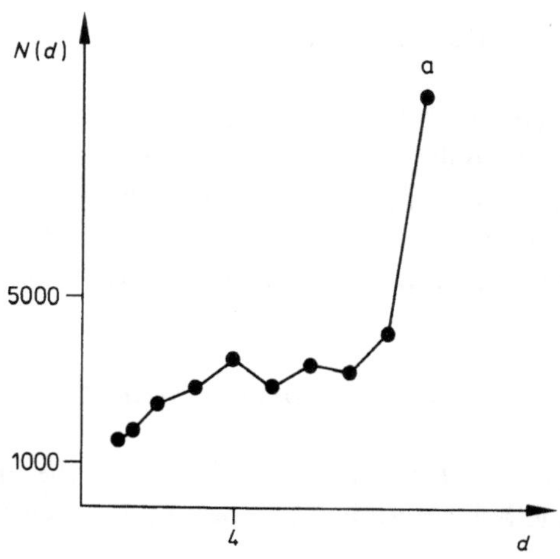

Fig. 3.34. Total brightness changes in the merging process on the image in Fig. 3.33

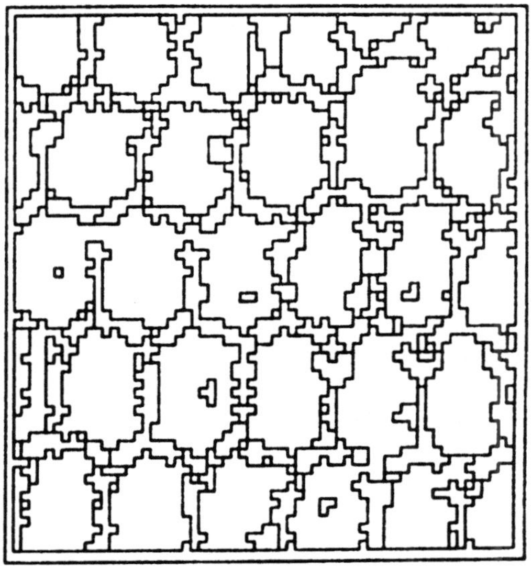

Fig. 3.35. Boundaries of extracted regions from image in Fig. 3.33

brightness change is large enough to separate different regions. If the process stops on the condition (a) or (b), the previous regions are the answer. If the process stops on condition (c) the current regions are the answer.

For the input images shown in Fig. 3.33, the total level changes in the merging processes are shown in Fig. 3.34. Figure 3.35 shows the boundaries of extracted regions obtained from the images in Fig. 3.33.

The region merging methods described above work on the basis of pixel properties of regions and simple heuristics. These methods are, however, not sufficiently powerful to be relied upon to detect all the regions we expect, and no more. The main reason is that they are independent of the kind of scene being observed. Yakimovsky and Feldman (1973) and Tenenbaum and Barrow (1977) used knowledge about scenes to guide region merging. These methods are described in Chap. 9.

3.5.2 Region Splitting

Region splitting starts with a single region and splits it into multiple regions. Each of these multiple regions is again similarly split into multiple regions. The key to this method is a criterion for deciding how a region should be split. Most techniques determine the criteria on the basis of statistics of pixel values within a region. Two representative methods are described below.

3.5.2.1 Region Splitting by Mode Methods

A typical statistic of pixel values is the histogram of the entire region. The mode method determines the threshold for region splitting on the basis of the histogram.

Since each uniform region contains many pixels of similar values, peaks in the histogram (called 'modes') are considered to correspond to such regions. If the histogram contains multiple peaks, the region is regarded as being composed of multiple uniform regions, and is split.

Now let us consider a simple case in which the histogram contains two peaks as shown in Fig. 3.36. A valley in the histogram between two peaks corresponds to a pixel value that occurs infrequently or does not occur. The value at the valley can be used as a threshold for region splitting. The region is split into two collections of pixels: those with pixel values below the threshold and those with pixel values above the threshold. Sometimes more than two connected regions are produced by this process. Each of these connected region is again examined in the same way as described above. This process is repeated until one or no peak is found in the histogram.

In practice the histogram is not as smooth as shown in Fig. 3.36. It is, therefore, useful to apply a smoothing operator such as an averaging operator before finding peaks and valleys. Only high peaks and deep valleys are located. They are determined by thresholding their levels or by comparing neighboring peaks and valleys. If the histogram contains more than two peaks, multiple thresholds may be derived from multiple valleys. There are two procedures for such a case. In the first, the region is simply split by multiple thresholds. In the second, the most prominent valley surrounded by high peaks is selected and the region split according to the corresponding threshold. The latter procedure is more reliable because the histogram of pixel values within a small region represents the property of the region more clearly than that within a larger region.

The technique is suitable for images that include uniform surfaces. A difficult example is shown in Fig. 3.37 where the histogram contains no prominent peaks because pixel values within each surface are not uniform.

The technique was extended to make use of multiple histograms by Tomita, Yachida, and Tsuji (1973) for texture images, and by Ohlander (1975) for color images. Ohlander used nine histograms of color features: *R*, *G*, *B*, brightness, hue, saturation, *Y*, *I*, and *Q* (see Sects. 2.3 and 2.4). Note that those features are not independent. Among the nine histograms, one is selected which contains the most

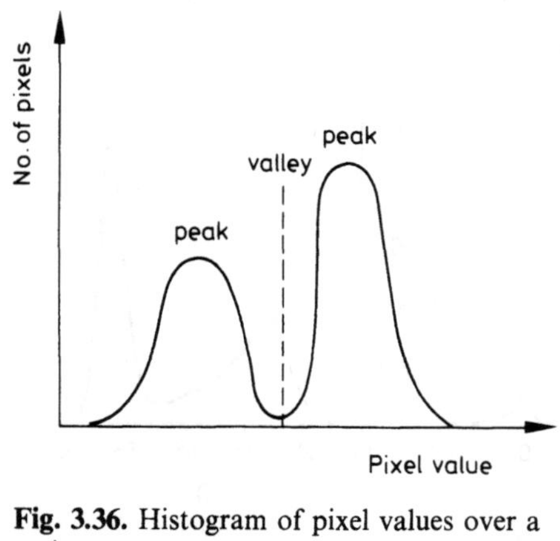

Fig. 3.36. Histogram of pixel values over a region

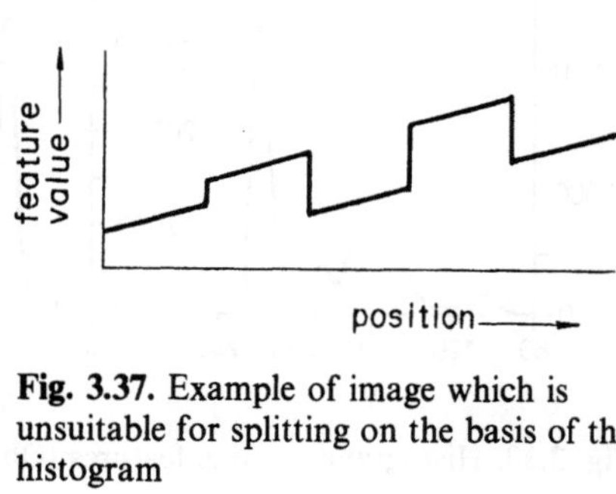

Fig. 3.37. Example of image which is unsuitable for splitting on the basis of the histogram

Fig. 3.38. Input image for region splitting (Ohlander, 1975)

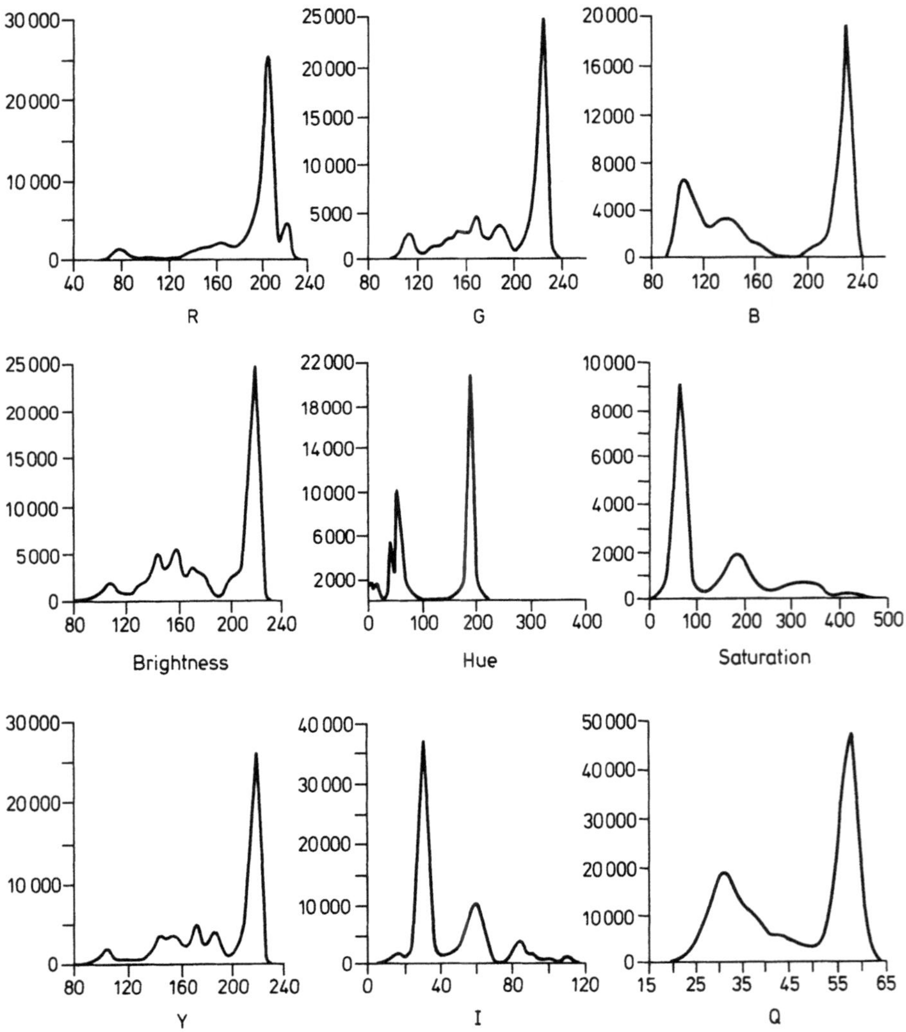

Fig. 3.39. Histograms of nine features (Ohlander, 1975)

Fig. 3.40. Result of thresholding for values of B (Ohlander, 1975)

prominent peaks and a valley. The region is then split according to the feature. For example, the histograms of nine features for the scene shown in Fig. 3.38 are shown in Fig. 3.39. The most prominent peaks and a valley are found in the histogram of B, and the entire image is split using B values of pixels with a threshold corresponding to the valley (about 173). Figure 3.40 shows the result, where white regions correspond to those with B values above the threshold and black regions to the others. Every time new regions are produced, the nine histograms are calculated and a decision is made on the basis of the results of those calculations. This process is repeated until no splitting is suggested by any histogram. The final result of the technique applied to Fig. 3.38 is shown in Fig. 3.41.

Again it must be noted that region splitting on the basis of features of pixels within the region is not sufficiently powerful to extract all regions we expect, because semantics of the image are not utilized.

3.5.2.2 Region Splitting Based on Discriminant Criterion

The mode methods are convenient to use if the histogram of the pixel values has prominent valleys. Otherwise, other methods are necessary. Figure 3.42 shows such an example. Although the histogram has no prominent peaks, we can perceive many blob-like regions. If *a priori* information is available about the image, e.g., 'the image contains a bright region with a known area', desired regions can be discriminated from the others (background). Without such information, we must use some criteria based on the distribution of the pixel value. The method described

Fig. 3.41. Result of region splitting for image in Fig. 3.38 (Ohlander, 1975)

here determines the best threshold of the pixel value according to a statistical criterion called the 'discriminant criterion' (Otsu, 1978).

Let a given image be represented by L levels (e.g., gray levels). Let p_i denote the normalized histogram of level i, i.e.,

$$\sum_{i=1}^{L} p_i = 1$$

The mean and the variance of the total image are given by

$$m_t = \sum_{i=1}^{L} i p_i \tag{3.49}$$

$$\sigma_t^2 = \sum_{i=1}^{L} (i - m_t)^2 p_i \tag{3.50}$$

Now suppose that the region is classified by a threshold k into two classes: C_1 with the pixel value less than or equal to k and C_2 with that greater than k. Let w_1 and w_2 denote the ratio of the area C_1 and C_2 to the total area, respectively ($w_1 + w_2 = 1$). The class mean and the class variance for C_j ($j = 1, 2$) are given by:

$$m_j = \sum_{i \in C_j} i p_i / w_j \tag{3.51}$$

$$\sigma_j^2 = \sum_{i \in C_j} (i - m_j)^2 p_i / w_j \tag{3.52}$$

The variance within a class, and the variance between classes, are defined as follows:

$$\sigma_w^2 = w_1 \sigma_1^2 + w_2 \sigma_2^2 \tag{3.53}$$

$$\sigma_b^2 = w_1 (m_1 - m_t)^2 + w_2 (m_2 - m_t)^2 = w_1 w_2 (m_1 - m_2)^2 \tag{3.54}$$

The threshold is good if σ_w^2 is small and σ_b^2 is large. Since the relation $\sigma_w^2 + \sigma_b^2 = \sigma_t^2$ holds, minimizing σ_w^2 also means maximizing σ_b^2. Therefore, the optimal threshold

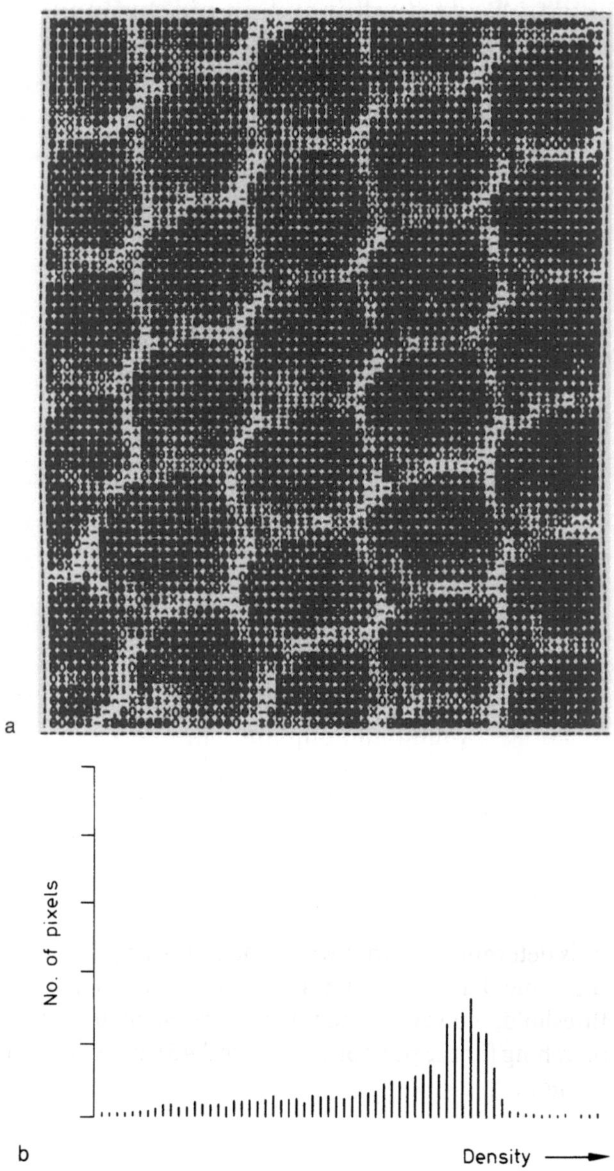

Fig. 3.42a, b. Example of an image unsuitable for mode methods: (**a**) image; (**b**) histogram of gray level

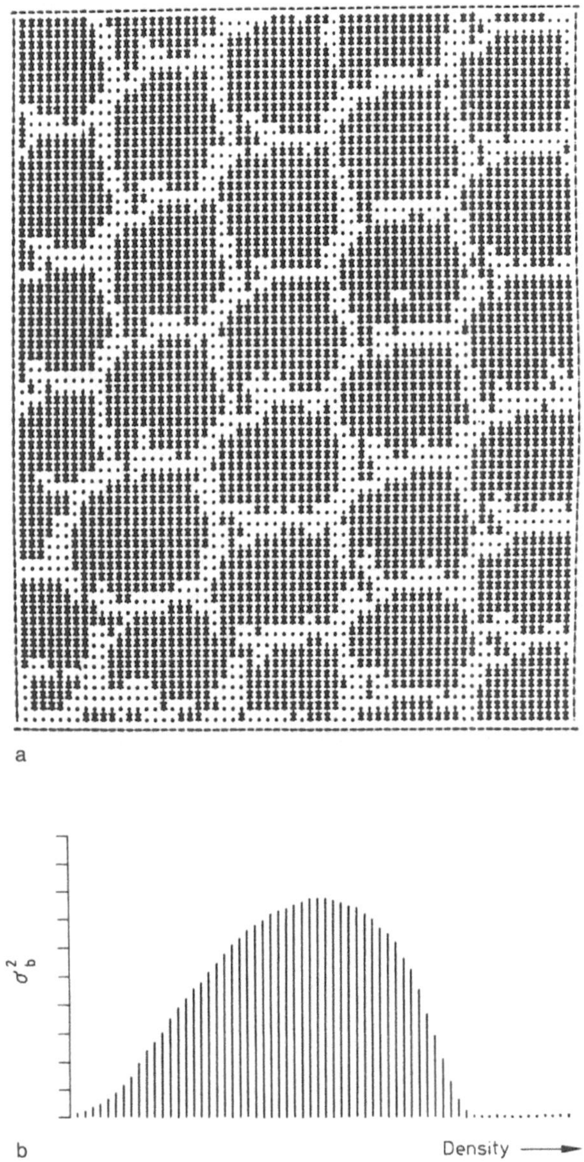

Fig. 3.43a,b. Result of region splitting for image in Fig. 3.42(a): (**a**) regions obtained by the discriminant criterion; (**b**) between-class variance of gray level versus density

k_0 is determined as that which maximizes σ_b^2. Because σ_b^2 is non-negative and takes the value 0 at $w_1=0$ and $w_1=1$, it has the maximum in the middle. The optimal threshold, however, cannot be derived analytically. It must be determined by searching for the peak of σ_b^2. Figure 3.43 shows an example of region splitting by this method.

4 Image Feature Description

The previous chapter describes methods of extracting boundaries of regions or regions themselves. Each boundary obtained by edge-following or region methods is represented by a sequence of boundary points, or each region is represented by a set of points in the region. Such representation is inadequate for use in high level processing. More abstract descriptions are necessary. This chapter introduces important descriptions of image features and describes how to build such descriptions.

4.1 Representation of Lines

It is often useful to represent a sequence of boundary points by equations of lines (including curves) to be used for interpretation of the image. The simplest equation is that of a straight line. Any curve can be approximated by piecewise linear lines. If something is known about a line, a better equation can be used. For example, circular edges in a three-dimensional space are approximated in the image by an ellipse.

Without *a priori* assumption, however, we cannot select the best equation. In practice, boundary points are extracted from an image, and the positions are not precisely determined. It is, therefore, not easy to choose the best equation among complex ones. For example, it is not easy to determine whether a sequence of points is better described by a part of an ellipse or a part of a hyperbola. For recognition of objects, line equations must be simple so that features of objects may be directly represented in terms of the coefficients of the equations. The following sections concentrate on simple description of lines such as straight lines, circles and ellipses, and explain how to divide a sequence of points into segments so that simple line equations may be fitted to them.

Representation of lines is also necessary for building models of objects. In such a case, we can use more complex curves because the line equations may be obtained interactively. The rest of this section introduces typical representations of curves.

4.1.1 Spline Functions

The spline function is most commonly used for approximating a curve passing through given points (Powell, 1970). Usually, the equation of a curve is represented in the x–y plane by $y=f(x)$, where the coordinate system is chosen such that the slope of the curve is not steep at any point. Let a sequence of given points be (x_0, y_0), $(x_1, y_1), \ldots, (x_n, y_n)$, and let $x_i < x_j$ if $i < j$ as shown in Fig. 4.1. Function $f(x)$ is said

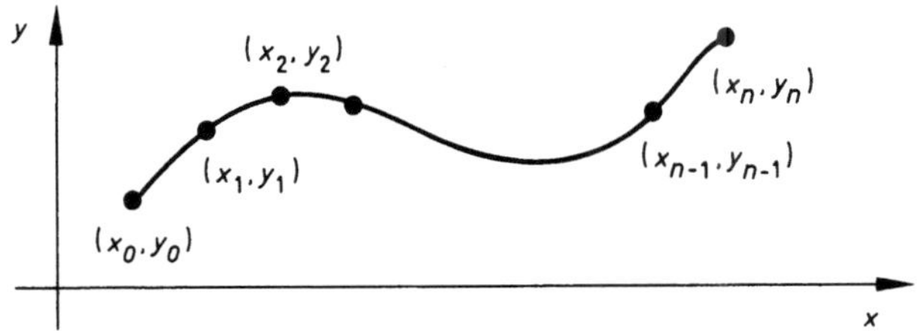

Fig. 4.1. Spline curve

to be a spline function with degree m if it satisfies the following conditions:

1. $f(x)$ is a polynomial function of order less than or equal to m at any interval $[x_{i-1}, x_i]$ $(i=1, \ldots, n)$
2. $f(x)$ and its derivatives up to $m-1$ order are continuous at the interval (x_0, x_n).

The spline function of degree one, for example, represents a piecewise linear line. The spline function of degree three is often used because both the tangent and the curvature of the spline are continuous.

Let $P_{m,i}(x)$ denote a spline function of degree m in the interval $[x_{i-1}, x_i]$ and $P_{m,i}^{(r)}(x)$ denote the rth order derivative. Points $(x_1, y_1), \ldots, (x_{n-1}, y_{n-1})$ are called knots. The condition of continuity is represented by

$$P_{m,i}^{(r)}(x_i) = P_{m,i+1}^{(r)}(x_i) \quad \text{for} \quad r=0,1,\ldots,m-1 \; ; \quad i=1,2,\ldots,n-1 \tag{4.1}$$

From Eq. (4.1) the following equation is derived:

$$P_{m,i+1}(x) = P_{m,i}(x) + c_i(x-x_i)^m \tag{4.2}$$

Now let us consider the property of the spline function. Generally, if an elastic string is slightly bent, the total energy stored in the string is proportional to the integral of the square of the curvature. The curvature of $f(x)$ is approximated by the second differential $f''(x)$ if the first differential $f'(x)$ is small. Neglecting a proportional constant, the total energy E is given by:

$$E = \int_{x_0}^{x_n} \{f''(x)\}^2 \, dx \tag{4.3}$$

It has been shown that E is minimum when $f(x)$ coincides with the spline function of degree three. More generally, the spline function of degree $2k-1$ minimizes the following generalized energy:

$$E_k = \int_{x_0}^{x_n} \{f^{(k)}(x)\}^2 \, dx \tag{4.4}$$

4.1.2 Smoothing Splines

The previous subsection describes splines passing through specified points. This subsection deals with a case where specified points involve some errors. The

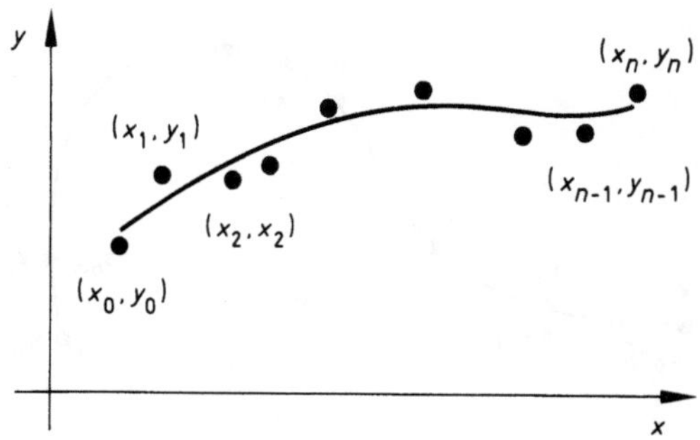

Fig. 4.2. Smoothing spline

problem is to obtain a curve $f(x)$ which satisfies the following two conditions: (1) it passes near specified points and (2) it is smooth (see Fig. 4.2). Since the slope of the curve is assumed to be small, the measure of the first condition may be based on the difference of y values of each point and the curve. Then the first condition can be formulated as minimization of the following square error:

$$E_y = \sum_{i=0}^{n} \{y_i - f(x_i)\}^2 \tag{4.5}$$

The second condition is formulated as minimization of Eq. (4.4). The best function is obtained by minimizing the weighted sum of the two:

$$T = E_k + \lambda E_y \tag{4.6}$$

where λ is a constant. If λ is large, the curve approaches a piecewise linear line passing through given points; and, if λ is small, it approaches a straight line. It has also been shown that the solution is a spline function of degree $2k-1$. This spline is called 'smoothing spline'.

4.1.3 Parametric Splines

In the previous two subsections the spline is represented by the curve $y = f(x)$. This formulation cannot represent curves with large slopes or with vertical segments (e.g., a circle). A parametric representation is suitable for such curves.

A two-dimensional curve is represented by a 1×2 matrix $[x(t)\ y(t)]$, where t is a parameter. A circle, for example, is represented by $[r\cos t\ \ r\sin t]$. Now let us define a parameter s to be the length of a curve from an end point to $\boldsymbol{x}(s)$ $(= [x(t)\ y(t)])$ as shown in Fig. 4.3. Let us represent the equation of the curve by a 1×2 matrix defined as:

$$\boldsymbol{P}(s) = [x(s)\ y(s)] \tag{4.7}$$

Note that $\boldsymbol{P}(s)$ can be regarded as a vector with two components. It is easily shown that $\boldsymbol{P}'(s)$ $(= [\mathrm{d}x(s)/\mathrm{d}s\ \ \mathrm{d}y(x)/\mathrm{d}s])$ represents the tangent vector at $\boldsymbol{x}(s)$, and $\boldsymbol{P}''(s)$ represents the vector toward the center of the tangential circle at $\boldsymbol{x}(s)$ with length equal to the curvature.

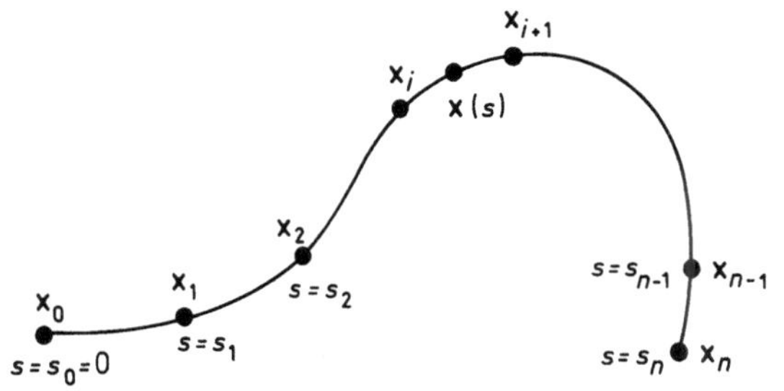

Fig. 4.3. Parametric spline

For a given sequence of points $\boldsymbol{x}_0, \boldsymbol{x}_1, \ldots, \boldsymbol{x}_n$, we can obtain a parametric spline function in the same way as described above. Suppose, for example, we want to obtain a spline with the first and second derivatives continuous at each knot. Then the spline is represented by a set of spline functions of degree three. Each spline function $\boldsymbol{P}_i(s)$ at $[\boldsymbol{x}_{i-1}\ \boldsymbol{x}_i]$ is given by

$$\boldsymbol{P}_i(s) = [s^3\ s^2\ s\ 1]\,\boldsymbol{M}_i \tag{4.8}$$

where $\boldsymbol{M}_i$ is a 4×2 coefficient matrix. Each $\boldsymbol{M}_i$ is obtained from the constraint that the curve passes through given points, and the first and second derivatives are continuous at the knots.

4.1.4 B-Splines

B-splines are piecewise polynomial curves guided by a sequence of points (DeBoor, 1978). They differ from the parametric splines described in the previous subsection in that they need not pass through given points (called 'control points'). B-splines are also classified according to the degree. Given a sequence of points $\boldsymbol{x}_0, \boldsymbol{x}_1, \ldots, \boldsymbol{x}_n$, a spline of degree m is defined by $n+1-m$ polynomials. Each polynomial is represented as a linear combination of $m+1$ points.

Cubic splines are the most frequently used since they are of the lowest degree in which the curvature is continuous. The ith cubic polynomial is given by:

$$\boldsymbol{P}_i(t) = B_0(t)\,\boldsymbol{x}_{i-1} + B_1(t)\,\boldsymbol{x}_i + B_2(t)\,\boldsymbol{x}_{i+1} + B_3(t)\,\boldsymbol{x}_{i+2} \tag{4.9}$$

where B_0, B_1, B_2, and B_3 are cubic polynomials with respect to parameter t $(0 \le t \le 1)$. In Fig. 4.4, each point $\boldsymbol{P}_i$ shows a knot corresponding to $t=0$ and $t=1$. We must determine 16 coefficients included in the four polynomials in Eq. (4.9). The

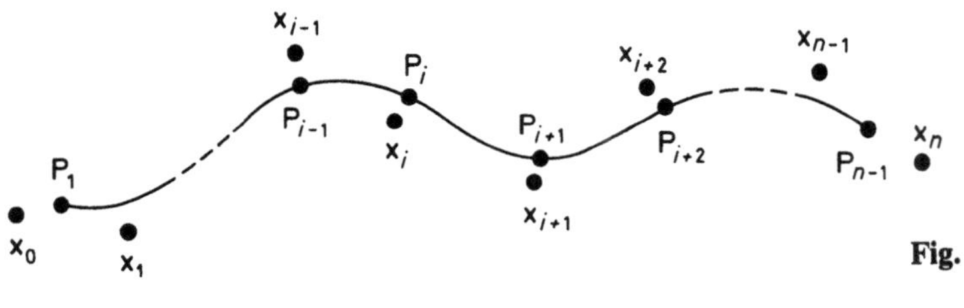

Fig. 4.4. B-spline $(m=3)$

condition that the adjacent curve segments $\boldsymbol{P}_i(t)$ and $\boldsymbol{P}_{i+1}(t)$ must be continuous up to the second derivatives for any $\boldsymbol{x}_k$, for $k=i-1, i, \ldots, i+3$, provides 15 equations. For example, $\boldsymbol{P}_i(1)=\boldsymbol{P}_{i+1}(0)$ is rewritten as:

$$B_0(1)\,\boldsymbol{x}_{i-1}+B_1(1)\,\boldsymbol{x}_i+B_2(1)\,\boldsymbol{x}_{i+1}+B_3(1)\,\boldsymbol{x}_{i+2}$$
$$=B_0(0)\,\boldsymbol{x}_i+B_1(0)\,\boldsymbol{x}_{i+1}+B_2(0)\,\boldsymbol{x}_{i+2}+B_3(0)\,\boldsymbol{x}_{i+3}$$

which provides the following five equations:

$$B_0(1)=0\ ,\quad B_1(1)=B_0(0)\ ,\quad B_2(1)=B_1(0)$$
$$B_3(1)=B_2(0)\ ,\quad B_3(0)=0$$

One more equation is provided by the condition that the shape of $\boldsymbol{P}_i(t)$ is invariant to the coordinate transformation:

$$B_0(t)+B_1(t)+B_2(t)+B_3(t)=1 \tag{4.10}$$

By solving those 16 equations, 16 coefficients are obtained as:

$$\begin{aligned} B_0(t)&=(1-t)^3/6\\ B_1(t)&=t^3/2-t^2+2/3\\ B_2(t)&=-t^3/2+t^2/2+t/2+1/6\\ B_3(t)&=t^3/6 \end{aligned} \tag{4.11}$$

It is easily shown that none of the four polynomials is negative. From this fact and Eq. (4.10), any point on the curve is an interpolation of the four control points. That is, the curve segment is included in the square determined by the control points. This is illustrated in Fig. 4.5. Generally, B-splines of degree m are included in polygons determined by $m+1$ control points. B-splines are used in practice because of this helpful property and the continuity of derivatives for any control points.

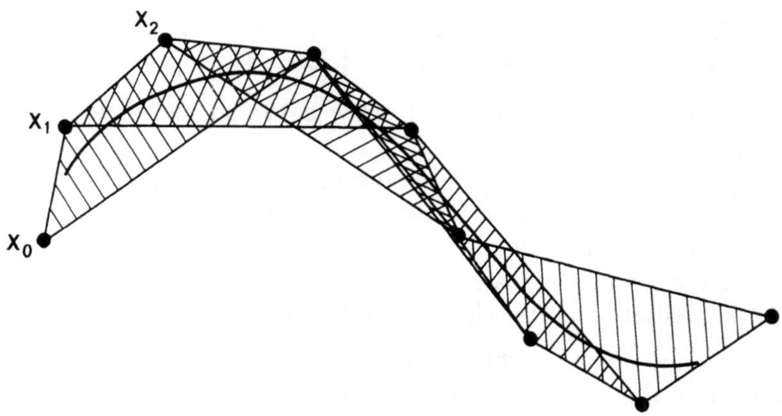

Fig. 4.5. B-spline included in convex hulls formed by consecutive control points ($m=3$)

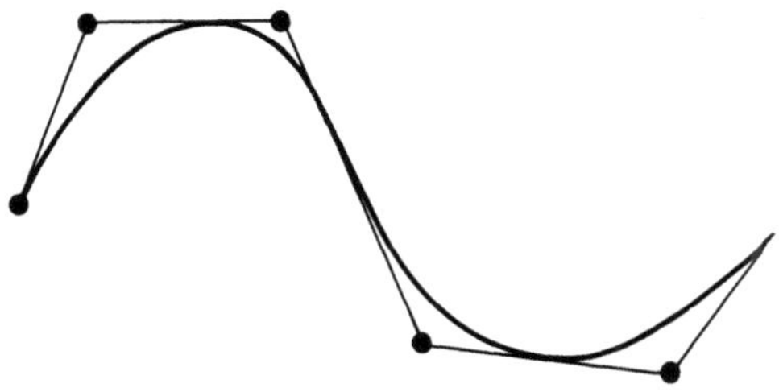

Fig. 4.6. Quadratic B-spline ($m=2$)

Quadratic B-splines are similarly defined. They pass through midpoints of lines between adjacent control points with tangents equal to the lines at $t=1/2$ (see Fig. 4.6).

4.2 Segmentation of a Sequence of Points

It is often useful to represent a sequence of boundary points by equations of lines (including curves) to be used for interpretation of the image. In general a sequence of points is not always represented by a single equation. It is then segmented into subsequences of points so that each of the subsequences may be well approximated by an equation.

4.2.1 Approximation by Straight Lines

Equations of lines may depend on the nature of boundaries in the image. If all boundaries are known to be straight lines, they are easily represented by equations of straight lines. In particular, boundary points obtained by edge following need not be segmented, for each sequence of points corresponds to a straight line. If boundaries are obtained by a region method, they require segmentation.

A curve may also be approximated by polygonal lines. The procedure for finding a suitable polygonal approximation to a given curve is to find corners or knots that yield the best polyline. There are many schemes for segmentation, as with region methods. Some of them can be applied to approximation by equations of curves. They are described below.

Here, a simple splitting scheme (Duda and Hart, 1973) is introduced. The recursive algorithm is explained with reference to Fig. 4.7:

1. Given a sequence of points, draw a straight line between its end points (Fig. 4.7(a)).
2. For every point, compute its distance from the approximating line. If it is everywhere within some threshold, exit. Otherwise, find the point farthest from the approximating line, make it a new knot, and segment the sequence into two new sequences (Fig. 4.7(b)).
3. Recursively apply the algorithm to the two new sequences (Figs. 4.7(c) and (d)).

Although this algorithm is simple, it is guaranteed to approximate a curve with a polyline within a specified tolerance. However, it is sensitive to local fluctuations of points and does not look good to the human eye in such cases.

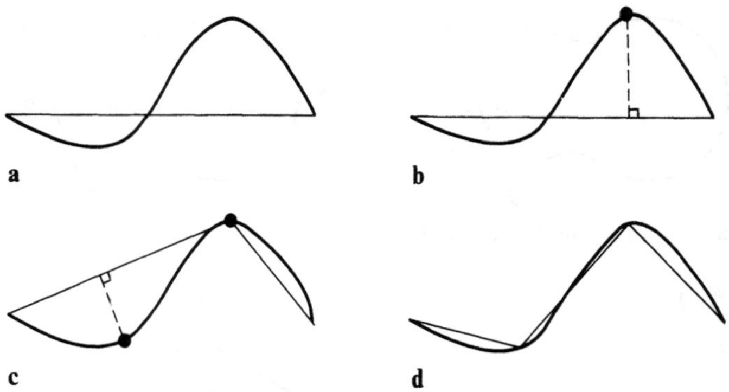

Fig. 4.7a–d. Stages in splitting algorithm: (**a**) sequence of points approximated by a line; (**b**) new knot; (**c**) second recursion; (**d**) final approximation

4.2.2 Approximation by Curves

A sequence of points is often better approximated by equations of curves. Types of equations may depend on the nature of boundaries in an image. Popular approaches try to fit spline functions to those points. However, it is not easy for humans to grasp the global shape of the curve only from a set of coefficients of these functions.

A simple way is to approximate the sequence of points by straight lines and arcs. Turner (1974) proposed the ψ–s curve for finding straight lines and arcs. For every point in the sequence, ψ is defined to be the direction of a tangent to the boundary. Since the boundary is not continuous, the tangent is approximated by the direction of the line between the point and the one that is several points behind (or ahead of) it. ψ is plotted against s, the arc length of the boundary traversed from the starting point. An example of the ψ–s curve is shown in Fig. 4.8.

For a closed boundary, the function is periodic, with discontinuous jumps between 0 and 2π. Horizontal straight lines in the ψ–s curve correspond to straight lines on the original boundary. Other straight lines correspond to arcs, since ψ is changing at a constant rate. Thus the problem of segmentation of the boundary into straight lines and arcs is reduced to that of segmentation of the ψ–s curve into straight lines.

Often included in images of the real world are many elliptic segments which are projections of arcs in the three-dimensional space. An elliptic segment yields a curve in the ψ–s curve. A better method is necessary for locating straight lines and simple smooth curves to be approximated by elliptic segments. Shirai (1978) proposed curvatures for finding such segments. The curvature at a point is approximated by the 'k-curvature', the angle made between the lines from the point to that k points ahead and to that k points behind (Fig. 4.9). The curvature φ is also plotted against s. An example of the φ–s curve is shown in Fig. 4.10.

Horizontal straight lines in the φ–s curve correspond to arcs on the original boundary (as a special case, $\varphi(s)=0$ corresponds to straight lines). Peaks in the φ–s curve correspond to points where the tangent is discontinuous. Based on these facts, segmentation of a sequence proceeds as follows.

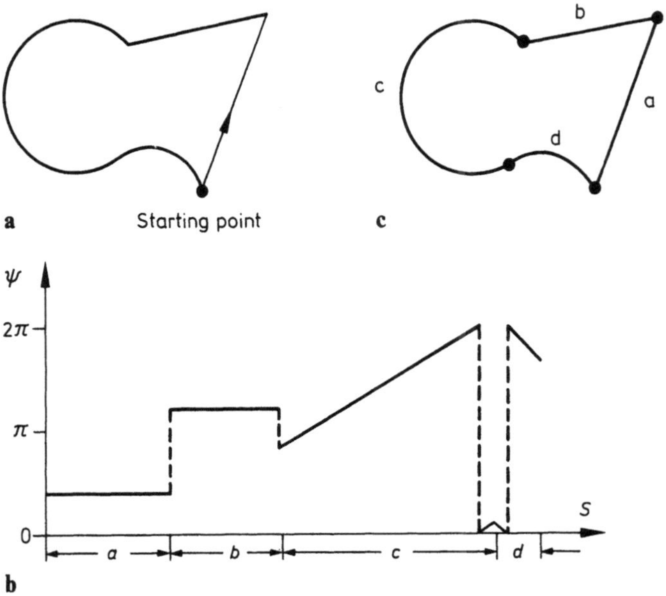

Fig. 4.8a–c. Segmentation by the ψ–s curve: (**a**) sequence of points; (**b**) ψ–s curve; (**c**) result of segmentation

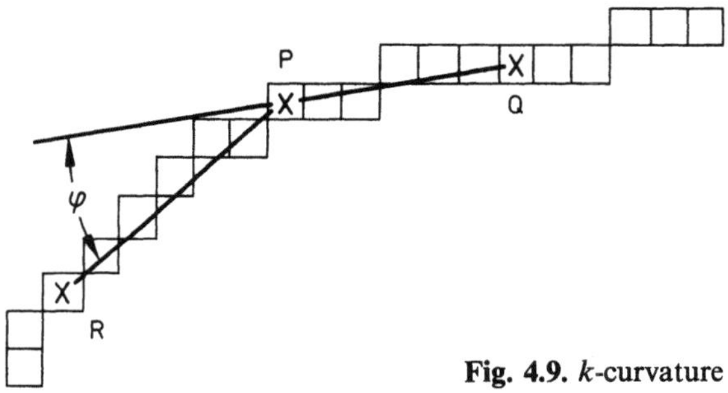

Fig. 4.9. k-curvature

1. Find obvious candidates for knots and segments.
2. Classify temporary segments into straight lines, curves, or unknown. Try to decompose long curves into straight lines and curves.
3. Merge adjacent segments if possible.
4. Determine positions of knots precisely.

The procedure is explained below, referring to Fig. 4.10. First, in the φ–s curve, intervals with large curvatures are found in order to locate obvious curves or knots with discontinuous boundary directions. These intervals are illustrated in Fig. 4.10(b) as $[L_i, R_i]$. The interval $[L_i, R_i]$ has the following property.

$$\varphi_m > \varphi_t \tag{4.12}$$

where $\varphi_m = \max_{s \in [L_i, R_i]} \{\varphi(s)\}$, and φ_t is a threshold.

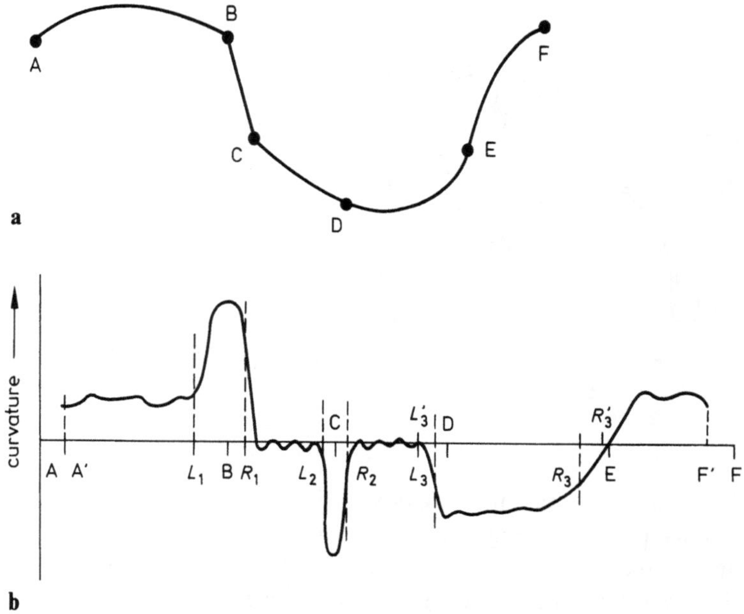

Fig. 4.10a, b. Segmentation by the φ–s curve: (**a**) sequence of points; (**b**) φ–s curve

$$|\varphi(s)| \begin{matrix} > h(\varphi_m) & \text{for} & s \in [L_i, R_i] \\ < h(\varphi_m) & \text{for} & s = L_i - 1 \quad \text{and} \quad s = R_i + 1 \end{matrix} \tag{4.13}$$

where $h(x)$ is a linear function of x ($h(x) < x$).

These intervals may correspond to either knots or curved segments. If an interval is short it is regarded as a knot candidate, otherwise as that for a curved segment. New knots are inserted at both ends of each curved segment (L_3' and R_3' in Fig. 4.10(b)). Now temporary segments are defined as the intervals between knot candidates (for example, $[A', L_1]$, $[R_1, L_2]$, $[R_2, L_3']$, $[L_3, R_3]$, and $[R_3', F']$ in Fig. 4.10(b)).

Step (2) classifies temporary segments (excluding curved segments found in step (1)) as straight lines or curves. The classification is based on the value of k (of k-curvature), the number of points (m) in the segment, and the sum S_φ of $\varphi(s)$ in the segment. The segment is approximated by an arc as shown in Fig. 4.11, and the degree of difference from a straight line is represented in terms of the fan angle θ of

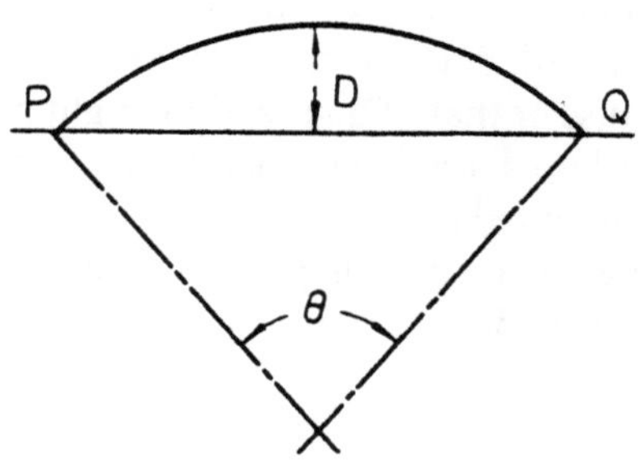

Fig. 4.11. Approximation of a segment by an arc

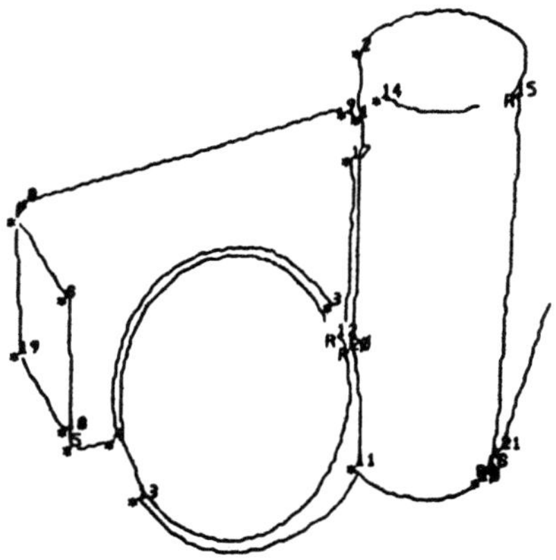

Fig. 4.12. Result of segmentation for Fig. 3.25

the arc and the maximum distance d between the arc and the line connecting the terminal points (see Fig. 4.11). Referring to the fact that $S=(m-2k)\varphi_a$ where φ_a is the average k-curvature, and that the difference of the tangent lines at two points which are k points distant is φ_a, the following equations hold:

$$\theta = S_\varphi(m-1)/\{k(m-2k)\} \tag{4.14}$$

$$d=(m/\theta)\,(1-\cos\theta/2) \tag{4.15}$$

Based on the arc assumption, the classification procedure is given as follows (with comments in braces { }).

If $m<2k$, then the segment is undefined {curvature cannot be computed};
else, if $d>d_u$, then curve {threshold d_u should be high enough to discriminate only an obviously curved segment};
  else, if $\theta<\theta_t$, then straight {d is small and curvature is also small};
    else, if $m<m_t$ and $d<d_l$, then straight {$d_l<d_u$};
      else, curve;

A curved segment is further examined to determine if it includes a straight line. If so, it is again divided into a line, and step (2) is repeated.

Step (3) tries to merge adjacent undefined or curved segments. The criterion for merging is based on the average curvature (θ/m) of each segment and that of the knot between them. If adjacent segments and the knot are similar in their average curvature, they are merged. This process is repeated until no more segments are merged. Small segments of a smooth curve created in step (1) because of the effect of noise or that of digitization might be merged to a single curve. In step (4), positions of knots are determined as intersections of adjacent segments. The intersection is computed from equations of lines fitted to segments. Figure 4.12 shows the result of the segmentation process applied to sequences of boundary points shown in Fig. 3.25.

4.3 Fitting Line Equations

The second part of the boundary representation is to fit a straight line or a curve equation to each segment. The problem is to determine the optimal equation for a set of n points with coordinates (x_i, y_i). The optimal equation depends on the evaluation function that represents the goodness of fit. Three typical evaluation functions are introduced and methods of fitting them are described below.

4.3.1 Using Errors Along a Single Axis

In this case the evaluation function includes only errors along a single axis, say the y-axis. The line equation is usually represented by

$$y = f(x) \tag{4.16}$$

Parameters of the equation are determined so that the following evaluation function is minimized.

$$S = \sum_{i=1}^{n} \{y_i - f(x_i)\}^2 \tag{4.17}$$

The solution is obtained by a conventional least-square method.

This evaluation function does not precisely reflect the distance of each point from the equation, especially if the direction of the perpendicular line from each point to the line $y = f(x)$ is very different from that of the y-axis. A modification is to choose a better axis along which errors are calculated. The choice depends on the distribution of boundary points. In fitting a straight line, for example, Eq. (4.16) is used if $|x_n - x_1| > |y_n - y_1|$. Otherwise, the equation of the line is represented by $x = g(y)$.

4.3.2 Using Errors of Line Equations with Two Variables

The equation of a line and the evaluation function are represented, respectively, as follows:

$$f(x, y) = 0 \tag{4.18}$$

$$S = \sum_{i=1}^{n} f^2(x_i, y_i) \tag{4.19}$$

This equation is convenient for fitting a curve because it is easily computed. However, the evaluation function does not precisely reflect the distance d_i of each point from the equation. Let us consider, for example, the problem of fitting a circle represented by:

$$f(x, y) = (x - a)^2 + (y - b)^2 - r^2 \tag{4.20}$$

If a point (x_i, y_i) is outside of the circle by distance d_i, then $f(x_i, y_i)$ is given as:

$$f^2(x_i, y_i) = \{(r+d_i)^2 - r^2\}^2 \tag{4.21}$$

This equation is obviously different from distance d_i.

4.3.3 Using Distance from Each Point to Fitted Line

The evaluation function is most suitable because it directly reflects the distance d_i of each point from the equation. First, the simplest case is described where a straight line is fitted. Let the equation of a line be denoted by

$$(y - y_0)\cos\theta - (x - x_m)\sin\theta = 0 \tag{4.22}$$

where y_0 and θ are parameters of the equation, and x_m is the mean of $\{x_i\}$. The evaluation function is given as the following.

$$S = \sum_{i=1}^{n} d_i^2 = \{(y_i - y_0)\cos\theta - (x_i - x_m)\sin\theta\}^2 \tag{4.23}$$

Equation (4.23) is easily minimized by differentiating it with respect to y_0 and θ. The solution is given as follows:

$$y_0 = \frac{1}{n} \sum_{i=1}^{n} y_i - y_m$$

$$\theta = \tfrac{1}{2} \arctan\{2\sigma_{xy}^2/(\sigma_x^2 - \sigma_y^2)\}$$

where y_m is the mean of $\{y_i\}$; σ_x^2 and σ_y^2 are the variance of $\{x_i\}$ and $\{y_i\}$, respectively; and σ_{xy}^2 is the covariance of $\{x_i\}$ and $\{y_i\}$. The direction θ is determined to be $-\pi/2 < \theta < \pi/2$ and the sign to be the same as σ_{xy}^2. The equation thus obtained passes through the center of gravity of a set of points, and the direction coincides with that of the principal axis.

Now let us consider the case of curve fitting. Unfortunately, parameters of the equation are generally not obtained analytically, because determination of the distance from a point (x_i, y_i) to the equation of a curve us not simple. For example, the distance to the circle defined by Eq. (4.20) is given by

$$d_i^2 = (x_i - a)^2 + (y_i - b)^2 - r^2$$

The evaluation function is obviously not linear in parameters a, b, and r.

A possible method is to approximate the distance d_i assuming that d_i is small. Let the equation of a line be $f(x, y) = 0$. The distance d_i from point (x_i, y_i) to the nearest point (X_i, Y_i) on the line is given by:

$$d_i^2 = \Delta x_i^2 + \Delta y_i^2 \tag{4.24}$$

where $\Delta x_i = x_i - X_i$, and $\Delta y_i = y_i - Y_i$. Assuming that Δx_i and Δy_i are small enough, $f(X_i, Y_i)$ is expanded as follows:

$$f(X_i, Y_i) = f(x_i, y_i) - \frac{\partial f(x_i, y_i)}{\partial x} \Delta x_i - \frac{\partial f(x_i, y_i)}{\partial y} \Delta y_i \tag{4.25}$$

where $\frac{\partial f(x_i, y_i)}{\partial x} = \left.\frac{\partial f(x, y)}{\partial x}\right|_{(x_i, y_i)}$

By minimizing d_i^2 under the constraint of Eq. (4.25), d_i is given by the following equation:

$$d_i = \frac{|f(x_i, y_i)|}{\sqrt{\left(\frac{\partial f(x_i, y_i)}{\partial x}\right)^2 + \left(\frac{\partial f(x_i, y_i)}{\partial y}\right)^2}}$$

$$= |f(x_i, y_i)| / |\mathrm{grad}\, f(x_i, y_i)|^2 \tag{4.26}$$

The evaluation function is, therefore,

$$S = \sum_{i=1}^{n} |f(x_i, y_i)|^2 / |\mathrm{grad}\, f(x_i, y_i)|^2 \tag{4.27}$$

Note that if grad $f(x_i, y_i)$ is constant, minimization of Eq. (4.27) is equivalent to minimization of Eq. (4.19).

Minimization of Eq. (4.27), however, is not performed analytically. Usually it is solved by iteration starting from an approximate equation. The method is explained by using a simple example. Suppose that the equation of a curve is represented as the following:

$$f(x, y;\, a, b, c) = 0 \tag{4.28}$$

where a, b, and c are parameters of the equation. Let a', b', and c' denote approximate values of these parameters. For point (X_i, Y_i) on the curve nearest to point (x_i, y_i), the following equation holds:

$$f(X_i, Y_i;\, a, b, c)$$
$$= f(x_i - \Delta x_i, y_i - \Delta y_i;\, a' - \Delta a,\, b' - \Delta b,\, c' - \Delta c) = 0 \tag{4.29}$$

where $\Delta a = a' - a$, $\Delta b = b' - b$, $\Delta c = c' - c$. Assuming that Δx_i, Δy_i, Δa, Δb, and Δc are small, Eq. (4.29) is expanded as:

$$f(x_i, y_i;\, a', b', c') - \frac{\partial f_i}{\partial x} \Delta x_i - \frac{\partial f_i}{\partial y} \Delta y_i - \frac{\partial f_i}{\partial a} \Delta a - \frac{\partial f_i}{\partial b} \Delta b - \frac{\partial f_i}{\partial c} \Delta c = 0$$
$$(i = 1, 2, \ldots, n) \tag{4.30}$$

where $\partial f_i/\partial x$ represents the value of $\partial f/\partial x$ with x_i, y_i; a', b', c'. The evaluation function is given by:

$$S=\sum_{i=1}^{n}(\Delta x_i^2+\Delta y_i^2) \tag{4.31}$$

Minimization of Eq. (4.31) is reduced to minimization of the following new function g, by introducing Lagrange's coefficients p_i and letting h_i denote the left hand side of Eq. 4.30.

$$g=\frac{1}{2}S-\sum_{i=1}^{n}p_ih_i \tag{4.32}$$

By differentiating Eq. (4.32) with respect to Δx_i, Δy_i, Δa, Δb, and Δc, respectively, and setting the results to be 0, the following equations are derived:

$$\partial g/\partial\Delta x_i=\Delta x_i+p_i\partial f_i/\partial x=0,\quad \partial g/\partial\Delta y_i=\Delta y_i+p_i\partial f_i/\partial y=0,\quad (i=1,2,\ldots,n) \tag{4.33}$$

$$\frac{\partial g}{\partial\Delta a}=\sum_{i=1}^{n}p_i\frac{\partial f_i}{\partial a}=0,\quad \frac{\partial g}{\partial\Delta b}=\sum_{i=1}^{n}p_i\frac{\partial f_i}{\partial b}=0,\quad \frac{\partial g}{\partial\Delta c}=\sum_{i=1}^{n}p_i\frac{\partial f_i}{\partial c}=0 \tag{4.34}$$

Now Eq. (4.32) has $(3n+3)$ variables, which are solved by $(3n+3)$ equations: n from Eq. (4.30), $2n$ from Eq. (4.33), and 3 from Eq. (4.34). Note that the solution is easy, because Eqs. (4.30) and (4.33) are analytically solved and three linear equations are derived with respect to Δa, Δb, and Δc. Starting from approximate values of parameters (a', b', and c'), better approximate values ($a'-\Delta a$, $b'-\Delta b$, and $c'-\Delta c$) are obtained. This process is repeated until sufficient approximation is obtained. Usually, the process terminates when Δa, Δb, and Δc become small enough.

Initially, approximate values of parameters must be determined. For a circle, for example, parameters a, b, and r in Eq. (4.20) can be initially determined by three

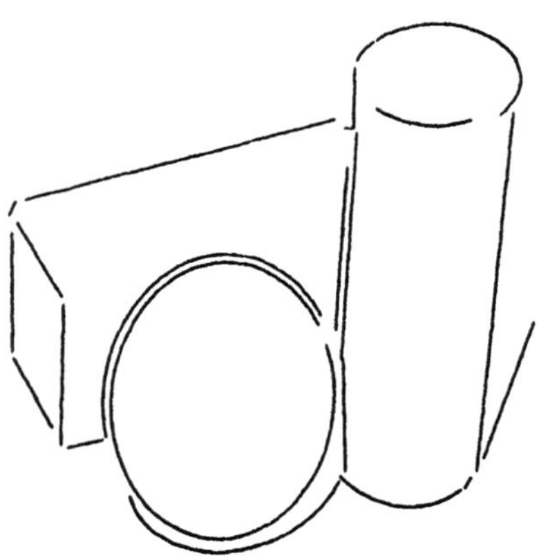

Fig. 4.13. Result of line fitting for Fig. 4.12

representative points in the sequence. The approximation is better if these representative points are selected so that the distances among them are almost the same. Of course, for an ellipse, five parameters are necessary. Initial values of these parameters are similarly obtained by five representative points. Then the iteration is performed by solving five linear equations in each stage.

Figure 4.13 shows the result of applying the iteration method for fitting straight lines and ellipses to sequences of points shown in Fig. 4.12.

4.4 Conversion Between Lines and Regions

It is often necessary to obtain border lines from regions extracted by a region method, or to obtain regions bounded by lines or edges extracted by an edge-following method. This section describes efficient methods for conversion between lines and regions.

4.4.1 Boundary Detection

The purpose of boundary detection is to detect boundary points for a given set of regions. We can assume without loss of generality that regions are given as a binary image, where points with pixel value 1 correspond to regions and those with value 0 correspond to the background.

There are many definitions of a boundary. The first two broad classifications are according to the definitions of the connectedness of regions described in Subsection 3.4.5 (four-connected and eight-connected). Figure 4.14 shows examples of boundary points in the two definitions. Next, the position of boundary points may be in the region, out of the region, or between the region and the background. Figure 4.15 shows an example of sets of these boundary points (four-connected). Usually, the position of the boundary points is in the region.

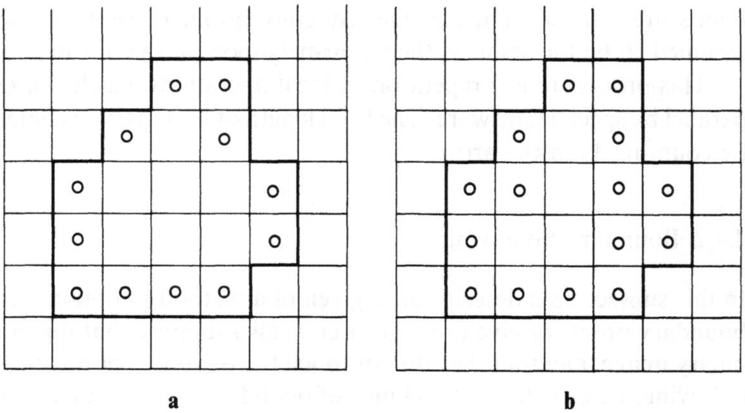

Fig. 4.14a, b. Two kinds of boundary points: (**a**) in the four-connected definition; (**b**) in the eight-connected definition

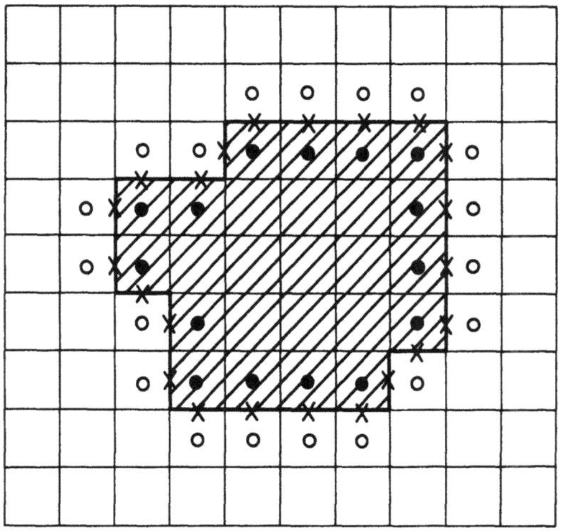

Fig. 4.15. Three different sets of boundary points

The boundary points are detected in a binary image $f(i,j)$ and stored in another binary image $g(i,j)$, where $g(i,j)=1$ if a point at (i,j) is a boundary point, and $g(i,j)=0$ otherwise. For simplicity, let the size of the input array $f(i,j)$ be $n \times n$. Let us further suppose that the periphery of the array is all 0 (regions do not touch the periphery). The procedure for obtaining four-connected boundary points is shown here. The input array is scanned by repeating local operations within the four-neighbors (denoted by I_4) in the following way:

for $j=2$ step 1 until $n-1$
for $i=2$ step 1 until $n-1$
  if $f(i,j)=1$ and there exist $(p,q) \in I_4$ such that $f(p,q)=0$,
    then $g(i,j) \leftarrow 1$;
  else $g(i,j) \leftarrow 0$;

Boundary points in the eight-connected definition are similarly detected (by replacing I_4 by eight-neighbors I_8). If regions touch the periphery, some of the boundary points in the periphery are not determined because the neighbors of those points are outside of the image. By convention, however, those neighbors are assumed to be the same as their four-neighbors in the image.

This procedure is a repetition of local operations which can be carried out in parallel by special hardware. The total length of boundaries is obtained from $g(i,j)$ by counting 1s in the array.

4.4.2 Boundary Following

In this subsection a description is given of a method to obtain series of connected boundary points of given regions. Let us also suppose that regions are given by a binary image, and that they do not touch the periphery of the image. In boundary following, we can choose two kinds of boundary series: four-connected and eight-connected boundary series. A series of four-connected boundary points is itself four-connected. Note that a set of boundary points of a four-connected region is not

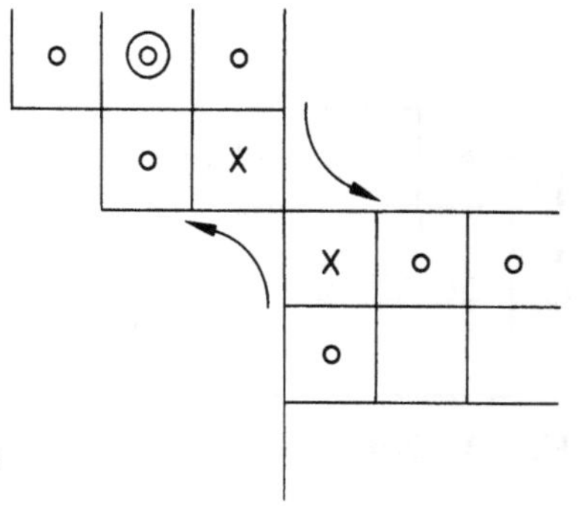

Fig. 4.16. Example of eight-connected boundary points

always four-connected itself (see Fig. 4.14(a) for example). On the other hand, boundary points of an eight-connected region may be four-connected (as shown in Fig. 4.14(b)) or eight-connected as shown in Fig. 4.16 (the pair marked by 'x'). In boundary following, eight-connected boundary series of eight-connected regions are usually chosen. That is, extra points are removed from a series of boundary points of eight-connected regions. For example, in Fig. 4.16, the boundary point marked by a double circle is removed because it does not change the connectivity of the series of boundary points.

There are two types of boundary-following procedure, depending on whether the input image may be changed or not. In the former procedure, the input image is used as a memory for determining the termination of boundary following (Rosenfeld and Kak, 1976). Otherwise, the termination condition must be checked in a more complex way. Although we assume that the input is a binary image, it may be a gray image. In boundary following, a gray image is equivalent to a binary image if a definition of regions is defined. A simple example is a threshold that determines whether a pixel is in the region or in the background. In such a case, the original gray image may be used for other purposes. Therefore, it is not allowed to change. In this subsection, the boundary following procedure which does not change the input image is described.

Let us consider the procedure of following eight-connected boundary points clockwise. The core of the procedure is to find the next boundary point for a given pair of a current boundary point and an adjacent background point. This procedure is as follows:

1. Examine the eight-neighbors of the current point in clockwise order, starting with the given background point.
2. The first encountered region point is the next point.
3. The last background point is the next background point.
4. Store the current point in the list of the boundary.

This procedure is illustrated in Fig. 4.17, where C_k is the current point and B_k is the given background point. The first encountered region point C_{k+1} is the next point, and the previous point B_{k+1} is the next boundary point. Repeating this procedure, boundary points are successively obtained.

Next, let us consider the termination condition of the boundary-following procedure. The principle is to check if the current point is the initial point. However,

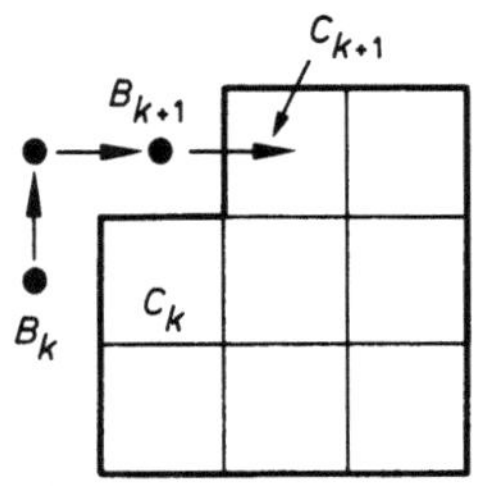

Fig. 4.17. Next boundary points

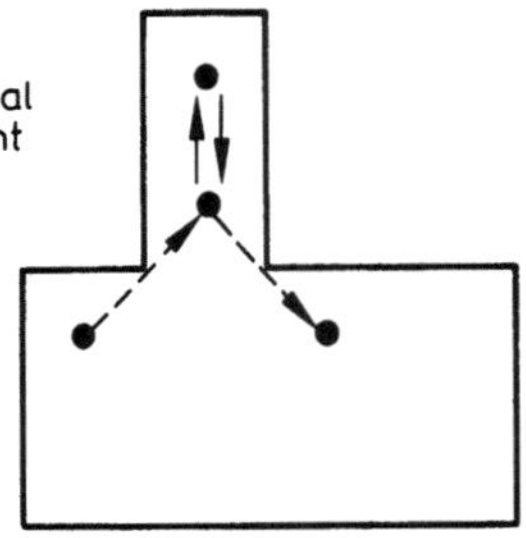

Fig. 4.18. Returning to the initial point

we must note that a boundary point may be found many times in the boundary-following process. Even if the current point coincides with the initial point, we cannot conclude that the entire boundary has been followed.

An example is shown in Fig. 4.18. When the initial point is found first, the process must be continued. It stops when the initial point is found for a second time. Considering this case, the termination condition becomes more complex. Now let the initial boundary point be denoted by C_1 and the second boundary point (if it exists) be denoted by C_2. The termination algorithm is as follows:

If the current point coincides with C_1
    and the next point coincides with C_2,
    then delete the current point from the series of boundary points,
        and stop.

Note that this condition works even if a region consists of a single point.

Now the final problem is how to find the initial point and an adjacent background point. The principle for finding the pair is to scan the image until a point in a region is found. The point is the initial point and the previous point is the adjacent background point. In a conventional TV scan, the adjacent point is to the left of the initial point. The boundary is followed from this initial condition.

If there is more than one region in the image, after the boundary of a region is followed, another boundary must be sought. This time, however, the first encountered region point may have already been followed. If we can see to which region the encountered point belongs from the value of the point, the check is easy. That is, we have only to check if the identified region has already been followed. Otherwise, the check is not simple. It may take a long time to check if this point coincides with any point in the lists of the boundaries obtained previously.

One way to avoid this check is to use another array (called a 'boundary array') to store the boundary points. Regions are numbered in the order of detection, and the same number is assigned to the boundary points. The number is stored in the corresponding points (elements) of the boundary array. Then the candidate point is checked by examining the corresponding point in the boundary array.

4.4.3 Labeling Connected Regions

The purpose of labeling connected regions is to obtain regions bounded by boundary points. Sequential numbers are assigned to different regions and they are

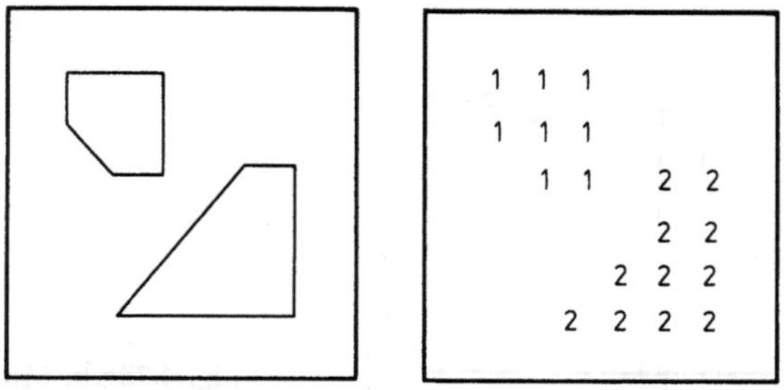

a b

Fig. 4.19a,b. Example of connected region labeling: (**a**) input (boundary); (**b**) output

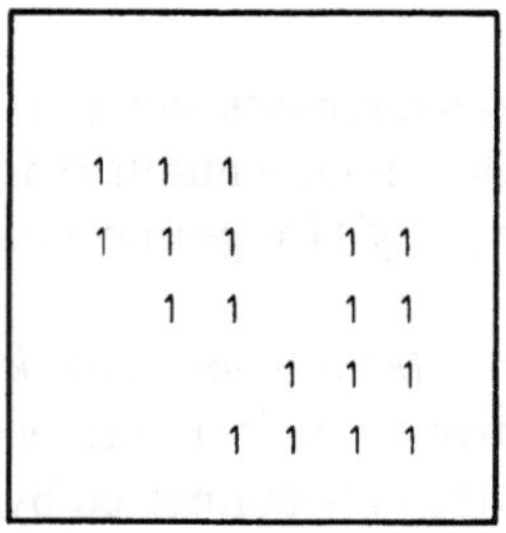

Fig. 4.20. Input binary image

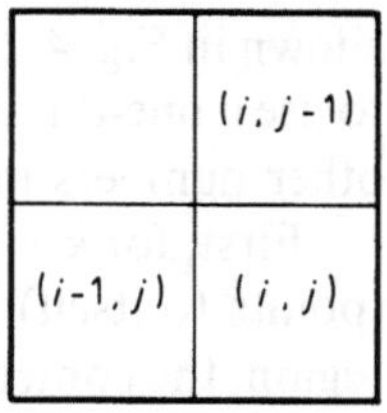

Fig. 4.21. Examined neighbors for four-connected regions

stored as an array whose elements $g(i,j)$ contain these numbers. Figure 4.19 shows an example of this processing.

It is convenient to consider first the problem of labeling connected components in the binary image. An example of an input is shown in Fig. 4.20. The output is the same as Fig. 4.19(b). An efficient labeling procedure is described here. It takes two passes.

In the first pass, tentative region numbers are assigned to the output array $g(i,j)$ by examining the two neighbors as shown in Fig. 4.21. The procedure for four-connected regions is shown below (with comments in braces { }).

```
k←0; {k is the number of regions.}
for j=2 step 1 until n−1
for i=2 step 1 until n−1
   if f(i,j)=0, then g(i,j)←0;
   else
      if g(i−1,j)=0 and g(i,j−1)=0,
         then g(i,j)←k; k←k+1; {new region found}
      else
         if g(i−1,j)=0, then g(i,j)←g(i,j−1);
         else if g(i,j−1)=0 then g(i,j)←g(i−1,j);
            else
               if g(i−1,j)=g(i,j−1), then g(i,j)←g(i,j−1);
               else g(i,j)←g(i,j−1); {Two regions merge here.}
                  record that g(i−1,j) and g(i,j−1) are in the same class;
```

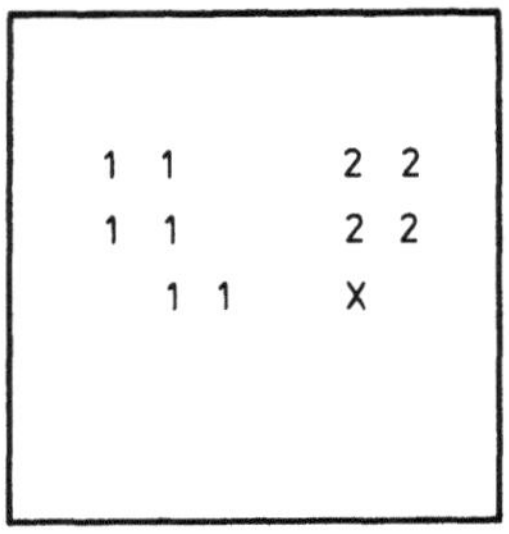

Fig. 4.22. Different regions merge at 'x'

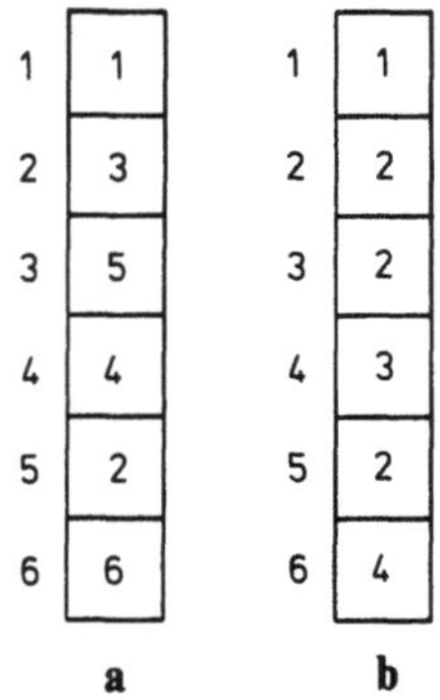

Fig. 4.23a, b. Modification of the region number array: (**a**) before; (**b**) after

The last case in the above procedure happens when two separated regions merge, as shown in Fig. 4.22, at 'x'. A convenient way to record equivalent region numbers is to use a one-dimensional array $h(k)$ (called a 'region number array') for pointers to other numbers in the same class.

First, for $k=1$ to M (the maximum number of the region) $h(k)$ is given value k (points to itself). When region numbers k_1 and k_2 are known to be in the same region, the content of $h(k_1)$ and that of $h(k_2)$ are exchanged (they are connected by the pointers). After the first pass is over, the equivalent classes are easily obtained by tracing the pointers. At the same time, new numbers are stored in the region number array in order to label correct region numbers in the second pass. The purpose of this processing is illustrated in Fig. 4.23. The result of the first pass is shown in Fig. 4.23(a), which shows that regions 2, 3, and 5 have been merged. By assigning the same region number to them and adjusting others, we can obtain the result shown in Fig. 4.23(b). This process is as follows:

```
q←0;  {q is the number of the connected regions.}
for p=1 step 1 until k  {k is the maximum number of tentative regions
                          obtained in the first pass.}
   if h(p)<p, then do nothing;  {h(p) was already updated.}
   else
      q←q+1; r←p;  repeat
                      next←h(r); h(r)←q; r←next
                   until h(r)=p
```

In the second pass, the output array is updated in a straightforward fashion. That is, if $g(i,j)>0$, then $g(i,j) \leftarrow h(g(i,j))$.

In order to label eight-connected regions, the first procedure must be slightly modified. Examination of four eight-neighbors is required as shown in Fig. 4.24. Note that at most two different numbers have been assigned to the neighbors. The processing is similar to the four-neighbor case except that $g(i,j-1)$ and $g(i-1,j)$ are never labeled by different numbers, and that $g(i+1,j-1)$ may be different from $g(i-1,j-1)$ or from $g(i-1,j)$.

Now let us consider the original problem: from boundary to region. Suppose that boundary points are given as a binary image (as shown in Fig. 4.25(b)). If all

$(i-1, j-1)$	$(i, j-1)$	$(i+1, j-1)$
$(i-1, j)$	(i, j)	

Fig. 4.24. Examined neighbors for eight-connected regions

a b

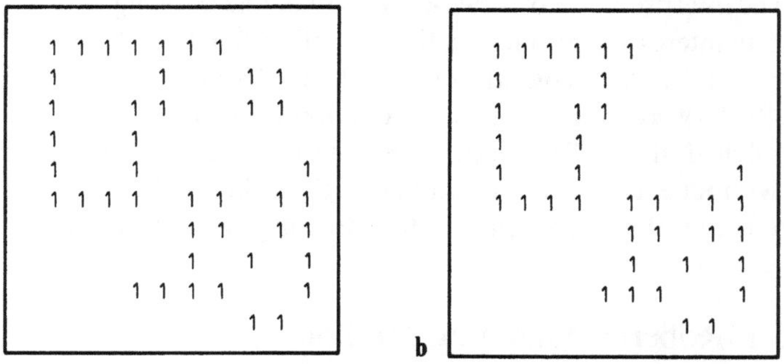

Fig. 4.25a, b. Binary image with open boundaries: (**a**) binary image with open boundary; (**b**) after open boundary is removed

boundaries are closed, then the binary image can be converted into that representing the regions (as shown in Fig. 4.20). This problem is called a 'painting problem', and is solved by one scan of the entire image.

If boundaries are not always closed, open boundaries must first be removed as shown in Fig. 4.25. This can also be performed in one pass by scanning the input image. An open end on a boundary is found by examining the neighbors of a boundary point. If a boundary point has less than two boundary points in the neighbor, it is an open end and it is removed (the value of the point is converted to 0). Then the neighboring boundary point (if it exists) is again examined in the same way. After a series of open boundary points is thus removed, the scanning is continued from the initial open end. When the entire image is scanned, open boundaries are all removed.

5 Interpretation of Line Drawings

The interpretation of a two-dimensional line drawing as a three-dimensional scene is an interesting problem in the field of artificial intelligence. The problem was first solved for the recognition of polyhedra from a real image. Later many research efforts were concentrated on developing theories of interpretation of complex polyhedral line drawings, where the line drawings are assumed to be complete (without extra edges and with no edges lacking). As an extension of the theoretical research, the realizability of line drawings was explored.

5.1 Roberts' Matching Method

One of the earliest researchers to be concerned with the interpretation of line drawings as three-dimensional objects was Roberts (1963). He extracted a line drawing from an image of a scene as described in Chap. 3, and interpreted the line drawing by matching it to models of simple polyhedra. The models are represented in a three-dimensional coordinate system. Figure 5.1 depicts a model of a cube. An object in a scene is considered to be created from the corresponding model by a transformation, and the image is considered to be created by a known imaging system. Suppose that a model is transformed to a scene by a transformation matrix Q, and that the object is transformed to the image by a transformation matrix P. Let $(X_i, Y_i, Z_i, 1)^t$ denote the homogeneous coordinate of the ith vertex of the model, and $(X_i', Y_i', Z_i', W_i')^t$ denote that of the image. The relation between both coordinates is given as follows:

$$(X_i', Y_i', Z_i', W_i')^t = PQ(X_i, Y_i, Z_i, 1)^t \tag{5.1}$$

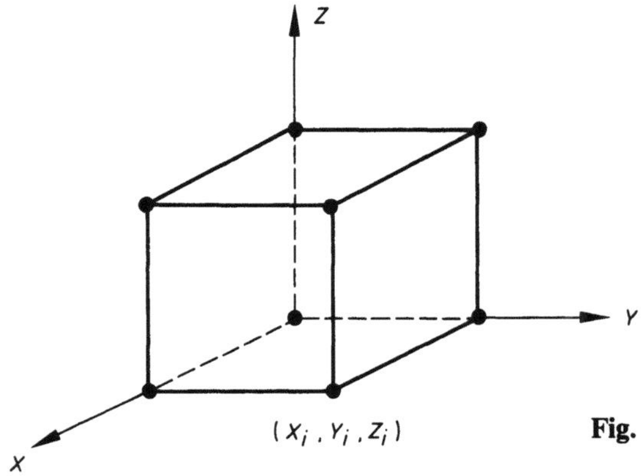

Fig. 5.1. Three-dimensional model of a cube

Now, as described in Sect. 2.1, P is generally a perspective projection matrix defined by the imaging system as given below:

$$P=\begin{pmatrix}1 & 0 & 0 & 0\\ 0 & 1 & 0 & 0\\ 0 & 0 & 1 & 0\\ 0 & 0 & -1/f & 1\end{pmatrix} \tag{5.2}$$

where f is the focal length of the imaging system. Although a scale change was considered by Roberts, it is excluded here for simplicity. The transformation Q consists of a rotation and a translation in the three-dimensional space.

$$Q=TR \tag{5.3}$$

The rotation can be regarded as successive rotations about three axes. The rotations by θ about the X axis, by φ about the Y axis, and by ψ about the Z axis are represented by the following homogeneous coordinate transformation matrices, respectively:

$$R_x=\begin{pmatrix}1 & 0 & 0 & 0\\ 0 & \cos\theta & -\sin\theta & 0\\ 0 & \sin\theta & \cos\theta & 0\\ 0 & 0 & 0 & 1\end{pmatrix},\quad R_y=\begin{pmatrix}\cos\varphi & 0 & \sin\varphi & 0\\ 0 & 1 & 0 & 0\\ -\sin\varphi & 0 & \cos\varphi & 0\\ 0 & 0 & 0 & 1\end{pmatrix},$$

$$R_z=\begin{pmatrix}\cos\psi & -\sin\psi & 0 & 0\\ \sin\psi & \cos\psi & 0 & 0\\ 0 & 0 & 1 & 0\\ 0 & 0 & 0 & 1\end{pmatrix} \tag{5.4}$$

The total rotation matrix R is given by:

$$R=R_zR_yR_x=\begin{pmatrix} & [R_t] & & 0\\ & & & 0\\ & & & 0\\ 0 & 0 & 0 & 1\end{pmatrix} \tag{5.5}$$

where R_t is a 3×3 matrix with respect to θ, φ, and ψ. The translation by (X_t, Y_t, Z_t) is represented by:

$$T=\begin{pmatrix}1 & 0 & 0 & X_t\\ 0 & 1 & 0 & Y_t\\ 0 & 0 & 1 & Z_t\\ 0 & 0 & 0 & 1\end{pmatrix} \tag{5.6}$$

Substituting R and T into Eq. (5.3),

$$Q=\begin{pmatrix} & [R_t] & & X_t \\ & & & Y_t \\ & & & Z_t \\ 0 & 0 & 0 & 1 \end{pmatrix} \tag{5.7}$$

The total transformation matrix H is defined as:

$$H=PQ \tag{5.8}$$

Now H has been represented by six unknown parameters: X_t, Y_t, Z_t, θ, φ, and ψ. The predicted coordinate of the vertex in the image is given by:

$$(x_i', y_i')^t = (X_i'/W',\ Y_i'/W')^t \tag{5.9}$$

Let (x_i, y_i) denote the position of the vertex obtained in the line drawing. In Roberts' matching process, a model of a block is first assumed, and then several vertices of the model and the corresponding junctions in the line drawing are selected for matching. A junction is a point of intersection of two or more lines. The selection is based on the correspondence of polygons in the line drawing to surfaces of the object, then the assumption is verified by finding the best transformation. In order to evaluate the goodness of the matching, the following function is defined:

$$f=\sum_{i=1}^{n} [(x_i'-x_i)^2+(y_i'-y_i)^2] \tag{5.10}$$

where n is the number of pairs of vertex and junction. The best transformation is determined so that it may minimize this evaluation function. The error E of the matching, therefore, is given as follows:

$$E=\min_H \{f\} \tag{5.11}$$

If E is not small enough, the assumed correspondence between vertices and junctions is wrong, or the assumed model is wrong. Then another assumption is made and verified again.

Roberts solved the minimization problem by the least-square method. Since Eq. (5.10) does not include Z_i', only 3×4 elements of H are necessary. Thus the solution was derived by a set of simultaneous linear equations.

Although Roberts' method can determine the transformation in a straightforward fashion, it presents a difficulty. That is, the elements of H are not independent; they obey a constraint determined by 6 independent parameters as described above. The elements obtained by the method are not guaranteed to satisfy the constraint.

The method was applied to scenes consisting of simple objects and compound objects. Figure 5.2(a) shows an example of an image with a compound object partially occluding a simple object. A simple object is the transformation (including

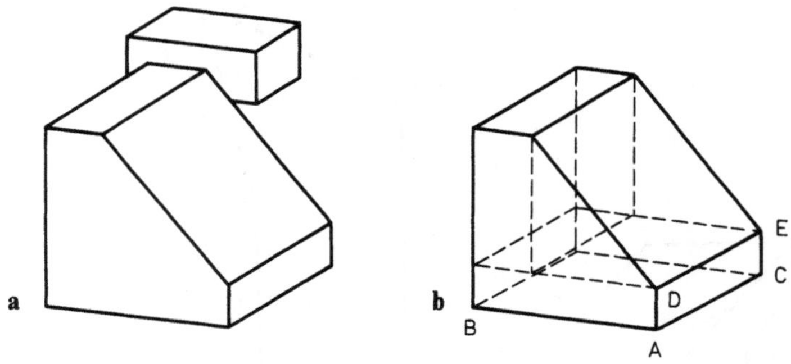

Fig. 5.2a,b. Compound object recognition: (**a**) scene with a compound object and a partially occluded simple object; (**b**) decomposition of a compound object

scale change) of a model, while a compound object is not. A compound object is regarded as the result of assembling several simple objects as shown in Fig. 5.2(b). In this example, a rectangular object at the bottom is first recognized by matching vertices A, B, C, D, and E to a cube model, and then it is removed from the compound object, and so on. An occluded simple object was also recognized by similar partial matching.

5.2 Decomposition of Line Drawings Into Objects

While Roberts' work enabled the recognition of known objects such as cubes and wedges, Guzman (1968) developed a program to analyze line drawings of polyhedra without using explicit models of objects. His program, called SEE, identifies objects even if they are partially occluded. For example, given a line drawing as shown in Fig. 5.3, SEE first locates regions surrounded by lines (numbers from 1 to 14 in the figure, where number 14 corresponds to the background), and then finds three bodies: the first consists of regions 1, 2, and 6, and so on.

Guzman paid attention to junctions of line drawings as clues to the determination of whether adjacent regions belong to the same body. Junctions are classified into types as shown in Fig. 5.4 according to the geometrical configuration of their incident lines. Regions around junctions may belong to the same body or to different bodies. For example, two regions of an Arrow junction with acute angles often belong to the same body, while the other region belongs to another (occluded) body. Thus, for each junction type in Fig. 5.4, regions are assigned to one region or another by such heuristics, and these heuristic rules are stored beforehand in the program.

According to these heuristic rules, SEE examines each junction in a line drawing, and links regions around the junction if these regions are assigned to the same body. Figure 5.5(a) shows links thus attached to regions at appropriate junctions. The result of linking is represented by a graph as shown in Fig. 5.5(b), where each node corresponds to a region and each arc to a link.

In the next stage, SEE merges nodes of a graph according to other heuristics and creates new nodes called 'nuclei'. For example, regions connected by two or more

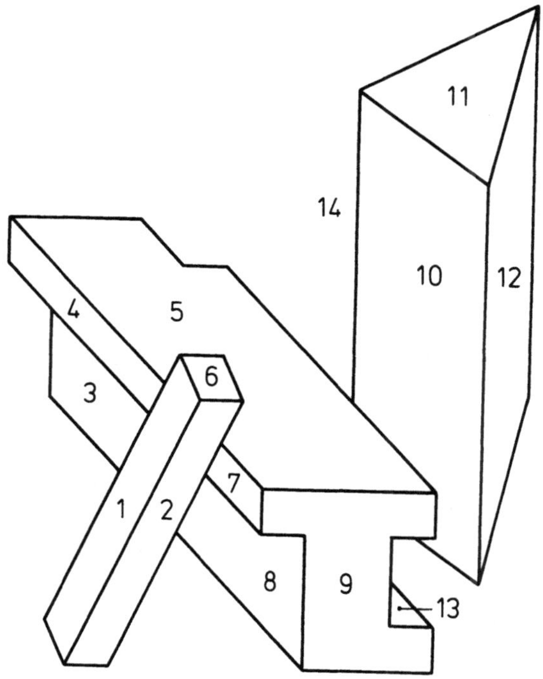

Fig. 5.3. Example of line drawing analyzed by SEE (Guzman 1968)

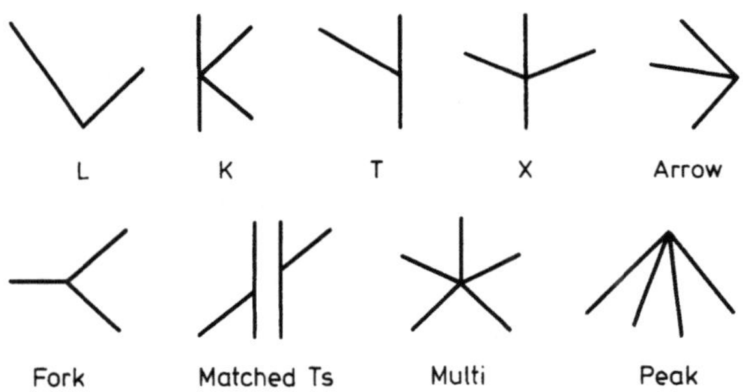

Fig. 5.4. Junction types

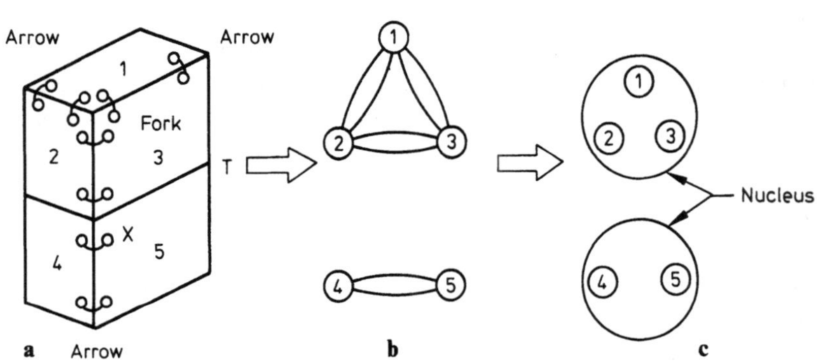

Fig. 5.5a–c. SEE body decomposition process: (**a**) links attached to line drawing; (**b**) graphic representation; (**c**) result of merging

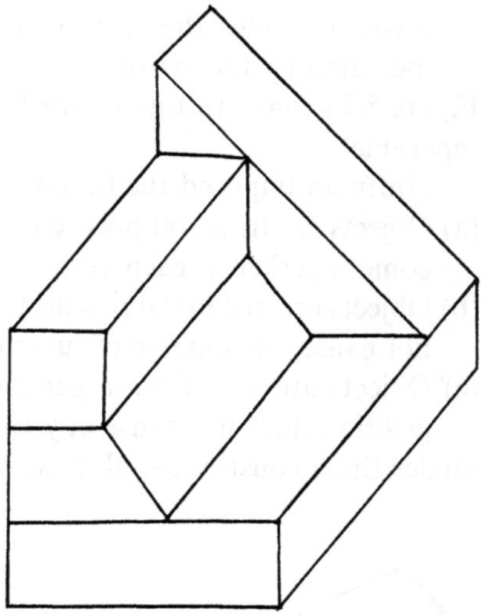

Fig. 5.6. Example of line drawing that is not correctly analyzed by SEE

links are merged. The result of the merging process is shown in Fig. 5.5(c), where two nuclei (which correspond to bodies) are obtained. In this way, fairly complex scenes are analyzed (like the one shown in Fig. 5.3).

However, SEE made mistakes for some line drawings. Figure 5.6 shows such an example. It is not easy to modify a program, because many heuristic rules have no theoretical foundation. Although Guzman's method has not been used in practice, his approach of using junction types as clues for line drawing analysis has greatly influenced later research work.

5.3 Labeling Line Drawings

In contrast to Guzman's heuristic approach, Huffman (1971) and Clowes (1971) independently took a more systematic approach to interpretation of polyhedral line drawings. They paid attention to the physical meaning of lines, and found useful constraints on types of lines at vertices. These constraints are used for interpretation of line drawings. In this section only Huffman's work will be described, since Clowes work is essentially the same.

5.3.1 Vertex Type

Huffman (1971) classified a line according to its physical meaning into three types and assigned labels to them as follows:

1. A convex edge, with both of its surfaces visible from the camera, is denoted by '+'.
2. A concave edge, with both of its surfaces visible from the camera, is denoted by '−'.
3. An occluding edge, with one of its surfaces occluding the other surface of another body, is denoted by '→' or '←'. The surface on the right side of the

arrow occludes the surface on the left side when we look in the direction indicated by the arrow.

Figure 5.7 shows Huffman's labeling for a rectangular prism stuck to a plane (not separable).

Huffman imposed the following constraints on the line drawings.

(a) Objects are trihedral polyhedra, i.e., polyhedra in which exactly three surfaces come together at each vertex.
(b) Objects are in general positions, i.e., a slight change of the object position does not cause any change of junction types in the line drawing.
(c) Objects are seen from a general position, i.e., a slight change of the camera position does not cause any change of junction types.

Under these constraints, all possible junction types were enumerated.

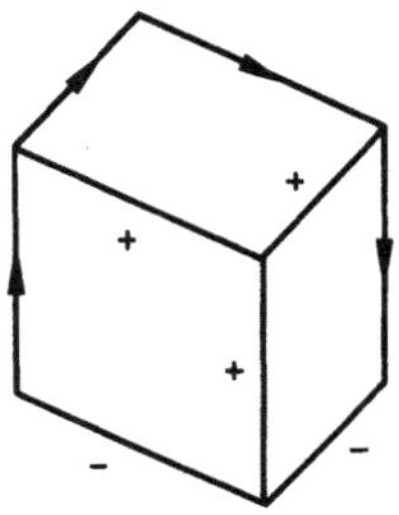

Fig. 5.7. Huffman's labeling for a rectangular prism

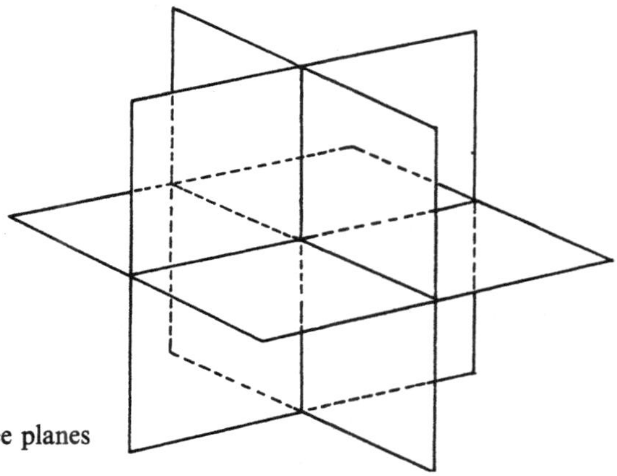

Fig. 5.8. Eight octants generated by three planes

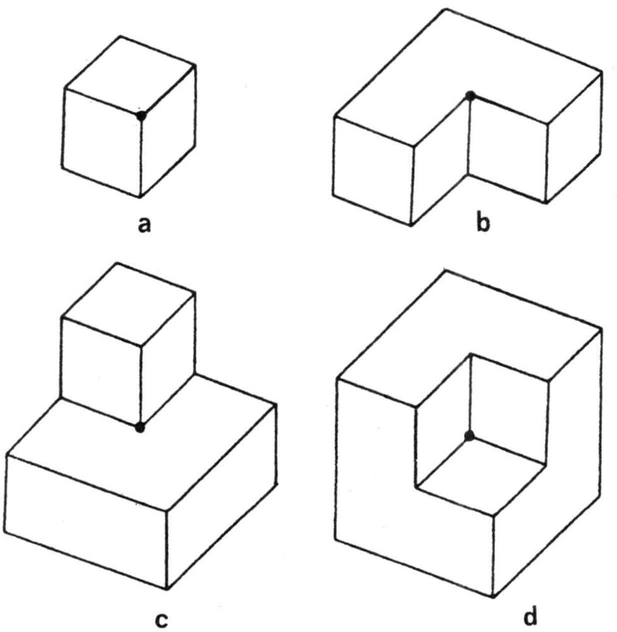

Fig. 5.9a–d. Vertex types: (**a**) one octant filled; (**b**) three octants filled; (**c**) five octants filled; (**d**) seven octants filled

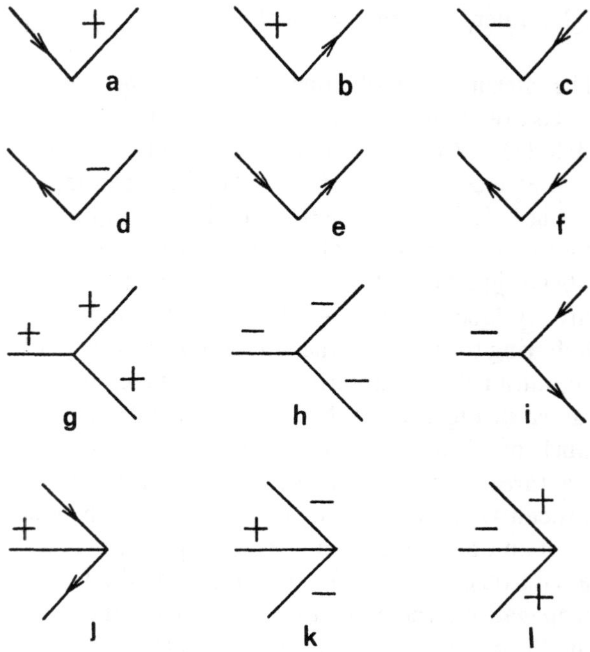

Fig. 5.10. Junction labels for a trihedral polyhedron

Fig. 5.11. Four labelings for a T type junction

A vertex is generated by three surfaces. These three surfaces partition the space into eight octants as shown in Fig. 5.8. Vertices are systematically generated by determining which octants are occupied by solid material. Figure 5.9 shows the four vertex types corresponding to the possible number of octants occupied by solid material. Note that other types are impossible because of either of two reasons: more than three surfaces meet, or the vertex disappears (as in the case where only two adjacent octants are filled). Next, junction types are enumerated by considering viewing directions. The vertex of Fig. 5.9(a) can be seen from seven vacant octants, while the vertex of Fig. 5.9(d) can be seen from only one octant. For each view, a type of junction and the labels of the incident lines are obtained. Enumeration of all cases results in only 12 junction labels as shown in Fig. 5.10.

A vertex thus corresponds to one of 12 junctions. However, we must consider junctions which do not correspond to any vertices. If an edge is partially occluded by another edge, it may be observed as a T junction (see Fig. 5.4). The label of the occluding line is already determined, but the label of the third line is arbitrary. Thus four different labelings are possible for a T type junction as shown in Fig. 5.11.

5.3.2 Interpretation by Labeling

The interpretation of a line drawing can be regarded as the assignment of possible labels to all lines in the drawing. Labels must be assigned so that all junctions may be included in the list of possible junction labels shown in Figs. 5.10 and 5.11.

Let us consider the problem of labeling a simple line drawing such as that shown in Fig. 5.12(a). Suppose that an object is not touching any other object. Then the contour lines must be labeled by arrows as shown in Fig. 5.12(b). At this stage, the label of junctions B, D, and F is determined to be 'f', since their incident lines are already labeled with '→'. Now, at junction A, two lines are labeled with '→'. Referring to Fig. 5.10, the junction label is seen to be 'j', and the label of the third line must be '+'. Similarly, the label of junctions C and E is determined. The result is shown in Fig. 5.12(c). Note again that the label of junction G is 'g', because the labels of all incident lines are already determined. The result of labeling suggests that three rectangular planes are seen and that they form three convex edges. It is not difficult to infer a rectangular prism from the result.

If an object is known to be on a plane, then a similar process will produce the labels as shown in Fig. 5.7. Huffman's method is regarded as a process of constraint propagation, where the constraint corresponds to the list of possible junction types and the propagation means that the label of a line does not change in the middle. In order to find all possible labeling for complex line drawings, systematic strategies are necessary. The following subsections describe two different methods: a sequential search method and a relaxation method.

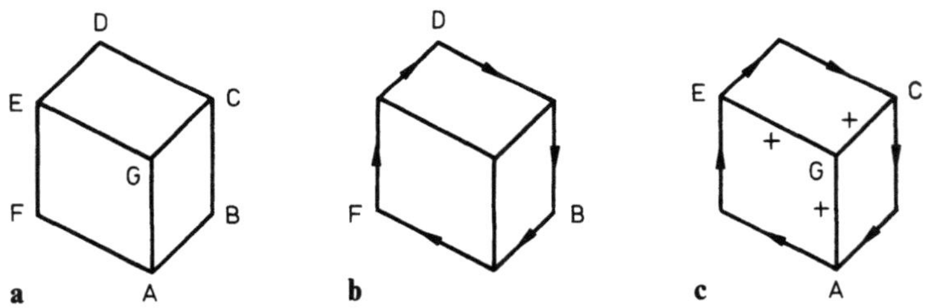

Fig. 5.12a–c. Example of labeling process: (**a**) line drawing of a rectangular prism; (**b**) contour lines are labeled by '→'; (**c**) Arrow type junctions are labeled

5.3.3 Sequential Labeling Procedure

A sequential labeling method assigns possible junction labels to one junction at a time. An efficient procedure is illustrated in Fig. 5.13. The problem is to assign possible labels to all lines in the figure. Let us suppose that junctions are assigned possible labels in the order A, B, . . . , H.

First, arrow junction A is given three possible labels 'j', 'k', and 'l'. The label of junction B is constrained by the adjacent junction A. For example, label 'b' is not compatible with any of the possible labels at A. In such a case, label 'b' at B is said to be incompatible with the possible junction labels at A. Such incompatible labels are

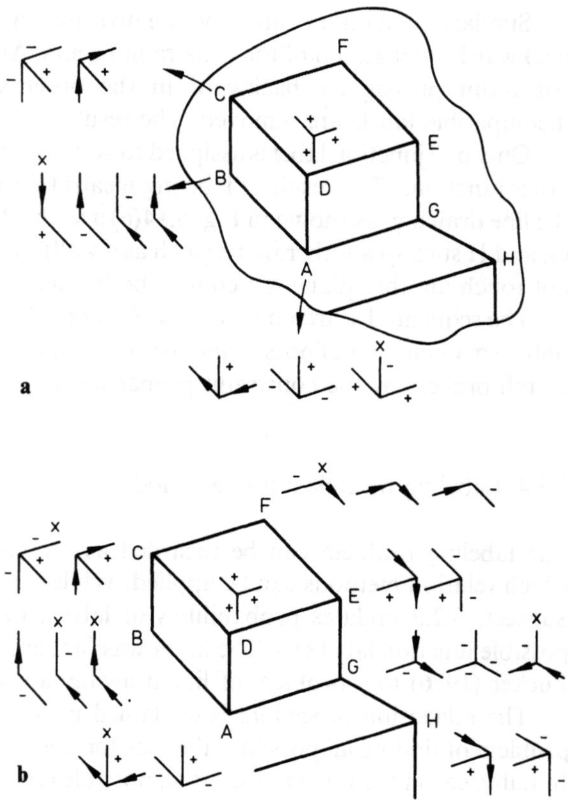

Fig. 5.13a, b. Sequential labeling procedure (a mark 'x' shows that the label is filtered out): (a) intermediate result after junction D is investigated; (b) result of labeling after junction H is investigated

removed from the six junction label candidates for junction B. That is, two of them are filtered out by the forward propagation of the constraint. Only four junction labels are possible at B as shown in Fig. 5.13(a).

Since the possible junction labels at A are all compatible with the possible junction labels at B, nothing happens at junction A. Similarly, junction C is assigned two labels as shown in the figure. Now, junction label 'a' at B is incompatible with the possible junction labels at C. Therefore it is removed from the possible label set. In this case, the constraint has propagated backward. Figure 5.13(a) shows the intermediate result when junction D is investigated.

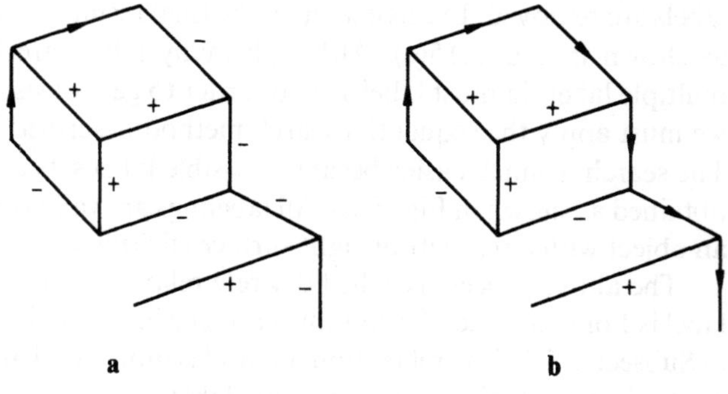

Fig. 5.14a, b. Two interpretations of a line drawing: (a) right vertices stick to another plane; (b) right vertices occlude another plane

Similarly, junctions are investigated through H. During the process no backward propagation of the constraint occurs. After H is assigned a label set, the constraint propagates backward in the order G, A, B, C, D, and F, and incompatible labels are removed. The result is shown in Fig. 5.13(b).

Only one junction label is assigned to A, B, C, and D. Two labels are assigned to other junctions. The result of labeling means that there are two interpretations of the line drawing, as shown in Fig. 5.14(a) and (b). In the former case, vertices E, F, G, and H stick to another plane (such as a wall). In the latter case, those vertices do not touch another plane. Of course, both interpretations are correct.

The sequential search method was first proposed by Waltz (1975). It maintains only a small number of possibilities because many of them are filtered out during the search process by the constraint propagation.

5.3.4 Labeling by Relaxation Method

The labeling problem can be regarded as a constraint-satisfaction problem, to which relation methods can be applied. While the relaxation method described in Subsect. 3.2.2 updates probabilities of labels, the method for labeling updates possible junction label sets. The latter was first applied by Rosenfeld, Hummel and Zucker (1976) to a problem of line drawing labeling.

The relaxation procedure is explained using a simple example. Consider the problem of finding all possible labelings for the line drawing shown in Fig. 5.12(a). Initially, each junction has a set of all possible junction labels. Figure 5.15(a) shows label sets at junctions A, B, and C.

In each iteration, the number of label sets at junctions is reduced by examining their compatibility with those of adjacent junctions. For example, the label set at junction B is updated on the basis of the compatibility of each member with label sets at junctions A and C. The first member of the label set at B is label 'a'. It is compatible with the label set at A because it fits to label 'l' at A (it shares with label 'l' the same label '+' for line AB). However, it is not compatible with the label set at C, because it fits to none of the member labels. Similarly, labels 'b' and 'e' are not compatible with A's label set. Those three junction labels are removed from the junction set at B. All junctions are thus examined. The resultant junction sets are as shown in Fig. 5.15(b).

This result is used for the second iteration. It is easily seen that label 'l' at A will be removed in the next iteration. The relaxation process terminates when no more labels are removed. In this example, the final result is obtained after three iterations as shown in Fig. 5.15(c). Although many labels are filtered out, there are still multiple labels in most label sets. In order to get consistent combinations of labels, we must apply the sequential search method described in the previous subsection. The search is much easier because possible label sets are small. Four labelings are obtained as shown in Fig. 5.16. All labelings are valid (the last two figures represent an object with a rear left or right surface sticking to the vertical wall, respectively).

The above process is called discrete relaxation because the probability of each label is 1 or 0, instead of a continuous value in the probabilistic relaxation described in Subsect. 3.2.2. The relaxation method is more efficient than the sequential search method, if parallel processing is available.

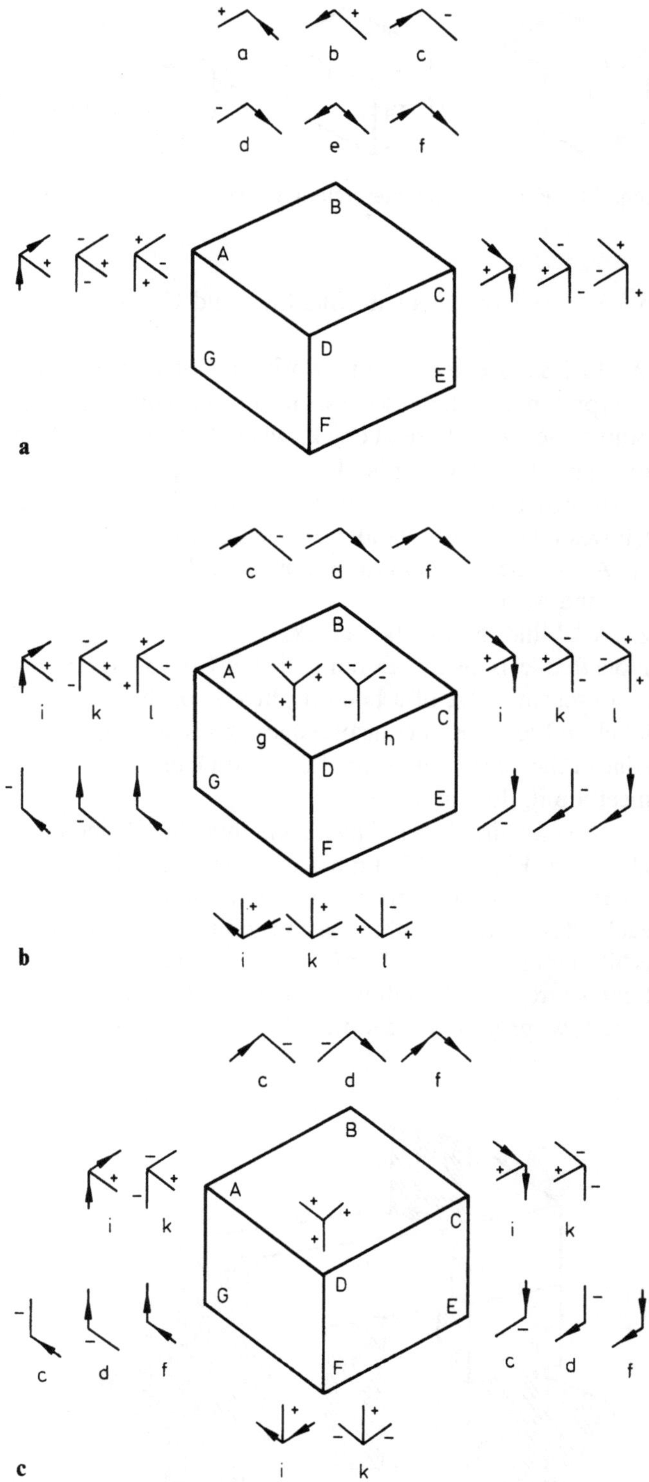

Fig. 5.15a–c. Labeling by relaxation method: **(a)** initial possible label sets at junctions A, B, and C; **(b)** label sets after one iteration; **(c)** final label sets after three iterations

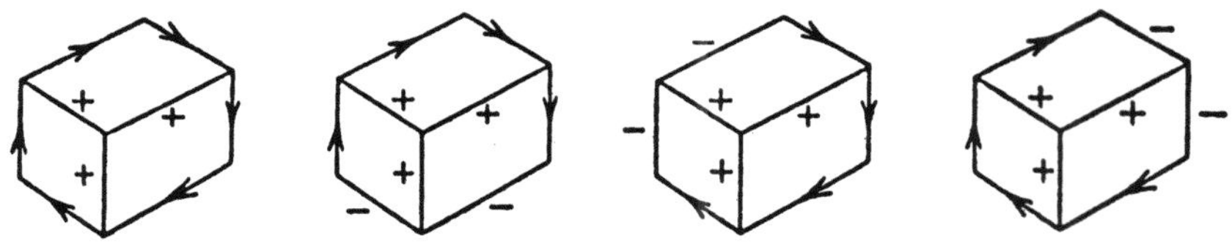

Fig. 5.16. Four possible interpretations obtained by relaxation

5.3.5 Line Drawings with Shadows and Cracks

Waltz (1975) extended the work of Huffman and Clowes described above to interpret more general scenes. He allowed a line drawing to include lines of shadow boundaries, and those of cracks where four or six surfaces meet. A typical example of such a line drawing is illustrated in Fig. 5.17.

In order to interpret line drawings with shadows and cracks, the Huffman-Clowes label set is extended to include the following labels:

1. A '↑' line represents a shadow boundary. The direction of the arrow shows the shadow region.
2. A 'c' line represents a crack.

Note that 'c' is always accompanied by '→' (or '←') because the line corresponds to an obscuring edge of a body (right side of the arrow). There are other composite labels in Fig. 5.18. A concave edge is given a composite label '⇉' if it is a bounding edge of the body (right side of the arrow), or a composite label '→←' if three bodies meet along the line.

Now 11 line labels have been introduced, including the original four from Huffman. Figure 5.19 summarizes the 11 labels.

In addition to the new labels, illumination conditions are also considered. For each side of a line, the illumination condition is classified into three types: the region is 'illuminated' directly from the light source (denoted by 'I'), turned away from the light source ('self-shadowed', denoted by 'SS'), or shaded by another surface ('shadow projected', denoted by 'SP'). Lines are classified according to the

Fig. 5.17. A line drawing with shadows and cracks

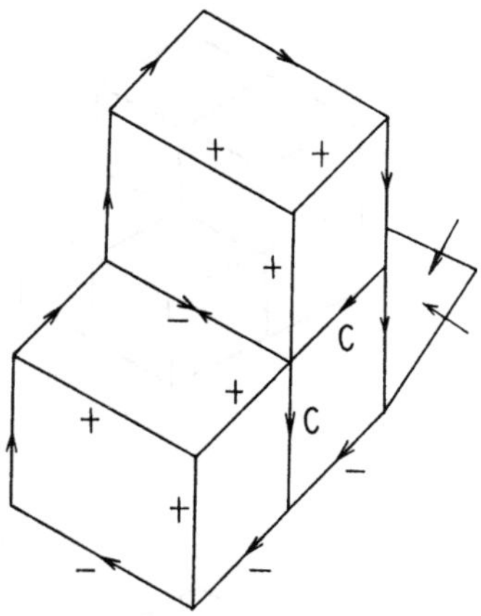

Fig. 5.18. Line labels used by Waltz

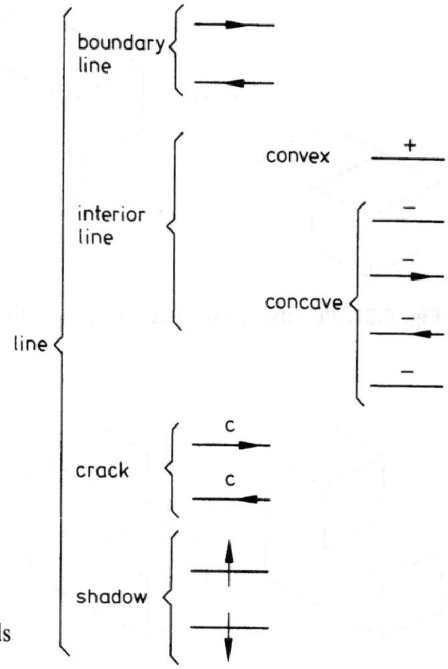

Fig. 5.19. List of line labels

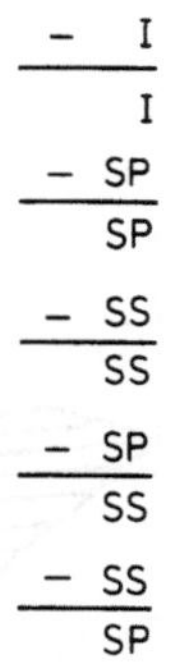

Fig. 5.20. Illumination types for a concave line

illumination types of both sides. Nine classes can be created by all combinations of illumination types. However, the possible class of a line depends on the label of the line. For example, a concave line ('−') is classified as one of the five classes shown in Fig. 5.20. If the illumination class is included in the label set, the number of line labels increases from 11 to 53.

In order to enumerate junction labels, vertex types are systematically generated in the same way as in Subsection 5.3.1. In this case, however, the four types shown in Fig. 5.9 are not enough. For example, vertex types shown in Fig. 5.21 are allowed. In addition, many possibilities must be considered for a certain geometry. The geometry made by filling three octants, for example, is further divided into four cases as shown in Fig. 5.22.

For each junction type, a viewing direction and an illumination direction are also assigned to one of the octants. Then junction types, shadows, and illumination conditions are completely determined.

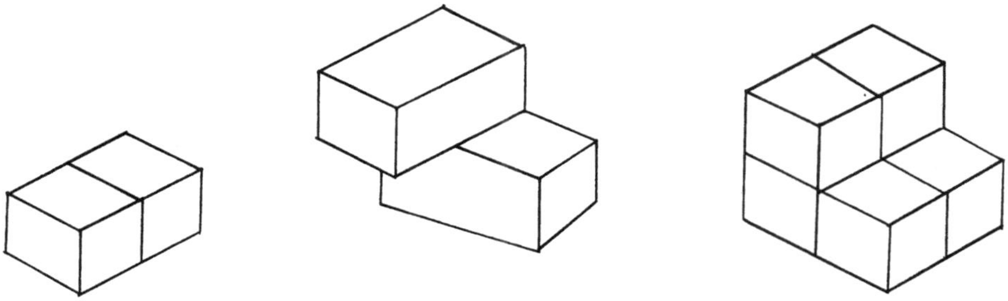

Fig. 5.21. Possible geometries for generation of vertex type

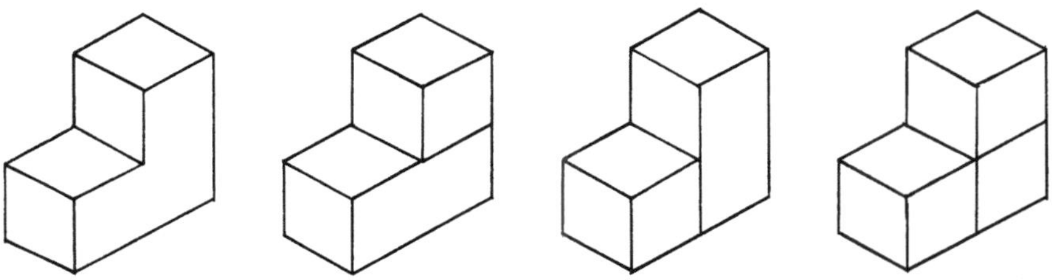

Fig. 5.22. Four vertex types for a geometry

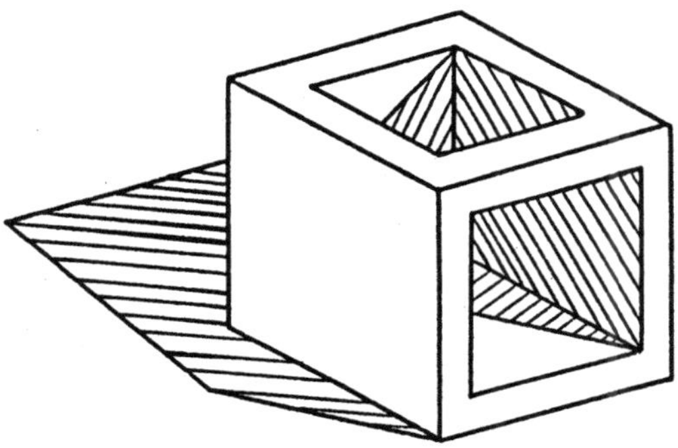

Fig. 5.23. Line drawing interpreted by Waltz (1975)

Waltz considered ten junction types and obtained possible junction labels for those junction types. Among these the Fork junction has the highest number of junction labels (836). The total number of labels is more than three thousand. This may expand the search space. But the number of line labels has also increased from 4 to 11. This imposes stronger constraints on the compatibility between adjacent junction types. The labeling procedure is the same as that described above. Although the large number of junction labels makes it difficult to simulate the process manually, the problem is not hard for computers. Most candidate labels that are initially assigned to junctions are filtered out very quickly by the strong constraints. Waltz showed that the amount of computation is approximately proportional to the number of junctions. Figure 5.23 shows an example of a line drawing interpreted by Waltz's program.

The labeling method showed that a set of simple local constraints can solve complicated problems with the constraint propagation technique. It also demonstrated that the greater the knowledge available, the more effectively the search space is constrained.

5.3.6 Interpretation of Curved Objects

It is natural to explore a way to extend the labeling technique to deal with curved objects. One of the difficulties is how to classify junction types. The number of junction types is expected to increase tremendously. For example, the shape of the Arrow type junction may expand to 27 types as shown in Fig. 5.24, where each line is classified to be straight, convex, or concave.

Moreover, the physical meaning of lines also increases. In a line drawing of polyhedra, a line corresponds to an edge or a shadow boundary. For curved objects, a line may correspond to a contour of a smooth surface (a horizon). The corresponding line on the curved surface changes as the line of sight changes. We need a new label for such lines. Let a double arrowed line '→→' denote an obscuring contour of a curved surface. The direction of the double arrow shows that the right side region occludes the left side region of the same surface.

Turner (1974) interpreted line drawings including polyhedra and objects with quadratic surfaces such as ellipsoids or cones. His approach was similar to that of Waltz. He made a junction dictionary of all possible labels for all types of junctions. In order to make the dictionary systematic, he modified junctions for polyhedra. That is, each plane of a junction is modified to a curved surface. A curved surface is classified as an ellipsoid, a hyperboloid, or a cone. Figure 5.25 shows the

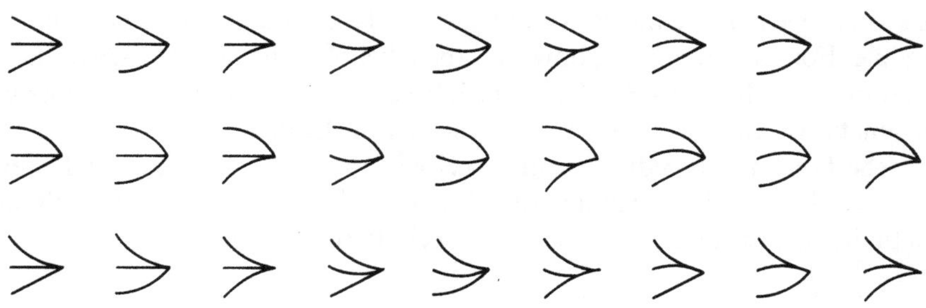

Fig. 5.24. Junction types of curved bodies modified from an Arrow junction

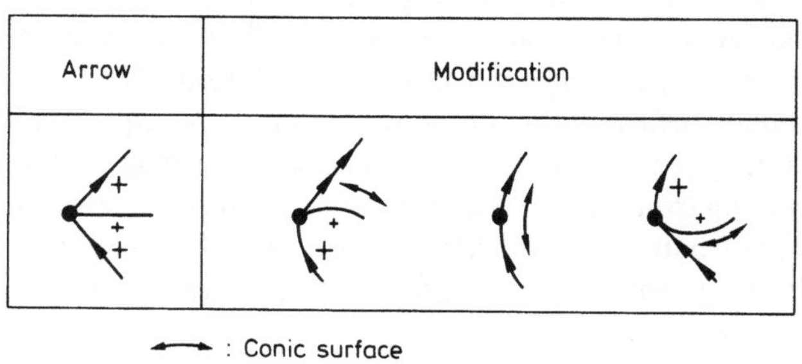

Fig. 5.25. Extension of polyhedral junction to curved body

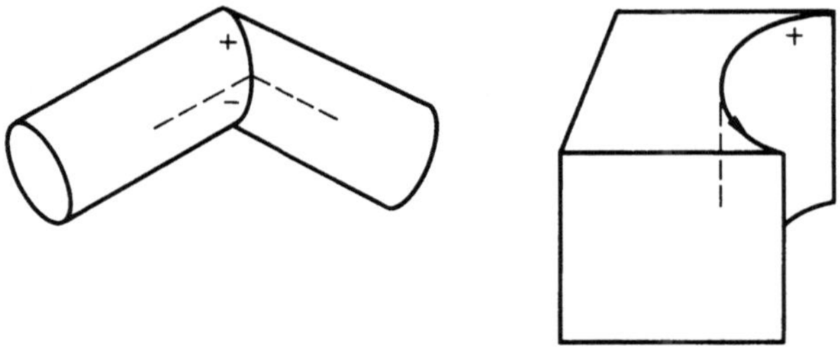

Fig. 5.26. Example of label change in a line

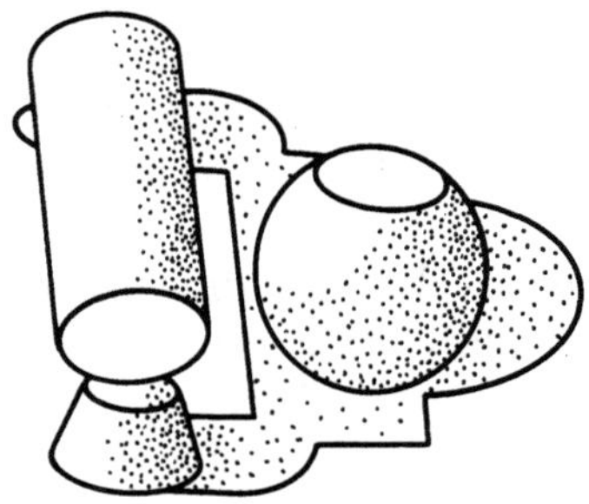

Fig. 5.27. Example of a scene analyzed by Turner (1974)

modification of planes in the Arrow junction to cones. Three junction labels are generated depending on which line of the junction is modified to the generating line of the cone. Similarly, planes are replaced by other types of curved surfaces.

Thus, more than five thousand junction types are generated. In order to enumerate junction labels involving shadows, shadow lines of each junction type are generated for all possible directions of the illumination. The junction dictionary contains all possible labels.

Another difficulty lies in the labeling problem. In labeling polyhedral line drawings, we can use the constraint that the label of a line does not change in the middle. For curved objects, however, the label of a line may change in the middle. Examples are shown in Fig. 5.26. The label change was examined for possible pairs of junctions, and the result was also stored in the dictionary.

The labeling procedure is, in principle, similar to that described previously. Figure 5.27 shows an example of a line drawing analyzed by Turner's program (actually, the input drawing does not include the shading).

5.3.7 Interpretation of Origami World

Origami is the traditional Japanese manual art of making various shaped objects by folding a sheet of square paper. The labeling method was extended by Kanade (1980) to the Origami world interpretation. The Origami world is composed of planar surfaces (which need not be sheets of paper!). It contains solids because we cannot distinguish a solid from a set of surfaces bounding an empty interior by looking from the outside. Therefore, more line drawings are allowed in the Origami world than in the trihedral world. Figure 5.28 shows such an example. The line drawing represents a box made of just five surfaces (the bottom is not seen).

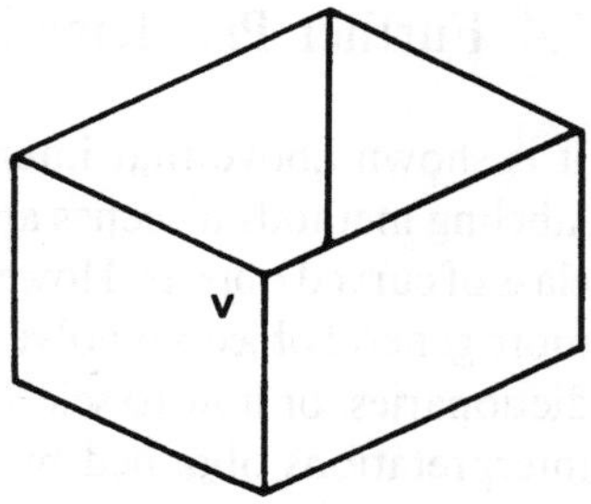

Fig. 5.28. Line drawing of a box

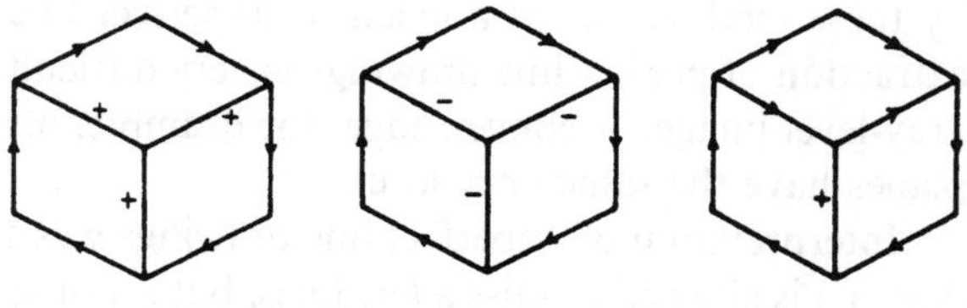

Fig. 29a–c. Interpretations of a cube-like line drawing: (**a**) convex corner; (**b**) concave corner; (**c**) triangular box

When we fold a sheet of paper along an edge, two vertices are generated at the ends of the edge. An example is vertex 'v' in Fig. 5.28. Such a vertex is formed by just two surfaces. In the Origami world, therefore, it is assumed that no more than three surfaces meet at a vertex (in the trihedral world exactly three surfaces are assumed). The junction dictionary can be constructed in the same manner as for the trihedral world. Table 5.1 shows the number of possible junctions in the Origami world, as compared with the trihedral junctions.

The labeling procedure used the augumented dictionary. Although many impossible labels are filtered out by this procedure, more interpretations remain than in the trihedral world. Some of them are not realizable, but many are. Figure 5.29 shows three interpretations of a line drawing: (a) a convex corner, (b) a concave corner, and (c) a triangular box (the top edge of the back surface is not flat, but L-shaped).

Table 5.1. Comparison of the junction dictionaries for L, ARROW, FORK, and T junction types

Junction type	Trihedral-world dictionary	Origami-world dictionary
L	6	8
ARROW	3	15
FORK	3	9
T	4	16

5.4 Further Problems in Line Drawing Interpretation

It is shown above that interpretation of line drawings is, in principle, solved by labeling methods if scenes are constrained to include only trihedral polyhedra or a class of curved objects. However, the extension of these methods to interpretation of more general objects involves many unsolved problems: how to make huge junction dictionaries, or how to select an appropriate interpretation from a large number of interpretations obtained by labeling methods.

Another important problem of the labeling methods is that they accept as input only perfect line drawings. We cannot predict what kind of results will be obtained by these methods when applied to imperfect line drawings. On the other hand, extraction of perfect line drawings is very difficult, especially if the input is just a gray-level image. A convex edge, for example, may not be detected if both of its planes have the same gray level.

Interpretation of imperfect line drawings was studied by Falk (1972). The line drawing is allowed to miss a few lines, but is not allowed to include extra lines (see Fig. 5.30 for example). He used nine models of objects such as rectangular solids and wedges. Unlike Roberts' models, which were allowed to change their sizes, Falk's models were completely specified in shape and size. His program proceeds as follows.

1. Segmentation. The line drawing is partitioned into bodies on the basis of a large set of heuristics.
2. Completion. Obvious lines or parts of lines are added.
3. Recognition. Each body is recognized by matching to the models.
4. Prediction. The expected line drawing is generated from the result of recognition.
5. Verification. The predicted line drawing is compared with the original one. If contradictions are found, these parts are analyzed again.

The difficulty of the method is that it is based on many heuristics that have no theoretical foundations. However, it suggested useful approaches: a hypothesis-and-test strategy, and a method of matching a part of the line drawing to three-dimensional models.

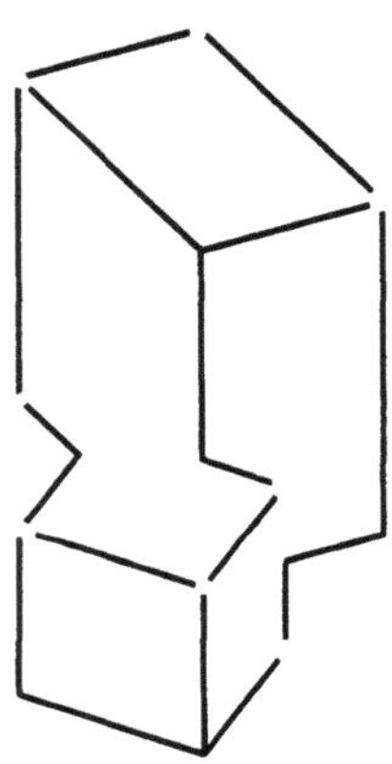

Fig. 5.30. Imperfect line drawing analyzed by Falk (1972)

Generally, it is impossible to obtain a unique interpretation of an imperfect line drawing. There are two approaches to this problem. One is to go back to the original image to examine doubtful regions more carefully, or to go back to the input system to collect more information such as color or range.

The other approach is to modify the imperfect line drawing so that it may have a consistent interpretation. The problem in this approach is that, even if some lines are added or deleted from a consistent line drawing, the result may also be consistent. That is, the modification is not uniquely determined. One solution is to introduce a suitable criterion for deciding which line drawing is best. The criterion may be a function of the number of modified lines, or shapes of surfaces. In any case, some heuristics are indispensable.

6 Realizability of Line Drawings

As shown above, the labeling technique is a powerful tool for the interpretation of perfect line drawings. If a line drawing is assumed to be extracted correctly from a real scene, at least one of the interpretations corresponds to the real scene. That is, the line drawing is realizable (in this interpretation). If a line drawing is not extracted correctly, or a line drawing is given by a human, it may not be realizable or may even not be interpreted. In the following section the case where line drawings have no interpretations is discussed. The subsequent sections introduce two approaches to the determination of the realizability of labeled line drawings.

6.1 Line Drawings Without Interpretations

Since the realizability of a line drawing is determined for a given interpretation, the realizability is undefined if the line drawing has no interpretation. That is, the line drawing is not realizable, or does not satisfy the constraints described in Sect. 5.3.

For example, the line drawings shown in Fig. 6.1 are not realizable, although each junction itself is valid. Suppose Fig. 6.1(a) is labeled from the contour to the internal junctions. The contour can be labeled with '→'; three arrow junctions on the contour are labeled, and then two fork junctions are labeled as shown in the figure. Now the label of junction A implies that line AB be labeled '→'. On the other hand, the label of junction B implies '−'. Figure 6.1(b) is similarly judged to be impossible.

Note that line drawings without consistent labeling may be realizable if the assumed constraints are relaxed. Figure 6.2 shows realizable line drawings that cannot be labeled by Huffman's label set. Figures 6.2(a) and (b) correspond to

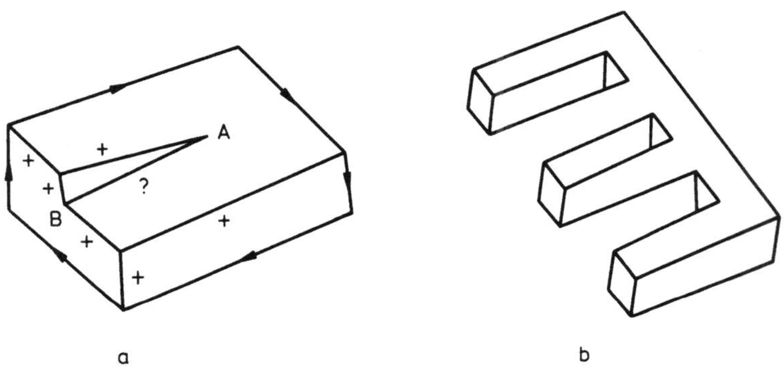

Fig. 6.1. Impossible line drawings that cannot be labeled

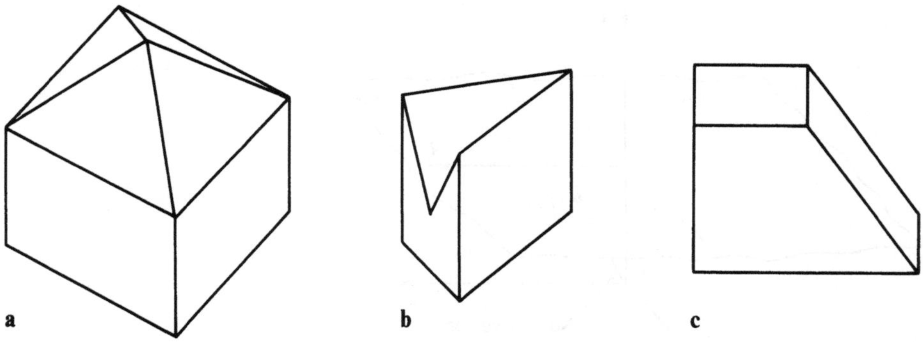

Fig. 6.2. Possible objects that cannot be labeled

polyhedra that have vertices with four surfaces (i.e., nontrihedral polyhedra). Figure 6.2(c) violates the constraint that the object be seen from a general position.

6.2 Use of Gradient Space

It has been shown that the susceptibility of a line drawing to labeling is a necessary condition for its realizability. However, it is not a sufficient condition. Research efforts have been made to obtain a systematic method for classifying line drawings as possible or impossible.

Huffman (1971) raised the problem of realizability of line drawings and introduced the idea of dual space for this problem. The projection of dual space onto a two-dimensional plane is called the 'dual picture'. Mackworth (1973) proposed a method to interpret line drawings in the dual picture. Instead of the dual picture, he used the name 'gradient space' because it represents gradients of object surfaces. Since three-dimensional dual space is not often useful, the 'gradient space' is used here.

6.2.1 Gradient Space

Let us suppose that line drawings are orthogonal projections of real space onto the x–y plane. A plane in (real) space can be denoted by:

$$-z = px + qy + c \tag{6.1}$$

The plane is represented in gradient space as a point (p, q). Note that a point in gradient space corresponds to an infinite number of planes of the same direction at different positions. Since the vector $(p, q, 1)$ is normal to the plane represented by Eq. (6.1), the gradient image of a plane can be regarded as the intersection of the normal vector at the origin with the horizontal plane at $z = 1$ (see Fig. 6.3).

To illustrate the concept of gradient space, imagine a polyhedron placed on the x–y plane as shown in Fig. 6.4. Suppose a plane A is parallel to the x–y plane. It is

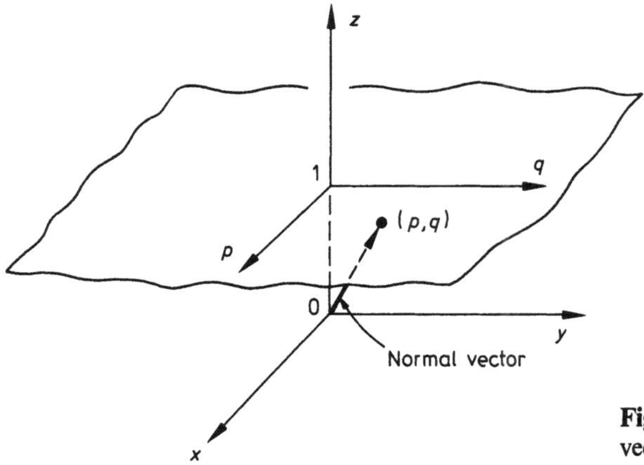

Fig. 6.3. Relation between a normal vector and the gradient image

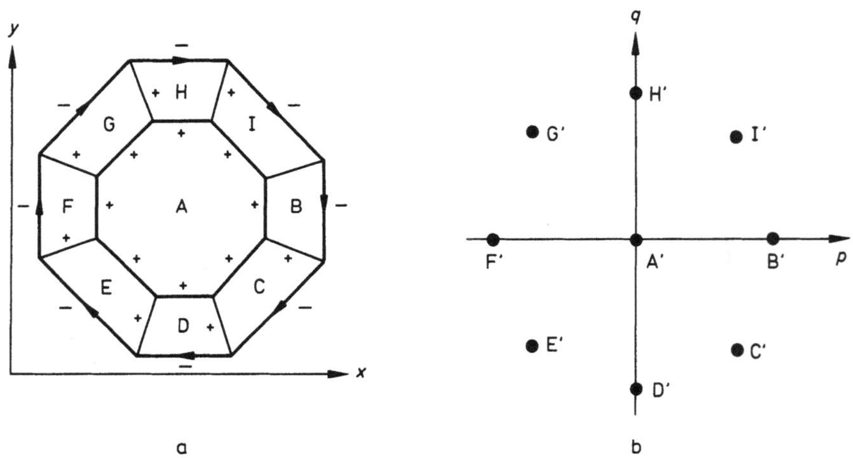

Fig. 6.4. (**a**) Polyhedron in real space; (**b**) gradient space images of the surfaces

then represented in gradient space by the point at the origin (A′ in Fig. 6.4(b)). Plane B, which tilts away from the viewer to the right, is mapped to the right of point A′. The other planes are similarly mapped onto gradient space. Notice that the spatial relation of planes is the same as that of corresponding points in gradient space. This is because all lines between two planes are convex.

Let us analyze the relation between real space and gradient space in more detail. Figure 6.5(a) shows that plane A meets another plane at line ST. Suppose that plane A is represented by A′ in gradient space as shown in Fig. 6.5(b). If the opponent plane faces in the same direction as plane A (B_1 in the figure), the gradient image is, of course, the same point (A′). If it tilts away to the upper right (B_2), i.e., ST is convex, then the gradient image (B_2') is at the upper right of A′. If it tilts to the opposite side (B_3), i.e., ST is concave, then the gradient image (B_3') is to the lower left of A′.

In both cases, the larger the tilt angle of the plane, the larger is the distance of the gradient image from A′. It is easily proved that B_2' and B_3' lie on the line

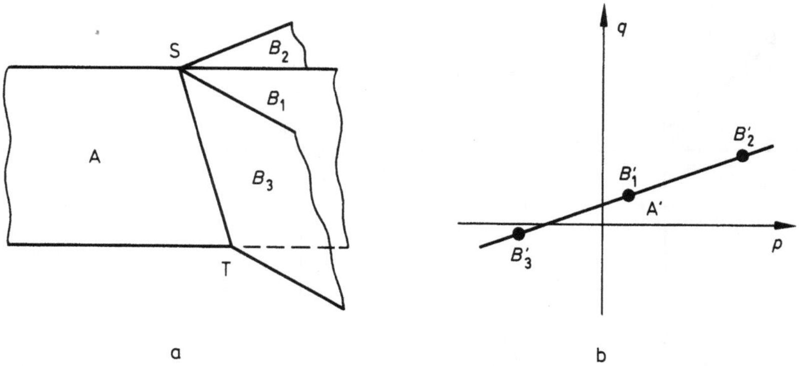

Fig. 6.5a, b. Gradients of two connected planes: **(a)** real space; **(b)** gradient space

perpendicular to line ST if the x–y coordinate system and p–q coordinate system are superposed. This property is used to map surfaces of polyhedra onto gradient space.

6.2.2 Construction of Gradient Image

Mackworth interpreted line drawings by constructing the image of each plane in gradient space. His program POLY first decides the type of edges: connecting edges (either convex or concave) and occluding edges. It then verifies the assumption by constructing the gradient image, i.e., it searches over a binary tree until the consistent dual picture is obtained.

Consider how POLY works for the example shown in Fig. 6.6. It first picks up an arbitrary region, say region A, and assigns an arbitrary gradient, say (0, 0), to it. The gradient image A′ is the origin of the gradient space. Next, region B is considered. Regions A and B have two common bounding lines (lines 1 and 2). Each line may be a connecting edge or an occluding edge. The program explores all combinations of the edge type.

It first assumes that line 1 is a connecting edge. In that case, the gradient image of B must be on the line that passes through A′ perpendicular to line 1. Again, two possibilities must be considered: the gradient image B′ is to the upper left and to the lower right of A′. Let us choose B′ at a fixed distance from A′, as shown in Figs. 6.7(a) and (b).

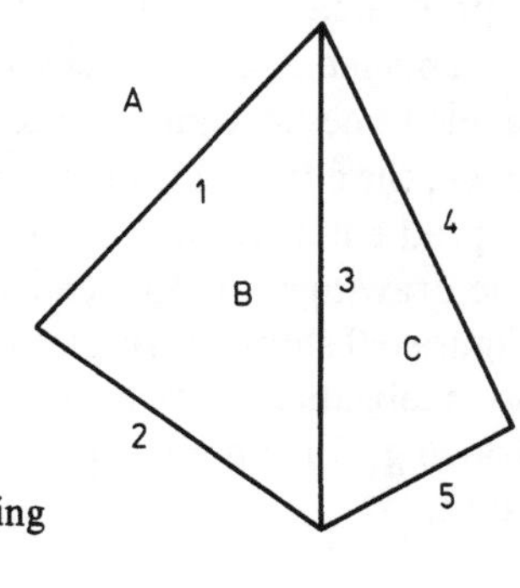

Fig. 6.6. A simple line drawing

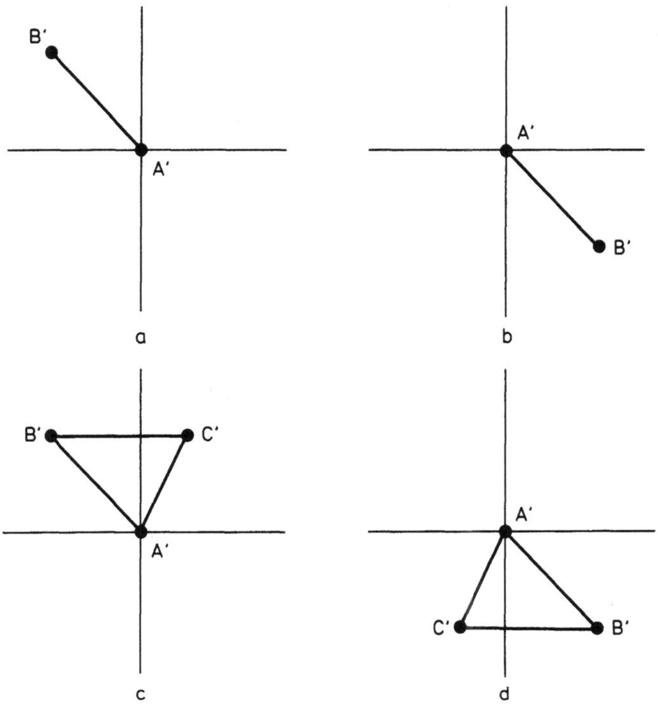

Fig. 6.7a–d. Construction of gradient image: (**a**) for convex line 1; (**b**) for concave line 1; (**c**) extension of (**a**); (**d**) extension of (**b**)

Next, POLY takes line 2. It cannot be a connecting edge, because if it were, line A′B′ would be perpendicular to line 2. Thus, line 2 has to be occluding.

POLY proceeds to lines 3 and then 4. Let us consider the case where both lines are connecting. The gradient image of region C must be on the line perpendicular to line 3 through B′ and the line perpendicular to line 4 through A′. These constraints completely determine C′ as shown in Figs. 6.7(c) and (d). Line 5 is similarly determined to be occluding. In the former interpretation, lines 1 and 4 are concave, and line 3 is convex, while in the latter, lines 1 and 4 are convex, and line 3 is concave.

Other interpretations are also obtained by verifying other assumptions. The method described above can reject line drawings such as those shown in Fig. 6.8, because their gradient images cannot be constructed. In both cases, the construction is prevented by two surfaces A and B connected by two different lines ‘a’ and ‘b’.

This method can easily be extended to the determination of the realizability of labeled line drawings. Since the interpretation of a labeled line drawing is already given, the construction of a gradient image requires no search process. Thus the use of gradient space can detect a class of unrealizable line drawings. However, some line drawings are not realizable even if their gradient images can be constructed. Figure 6.9 shows examples of such line drawings. It is clear that the first drawing is not realizable because two planes A and B meet at parallel lines. In the second drawing, three convex edges among three planes A, B, and C do not meet at one point.

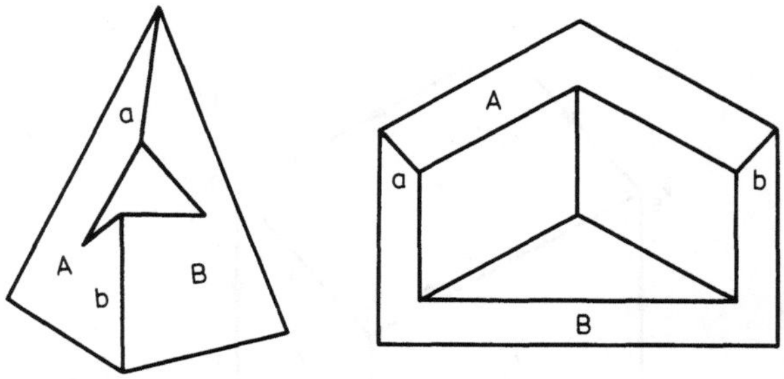

Fig. 6.8. Line drawings that have no gradient images

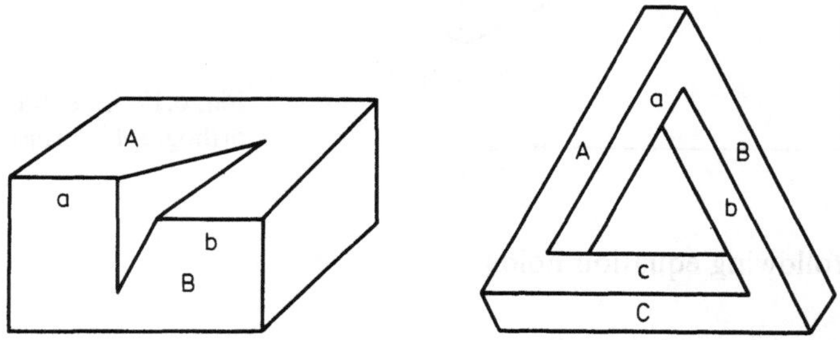

Fig. 6.9. Impossible line drawings that have gradient images

Although the construction of a gradient image is not a sufficient condition for a line drawing to be realizable, the idea of gradient space plays an important role as a compact representation of planes.

6.3 Use of Linear Equation Systems

A straightforward approach to the determination of the realizability of a line drawing is to construct polyhedra in real space so that their images coincide with the line drawing. In the following subsections a quantitative method and a qualitative one are described.

6.3.1 Solving Linear Equation Systems

Let us assume that line drawings are projections of three-dimensional scenes along the z axis and that they are already labeled. Let us, furthermore, assume that polyhedra are put in general postures: no faces of polyhedra are parallel to the z axis. Let (x_i, y_i, z_i) denote the coordinate of vertex v_i, and

$$a_j x + b_j y + z + c_j = 0$$

denote the equation of face f_j (see Fig. 6.10). Since x_i and y_i are given by the line drawing, the only variables are the z_i, a_i, b_i, and c_i. If vertex v_i lies on face f_j the

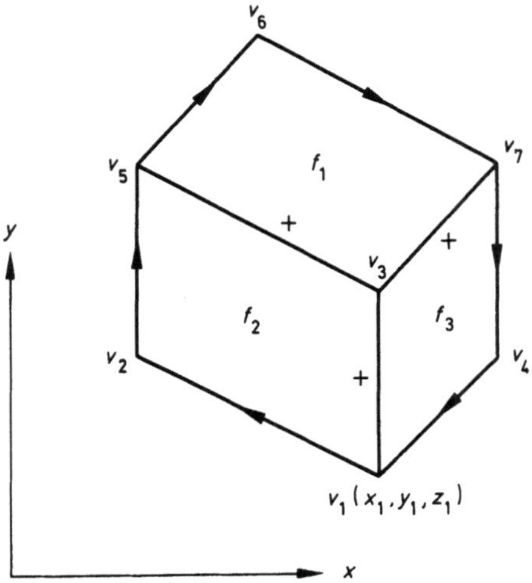

Fig. 6.10. Line drawing produced by orthographic projection

following equation holds:

$$a_j x_i + b_j y_i + z_i + c_j = 0 \tag{6.2}$$

This is a linear equation with respect to z_i, a_j, b_j, and c_j. Suppose that the line drawing has n vertices and m faces, and that face j has l_j visible vertices. We can get l_j linear equations for the l_j vertices on the face f_j. As a whole the number of equations is given by

$$l = l_1 + l_2 + \ldots + l_m$$

The number of unknown variables k is given by:

$$k = n + 3m \tag{6.3}$$

Let $\boldsymbol{w}$ denote a vector whose components correspond to k unknown variables, that is, $\boldsymbol{w} = (z_1 \ldots z_n\, a_1\, b_1\, c_1 \ldots a_m\, b_m\, c_m)^t$; then the equation system can be rewritten as:

$$A\boldsymbol{w} = 0 \tag{6.4}$$

where A is a coefficient matrix. This equation system is called a fundamental equation system.

Now care must be taken that the fundamental equation system has a trivial solution in which every face is identical. Indeed, if we let $a_i = a$, $b_i = b$, and $c_i = c$, for any i, then the following solution satisfies the equation system:

$$z_i = -ax_i - by_i - c\,, \quad \text{for} \quad i = 1, \ldots, m$$

This trivial solution, however, does not give the labeled line drawing because all planes are reduced to a single plane.

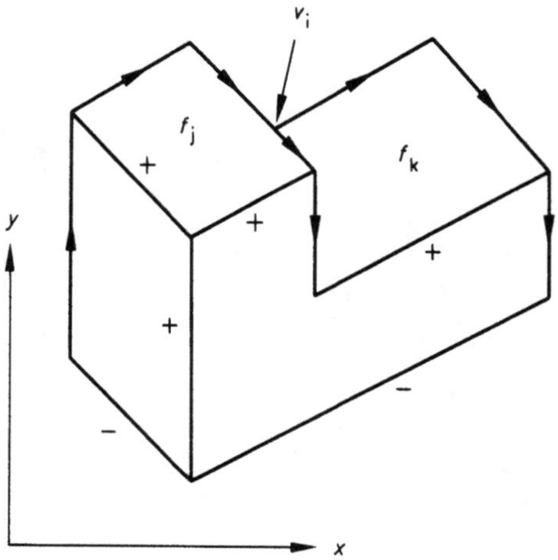

Fig. 6.11. Constraint on obscuring line

Now in order to obtain an appropriate solution, let us introduce another constraint: every plane must be consistent with the labeling of lines. In Fig. 6.10, for example, faces f_1 and f_2 must meet along a convex edge; that is, vertex v_1 must be behind face f_1. This fact is represented by the following inequality.

$$a_1x_1+b_1y_1+z_1+c_1<0 \tag{6.5}$$

Such inequalities are obtained for convex and concave edges.

If there are T-shaped junctions along obscuring lines, an extra vertex is introduced on the obscured edge, as shown in Fig. 6.11. Vertex v_i on face f_k must be behind face f_j. This is similarly represented by the following inequality:

$$a_jx_i+b_jy_i+z_i+c_j<0 \tag{6.6}$$

A set of these inequalities can be reduced to

$$\boldsymbol{B}\boldsymbol{w}<0 \tag{6.7}$$

where $\boldsymbol{B}$ is a coefficient matrix.

It has been shown that a labeled line drawing is realizable if and only if Eq. (6.4) has a solution that satisfies constraint (6.7). An efficient algorithm has been developed in the field of mathematical programming to determine whether or not the solutions exist and to obtain them if they do exist. Now the problem of realizability seems to be solved. However, this is not a practical solution, because the existence of the solution may be affected by the slightest change of the positions of vertices. It is impossible to input the coordinates of vertices without error.

6.3.2 Position-Free Line Drawings

The purpose of this subsection is to introduce position-free line drawings for the determination of the realizability of line drawings in more practical situations. A

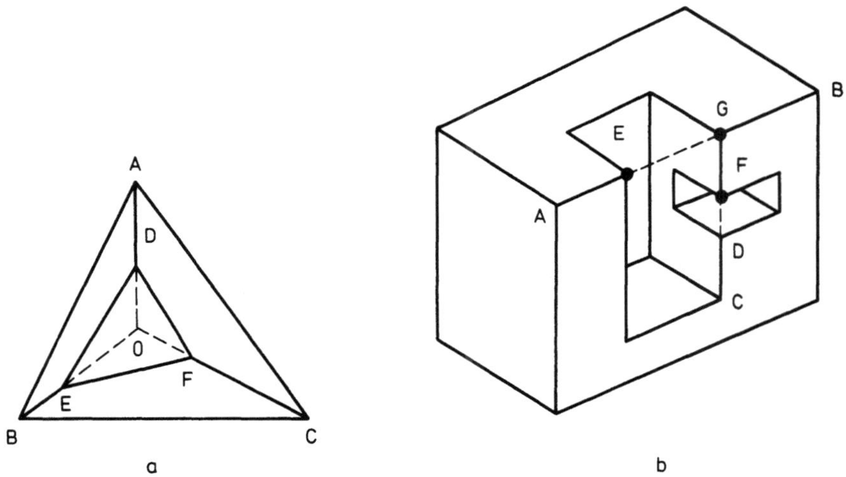

Fig. 6.12a, b. Position-constrained line drawings: (**a**) three lines must meet at a point (O); (**b**) two lines must be colinear

line drawing is called position-free if its fundamental equation system and inequality system have a solution even when any vertices are moved slightly in an arbitrary direction. Examples of position-free line drawings are shown in Figs. 6.10 and 6.11. A counter-example is shown in Fig. 6.12. When a vertex, say vertex F, moves out of line CO, its fundamental equation system has no solution, and thus the line drawing is not realizable. Such a line drawing is called position-constrained.

The principle of discriminating position-free line drawings is intuitively explained as follows. If a line drawing of polyhedra includes more than one face, four vertices can be given arbitrary z values (we say that the line drawing has four degrees of freedom). In Fig. 6.10, for example, when vertices v_1, v_2, and v_3 are given arbitrary z values, face f_2 is fixed. The z values of the other vertices (in this example, vertex v_5) are also determined. We can give an arbitrary z value to another vertex on another face. Suppose we choose vertex v_4 and give an arbitrary z value that satisfies the label of the incident line (in this case, label '+' of the vertical line); then face f_3 is determined (together with vertices v_1 and v_3). The z value of vertex v_7 is also determined. Finally, face f_1 is determined (by vertices v_3, v_5, and v_7). Thus, we can show that the line drawing is realizable by generating a corresponding polyhedron. Since this process is not affected by the positions of the junctions, the line drawing is position-free.

Now let us consider a formal method to determine whether a line drawing is position-free or not, by using the number of variables (k) and the number of equations of the fundamental equation system (l). Let s be defined as:

$$s = k - l \tag{6.8}$$

The value of s represents the degree of freedom if the fundamental equation system is linearly independent. In Fig. 6.10, for example, $l = l_1 + l_2 + l_3 = 12$, $k = 7 + (3 \times 3) = 16$, and $s = k - l = 4$. We can give arbitrary values to 4 variables in

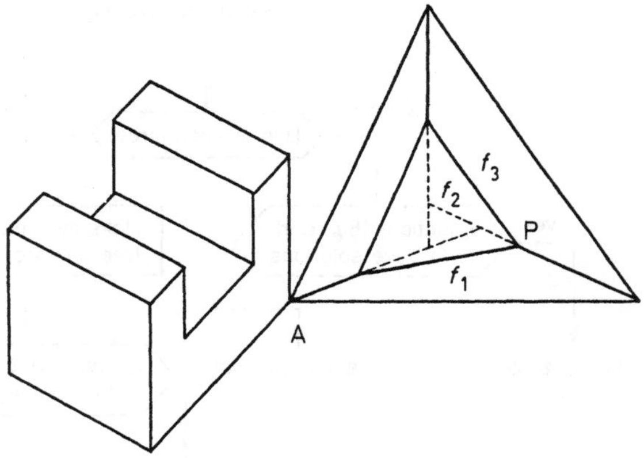

Fig. 6.13. An impossible line drawing with $s=7$

the fundamental equation system. Then, the number of variables is the same as that of equations. Therefore, the fundamental equation system of the drawing always has a solution even if positions of vertices change.

There are line drawings with s values greater than four. Figure 6.11 shows an example of a line drawing with $s=5$, where we can give arbitrary z values to five vertices. This line drawing is also position-free. If a position-free line drawing satisfies the fundamental equation system (6.4) and inequalities (6.7), it is realizable. Otherwise, it is not realizable.

If a line drawing of polyhedra including more than two faces has an s value less than four, the line drawing is position-constrained. A position-constrained line drawing must satisfy some constraints in order to be realizable. Figure 6.12(a) shows an example with $s=3$. The constraint is that lines AD, BE, and CF must intersect at a point. Figure 6.12(b) shows a line drawing with more constraints. The constraints are that junctions A, E, G, B must be on a line and that junctions C, D, F, and G must be on a line. That is, when junctions A, B, C, and D are given, junctions E and F must be on lines AB and CD respectively and junction G is uniquely determined as the crosspoint of the two lines.

The s value for a line drawing, however, does not give a sufficient condition for it to be position-free. Figure 6.13 shows such an example. The line drawing represents two polyhedra touching at junction A. If it is separated at A, the s value of the left is 5, and that of the right side is 3. Since they share common junction A, the s value of the whole drawing is 7. Actually, the line drawing is not realizable because the right side is position-constrained as mentioned above. Thus, for a line drawing with more than one face to be position-free, the s value of any part of the drawing must be greater than or equal to 4. For more rigorous discussion, see Sugihara (1982).

6.3.3 Realizability of Position-Constrained Line Drawings

It has been shown that the realizability of a position-free line drawing is not influenced by slight changes in the vertex positions. If a practical method is available for the determination of the realizability of position-constrained line drawings, we can determine the realizability of any labeled line drawing. Figure 6.14 shows a flowchart of the method (Sugihara, 1982).

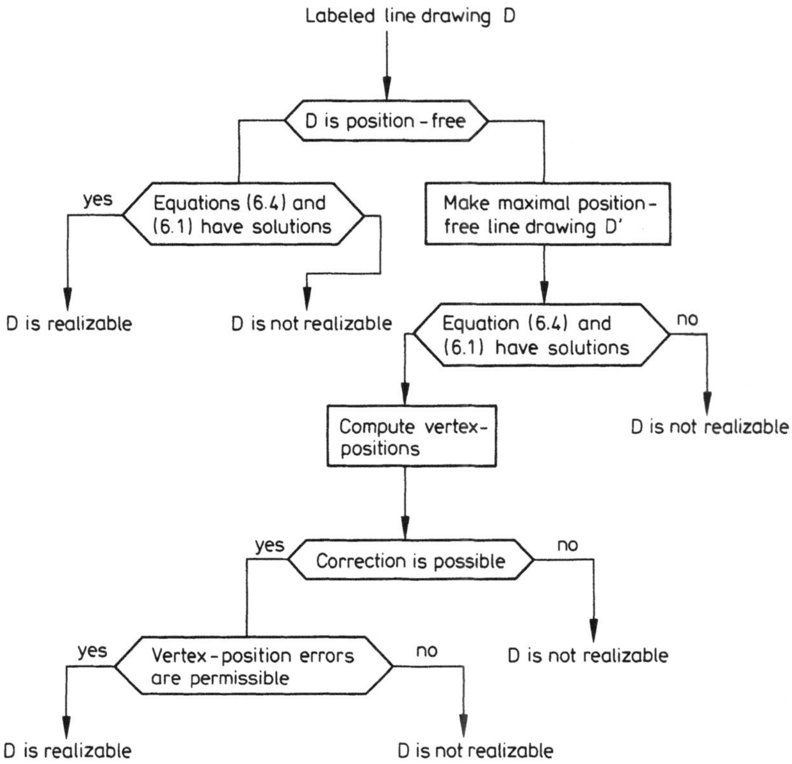

Fig. 6.14. Flowchart for the determination of realizability

Recall that a position-constrained line drawing has some parts that have less than 4 degrees of freedom. The fundamental equation system of such a drawing has excess equations. If some of the equations are removed, the drawing becomes position-free. In Fig. 6.13, for example, junction P is on three faces. Let us assume that junction P is on only two faces, f_1 and f_2 (that is, P is detached from face f_3). This means that the equation that junction P is on face f_3 is removed. The drawing then becomes position-free. Although we can remove more equations, one equation is sufficient for generating a position-free line drawing.

Let us define a maximal position-free line drawing to be the one derived by removing minimal equations. It is obvious that a position-constrained line drawing is not realizable if a maximal position-free line drawing of it is not realizable. Figure 6.9(b), for example, is not realizable because a maximal position-free line drawing generated by removing any one vertex–face pair from it does not satisfy the inequalities in Eq. (6.7).

On the other hand, the position-free line drawing derived from Fig. 6.13 is realizable. Thus the line drawing can be corrected by modifying the removed vertex–face pairs. The positions of junctions (in the line drawing) are derived from the equations representing the maximal position-free line drawing. In the previous example, the position of junction P is determined so that it may be at the intersection of faces f_1, f_2, and f_3.

Based on the modified line drawing, we can determine whether the original line drawing is realizable or not. The fundamental equation of the modified line drawing obviously has a solution. It is then compared with the original line drawing. If any corresponding vertex pair has different types, the original drawing is not realizable. Otherwise, the drawing is realizable, or can be corrected without changing a vertex type. Therefore, if position errors of junctions are permissible, the drawing is determined to be realizable.

Note that the correction is not unique. Figure 6.13, for example, becomes correct if any junction of the right side is moved. Instead of moving only one junction, we can apply the least-squares method to modify the drawing so that the sum of squares of position changes may be minimized. Another possibility is to move the least reliable junctions. In any case, we can determine the realizability of a position-constrained line by applying a predetermined criterion.

7 Stereo Vision

If the same object is seen from two different positions, its three-dimensional position can be measured. This technique is called 'stereo vision' or 'binocular vision'. It is the most important way in which humans capture range information. In computer vision, stereo vision is also important because it works in a variety of conditions. For example it has been used for obtaining terrain shapes from aerial photographs, where active ranging methods (see Sect. 2.5) cannot be applied.

Stereo vision has another advantage: it does not need any special equipment. This is one of the reasons why the study of stereo vision commenced earlier than that of other ranging methods. There have been two basically different approaches: (1) to understand the human binocular system, and (2) to find practical ways for range data acquisition. In the first approach attempts are made to obtain a computational model of the human binocular system, with the consequent requirement of a great deal of computation. On the other hand, the second approach is to develop stereo vision systems for use in specific applications. These practical methods for specific domains often lack general applicability.

Since stereo vision usually requires much computation, it has not been used in practice. Recently, however, it has again attracted considerable attention because the computation problem is expected to be solved by employing special purpose processors, and interaction between the two approaches described above is assisting the development of more powerful stereo models.

The main problem in stereo vision is to find corresponding points in left and right images. Once correspondences are determined, the three-dimensional positions of those points are easily computed from the pairs of points in both images. This geometrical calculation is described in the next section, and the subsequent sections are all devoted to the correspondence problem.

7.1 Stereo Image Geometry

Monocular image geometry as described in Sect. 2.1 is easily extended to stereo vision. Let us assume that two cameras with the same focal length f are placed so that the distance between the centers of their lenses O_1 and O_2 is d, as shown in Fig. 7.1, and the angle between the two optic axes is 2θ. Coordinate systems X_1–Y_1–Z_1 and X_2–Y_2–Z_2 are defined for these cameras respectively as shown in the figure (note that the Y_1 and Y_2 axes are perpendicular to the plane of the figure). Let us define a coordinate system X–Y–Z so that the Z axis bisects the angle between the Z_1 axis and Z_2 axis as shown in the figure.

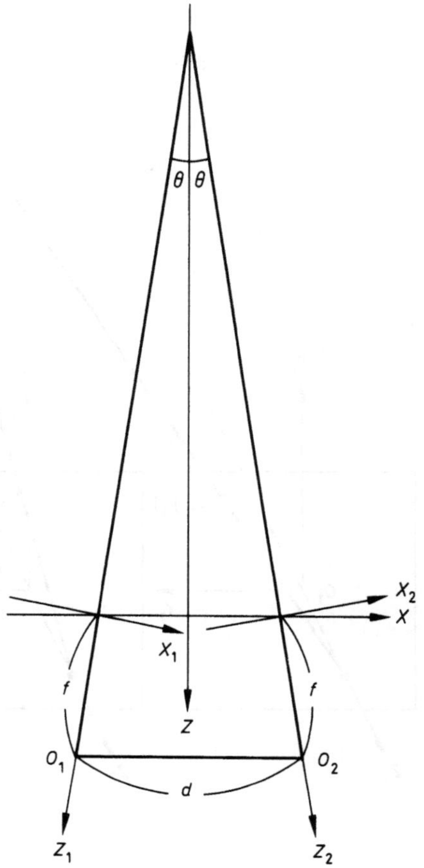

Fig. 7.1. Geometry of stereo vision

The relations between these coordinate systems are given as follows:

$$\begin{pmatrix} X_1 \\ Y_1 \\ Z_1 \end{pmatrix} = \begin{pmatrix} \cos\theta & 0 & \sin\theta \\ 0 & 1 & 0 \\ -\sin\theta & 0 & \cos\theta \end{pmatrix} \begin{pmatrix} X + d/2 - f\sin\theta \\ Y \\ Z \end{pmatrix} \tag{7.1}$$

$$\begin{pmatrix} X_2 \\ Y_2 \\ Z_2 \end{pmatrix} = \begin{pmatrix} \cos\theta & 0 & -\sin\theta \\ 0 & 1 & 0 \\ \sin\theta & 0 & \cos\theta \end{pmatrix} \begin{pmatrix} X - d/2 + f\sin\theta \\ Y \\ Z \end{pmatrix} \tag{7.2}$$

Suppose that a point P at (X, Y, Z) is observed by two cameras at (x_1, y_1) and at (x_2, y_2) on the image planes, respectively. Their relationship is given as follows:

$$\left.\begin{array}{l} x_i = fX_i/(f - Z_i) \\ y_i = fY_i/(f - Z_i) \end{array}\right\} \quad \text{for} \quad i = 1, 2 \tag{7.3}$$

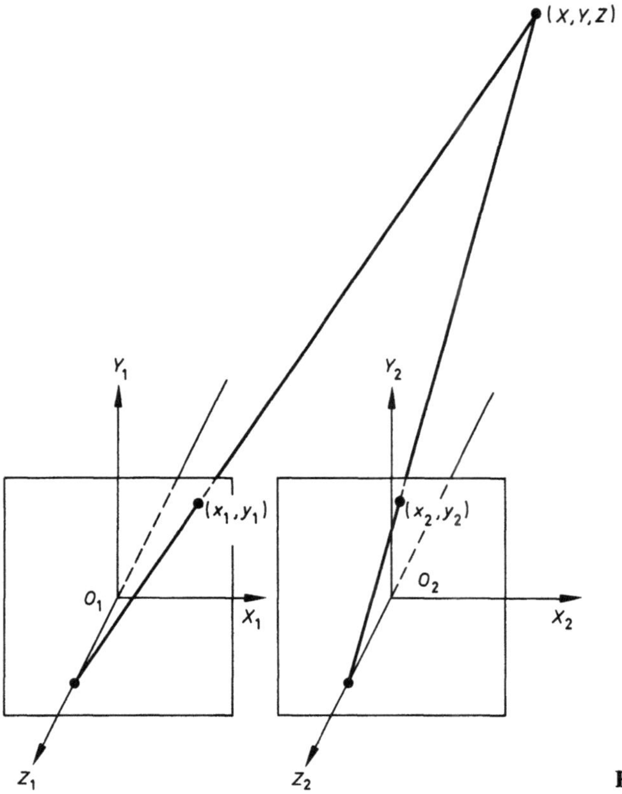

Fig. 7.2. Stereo imaging system

If two corresponding points at (x_1, y_1) and at (x_2, y_2) are obtained in the two image planes respectively (as shown in Fig. 7.2), the three-dimensional position (X, Y, Z) of the point is derived from Eqs. (7.1), (7.2), and (7.3). Note that there are 10 equations and 9 variables. This reflects a constraint on the relation between two points in the image planes. A point at (x_1, y_1) corresponds to a line of sight that passes through O_1 and (x_1, y_1). The line of sight is observed on the other image plane as a line which is called an 'epipolar line'. If θ is 0, for example, the epipolar line is a horizontal line at the same height as the point at (x_1, y_1). If θ is positive, the epipolar line is tilted in the upper right direction.

The analytical solution of the previous equations is rather complicated. Let us assume, for simplicity, that $\theta = 0$ (note, in this case, $Z_1 = Z_2 = Z$). Then the depth $(f - Z)$ is given as:

$$f - Z = fd/(x_1 - x_2) \tag{7.4}$$

Once Z is determined, X and Y are easily obtained by Eq. (7.3). Since f and d in Eq. (7.4) are fixed, the depth is inversely proportional to $(x_1 - x_2)$, the difference of the x coordinates of the two image planes. This difference is called disparity.

7.2 Area-Based Stereo

Area-based stereo techniques find corresponding points on the basis of the similarity of the corresponding areas in left and right images. The process consists of extracting feature points in one image (usually the left image), and finding their corresponding points in the other image.

7.2.1 Feature Point Extraction

It is usually not good practice to try to find corresponding points for all pixels. For example, a point in a uniform region in one image may correspond to many points in the corresponding region in the other image. Feature points are selected so that unambiguous matches might be obtained.

Feature points are extracted on the basis of the gray level variation in their neighboring regions. A point is regarded as a feature point if the gray level changes considerably in the neighboring region. When two cameras are placed in a

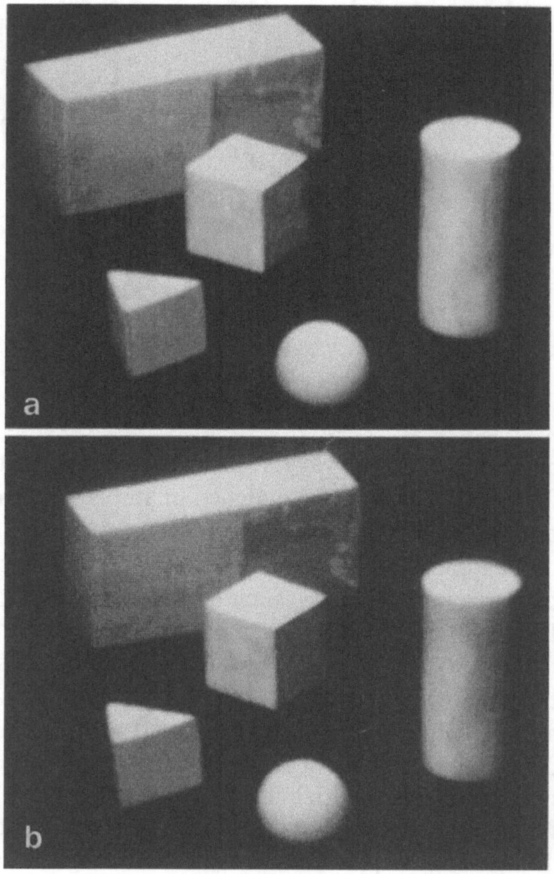

Fig. 7.3a, b. Example of stereo pair of images: (**a**) left image; (**b**) right image

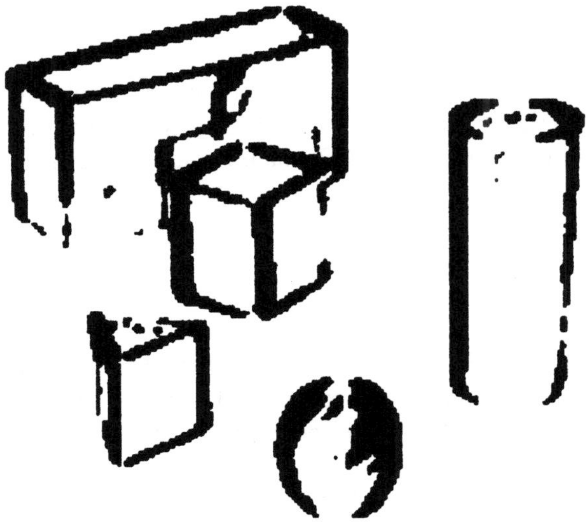

Fig. 7.4. Feature points extracted by applying the horizontal gradient operator to Fig. 7.3(a)

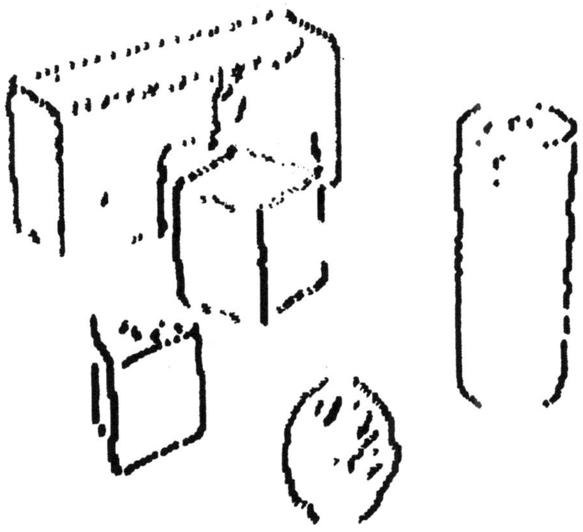

Fig. 7.5. Local maxima of the gradients shown in Fig. 7.4

horizontal line, the gray level must change horizontally. Points on a horizontal edge, for example, cannot be matched unambiguously if the gray level does not change horizontally in their neighbors.

A typical way to find feature points is to apply operators that are sensitive to horizontal variance, such as the horizontal gradient operator G_x defined by Eq. (3.13) or (3.15). Feature points can be obtained by thresholding the absolute values of G_x for all pixels, or for every $m \times m$ pixels (m is approximately the same as the window size for the G_x operator). Figure 7.4 shows feature points obtained by applying the G_x defined by Eq. (3.15) to the left image shown in Fig. 7.3. We can decrease the number of feature points by extracting only those points that are local maxima of their horizontal neighbors. Figure 7.5 shows local maxima obtained from Fig. 7.4. Note that this procedure is equivalent to applying the horizontal one-dimensional Laplacian and then extracting the zero-crossings.

7.2.2 Similarity Measures

Given a feature point in one (left) image, the corresponding point is sought on the basis of the similarity of the neighboring regions. The neighboring region is called a 'window'. When the correspondence of two points is examined, the windows are usually set so that each point is in the center of its window.

Many similarity functions have been proposed for specific applications. The most popular is the correlation of light intensity between the left and right windows. Let us assume that both windows are rectangular and that they consist of $m \times n$ pixels. Let $I_L(i,j)$ and $I_R(i,j)$ denote the light intensity of the pixel at the ith column and jth row in the left and right image, respectively. The correlation, C, is defined as follows.

$$C = \frac{\sigma_{LR}^2}{(\sigma_L^2 \sigma_R^2)^{\frac{1}{2}}} \tag{7.5}$$

where σ_L^2 and σ_R^2 represent the variance of the light intensity in the left and right window, given as:

$$\sigma_k^2 = \sum_{j=1}^{n} \sum_{i=1}^{m} \{I_k(i,j) - \mu_k\}^2/(mn) \,, \qquad \text{for} \quad k = \text{L or R}$$

where μ_k is the mean of the light intensity in the respective window, and σ_{LR}^2 is the covariance of $I_L(i,j)$ and $I_R(i,j)$ given as:

$$\sigma_{LR}^2 = \sum_{j=1}^{n} \sum_{i=1}^{m} [\{I_L(i,j) - \mu_L\} \{I_R(i,j) - \mu_R\}]/(mn)$$

The simplest evaluation function may be just the sum of the light intensity difference given as follows:

$$D = \sum_{j=1}^{n} \sum_{i=1}^{m} \{I_L(i,j) - I_R(i,j)\}^2 \tag{7.6}$$

Note that the higher the similarity, the lower is the value of D.

While D is computed sequentially, the intermediate value of the right hand side in Eq. (7.6) increases monotonically. Making use of this fact, we can stop calculation in the middle when the intermediate value is large enough. This idea was first proposed for image registration (Barnea and Silverman, 1972), and the algorithm was called 'SSDA' (Sequential Similarity Detection Algorithm). SSDA can be applied to stereo vision in the following way.

Let the difference function for window pairs be defined by:

$$D_s = \sum_{j=1}^{n} \sum_{i=1}^{m} |I_L(i,j) - I_R(i,j)| \tag{7.7}$$

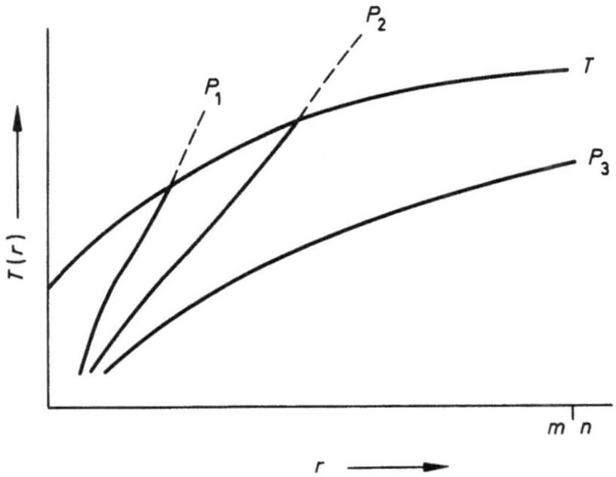

Fig. 7.6. SSDA with a monotonically increasing threshold

The idea is, instead of executing subtractions and additions nm times, to check, after r iterations, if D_s is large enough to be rejected as a corresponding point. Let the difference function after r iterations be denoted by $D_s(r)$. A constant threshold method rejects the window pair if $D_s(r)$ is greater than a threshold. The check is usually made at a constant interval, for example, every 10 iterations.

The threshold T can be a function of r, usually monotonically increasing with respect to r. An example of $T(r)$ is shown in Fig. 7.6. The rejection condition is similarly given as follows:

$$D_s(r) > T(r) \tag{7.8}$$

The rejection condition is satisfied earlier for rapidly increasing $D_s(r)$, while the decision is delayed for an ambiguous state.

Although SSDAs are efficient for registration of uniform images, they have some difficulties in stereo vision. One difficulty is that the values of difference function defined by Eq. (7.6) or (7.7) for corresponding window pairs usually becomes larger if contrasts of light intensities in their windows are high. One way to compensate for the effect of the contrast is to normalize light intensities with variances. An example of the difference function normalized with variances is given as:

$$D_v' = \sum_{j=1}^{n} \sum_{i=1}^{m} \{I_L(i,j) - I_R(i,j)\}^2 / (\sigma_L \sigma_R)$$

If we simply normalize with only one variance, another difference function is given as:

$$D_v = \sum_{j=1}^{n} \sum_{i=1}^{m} \{I_L(i,j) - I_R(i,j)\}^2 / \sigma_L^2 \tag{7.9}$$

Note that SSDAs cannot effectively be applied to the determination of similarities based on D_v', because the variance of both images must be computed.

The computation of D_v is much faster because the variance in the left window alone is enough for the determination of the corresponding point in the right image, while computation of D_v' requires the variance in the right window for every candidate position.

Another difficulty arises if the characteristics of the two cameras are different. Light intensities of a window pair for the same point may be different. One way to overcome this difficulty is to normalize with averages and variances as given in the following.

$$D_n = \sum_{j=1}^{n} \sum_{i=1}^{m} [\{I_L(i,j) - \mu_L\}/\sigma_L - \{I_R(i,j) - \mu_R\}/\sigma_R]^2 \tag{7.10}$$

SSDAs cannot effectively be used for the above criterion either. Note that D_n can be related to the correlation by the following simple transformation.

$$\begin{aligned} D_n = \sum_{j=1}^{n} \sum_{i=1}^{m} & [\{I_L(i,j) - \mu_L\}^2/\sigma_L^2 + \{I(i,j) - \mu_R\}^2/\sigma_R^2 \\ & -2\{I_L(i,j) - \mu_L\}\{I_R(i,j) - \mu_R\}/\sigma_L\sigma_R] \\ =\ & 2 - 2C \end{aligned} \tag{7.11}$$

Equation (7.11) means that minimizing D_n is equivalent to maximizing C.

In summary, correlation is generally a good similarity criterion: the difference defined by Eq. (7.9) is effective if the two cameras have similar characteristics; the difference defined by Eq. (7.7), which is most efficiently used by SSDAs, is applicable if images are uniform and taken by similar cameras.

7.2.3 Finding Correspondence

This subsection deals with the most difficult problem in stereo vision: how to find a corresponding point (in a right image) for a given feature point (in a left image). The corresponding point must be on the epipolar line if it exists. The fundamental strategy is to compute values of a similarity measure at all candidate points and to find the maximum. There are two problems: selection of the window size, and decision on the existence of corresponding points.

Generally, larger windows are suitable for obtaining global range information. For example, feature point L in a left image is to be matched to candidate points (on a horizontal line) as shown in Fig. 7.7. Suppose that correspondence is determined on the basis of the difference D_v defined by Eq. (7.9). Let $D_v(p)$ denote the value of D_v at p along the horizontal line. If the window size is small, the difference function $D_v(p)$ has a narrow-bottomed valley at the corresponding point p as shown in the upper graph in Fig. 7.7(c). An example is shown in Fig. 7.8. However, it is sensitive to noise, and the ratio of the value of $D_v(p)$ at p_0 to values at other distant points may not be large. Moreover, the difference function may have multiple valleys if local images around other points are similar to that at point p_0. Figure 7.9 shows an example of $D_v(p)$ with two valleys.

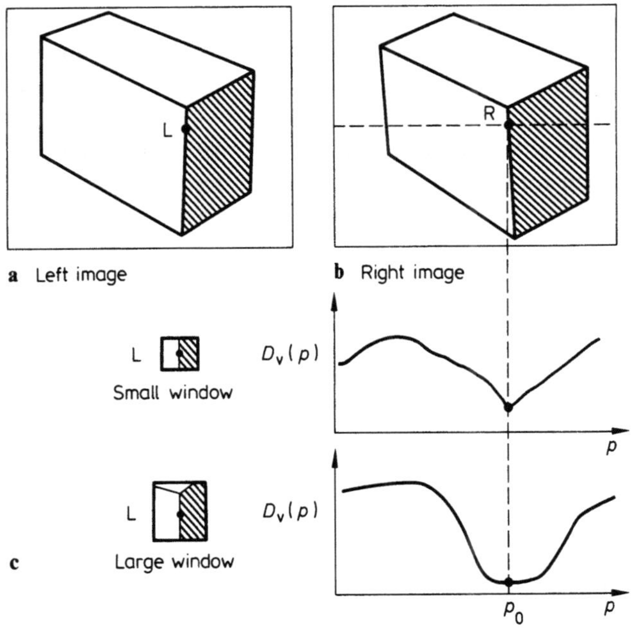

Fig. 7.7. Effect of window size

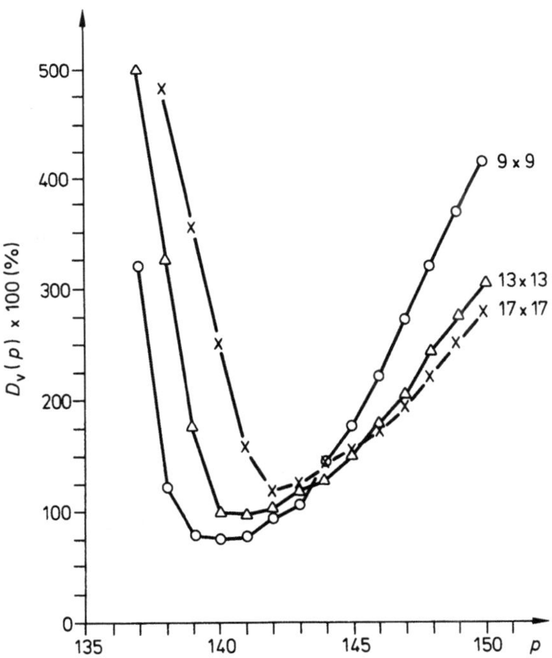

Fig. 7.8. Example of $D_v(p)$ computed with various window sizes

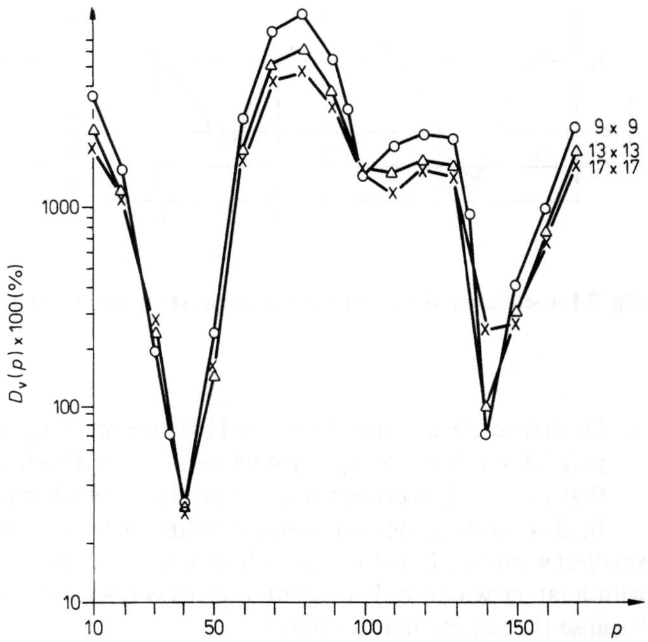

Fig. 7.9. Example of $D_v(p)$ with two valleys

On the other hand, with a larger window, $D_v(p)$ changes smoothly as shown in Figs. 7.7(c) and 7.8. Since it has a broad bottom around p_0, the corresponding point cannot be determined accurately. Another disadvantage is that more computation is required for obtaining $D_v(p)$ with a larger window. However, the difference function is less sensitive to noise, and the correspondence is more easily determined because it reflects the light intensity profile in a larger region (see Fig. 7.9).

Another problem is how to avoid a false match when the corresponding point does not exist. In Fig. 7.3, for example, three vertical edges of the prism are seen in the left image, but the leftmost edge is not seen in the right image. For any feature point on the leftmost edge, the corresponding point would not be found. Thus, the minimum of $D_v(p)$ does not always indicate the corresponding point. The value of the minimum and other valleys must be taken into consideration.

To solve these problems, the following method was proposed (Yasue and Shirai, 1973). Let the window be a square that consists of $n \times n$ pixels, and let n be odd so that a matching point may be in the center. The strategy is to try to find a corresponding point with the smallest window, and try again with a larger window if the result is ambiguous. Let the size of the smallest window and the largest one be n_0 and n_m respectively (in the example, $n_0 = 9$ and $n_m = 19$). The matching algorithm is as follows.

1. Let n be n_0.
2. Compute $D_v(p)$ for candidate points.
3. If $D_v(p)$ has only one valley such that $D_v(p) < d_1$, then p_0 is determined to be the corresponding point (see Fig. 7.10(a)).
4. If min $\{D_v(p)\} > d_2$ as shown in Fig. 7.10(c), there is no corresponding point.

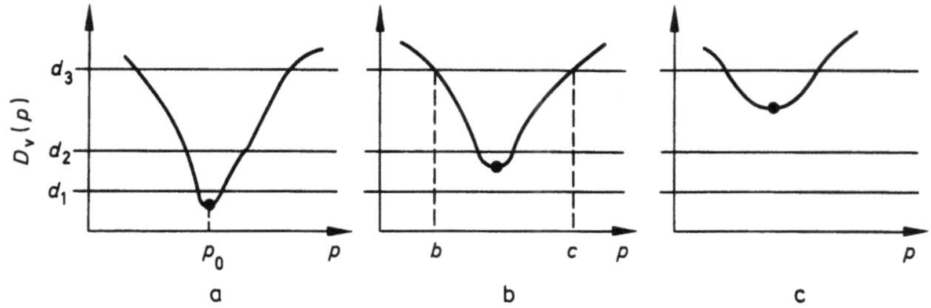

Fig. 7.10a–c. Search for corresponding point: (**a**) found; (**b**) retry; (**c**) not found

5. Otherwise, if n has already reached the maximum, n_m, there is no corresponding point. If n is less than n_m, then let $n \leftarrow n+2$, and limit the candidate points such that $D_v(p) < d_3$ (between b and c in Fig. 7.10(b)), and go to (2).

In this method, obvious corresponding pairs are obtained quickly with the smallest windows. It is also reliable because, in ambiguous cases, matching is retried with a larger window. The iteration process does not require much computation because the search area is limited.

Figure 7.11 shows the matched points in the right image obtained by applying the process to the feature points shown in Fig. 7.5. The three-dimensional positions of these feature points are computed by triangulation. Figure 7.12 shows the projection of these points onto a horizontal plane. The number of feature points in the left image is 996, and 136 points have no matching partners. Among matched pairs, 607 pairs are obtained with $n=9$, 226 pairs with $n=11$; 17, 4, 3, and 3 pairs with $n=13$, 15, 17, and 19, respectively.

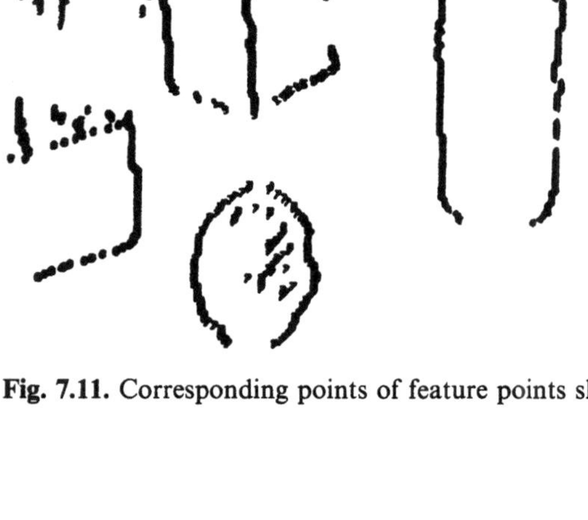

Fig. 7.11. Corresponding points of feature points shown in Fig. 7.5

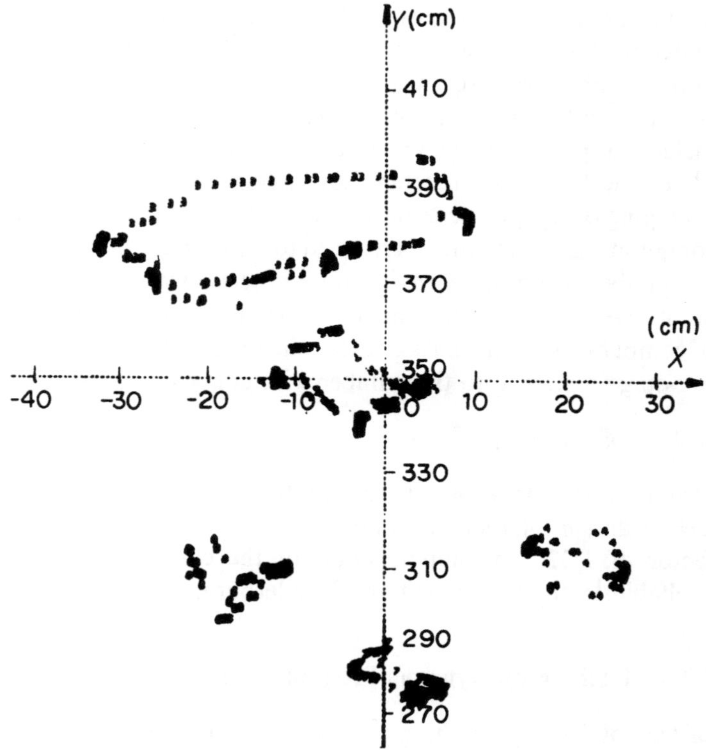

Fig. 7.12. Projection of three-dimensional points onto a horizontal plane

7.2.4 Multistage Matching

The computational cost of finding correspondence can be reduced by using a method of multistage matching. The strategy of multistage matching is to use low resolution images for coarse matching, and then to use higher resolution images for fine matching. Fine matching can be executed more quickly, because the search area is restricted by the result of the previous matching.

A typical method makes low resolution images by dividing images into small blocks of equal size, and averaging over each block. Matching pairs are obtained in a way similar to that described in the previous subsection. Suppose that a block consists of $m \times m$ pixels; then the number of feature points and the number of candidate points per feature point may be reduced to approximately $1/m^2$ and $1/m$, respectively.

Next, matching pairs are again obtained in higher resolution images. The feature extraction, during this stage, is applied only to those pixels whose corresponding pixels in the previous lower resolution image have matching partners. Suppose that each pixel in the previous image corresponds to $k \times k$ pixels in the current image. The search area is restricted to the interval whose center is determined by the disparity in the previous stage and whose length is k pixels. This process can be repeated until matching pairs are found in full-resolution images.

Let us compare the cost of the two-stage matching and that of conventional matching. Suppose that the size of images is $n \times n$ and, for simplicity, that a feature point is obtained everywhere. The conventional method must compute the similarity of two windows everywhere. Since the search area for each feature point includes approximately n pixels, the total number of computations of similarity is n^3. In the two-stage matching, averaging is necessary at first, but the cost of averaging is negligible compared with the rest of the computation. The number of computations of similarity is reduced to n^3/m^3 in the first stage. In the second stage, the number of computations is m ($m=k$ for the two-stage matching) for each feature point. Even if a matching pair is obtained for every feature point, the total number of computations is n^2m. As a result, the ratio of the number of computations with two-stage matching to the number with conventional matching is:

$$(n^3/m^3+n^2m)/n^3=1/m^3+m/n$$

Usually $n \gg m$ and $m^3 \gg 1$. Therefore, the ratio is much less than 1. For example, if $n=256$ and $m=4$, then the number of computations is reduced by approximately a factor of 1/32. The minimization of the computation cost has been studied probabilistically (Rosenfeld and Vanderburg, 1977).

7.2.5 Matching by Dynamic Programming

Instead of finding matching pairs independently in the images, a set of pixels on a horizontal scan line can be matched on the basis of one criterion to the corresponding set of pixels on the horizontal scan line in the other image.

The problem of obtaining a correspondence between two profiles can be formulated as a path-finding problem on a two-dimensional plane as shown in Fig. 7.13. The vertical axis shows the position on the left scan line and the horizontal one shows that on the right scan line. A point P at (i,j) on the path shows the

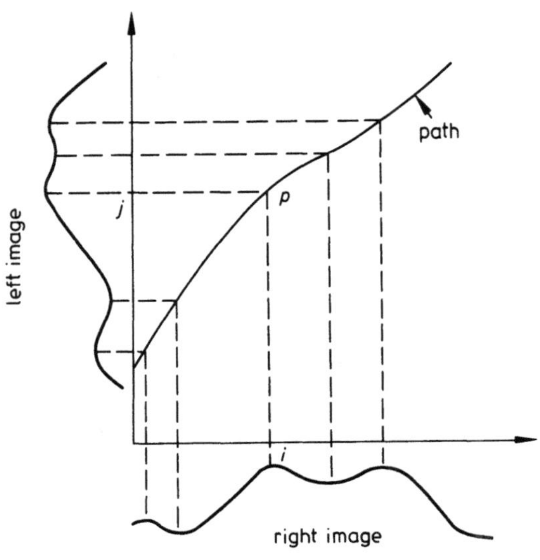

Fig. 7.13. Concept of DP matching

correspondence between the right image at i and the left image at j. The problem is to find the best path, i.e., the path with minimum cost. The cost corresponds to the integral of the difference described in Subsection 7.2.2 along the scan line. This sort of problem is efficiently solved using a dynamic programming (DP) technique, if the path is continuous. The method has been used for speech pattern matching, and called DP matching. If a surface in the scene is continuous and every part of the surface is observed in both images, then the path is continuous and monotonically increasing.

Let $D(i,j)$ denote the difference between the light intensity profile around i in the right image and that around j in the left. The cost of a path can be defined as the sum of the difference along it. Let $F(i,j)$ denote the minimum cost associated with the optimum path from the start to (i,j). The DP computation algorithm can be formulated as follows:

(1) $F(i,1) \leftarrow D(i,1)$

$F(1,j) \leftarrow D(j,1)$

(2) For $2 < i,j < n$

$$F(i,j) \leftarrow D(i,j) + \min\{D(i-1,j-1),\ F(i-2,j-1) + D(i-1,j),\ F(i-1,j-2) + D(i,j-1)\}$$

where n is the number of pixels included in the scan line. In step (2), computation proceeds from small i and j to larger ones. One proper way is to follow the sum $(i+j)$. In this matching algorithm, only three arcs are allowed in each step of the iteration as shown in Fig. 7.14. Of course, we may allow more arcs of various directions. In any case, by constraining the direction, the search area in each step of the DP is severely restricted. The restriction is due to the constraint of continuity. Stereo with DP matching is most suitable for obtaining continuous terrain shapes from aerial stereo images.

If a scene includes discontinuous surfaces, step (2) of the algorithm must be modified. If a part of a surface is observed in the left image and not observed in the right image, the arc corresponding to this part must be vertical. In the opposite case, it must be horizontal. Therefore, more paths must be considered in step (2). The difficult problem is the definition of the cost at discontinuous parts because the difference at these parts cannot be defined. Discontinuous parts should be detected by other suitable methods. The DP matching technique can be applied to a surface region only when the region is known to be continuous.

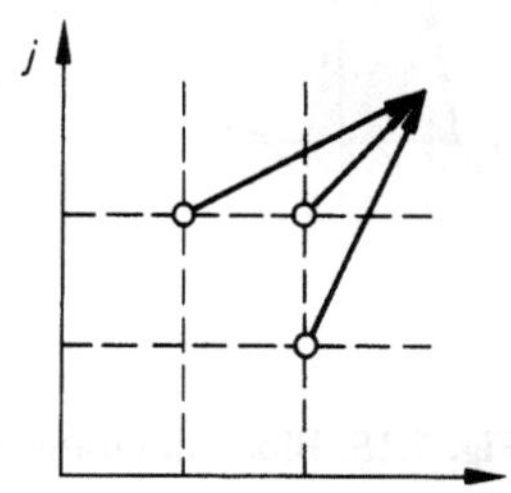

Fig. 7.14. Possible arcs

7.3 Feature-Based Stereo

Feature-based stereo techniques match features in the left image to those in the right image. Features are selected as the most prominent parts, such as edges, and they are detected in a way similar to that of area-based techniques. The characteristics of feature-based stereo are as follows.

1. Feature-based stereo is faster than area-based stereo, because candidates for corresponding points are much fewer.
2. Matching is less sensitive to photometric variations of imaging systems, since features represent properties of a scene.
3. Matching pairs are found only if both features are extracted in both images.

7.3.1 Feature-Based Stereo for Simple Scenes

One of the most simple features is the edge that represents light intensity change. A fast way to detect such edges is to differentiate the video signal and to threshold the result. One of the difficulties with the method is that it cannot detect edges which exhibit gradual intensity changes. However, if we have only to locate clear edges, the method is powerful. That is, image processing can be executed very quickly by a special hardware system, since the process is simple.

The idea was tested experimentally in relation to an obstacle detector for a car (Tsugawa et al., 1979). Figure 7.15 shows a block diagram of the arrangement. Two cameras are placed at vertically distant positions. Each camera is rotated 90° about the optical axis so that the scanning lines may be vertical. Edges are detected from the video signals and corresponding pulse trains are generated. One of the pulse trains is delayed for a certain time corresponding to a disparity of obstacles to be detected. The two pulse trains are checked to ascertain if any of their parts are similar. If any parts are matched, the distance of the corresponding surface in the scene is determined by the disparity (delay). The length of the surface is estimated on the basis of the distance and the length of the matched pulse train.

In order to detect obstacles in a certain range, the above process must be repeated with different delays. The image processing was executed online (at the

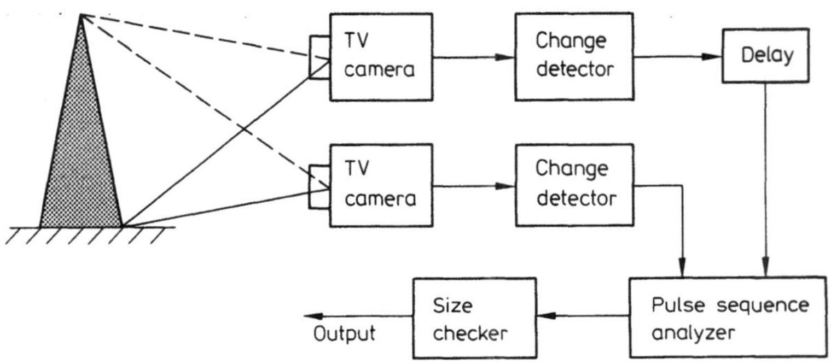

Fig. 7.15. Block diagram of edge-based stereo for obstacle detector

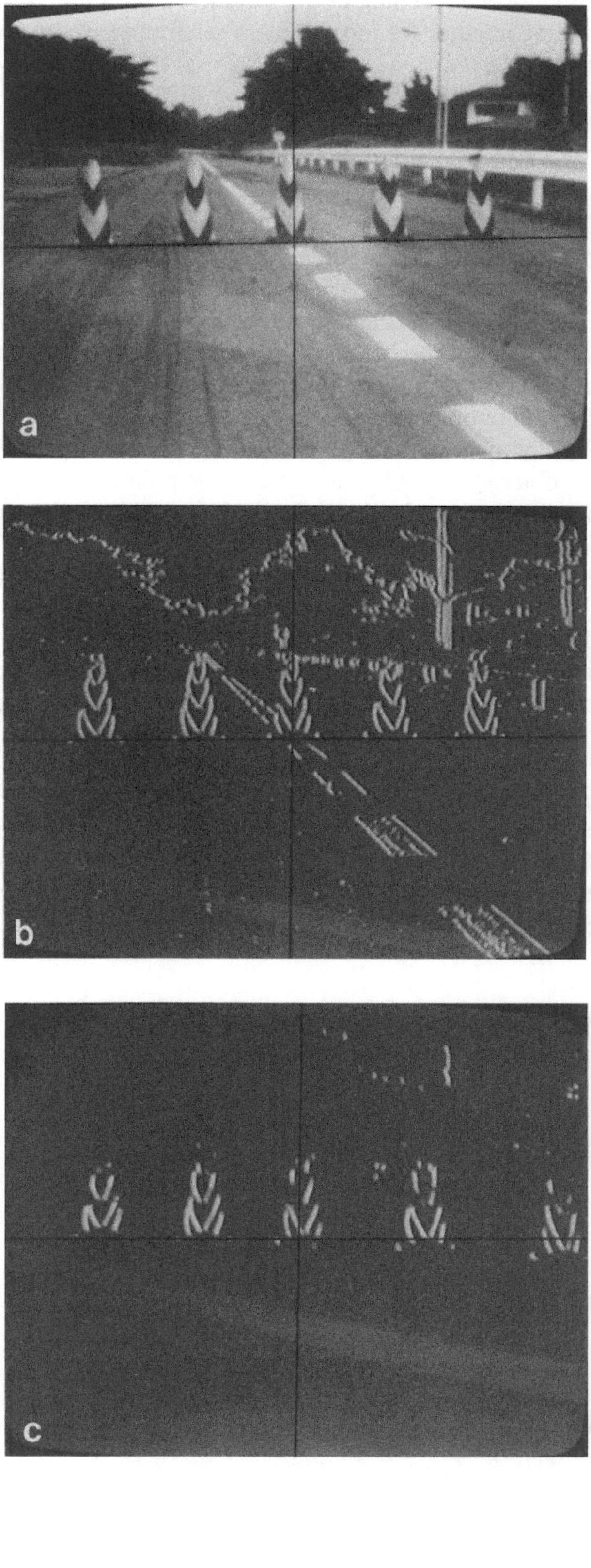

Fig. 7.16a–c. Result of obstacle detector experiment (Tsugawa et al., 1979): (**a**) one of the original images; (**b**) extracted edges; (**c**) detected obstacles

speed of the scanning of a TV camera), but pulse train check was processed by a microcomputer (at most 100 ms per frame). An experimental result is shown in Fig. 7.16.

7.3.2 Marr-Poggio-Grimson Algorithm

There have been many studies of the mechanism of human stereo vision. The central problem is the fusion mechanism: how regions in two images corresponding to a part of a scene are matched. One of the most famous theories is that of Marr and Poggio (Marr, 1982). They proposed a computational theory of depth perception and tested it experimentally by computer. In their theory, the matching conditions between two binary images were represented by the following three rules.

1. Compatibility: black dots can match only black dots.
2. Uniqueness: every point in the image can almost always (except for transparent objects) match no more than one point.
3. Continuity: the disparity of the matches varies smoothly almost everywhere over the image.

An algorithm of human stereo vision was proposed (Marr and Poggio, 1979) on the basis of the computational theory, and its computer implementation was developed (Grimson and Marr, 1979; Grimson, 1981). The strategy of matching is similar to that of the multistage matching described in Subsection 7.2.4, i.e., matching coarse features first, and then repeating the matching process at finer resolution.

Features are extracted from both images by the zero-crossing method described in Subsection 3.1.7. The parameter σ of the operator $\nabla^2 G$ is given a large value for coarse matching, and is given smaller values for finer matching. Figure 7.17 shows the zero-crossing operation with a larger σ value (see Fig. 3.12 for comparison). The zero-crossings are characterized by the sign of their intensity change and their rough orientation in the image. If the orientation of a zero-crossing is defined so that the

Fig. 7.17. Zero-crossing applied to Fig. 3.12(a) with $\sigma = 3$ pixels

intensity increases from left to right, the orientation is also signed. Two zero-crossings are matchable if their local orientations are within 30° of each other.

First, the coarse features are matched; this result is used as the starting point of the disparity for the matching of the finer features. At each stage, the eye positions are first fixed, and then matching of a certain region is performed. In the first stage, the offsets of the two eyes are arbitrarily set to zero, and features in the entire image are matched. In the succeeding stages, the offsets are determined by the disparity of the corresponding regions obtained in the previous stage.

The algorithm of matching in each stage is now formulated as follows:

1. Locate a zero-crossing in one image.
2. Find possible matching partners on the epipolar line in another image.
3. Obtain a matching pair.
4. Disambiguate any ambiguous matches.

These steps may be repeated several time to obtain enough matching pairs in the region.

In step (2), the search region is determined on the basis of the parameter w of the zero-crossing operator. According to statistical analysis, within the disparity range $-w/2 \leq d \leq w/2$ only one matching candidate is found with probability 95%. We may enlarge the range to $-w \leq d \leq w$ to get more matching pairs. In this case, it is known statistically that about half of the matching candidates are correct and unambiguous. The candidates are classified according to their disparity into three categories: nearly zero $(-1 \leq d \leq 1)$, convergent $(1 < d)$, and divergent $(d < -1)$.

In step (3), if a single candidate is found in only one of the three categories, the match is established. If multiple candidates are found, then no decision is made and the zero-crossing is marked as an ambiguous match.

Step (4) can be executed after the first iteration when the disparity of the neighborhood is determined. Here, for a zero-crossing with multiple matching candidates, a unique match is attempted by referring to the neighborhood. The disparity of the neighborhood is examined and the dominant category of the disparity is determined. If there is a single candidate in the same category as the dominant one, the match is established (this is called the 'pulling effect'). This is illustrated in Fig. 7.18, where arrows indicate the positions of zero-crossings in the left and right images. At first, matching is not established at a zero-crossing P in the left image because it has two matching candidates, R and S. When the matching is established between a zero-crossing Q and S, then a matching pair P and R is determined in the next iteration by the pulling effect.

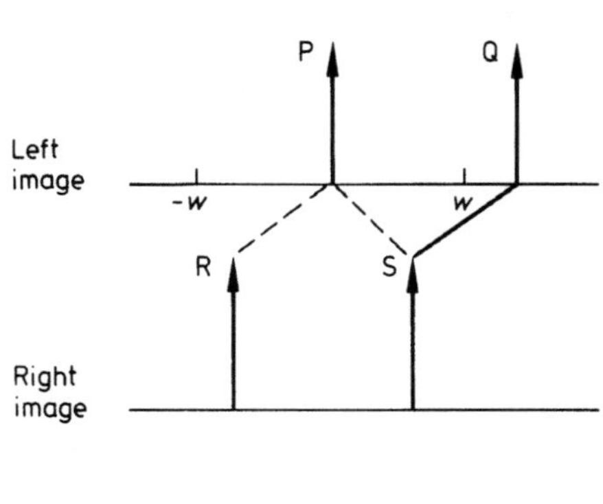

Fig. 7.18. Pulling effect

After the matching process is finished in the region under consideration, a check is made on whether the region lies within the assumed disparity range ($-w \leq d \leq w$). By a statistical analysis, the probability of a zero-crossing having at least one candidate match is roughly estimated to be 0.7. If the ratio of matched points to all the zero-crossings in the region is less than 0.7, then the region is determined to be out of range. The size of the region is proportional to the density of the zero-crossing, that is also proportional to w. Typically, the region is about 25 pixels on a side, for $w=9$ (Grimson, 1981).

This algorithm has some problems which must be solved for practical use. One of the most important problems is the scheme of multistage matching, which starts from global matching using zero-crossing extracted with a larger window. Suppose a surface has approximately uniform brightness with small scratches. Then zero-crossings extracted with a larger window are unreliable compared with those extracted with a smaller window. It seems, therefore, that the sequence of matching should not be fixed to proceed from rough to fine.

Another problem is how to deal with discontinuity of depth. If a zero-crossing corresponds to an obscuring edge, one side of the neighbor is discontinuous. Even if some zero-crossings are obtained, the depth of the neighbors cannot be interpolated from the known depth.

Another problem is how to execute the algorithm fast enough for practical applications. Although detection of zero-crossing can be performed quickly by special hardware, the matching algorithm is too complex for current hardware.

The computational model of feature-based stereo has not been studied for long. Since we have evidence of powerful stereo vision in humans, the problems of feature-based stereo are all very interesting research themes.

8 Shape from Monocular Images

It is in principle impossible to capture three-dimensional information from a monocular image. However, if something is known about the scene, a monocular image or multiple monocular images (viewed from the same position) may often provide information on three-dimensional surface orientations, though not complete range information. The shape of objects can be inferred from surface orientations. Methods of shape recovery depend on the constraints on the scene and the input information available. They are called, according to the constraints available, shape from shading, shape from shape, and shape from texture.

8.1 Shape from Shading

We can infer shape information from a monocular image if the illumination and the surface properties are known. If multiple images are available under different illumination conditions, surface orientations at any point in the image can be obtained. Such a process is called shape from shading. In this section, the relation between surface direction and the observed light intensity is first formulated, and then a few typical methods for obtaining shape from shading are introduced.

8.1.1 Reflectance Map

Let us consider a surface element S at (x, y, z) with surface normal $\boldsymbol{n}$ illuminated by a light source from direction $\boldsymbol{s}$ and observed by a camera from direction $\boldsymbol{v}$ as shown in Fig. 8.1. The central line of sight of the camera is the z axis as described in Sect. 2.1. Let $a(x, y, z)$ denote the incident light intensity at (x, y, z), and $\phi(\boldsymbol{n}, \boldsymbol{s}, \boldsymbol{v})$ denote the reflectance. Let $I(x', y')$ denote the light intensity of the image corresponding to the surface element. $I(x', y')$ can be represented by:

$$I(x', y') = ka(x, y, z)\phi(\boldsymbol{n}, \boldsymbol{s}, \boldsymbol{v}) \tag{8.1}$$

where k is a constant determined by the characteristic of the camera.

Generally, Eq. (8.1) is nonlinear and cannot be solved analytically. Now let us assume, for simplicity, that the light source is distant. Then $a(x, y, z)$ and $\boldsymbol{s}$ are constant at any position in the scene. Equation (8.1) is reduced to:

$$I(x, y) = ka\phi(\boldsymbol{n}, \boldsymbol{s}, \boldsymbol{v}) \tag{8.2}$$

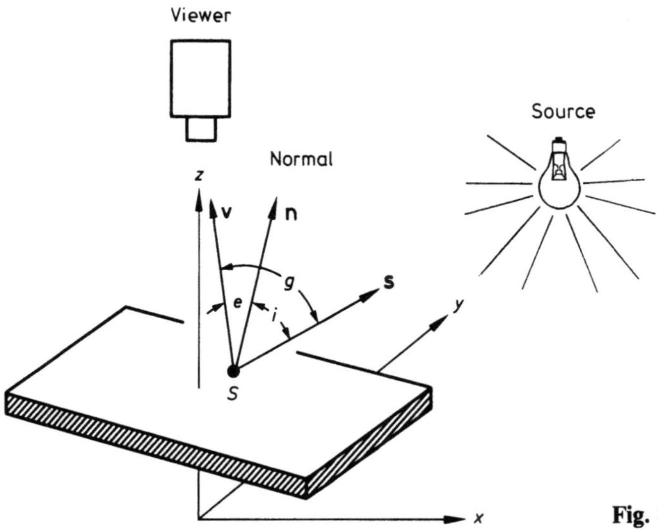

Fig. 8.1. Geometry of reflection

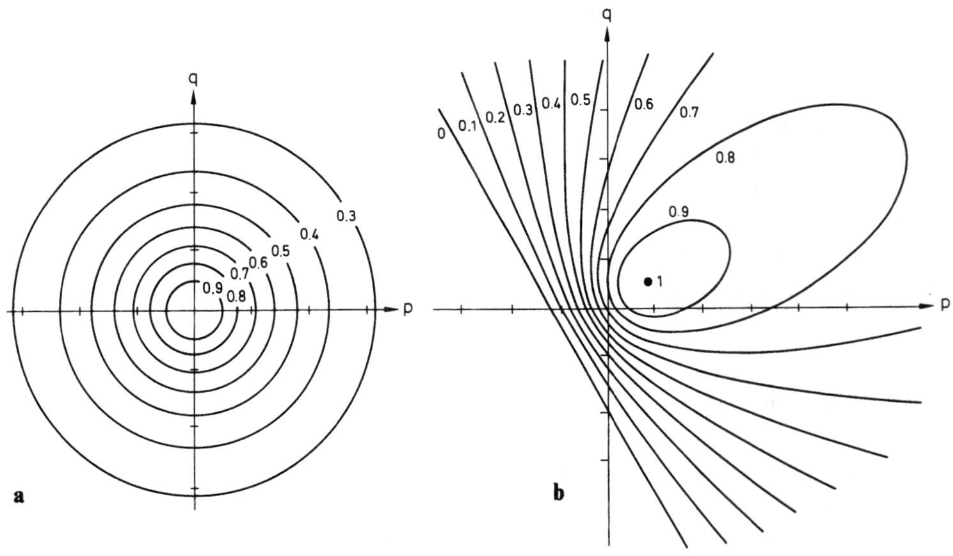

Fig. 8.2a, b. Reflectance map for a perfectly diffusing surface: (**a**) the light source direction is $(p_s, q_s)=(0, 0)$; (**b**) $(p_s, q_s)=(\sqrt{3}/2, 1/2)$

where a is the incident light intensity. It is convenient to express Eq. (8.2) as:

$$E(x, y)=\phi(\boldsymbol{n}, \boldsymbol{s}, \boldsymbol{v}) \tag{8.3}$$

where

$$E(x, y)=\frac{I(x, y)}{ka} \tag{8.4}$$

Now let us consider the reflectance function $\phi(\boldsymbol{n}, \boldsymbol{s}, \boldsymbol{v})$. One of the simplest reflectance models is a perfectly diffusing surface, in which the reflection is uniform for all viewer directions, and the reflectance is proportional to the cosine of the incident angle i:

$$\phi(\boldsymbol{n}, \boldsymbol{s}, \boldsymbol{v}) = \varrho \cos i \tag{8.5}$$

where ϱ is the reflectivity constant. Note that $\phi(\boldsymbol{n}, \boldsymbol{s}, \boldsymbol{v})$ is 0 for negative i (this case is excluded from the equation to avoid complexity).

Since $\boldsymbol{s}$ is fixed, i depends only on $\boldsymbol{n}$. In Sect. 6.2, we have seen that a plane is represented in gradient space as (p, q), and that the vector $(p, q, 1)$ is normal to the plane. The reflectance is, therefore, a function of p and q.

$$\phi(\boldsymbol{n}, \boldsymbol{s}, \boldsymbol{v}) = R(p, q) \tag{8.6}$$

Since $R(p, q)$ determines image intensity as a function of p and q, it is called a reflectance map.

Let vector $(p_s, q_s, 1)$ denote the direction of the light source; it can also be represented in gradient space as (p_s, q_s). The expression for $\cos i$ can be derived using a normalized inner product of two vectors $(p, q, 1)$ and $(p_s, q_s, 1)$.

$$\cos i = \frac{1 + pp_s + qq_s}{(1 + p^2 + q^2)^{\frac{1}{2}}(1 + p_s^2 + q_s^2)^{\frac{1}{2}}} \tag{8.7}$$

The reflectance map corresponding to $\phi(\boldsymbol{n}, \boldsymbol{s}, \boldsymbol{v})$ defined by Eq. (8.6) is given by:

$$R(p, q) = \frac{\varrho(1 + pp_s + qq_s)}{(1 + p^2 + q^2)^{\frac{1}{2}}(1 + p_s^2 + q_s^2)^{\frac{1}{2}}} \tag{8.8}$$

It is convenient to represent $R(p, q)$ as a series of contours of constant light intensity in gradient space. Figure 8.2 illustrates two reflectance maps for the case $(p_s, q_s) = (0, 0)$, i.e., $\boldsymbol{s} = \boldsymbol{v}$, and $(p_s, q_s) = (0.866, 0.5)$. Here, we assume that $\varrho = 1$ unless specified.

The characteristics of the reflectance map shown in Fig. 8.2(b) are analyzed as follows. A contour of intensity c is given by:

$$c = \frac{(1 + pp_s + qq_s)}{(1 + p^2 + q^2)^{\frac{1}{2}}(1 + p_s^2 + q_s^2)^{\frac{1}{2}}} \tag{8.9}$$

It is convenient to introduce a new coordinate systen p'–q' such that the p' axis may pass (p_s, q_s) as shown in Fig. 8.3. Then the relation between (p, q) and (p', q') is given by:

$$p = p' \cos\theta - q' \sin\theta \tag{8.10}$$

$$q = p' \sin\theta + q' \cos\theta \tag{8.11}$$

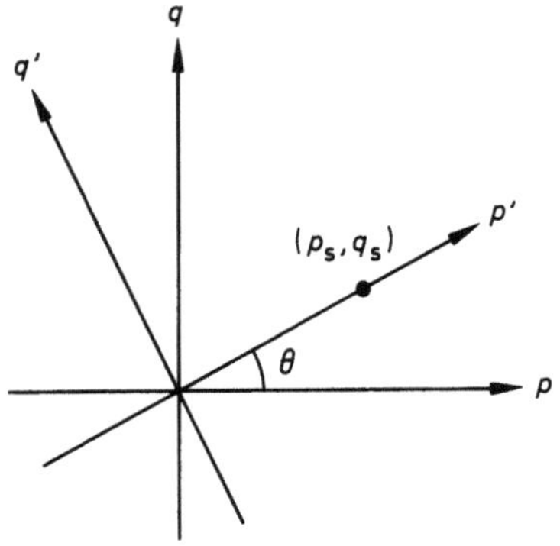

Fig. 8.3. Transformation of coordinate system

where $\theta = \arctan(p_s/q_s)$. In the new coordinate system, the direction of the light source (p'_s, q'_s) is given by $((p_s^2+q_s^2)^{\frac{1}{2}}, 0)$. Then, Eq. (8.9) is reduced to:

$$c = \frac{(1+p'p'_s)}{(1+p'^2)^{\frac{1}{2}}(1+p'^2_s+q'^2_s)^{\frac{1}{2}}} \tag{8.12}$$

or

$$\{c^2(1+p'^2_s)-p'^2_s\}p'^2-2p'_sp'+c^2(1+p'^2_s)q'^2+c^2(1+p'^2_s)-1=0 \tag{8.13}$$

The types of contour curve represented by Eq. (8.11) are as follows:

point	if	$c=1$
ellipse	if	$p'_s/(1+p'^2_s)^{\frac{1}{2}}<c<1$
parabola	if	$c=p'_s/(1+p'^2_s)^{\frac{1}{2}}$
hyperbola	if	$0<c<p'_s/(1+p'^2_s)^{\frac{1}{2}}$
line	if	$c=0$

Figure 8.4 illustrates a reflectance map with a p'–q' coordinate system for the case $(p'_s, q'_s)=(1,0)$.

Reflectance maps can be computed for other types of reflection, if images are formed by an orthogonal projection or a camera is distant compared with the size of objects. In this case, the reflectance depends only on $\boldsymbol{n}$, because both $\boldsymbol{s}$ and $\boldsymbol{v}$ are constant. Consider, for example, perfectly specular or mirror-like reflection. In specular reflection, the incident vector $\boldsymbol{s}$, the normal vector $\boldsymbol{n}$, and the emergent vector $\boldsymbol{e}$ lie in the same plane, and $\boldsymbol{s}$ and $\boldsymbol{e}$ are symmetrical with respect to $\boldsymbol{n}$. The reflectance function is expressed by:

$$\phi(\boldsymbol{n}, \boldsymbol{s}, \boldsymbol{v}) = \begin{cases} 1 & \text{if} \quad \boldsymbol{s}+\boldsymbol{v}=2\boldsymbol{n} \\ 0 & \text{otherwise.} \end{cases} \tag{8.14}$$

In gradient space, only a point at $(\alpha p_s, \alpha q_s)$ has intensity value 1, and the other part has value 0, where $\alpha = 1/(1+p_s^2+q_s^2)^{\frac{1}{2}}$.

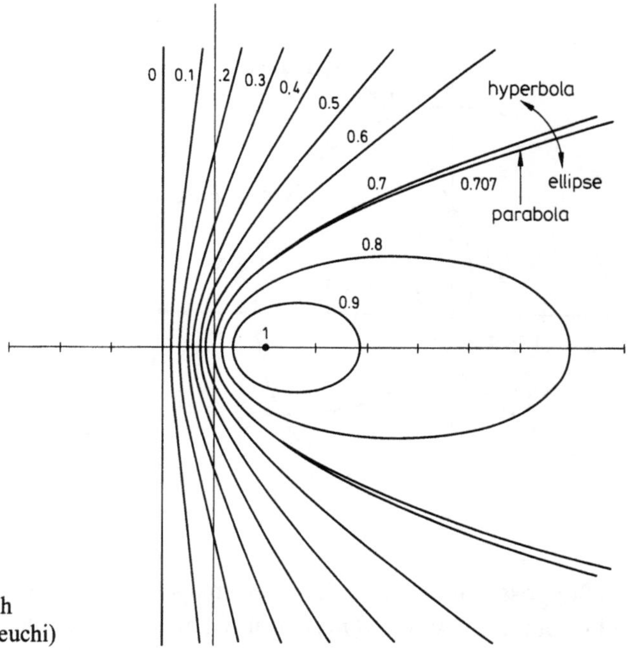

Fig. 8.4. Reflectance map with $(p_s', q_s') = (1, 0)$ (courtesy of Ikeuchi)

Reflection from glossy objects is not perfectly specular. The strongest reflection occurs toward $\boldsymbol{v}_0 = 2\boldsymbol{n} - \boldsymbol{s}$. The reflection decreases as the angle between $\boldsymbol{v}$ and $\boldsymbol{v}_0$ increases. The reflectance function of such imperfect specular surfaces can often be expressed as:

$$\phi(\boldsymbol{n}, \boldsymbol{s}, \boldsymbol{v}) = \cos^m d \tag{8.15}$$

where d is the angle between $\boldsymbol{v}$ and $\boldsymbol{v}_0$, and m is a constant $(m > 1)$. Note that if m is infinitely large, Eq. (8.15) is reduced to Eq. (8.14). Equation (8.15) also represents a reflectance map, since d is determined by $\boldsymbol{n}$.

Reflection from most surfaces is characterized by a mixture of specular and diffuse reflection. The reflectance function for such surfaces is expressed by:

$$\phi(\boldsymbol{n}, \boldsymbol{s}, \boldsymbol{v}) = \varrho_1 \cos i + \varrho_2 \cos^m d \tag{8.16}$$

In computer graphics, glossy surfaces are displayed with their light intensity computed by Eq. (8.16). Various kinds of material are depicted by changing parameters ϱ_1, ϱ_2, and m.

8.1.2 Photometric Stereo

The reflectance map defined by Eq. (8.6) constrains the possible surface orientation to a contour of intensity as shown in Fig. 8.2. If multiple images from different illumination conditions are available, the surface orientation is further constrained.

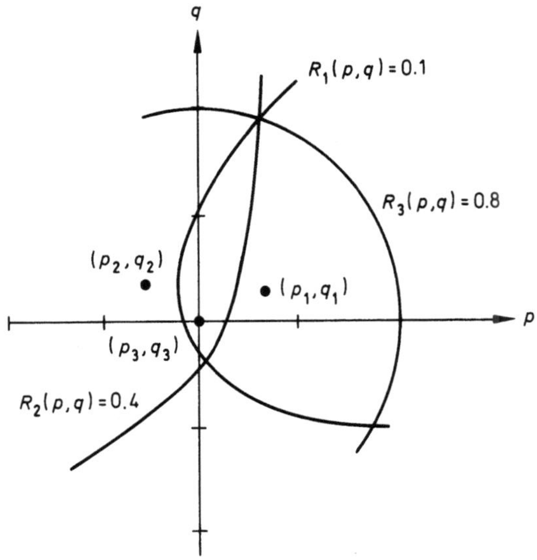

Fig. 8.5. Example of photometric stereo

Suppose, for example, that two images of diffusing surfaces are obtained with light source directions (p_1, q_1) and (p_2, q_2), and that $E_1(x,y)$ and $E_2(x,y)$ are obtained at (x,y) in the two images. Then two contours for $E_1(x,y)$ and $E_2(x,y)$ in the gradient space are determined as $R_1(p,q)$ and $R_2(p,q)$ as shown in Fig. 8.5. The surface orientation corresponds to the intersection of two curves. Since the two curves are generally conic sections, there are two intersections. That is, the surface orientation is constrained to two candidate directions. We can often select one of them by another constraint on the scene.

This method is called photometric stereo (Woodham, 1978), since three-dimensional information is computed from the light intensity of multiple images with different light source directions.

If three images are available, the surface orientation can be uniquely determined. In Fig. 8.5, for example, the surface orientation is determined as the intersection of the third contour $R_3(p,q)$ with the other two contours. Of course, the surface point must not be in shadow for any of the light sources. Since the surface direction has only two degrees of freedom (p and q), three contours provide extra constraints. Therefore, we can introduce one more unknown variable: ϱ. For each light source direction $\boldsymbol{s}_k$, the following equation holds at (x,y) in the image:

$$\begin{aligned} E(x,y) &= \varrho \cos i_k \\ &= \varrho(\boldsymbol{s}_k \cdot \boldsymbol{n}), \quad \text{for} \quad k=1,2,3 \end{aligned} \tag{8.17}$$

where the dot denotes the inner product of vectors. In matrix form

$$\boldsymbol{E} = \varrho S \boldsymbol{n} \tag{8.18}$$

where $\boldsymbol{E} = (E_1(x,y), E_2(x,y), E_3(x,y))^t$, and

$$S = \begin{pmatrix} s_{11} & s_{12} & s_{13} \\ s_{21} & s_{22} & s_{23} \\ s_{31} & s_{32} & s_{33} \end{pmatrix} \tag{8.19}$$

where s_{ij} denotes the jth component of $\boldsymbol{s}_i$. As long as the three vectors $\boldsymbol{s}_1$, $\boldsymbol{s}_2$, and $\boldsymbol{s}_3$ are not coplanar, the matrix S has an inverse S^{-1}. Then ϱ can be found from Eq. (8.18) as:

$$\varrho = |S^{-1}\boldsymbol{E}| \tag{8.20}$$

and then $\boldsymbol{n}$ can also be obtained as:

$$\boldsymbol{n} = (1/\varrho)S^{-1}\boldsymbol{E} \tag{8.21}$$

If four images are available, we can introduce another unknown variable. For example, we can detect regions in the image where the assumption of perfectly diffuse reflection is violated (Coleman and Jain, 1981).

8.1.3 Use of Surface Smoothness Constraint

We have seen that a reflectance map provides a constraint on the surface orientation. Another constraint is necessary for recovery of three-dimensional shape from a monocular image. Horn (1975) first formulated the photometric approach to recovery of the surface orientation from a monocular image in the form of a nonlinear first-order partial differential equation, assuming that the surface is smooth. If the boundary condition (a set of surface normals) is given, the equation may be solved numerically. A problem with the method is that it is sensitive to noise or measurement errors.

A more robust approach has been proposed (Ikeuchi and Horn, 1981) which assumes continuity and smoothness of the surface. Smoothness can be, in principle, defined as follows. Let $\boldsymbol{n}(x, y)$ denote the surface normal at (x, y) in an image, and $\bar{\boldsymbol{n}}(x, y)$ denote the average of the surface normals of the four-neighbors. The departure from smoothness at (x, y) may be defined by $|\boldsymbol{n}(x, y) - \bar{\boldsymbol{n}}(x, y)|$. A unit vector $\boldsymbol{n}$ can be represented by a point in a two-dimensional plane, such as (p, q) in the gradient space.

In the gradient space, however, $\boldsymbol{n}(x, y)$ cannot be approximated from the average of (p, q) of the four-neighbors. For large p or q, a small difference of the surface normal corresponds to a long distance in the gradient space (see Fig. 8.2). The ideal space is such that $|\boldsymbol{n} - \bar{\boldsymbol{n}}|$ is proportional to the distance between two points corresponding to $\boldsymbol{n}$ and $\bar{\boldsymbol{n}}$, respectively, in the space. Unfortunately, there is no such ideal space.

A better solution to this problem is the use of stereographic projection as shown in Fig. 8.6. A point on the Gaussian sphere (with unit radius) represents the surface normal of the same orientation. A point on the Gaussian sphere is projected onto a plane tangent at the north pole (N) from the south pole (S). The axes f and g are defined in the stereographic plane in the same way as p and q axes in the gradient space (parallel to x and y axes). The relation between (f, g) in the stereographic plane and (p, q) in the gradient space is given as follows:

$$\begin{aligned} f &= 2p\{(1+p^2+q^2)^{\frac{1}{2}} - 1\}/(p^2+q^2) \\ g &= 2q\{(1+p^2+q^2)^{\frac{1}{2}} - 1\}/(p^2+q^2) \end{aligned} \tag{8.22}$$

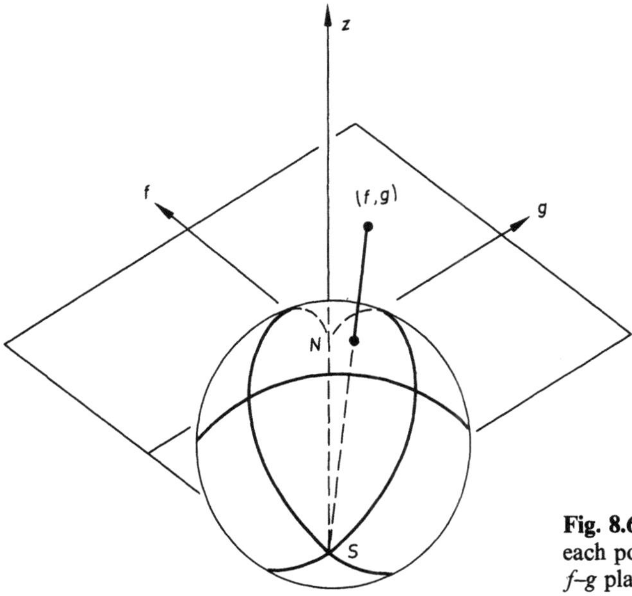

Fig. 8.6. Stereographic projection of each point on a unit surface to the f–g plane

The stereographic projection maps circles on the Gaussian sphere into circles on the plane. That is, this projection preserves shapes of small figures. Therefore, the distance between two points in the stereographic projection is a better approximation of the angle between their corresponding surface normals. The average surface normal can be better approximated by:

$$\begin{aligned}\bar{f}(x,y)&=\{f(x+1,y)+f(x,y+1)+f(x-1,y)+f(x,y-1)\}/4\\ \bar{g}(x,y)&=\{g(x+1,y)+g(x,y+1)+g(x-1,y)+g(x,y-1)\}/4\end{aligned} \tag{8.23}$$

The measure of smoothness is given by

$$e_1=\sum_x\sum_y [\{f(x,y)-\bar{f}(x,y)\}^2+\{g(x,y)-\bar{g}(x,y)\}^2] \tag{8.24}$$

where summation is computed over all the image except the periphery.

Another measure is defined as the error in the light intensity:

$$e_2=\sum_x\sum_y \{E(x,y)-R[f(x,y),g(x,y)]\}^2 \tag{8.25}$$

where $R(f,g)$ is the reflectance determined by f and g. Note that $R(f,g)$ can easily be computed from $R(p,q)$ or $\phi(\boldsymbol{n},\boldsymbol{s},\boldsymbol{v})$. For example, the reflectance of a perfectly diffusing surface is given by

$$R(f,g)=\frac{\{16(ff_s+gg_s)+(4-f^2-g^2)(4-f_s^2-g_s^2)\}}{(4+f^2+g^2)(4+f_s^2+g_s^2)} \tag{8.26}$$

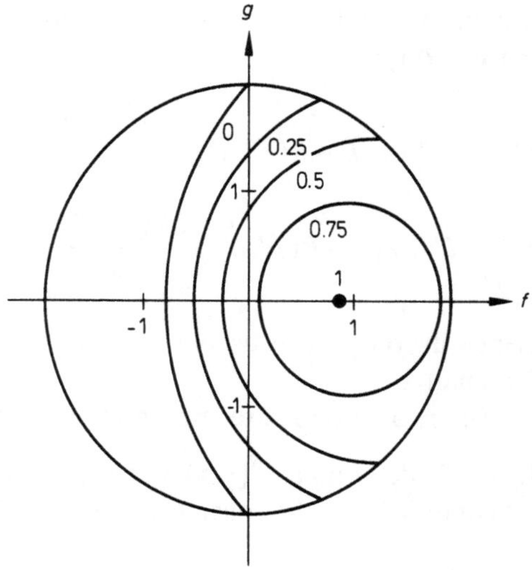

Fig. 8.7. Reflectance map in the f–g plane

where f_s and g_s denote the light source direction. Figure 8.7 shows the reflectance map for the light source direction 45°. The contours are all circular because circles on the Gaussian sphere are mapped into circles.

Now let us consider the error in the smoothness and that in the light intensity. The total error can be defined as:

$$e = e_1 + \lambda e_2 \tag{8.27}$$

where λ is a constant to adjust the two kinds of error to be in reasonable balance. Equation (8.27) is minimized by differentiating with respect to f and g (hereafter (x, y) is omitted in functions f, g, and E). Then the following equations are derived:

$$\begin{aligned} f &= \bar{f} + \lambda[E - R(f, g)] \frac{\partial R(f, g)}{\partial f} \\ g &= \bar{g} + \lambda[E - R(f, g)] \frac{\partial R(f, g)}{\partial g} \end{aligned} \tag{8.28}$$

These equations are solved by relaxation: iteratively computing the values of f and g on the $(n+1)$th iteration from the values of the nth iteration. The relaxation process might be formulated as:

$$\begin{aligned} f^{n+1} &= \bar{f}^n + \lambda[E - R(f^n, g^n)] \frac{\partial R(f^n, g^n)}{\partial f} \\ g^{n+1} &= \bar{g}^n + \lambda[E - R(f^n, g^n)] \frac{\partial R(f^n, g^n)}{\partial g} \end{aligned} \tag{8.29}$$

The relaxation process based on Eqs. (8.29) may not converge because of the observation error on E or instability of the numerical calculation. To avoid the instability, f and g in Eq. (8.29) are substituted by the average f and g (Ikeuchi and Horn, 1981):

$$f^{n+1}=\bar{f}^n+\lambda(E-R(\bar{f}^n,\bar{g}^n))\frac{\partial R(\bar{f}^n,\bar{g}^n)}{\partial f}$$
$$g^{n+1}=\bar{g}^n+\lambda(E-R(\bar{f}^n,\bar{g}^n))\frac{\partial R(\bar{f}^n,\bar{g}^n)}{\partial g} \quad (8.30)$$

Generally, the process becomes unstable for large values of λ, and converges slowly for small λ.

The relaxation is executed by the following procedure:

1. $n \leftarrow 0$; determine $f^0(x,y)$ and $g^0(x,y)$ if they are computed from a boundary condition; let the other $f^0(x,y)$ and $g^0(x,y)$ be 0.

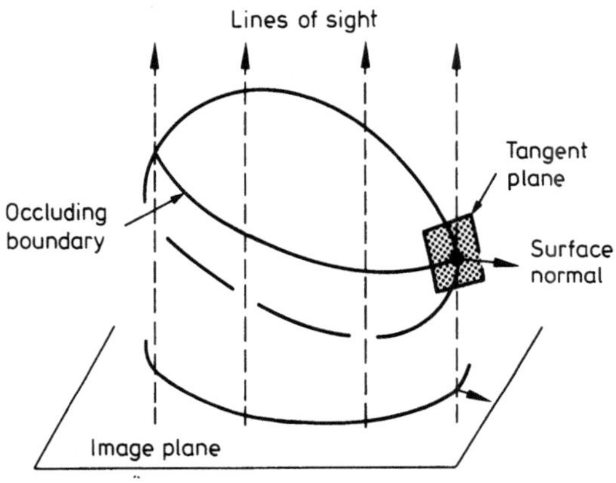

Fig. 8.8. Surface normal on the occluding boundary

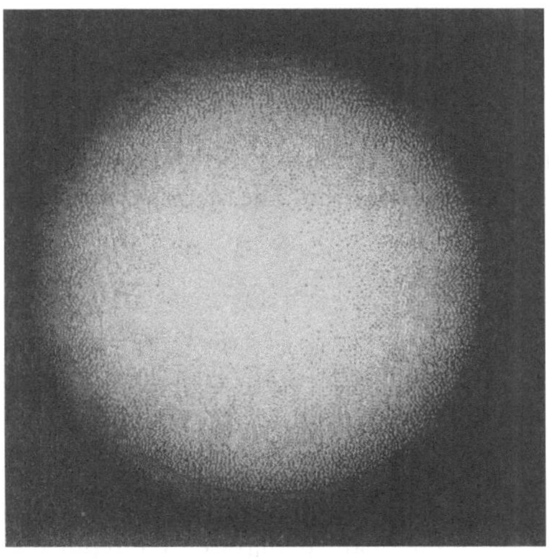

Fig. 8.9. Synthesized image of a sphere illuminated by a single distant light source (Ikeuchi and Horn, 1981)

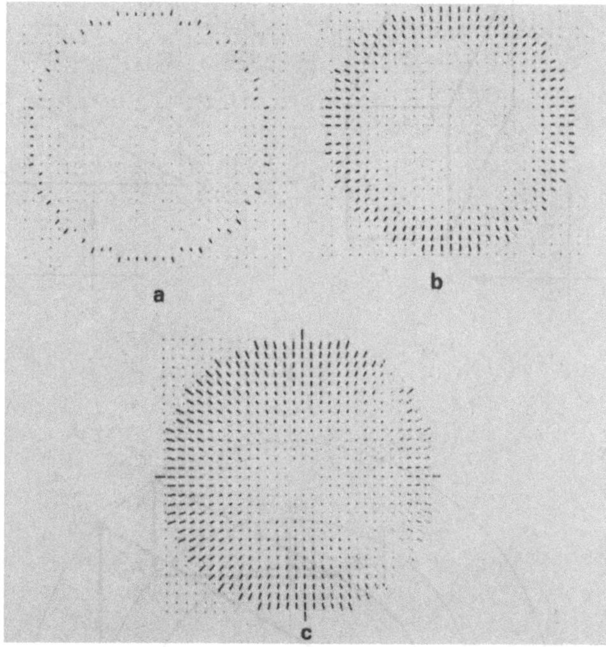

Fig. 8.10. Needle maps obtained at various stages of the relaxation process (Ikeuchi and Horn, 1981)

2. For nonboundary points, compute new values for f^{n+1} and g^{n+1} using Eq. (8.30); $n \leftarrow n+1$.
3. If the change of all f^n and g^n is small enough, stop; otherwise, go to (2).

The boundary condition is supplied by various constraints. If the surface is smooth, then the occluding boundary that is observed in the image determines the surface normal on the boundary. This is illustrated in Fig. 8.8. The surface normal at a point on the occluding boundary must be perpendicular to the line of sight through the point, and the projection of the surface normal onto the image plane must be perpendicular to the tangent of the boundary at the point.

An experiment carried out using a synthesized image of a sphere illuminated by a single distant light source is illustrated in Fig. 8.9. Figure 8.10 shows the needle maps (representing the surface normal at each point) obtained at various stages of the relaxation process.

8.1.4 Use of Shading and Line Drawing

The shape of a polyhedron can be recovered from the shading and the line drawing obtained from a monocular image. As described in Sect. 6.2, a line drawing provides a constraint on the gradient image. Now let us suppose that a line drawing is obtained as shown in Fig. 8.11(a). One of the gradient images can be constructed as shown in Fig. 8.11(b), where sides of the triangle are perpendicular to edges between corresponding planes in the line drawing. Note that the location and the size of the triangle are ambiguous.

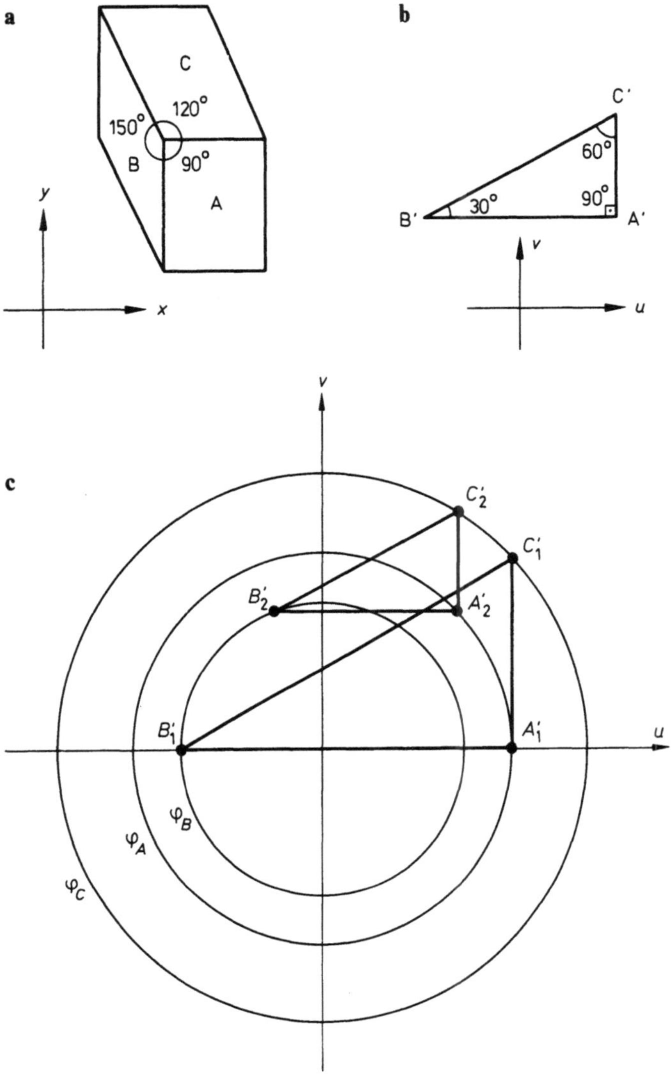

Fig. 8.11a–c. Use of gradient image and reflectance map (Horn, 1977): (**a**) line drawing; (**b**) gradient image; (**c**) contours corresponding to the reflectance of three planes and a triangle with shape similar to (**b**)

On the other hand, directions of the three planes are constrained by their shading to contours of constant reflectance on the reflectance map corresponding to the reflectances of the three planes. If we use the two types of constraints (the triangle and the contours), we may be able to recover the orientation of the planes. The principle is to put a triangle similar to Fig. 8.11(b) on the reflectance map so that each corner lies on the three contours as shown in Fig. 8.11(c).

In practice, the surface directions are obtained by solving simultaneous equations. Generally, two sets of solutions are derived, because the equations are quadratic. An example of the numerical solution is described in Horn (1977).

8.2 Use of Polarized Light

Photometric stereo may conveniently be used to obtain the normal of diffusing surfaces. Glossy surfaces, however, have little shading information, since they dominantly reflect specular rays. If glossy surfaces are completely smooth like a mirror, then the normals may be obtained by using known distributions of illumination sources (Ikeuchi, 1981a). Other glossy surfaces such as those of plastics are very difficult to deal with in a conventional way. A polarimetric approach was proposed for determining surface normals of such glossy surfaces (Koshikawa, 1979).

The observing system is depicted in Fig. 8.12. Objects are illuminated by many light sources of circular polarization, and observed by a TV camera through a retarder and an analyzer. Let us suppose that a surface with the normal vector $\boldsymbol{n}$ is illuminated by a light source from direction $\boldsymbol{s}$ and the light reflected at P is observed from direction $\boldsymbol{v}$ by a camera with coordinate system ξ–η–ζ as shown in Fig. 8.13. The direction of the surface normal $\boldsymbol{n}$ is determined by the incident angle ψ and the inclination angle φ in the figure.

The polarization state is represented by three parameters L, X, and O, which denote the difference between the horizontal and vertical components of polarized

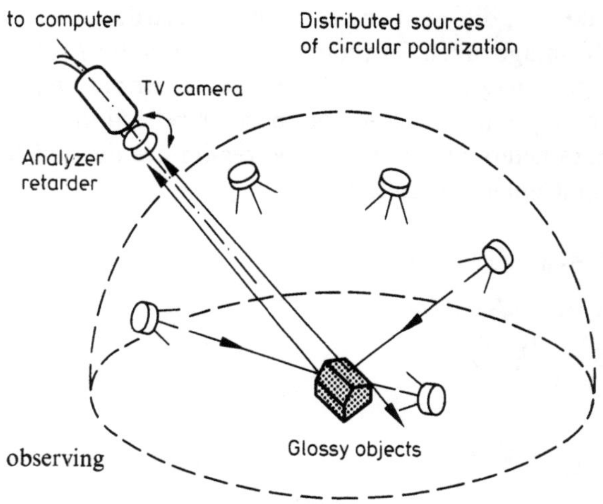

Fig. 8.12. Schematic diagram of an observing system

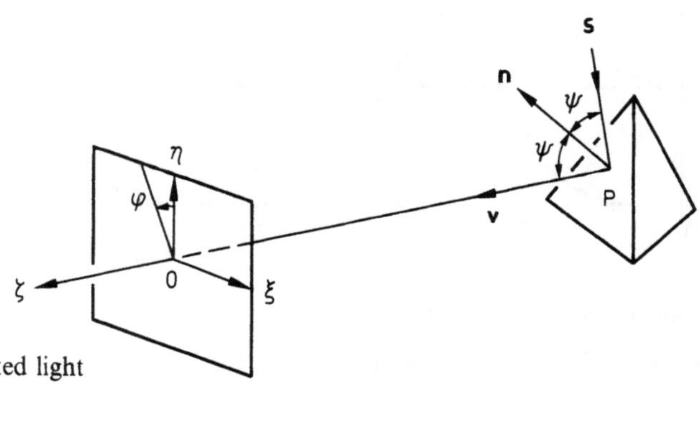

Fig. 8.13. Geometry of reflected light

light, that between +45° and −45° components, and that between clockwise and anticlockwise components, respectively. The intensity of the polarized component is given by:

$$I_p = L + X + O \tag{8.31}$$

The parameters for a right circular ray are derived theoretically from Clarke et al. (1971) as follows:

$$L/I_p = P\cos(2\varphi) - V\sin(2\varphi) \tag{8.32}$$

$$X/I_p = P\sin(2\varphi) + V\cos(2\varphi) \tag{8.33}$$

$$O/I_p = U \tag{8.34}$$

where P, U, and V are functions of ψ and the surface property of the reflecting point. Theoretical curves of P, U, and V are illustrated in Fig. 8.14. For a given surface material, parameter values of these curves may be obtained experimentally. The curves must in any case be obtained to be used for determining the direction of surfaces.

In order to compute precisely the polarization parameters, eight images are taken for different angles, θ, of the retarder. Let J_k denote the intensity of a pixel in the image taken for retarder angle $k\pi/4$, for $k = 0, 1, \ldots, 7$. An example of a set of eight images is shown in Fig. 8.15. Bright regions in any of the eight images correspond to regions of specular reflection from the surface. The polarization parameters at a point in the region are derived from the light intensities of the eight images as follows.

$$\begin{aligned} L &= J_0 - J_2 + J_4 - J_6 \\ X &= J_1 - J_3 + J_5 - J_7 \\ O &= -J_2 + J_6 \end{aligned} \tag{8.35}$$

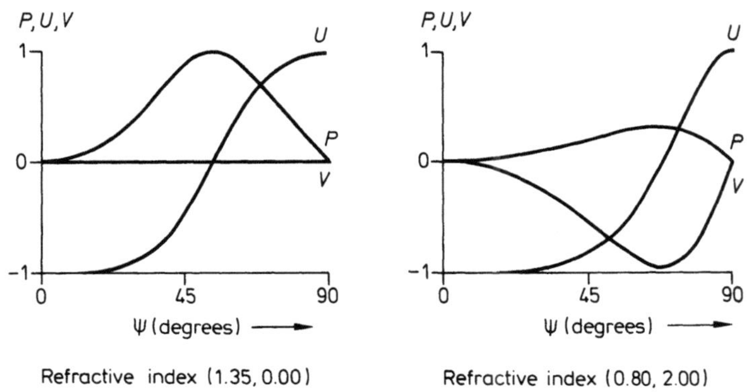

Fig. 8.14. Theoretical curves of P, U, and V

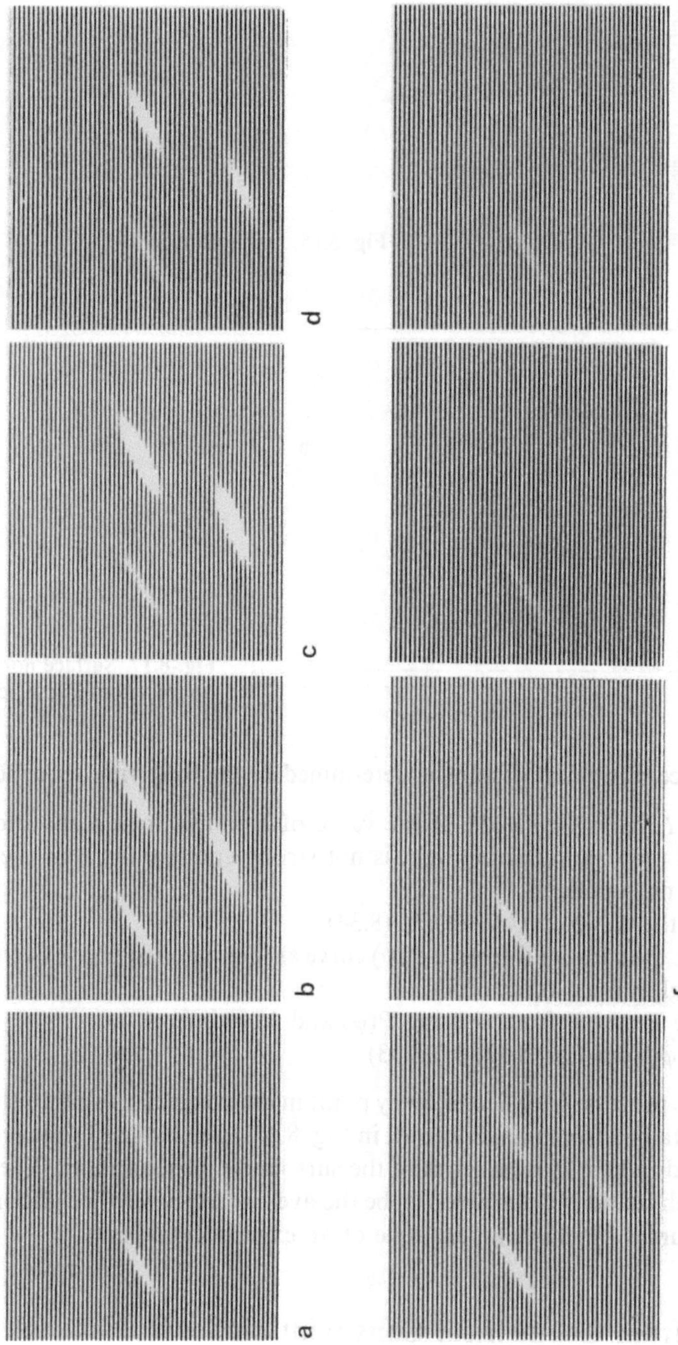

Fig. 8.15a–h. Eight images for different retarder angles:
(a) $\theta = 0$; **(b)** $\theta = \pi/4$; **(c)** $\theta = \pi/2$; **(d)** $\theta = 3\pi/4$;
(e) $\theta = \pi$; **(f)** $\theta = 5\pi/4$; **(g)** $\theta = 3\pi/2$; **(h)** $\theta = 7\pi/4$

Fig. 8.16. Image of I_p

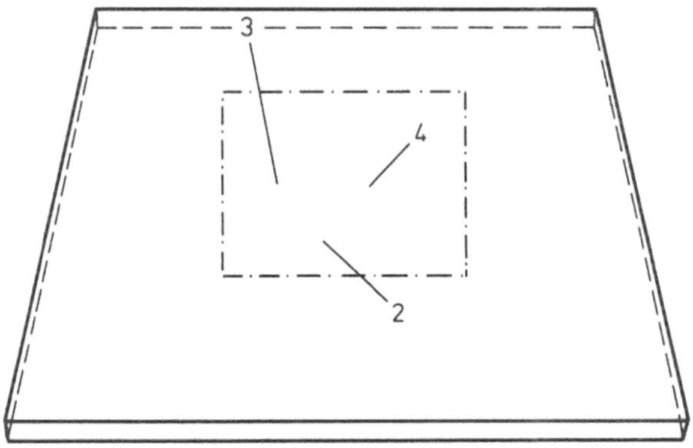

Fig. 8.17. Surface normals derived from Fig. 8.15

The surface normal at a point is determined in the following sequence.

1. Compute I_p from Eq. (8.31). If the value of I_p is less than a threshold, it is concluded that the reflecting light is not strong enough and that the surface normal is not obtained.
2. Compute the value of U from Eq. (8.34).
3. Determine the value of ψ from a $U(\psi)$ curve as illustrated in Fig. 8.14 (note that U is a single-valued function of ψ).
4. Determine P and V from ψ using $P(\psi)$ and $V(\psi)$ curves.
5. Compute φ from Eq. (8.32) or (8.33).

The above process is applied to every point in the image. Figure 8.16 shows the value of I_p obtained from images shown in Fig. 8.15. Usually, the I_p image consists of small islands where I_p is larger than the surrounding background. The surface normal of each island is determined to be the average of those of neighbors of the centroid. Figure 8.17 shows an example of an experimental result.

8.3 Shape from Geometrical Constraint on Scene

Humans use geometrical information about known objects to recover their shapes or orientations. For example, if we know that two lines in the image are parallel in the scene, we can constrain the orientation of the plane which includes the parallel lines.

The method of shape recovery from geometrical constraint can be formulated as follows. Let $\boldsymbol{X}$ denote a vector (x, y, z) that represents the position of a point in the scene and $\boldsymbol{x}$ denote a vector (x', y') that represents the corresponding point in the image. Usually $\boldsymbol{x}$ is a perspective projection of $\boldsymbol{X}$. This relation can generally be represented by:

$$\boldsymbol{x} = f(\boldsymbol{X}) \tag{8.36}$$

Let us suppose that geometrical constraints in the scene are represented by m equations with respect to n points in the scene:

$$\left.\begin{aligned} &h_1(\boldsymbol{X}_1, \boldsymbol{X}_2, \ldots, \boldsymbol{X}_n) = 0 \\ &h_2(\boldsymbol{X}_1, \boldsymbol{X}_2, \ldots, \boldsymbol{X}_n) = 0 \\ &\vdots \\ &h_m(\boldsymbol{X}_1, \boldsymbol{X}_2, \ldots, \boldsymbol{X}_n) = 0 \end{aligned}\right\} \tag{8.37}$$

$$\left.\begin{aligned} &\boldsymbol{x}_1 = f(\boldsymbol{X}_1) \\ &\boldsymbol{x}_2 = f(\boldsymbol{X}_2) \\ &\vdots \\ &\boldsymbol{x}_n = f(\boldsymbol{X}_n) \end{aligned}\right\} \tag{8.38}$$

We can get some information about three-dimensional geometry by solving the above simultaneous equations with respect to the $\boldsymbol{X}$ vectors.

Some representative constraints available for shape recovery are described below.

8.3.1 Surface Orientation from Parallel Lines

If we know that two lines on a plane are parallel in the scene, we can constrain the direction of the surface. This is best explained by using a vanishing point.

Suppose parallel lines on surface S are projected on the image by a perspective transformation. The lines (L_1 and L_2) in the image generally intersect at a point (P) as shown in Fig. 8.18. This intersection is called a vanishing point. Since the vanishing point corresponds, in the scene, to a point that is infinitely far away on surface S, the line of sight through the point is parallel to S. Let f denote the focal length of the camera model. The direction of the line of sight is represented by vector $(x', y', -f)$. The direction of the surface normal of S can be represented by vector $(p, q, 1)$, where (p, q) correspond to the gradient image of the surface. Since these two vectors are perpendicular,

$$x'p + y'q - f = 0 \tag{8.39}$$

This means that the surface normal is constrained on the line.

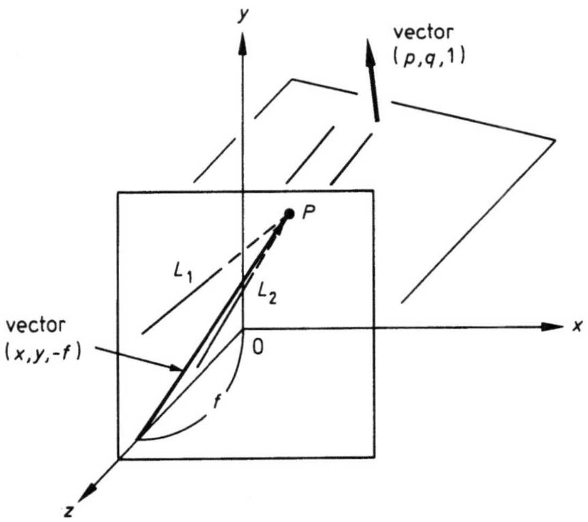

Fig. 8.18. Parallel lines intersect in the image at a vanishing point

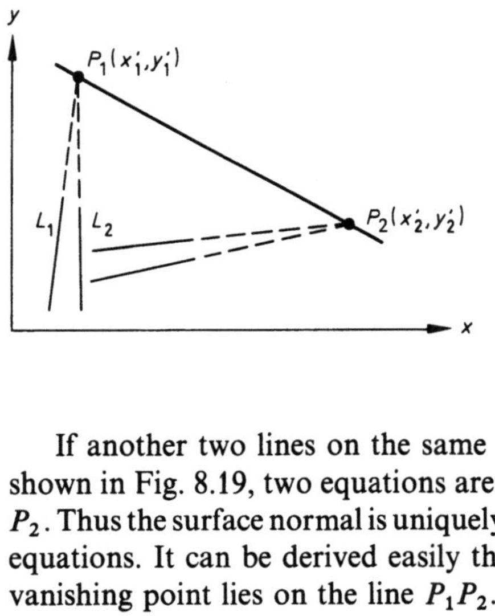

Fig. 8.19. Two sets of parallel lines projected on the image

If another two lines on the same surface S are also known to be parallel, as shown in Fig. 8.19, two equations are obtained from two vanishing points P_1 and P_2. Thus the surface normal is uniquely determined by solving the two simultaneous equations. It can be derived easily that for any parallel lines on the surface, the vanishing point lies on the line P_1P_2.

It is shown above that a surface normal can be obtained from the vanishing points of parallel lines. A surface normal can also be derived from Eqs. (8.37) and (8.38). Suppose that two sets of parallel lines are obtained in the image as shown in Fig. 8.20. Since Eq. (8.37) describes relations between points in the scene, we must select some points in the image to describe the parallelism. We need four points to describe the parallelism between two lines. A minimum number of points are selected as intersections of four lines as shown in Fig. 8.20.

The relations which establish that those points are on the intersections of two sets of parallel lines are formulated as:

$$\boldsymbol{X}_2 - \boldsymbol{X}_1 = \boldsymbol{X}_4 - \boldsymbol{X}_3 \qquad (8.40)$$

Equation (8.40) is equivalent to three equations with respect to the x, y, and z components of the 3D vectors. We have four more equations corresponding to

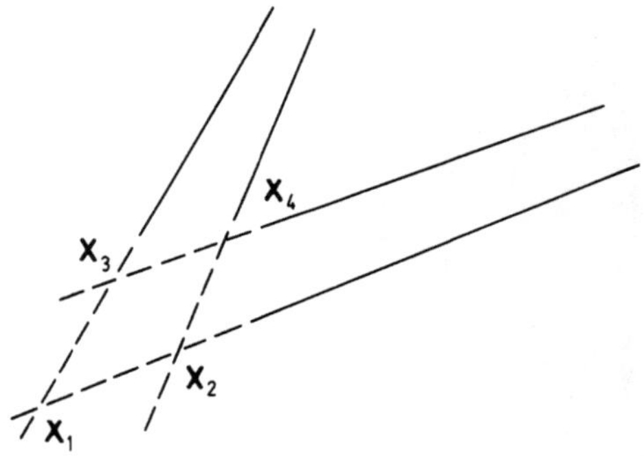

Fig. 8.20. Selected intersections of $\boldsymbol{X}$ vectors

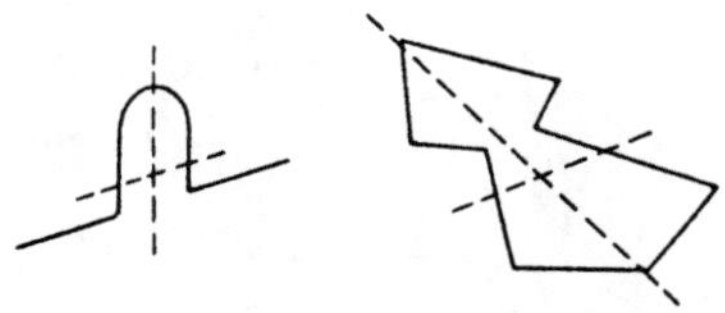

Fig. 8.21. Perpendicular symmetry axes

Eq. (8.38). Each equation is equivalent to two equations with respect to the x_i' and y_i' components of $\boldsymbol{x}_i$. The number of unknowns is 12, while the total number of equations is 11 ($=3+8$). The simultaneous equations are not solved completely. However, the relative values of the $\boldsymbol{X}$ vectors are obtained, i.e., the surface normal is obtained.

We have seen that the formulation with Eqs. (8.37) and (8.38) can be used in a straightforward manner, although the principle is better explained with vanishing points. We can use not only parallel relations but also perpendicular relations. Kanade (1980) used two perpendicular symmetry axes as shown in Fig. 8.21.

8.3.2 Shape from Texture

Texture was known to be a good clue for shape recovery. The orientation or distance of surfaces can be estimated from a so-called texture gradient: the change of density and size of texture elements. Although the possibility of shape recovery from texture has been pointed out by many researchers, there have been few works that actually demonstrate the usefulness of the texture.

The principle of the method of shape recovery from texture is similar to that described in the previous subsection: to make use of geometrical constraints in the scene.

8.3.2.1 Shape from Shape of Texture Elements

The simplest case is to use assumptions about the shape of texture elements. For example, if we know that a surface contains circular texture elements, the three-dimensional shape of the surface can be estimated from the observed shape of the elements. This was demonstrated by Ikeuchi (1984) with a painted golf ball as shown in Fig. 8.22. The direction of a plane that includes a circle can be computed from the shape observed in the image (generally elliptic) by the method described previously. First, for each texture pattern, the direction of the surface element is obtained. Then, assuming that the surface is smooth, the spherical surface is recovered by the relaxation method described in Subsection 3.2.2.

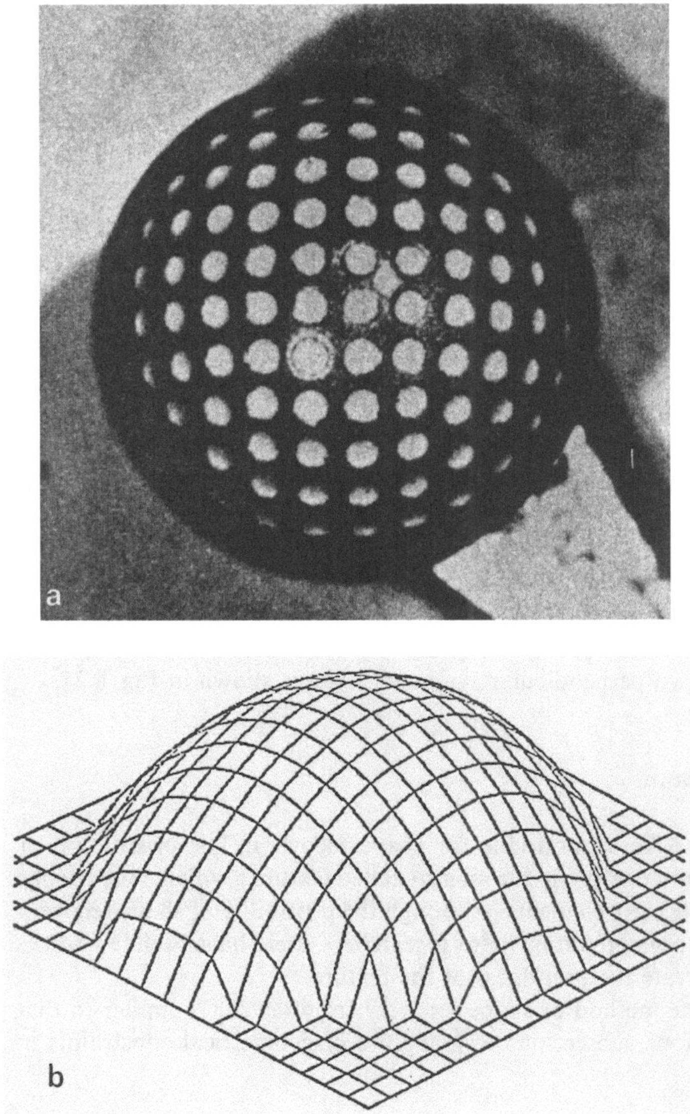

Fig. 8.22a, b. Shape estimation from known texture elements (Ikeuchi, 1984): (**a**) golf ball with circular texture elements; (**b**) estimated shape

8.3.2.2 Shape from Parallel Lines in Texture

A method of determining surface orientations from converging lines that are known to be parallel in the scene is described in Subsection 8.3.1. Parallel lines can also be found in regular texture patterns. Typical examples are lines formed by boards on a ceiling or windows on the wall of a building. Kender (1979) proposed a method of extracting converging lines in the image.

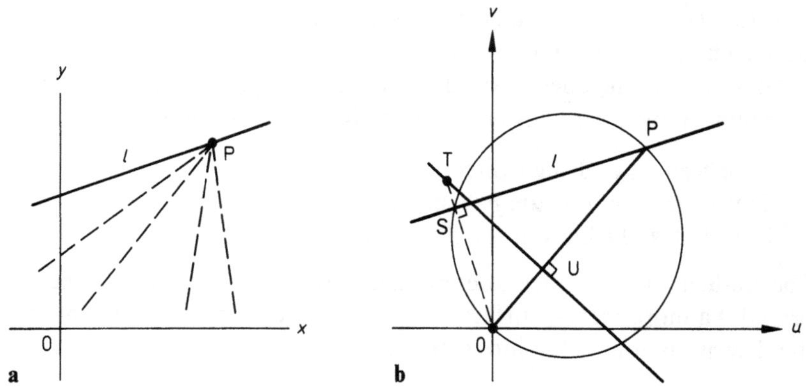

Fig. 8.23a, b. Extraction of converging lines: (**a**) converging lines in the image; (**b**) aggregation transform

Suppose that lines converge at P in the image as shown in Fig. 8.23(a). The equation of a line is represented by:

$$p = x\cos\theta + y\sin\theta \qquad (8.41)$$

Each line is transformed to a new parameter space. The line represented by Eq. (8.41) is transformed to a point T in u–v space where the coordinate (u, v) is defined by:

$$(u, v) = ((K/p)\cos\theta, (k/p)\sin\theta) \qquad (8.42)$$

This transformation is called 'aggregation transformation'.

By the aggregation transformation, a set of lines that converge to a point P in the image is mapped to the points lying in a single line in the u–v space. The reason for this is illustrated in Fig. 8.23(b), where the line l and the point P in the image are superposed. First, think of a perpendicular line from the origin O to the line l. The leg of the perpendicular line S is represented in the x–y coordinates as $(p\cos\theta, p\sin\theta)$. Note that T $(=(u, v))$ is on the line OS.

Next think of a perpendicular line from T to the line OP, and let U denote the leg as shown in Fig. 8.23(b). Since the triangle OUT and the triangle OSP are similar figures, the following relation holds for the length of the sides of the triangles:

$$\mathrm{OU}/\mathrm{OT} = \mathrm{OS}/\mathrm{OP} \qquad (8.43)$$

Substituting the relations $\mathrm{OS} = p$ and $\mathrm{OT} = K/p$ into Eq. (8.43), OU is given by:

$$\mathrm{OU} = K/\mathrm{OP} \qquad (8.44)$$

This means that the point U is fixed. It turns out that all lines that pass through a point P in the image are transformed in the u–v space to points on the line through U perpendicular to the line OP. If K is chosen to be equal to f, the focal length of the camera, the u–v plane coincides with the gradient space. That is, the line UT is equivalent to the one represented by Eq. (8.39).

If a surface includes more than two sets of parallel line segments as texture elements, converging lines are detected in the following steps.

1. Detect edges and their direction.
2. Transform them to the p–q space.
3. Detect straight lines in the p–q space.

The gradient of the surface is determined as the intersection of the lines. The method provides a more precise surface normal because many line segments contribute to the determination of the intersection.

8.3.2.3 Shape from Parallel Lines Extracted from Texture

Parallel lines can be obtained from a texture with some constraints even if no lines exist in the texture. Those constraints may be on the shape of the texture elements or on the distribution of the elements.

Figure 8.24 shows a simple example of a texture with circular elements of the same size. Since the image is formed by a perspective transformation, the shape of the texture elements is deformed. A vanishing point is obtained from a pair of elements. It is on the line passing through the mass centers of the elements. Let d_1 and d_2 denote the distance from a vanishing point P to the mass center of the smaller element O_1 and to that of the larger O_2, respectively, as shown in Fig. 8.25. Their ratio can be computed from the area of the two elements S_1 and S_2 (Ohta, Maenobu and Sakai, 1981) by the following equation:

$$d_1^3/d_2^3 = S_1/S_2 \tag{8.45}$$

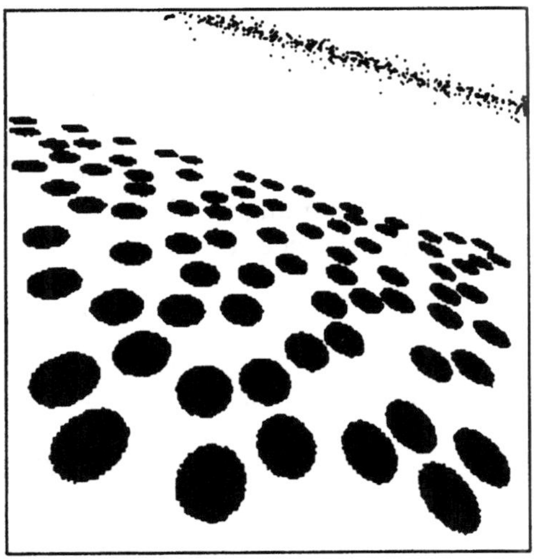

Fig. 8.24. Texture with circular patterns (Ohta, 1981)

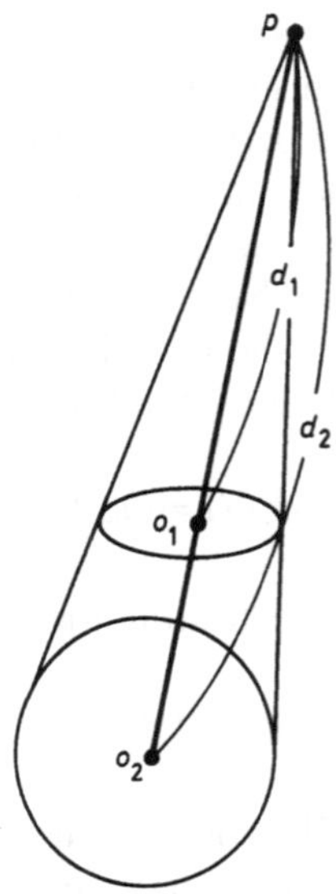

Fig. 8.25. Calculation of vanishing point

Fig. 8.26. Texture with many kinds of patterns (Ohta, 1981)

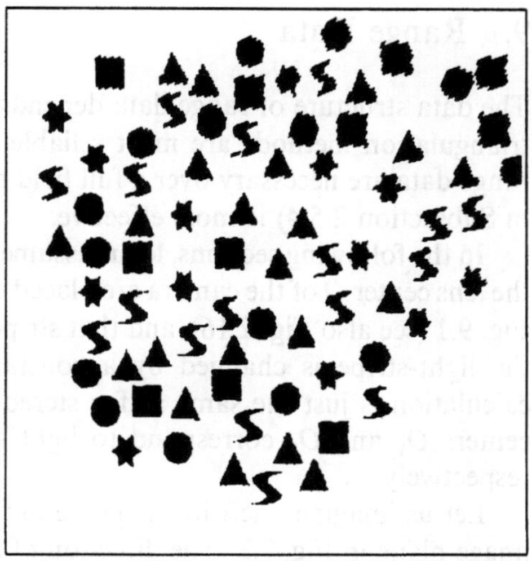

Fig. 8.27. Texture transformed from Fig. 8.25 (Ohta, 1981)

In Fig. 8.24, vanishing points obtained by 1515 pairs of those virtual parallel lines are plotted. If a line is fitted to those points, the surface normal is derived from the line as described in the previous section.

Next let us consider a case where the texture includes many kinds of patterns as shown in Fig. 8.26. First an arbitrary pair of texture elements is selected. Based on the assumption that they belong to the same class, the vanishing point is obtained. Then the assumption is verified by applying the transformation derived from the vanishing point to one element to see if the transformed element coincides with the other element. If they do not coincide, the assumption is discarded. Vanishing points are obtained from successful pairs of elements. The texture shown in Fig. 8.26 is processed by this method, and the result is shown in Fig. 8.27 which demonstrates the texture facing the camera.

We must note that the method is not effective if the orientation of texture elements is not uniform.

9 Range Data Processing

This chapter describes range data processing for the extraction of three-dimensional features and building scene descriptions. In three-dimensional computer vision, the main purpose of feature extraction is to extract geometrical features from images. While extraction of those features from monocular images is not easy, that from range data is much more reliable because the geometry of a scene is directly related to range data.

9.1 Range Data

The data structure of range data depends on the ranging device. Currently active triangulation methods are most reliable and are used for object recognition. If range data are necessary over a full field of sight, a light-stripe method (described in Subsection 2.5.4) is most effective.

In the following sections, let us assume for simplicity that the light source S and the lens center O of the camera are placed on a line parallel to the x axis as shown in Fig. 9.1 (see also Fig. 2.16), and that stripe images are taken while the direction of the light-stripe is changed by a constant angle. The principle of range data calculation is just the same as for stereo vision, depicted in Fig. 7.2, where lens centers O_1 and O_2 correspond to light source S and lens center O in Fig. 9.1, respectively.

Let us imagine a left image plane in front of the light source just like the left image plane in Fig. 7.2. The direction of a light beam is specified by the position (x_1, y_1) in the left image. In this configuration, if the light beam (x_1, y_1) is observed at (x_2, y_2) in the image (which may be called the right image to avoid confusion),

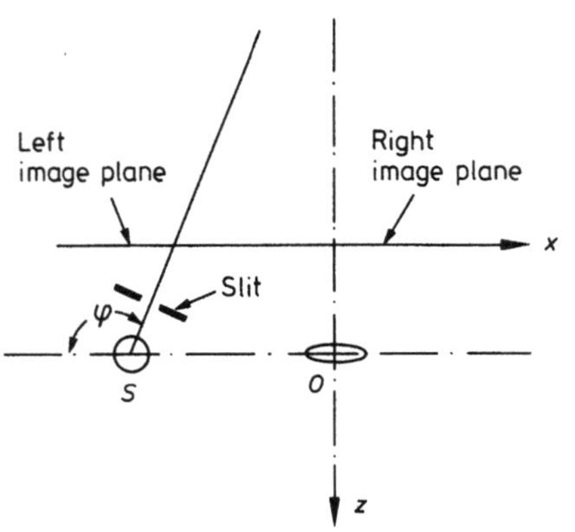

Fig. 9.1. Geometry of rangefinder

$y_1 = y_2$ holds. Since x_1 is known from the direction of the light-stripe and (x_2, y_2) is obtained from the observed stripe image in the right image plane, the reflecting surface position is easily computed.

The data structure of the range data is similar to that of monocular images: the direction of the light beam is specified by (i, j) where i indicates that the light-stripe is the ith projection and j denotes the vertical position in the stripe image, and the pixel value $\boldsymbol{x}(i, j)$ corresponds to the position of the surface that reflects the light beam. Since $\boldsymbol{x}(i, j)$ can be derived from the direction of the light beam (i, j) and the horizontal coordinate value $f(i, j)$ in the right image, $f(i, j)$ can also be used as the pixel value instead of $\boldsymbol{x}(i, j)$. The set of range data of this data structure is called a range image.

An important difference between the range image and monocular images is that the range is not always available, because the projected light-stripe may not be observed from the camera position. This lack of data may be a good clue to the detection of an occlusion.

9.2 Edge Point Detection Along a Stripe Image

Some important edge points are extracted by analyzing range data along a stripe image. Figure 9.2 shows types of feature points along such an image. Let us consider extraction of those feature points in an arbitrary stripe image. In this case, in dealing with range data, $f(j)$ may be used instead of $f(i, j)$ (because i is fixed), to denote the horizontal position of the jth point of the stripe image. Note that $f(j)$ is approximately proportional to the distance of the corresponding point in the scene from the image plane. Therefore, instead of $f(j)$, the depth of the point ($= -z$) can be used. However, $f(j)$ is advantageous because three-dimensional coordinates of stripe images need not be computed.

9.2.1 One-Dimensional Jump Edge

A jump edge (J in Fig. 9.2) means that either of the adjacent data ($f(j-1)$ or $f(j+1)$) is not available (of course $f(j)$ is given). Let us define the direction of a jump edge. Remember that the direction of the occluding edge in a line drawing is

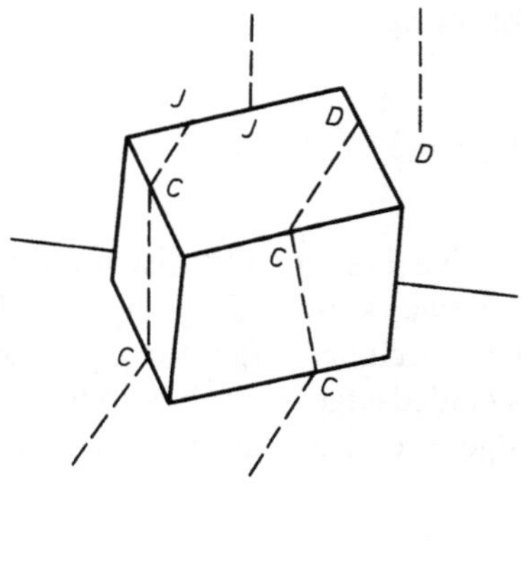

Fig. 9.2. Types of edges along stripe image

determined such that the object is on the right-hand side. The direction of a jump edge is similarly defined such that the available data point may be on the right. That is:

$$\begin{cases} \text{right} & \text{if only } f(j-1) \text{ is lacking} \\ \text{left} & \text{if only } f(j+1) \text{ is lacking} \\ \text{undefined} & \text{if both are lacking} \end{cases}$$

Note that it is not known from a single stripe image whether a jump edge corresponds to a discontinuous edge point (the left J in Fig. 9.2) or an occluded edge (the right J).

9.2.2 One-Dimensional Discontinuous Edge

A discontinuous edge (D) means that the value of f changes abruptly along the stripe image. A simple edge operator is given as follows:

$$D(j)=f(j+1)-f(j) \tag{9.1}$$

If $|D(j)|$ is above a certain threshold, a point j is determined as a discontinuous edge. Note that the next point, $j+1$, is also determined as a discontinuous edge. An occluding edge and an occluded edge are easily discriminated by the sign of $D(j)$. Since the smaller the z value the nearer is the point to the camera, $D(j)>0$ means that a point at j corresponds to an occluding edge.

A more general operator is defined as:

$$D_{d_1,d_2}(j)=\sum_{k=d_1}^{d_2} [\{f(j+k)-f(j-k)\}/2k] \tag{9.2}$$

where d_1 and d_2 are parameters (usually $d_1<d_2<3$, typically $d_1=d_2=2$). A point j is similarly determined as an edge candidate if $|D_{d_1,d_2}(j)|$ is large enough. If an isolated edge candidate is found, it is determined as an edge. Otherwise (if a series of candidates is found), a point with the local maximum of $|D_{d_1,d_2}|$ is selected as an edge point. If it is determined as an edge, the adjacent edge point is selected in the following way:

$$|f(j+d_1)-f(j)|-|f(j-d_1)-f(j)| \begin{cases} >0 & \text{point at } (j+1) \\ <0 & \text{point at } (j-1) \end{cases} \tag{9.3}$$

The direction of a discontinuous edge in the left image can be determined in the same way as that for a jump edge. If a point j is an occluding edge and a point $(i, j-1)$ is an occluded edge, the direction of the occluding edge is right and that of the occluded edge is left. If a point j is an occluded edge and a point $j-1$ is an occluding edge, the directions are left and right, respectively.

9.2.3 One-Dimensional Corner Edge

A corner edge (C) is a junction between two lines with different slopes. It corresponds to a convex or concave edge point as shown in Fig. 9.2. A simple operator for corner edge detection is given as follows:

$$DD(j)=\{f(j+1)+f(j-1)-2f(j)\}/2 \tag{9.4}$$

If $|DD(j)|$ is large, a point j is similarly determined as a corner edge. If $DD(j)$ is positive, the point corresponds to a convex edge, and vice versa. A more general operator is similarly defined as:

$$DD_{d_1,d_2}(j)=\sum_{k=d_2}^{d_1}[\{f(j+k)+f(j-k)-2f(j)\}/2k] \tag{9.5}$$

where d_1 and d_2 are parameters.

Feature extraction along a stripe image is very simple and needs little computation space. One disadvantage of the method is that it is not sensitive to vertical edges. For example, an edge point along a vertical edge is hardly detected. It is even less sensitive to slanted edges than to horizontal edges. That is, the output of operators along a stripe image does not precisely reflect geometrical features. Therefore, if the direction of edges is not known, two-dimensional operators are necessary to detect geometrical features more precisely.

9.3 Two-Dimensional Edge Operators for Range Images

One important advantage of two-dimensional edge operators is that they are less sensitive to the orientation of edges. Similar types of edge points are detected as described in the previous section.

9.3.1 Two-Dimensional Jump Edge

Two-dimensional operators can detect more general jump edges. That is, an edge is called a jump edge if any of its neighbors has no range data. There are two definitions of the neighbor: four-neighbor and eight-neighbor as described in Subsection 3.4.5. There are, therefore, two definitions of the jump edge depending on the definition of the neighbor.

The direction of a jump edge in the left image plane can also be defined by extending the definition of the one-dimensional jump edge described in the previous section. In order to determine in which direction range data is missing, the neighbor points are examined to see if range data is obtained there, and then the centroid of those which are missing range data is computed. Figure 9.3 illustrates a case where two neighbors, $(i-1,j)$ and $(i,j-1)$, have no range data. Let $\boldsymbol{t}(i,j)$ denote a vector from (i,j) to the center of gravity. The direction of the edge is $\angle\boldsymbol{t}(i,j)+\pi/2$, where directions are measured clockwise from the x axis in the left image plane, and $\angle\boldsymbol{t}(i,j)$ denotes the direction of $\boldsymbol{t}(i,j)$.

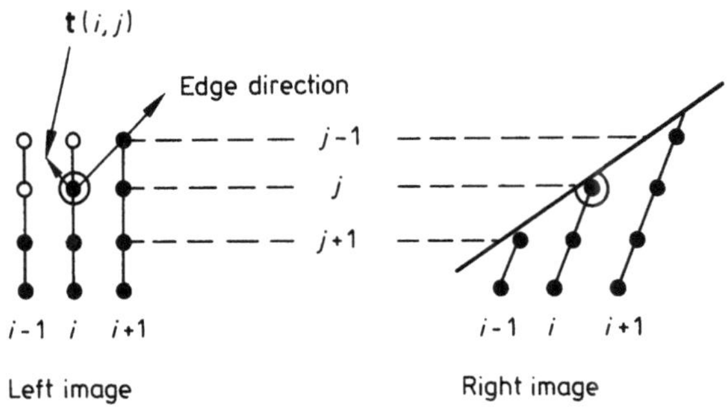

Fig. 9.3. Direction of jump edge

9.3.2 Two-Dimensional Discontinuous Edge

A discontinuous edge for two-dimensional operators means that the value of f changes abruptly in the neighbor. Let us consider, for simplicity, a four-neighbor case. A typical method is to detect discontinuities between the edge and the neighbors. A simple method uses the operator defined by Eq. (9.1) to obtain the discontinuity in the downward direction. Let $D(i,j)$ in Eq. (9.1) be denoted by $D(i,j;\pi/2)$, where $\pi/2$ represents the downward direction. The discontinuity in the right direction is defined in a similar way:

$$D(i,j;0)=f(i+1,j)-f(i,j) \tag{9.6}$$

The discontinuity in the upper direction $D(i,j;3\pi/2)$ and the left direction $D(i,j;\pi)$ are similarly defined. The two-dimensional operator takes the maximum discontinuity:

$$D_2(i,j)=\max_{k=0,1,2,3}\{|D(i,j;k\pi/2)|\} \tag{9.7}$$

If $D_2(i,j)$ is above a threshold, the point (i,j) is determined as a discontinuous edge. An occluding edge and an occluded edge are discriminated by the sign of $D(i,j;k_m\pi/2)$ where k_m is determined so that it maximizes Eq. (9.7).

The determination of the direction of a discontinuous edge in the image plane is not simple if the edge point has many discontinuous neighbors. Let us say that the edge (i,j) has a discontinuous neighbor in direction $k\pi/2$ if $|D(i,j;k\pi/2)|$ is above a certain threshold. In order to determine the edge direction, only those neighbors have to be considered that produce the same sign of $D(i,j;k\pi/2)$ as that of $D(i,j;k_m\pi/2)$. Let $\boldsymbol{t}(i,j)$ denote a vector from (i,j) to the center of gravity of those neighbors just as in the case of the jump edge. The direction of the edge is similarly determined as $\angle \boldsymbol{t}(i,j)+\pi/2$.

The operator D_2 can be extended so that it reflects data at more distant points as given in Eq. (9.2). That is, a vertical discontinuity $D_{d_1,d_2}(i,j;\pi/2)$ is the same as $D_{d_1,d_2}(i,j)$ defined by Eq. (9.2). A horizontal discontinuity is similarly defined as follows:

$$D_{d_1,d_2}(i,j;0)=\sum_{k=d_2}^{d_1}[\{f(i+k,j)-f(i-k,j)\}/2k] \tag{9.8}$$

A two-dimensional operator may also take the maximum of the two:

$$D_{2\,d_1,d_2}(i,j) = \max\{|D(i,j;0)|,\ |D(i,j;\pi/2)|\} \tag{9.9}$$

If multiple edges are found along the direction of maximum discontinuity, the local maximum is selected just as in the one-dimensional case. The direction of the edge is determined in the same way as that for $D_2(i,j)$.

Since edge operators have been defined using four-neighbors, we have considered only geometrical properties along horizontal and vertical directions. Those operators can easily be extended to the case of eight-neighbors by considering diagonal directions.

9.3.3 Two-Dimensional Corner Edge

A corner edge for two-dimensional operators means that two different surfaces meet there. A typical method computes the difference of the surface orientation in the neighbor. The surface orientation at (i,j) is represented by a vector $\boldsymbol{n}(i,j)$ defined by:

$$\boldsymbol{n}(i,j) = (\partial f(i,j)/\partial x,\ \partial f(i,j)/\partial y,\ -1) \tag{9.10}$$

In order to compute partial derivatives, three-dimensional coordinate values are necessary. Let $g(i,j)$ and $h(i,j)$ denote x and y components of $\boldsymbol{x}(i,j)$. Then the partial derivatives are approximated by:

$$\partial f(i,j)/\partial x = \{f(i+k,j) - f(i-k,j)\}/\{g(i+k,j) - g(i-k,j)\} \tag{9.11}$$

$$\partial f(i,j)/\partial y = \{f(i,j+k) - f(i,j-k)\}/\{h(i,j+k) - h(i,j-k)\} \tag{9.12}$$

where k is a parameter $(0 < k < 3)$. The three-dimensional angle $\alpha(i,j)$ between surface orientations of horizontally distant points (see Fig. 9.4) and the angle $\beta(i,j)$ between those of vertically distant points are given by the following equations:

$$\cos\alpha(i,j) = \frac{\boldsymbol{n}(i+k,j)\cdot\boldsymbol{n}(i-k,j)}{|\boldsymbol{n}(i+k,j)|\,|\boldsymbol{n}(i-k,j)|} \tag{9.13}$$

$$\cos\beta(i,j) = \frac{\boldsymbol{n}(i,j+k)\cdot\boldsymbol{n}(i,j-k)}{|\boldsymbol{n}(i,j+k)|\,|\boldsymbol{n}(i,j-k)|} \tag{9.14}$$

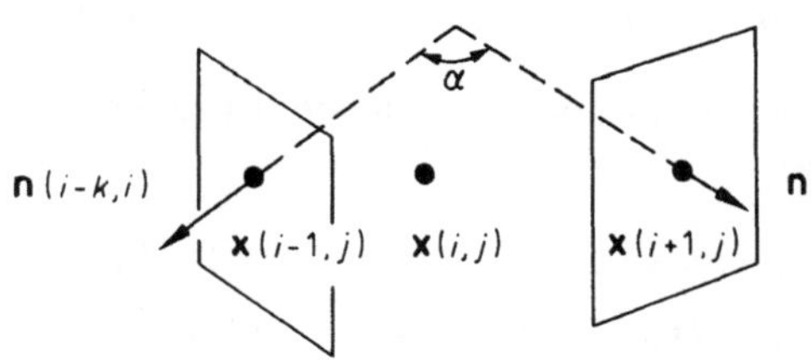

Fig. 9.4. Angle between surface orientations of horizontally distant points

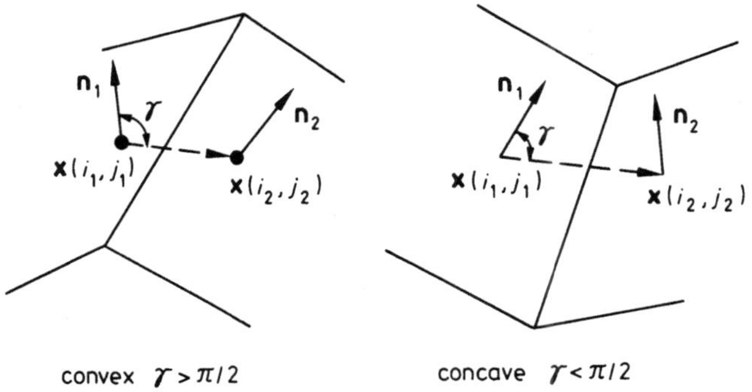

Fig. 9.5. Determination of convexity

where · denotes inner product, and both angles are normalized to be $0 \leq \alpha, \beta \leq \pi$. A two-dimensional corner edge operator is given as:

$$DD_2(i,j) = \max\{\alpha(i,j), \beta(i,j)\} \tag{9.15}$$

The direction of the edge in the three-dimensional scene is obtained from the pair of surface normals that maximize Eq. (9.15). Let $\boldsymbol{n}_1$ and $\boldsymbol{n}_2$ denote the surface normals of the pair; the direction $\boldsymbol{\theta}$ of the edge is defined as their cross-product:

$$\boldsymbol{\theta}(i,j) = \boldsymbol{n}_1 \times \boldsymbol{n}_2 \tag{9.16}$$

where × denotes cross-product. Convexity of the edge is also determined. Let a pair of surface normals $\boldsymbol{n}_1$ and $\boldsymbol{n}_2$ be obtained at $\boldsymbol{X}(i_1, j_1)$ and $\boldsymbol{X}(i_2, j_2)$ (see Fig. 9.5). If the inner product of normal $\boldsymbol{n}_1$ and a vector from $\boldsymbol{X}(i_1, j_1)$ to $\boldsymbol{X}(i_2, j_2)$ is negative, the edge is convex. That is:

$$\{\boldsymbol{X}(i_2, j_2) - \boldsymbol{X}(i_1, j_1)\} \cdot \boldsymbol{n}_1 \begin{cases} <0 & \text{convex} \\ >0 & \text{concave} \end{cases}$$

It is convenient to define the sign of the strength of an edge depending on the convexity of the edge as follows.

$$DD_2'(i,j) = \begin{cases} DD_2(i,j) & \text{if convex} \\ -DD_2(i,j) & \text{if concave} \end{cases}$$

Since the operator DD_2 requires much computation, we may use a more simple operator, like $DD(j)$ defined in Eq. (9.4). Let $DD(i,j;\pi/2)$ denote $DD(j)$ of the ith stripe (remember that $DD(j)$ represents the second-order derivative in the vertical direction). The horizontal derivative $DD(i,j;0)$ is similarly defined as:

$$DD(i,j;0) = \{f(i+1,j) + f(i-1,j) - 2f(i,j)\}/2 \tag{9.17}$$

The result of this operator may be either the maximum or the root mean square of the two:

$$DD_1(i,j) = \max\{|DD(i,j;0)|, |DD(i,j;\pi/2)|\} \tag{9.18}$$

$$DD_1'(i,j) = \{DD^2(i,j;0) + DD^2(i,j;\pi/2)\}^{\frac{1}{2}} \tag{9.19}$$

Convexity can be derived from the sign of the derivatives. For example, the edge is convex if $DD(i,j;0)+DD(i,j;\pi/2)$ is positive, and vice versa.

Another operator may also be defined, using Eq. (9.5) as the vertical derivative, with the horizontal derivative similarly given. Note that simple operators are unable to detect three-dimensional directions of edges. However, the direction in the image plane can be defined. For DD_1, the direction θ_z is perpendicular to the direction of the derivative that gives the maximum of Eq. (9.18). If, for example, $DD(i,j;0)$ is larger, $\theta_z(i,j)=\pi/2$. Note that four directions are discriminated if eight-neighbors are considered. The diagonal operators are given as:

$$DD(i,j;\pi/4)=\{f(i+1,j+1)+f(i-1,j-1)-2f(i,j)\}/2 \tag{9.20}$$

$$DD(i,j;3\pi/4)=\{f(i-1,j+1)+f(i+1,j-1)-2f(i,j)\}/2 \tag{9.21}$$

For DD_1' the direction is defined as

$$\theta_z'(i,j)=\arctan\{DD(i,j;\pi/2)/DD(i,j;0)\}+\pi/2 \tag{9.22}$$

9.4 Scene Segmentation Based on Stripe Image Analysis

It is shown above that stripe images themselves are useful for understanding scenes. Looking at Fig. 9.6, for example, we may recognize a block on a plane in front of a wall. An intuitive way to recognize polyhedra is, first, to describe stripe images by lines, and then to classify them into groups corresponding to planes. Since this method requires less computation, it is practicable for analysis of simple scenes. In the following subsections a description is given of procedures involving this method (Shirai, 1972).

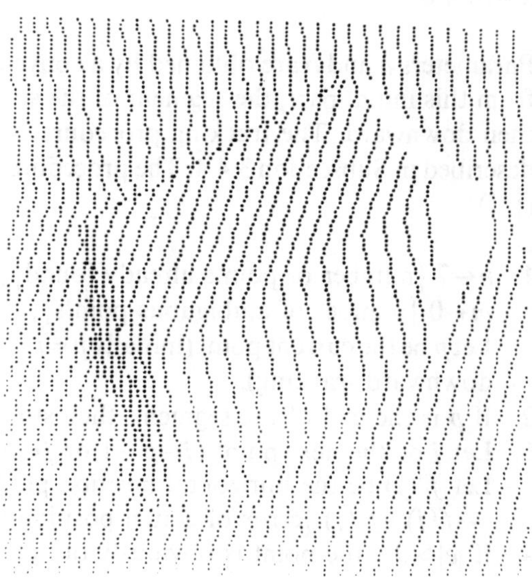

Fig. 9.6. Stripe image of a block

9.4.1 Segmentation of Stripe Image

In this procedure each stripe image is segmented into straight lines. First, jump edges and discontinuous edges are detected along a stripe image by operators for those edges as described in Sect. 9.2. These edges split a stripe image into multiple continuous segments.

Each continuous segment is further segmented at corner edges into straight line segments. Corner edge detection along a continuous segment is not easy because a conventional local operator may be sensitive to noise. In order to reflect a more global geometry, line tracking is performed. The line tracking process consists of two stages: finding a starting point, and tracking the segment upward and downward until terminal points are found.

Let us consider the tracking process for a continuous segment in an arbitrary stripe image. Let $f(j)$ denote the horizontal position of the jth point of the stripe image. As described in Sect. 9.1, $(f(j), j)$ denotes the position of the point in the right image plane. The starting point of line tracking must be on a straight part of the segment so that the initial estimation of the line equation may be precise. The straight part is defined as a sequence of points $\{j-3, j-2, j-1, j, j+1, j+2, j+3\}$ which satisfies the following two equations.

$$|d(1)+d(-1)|+|d(2)+d(-2)|+|d(3)+d(-3)|<\theta_s \tag{9.23}$$

$$|\{(d(1)-d(-1)\}+\{d(2)-d(-2)\}-\{d(3)+d(-3)\}|<\theta_l \tag{9.24}$$

where $d(i)=f(j+i)-f(j)$, and θ_s and θ_l are thresholds. Equation (9.23) provides the measure of symmetry at point j, and Eq. (9.24) provides the measure of linearity.

A straight part is sought by scanning the segment downward. When it is found, a line equation is fitted to the seven points. Since lines are nearly vertical, the line equation is represented as follows:

$$x=ay+b \tag{9.25}$$

Parameters a and b are obtained by a conventional least-squares method. Starting from this initial part, the segment of the stripe image is tracked first upward and then downward. The tracking procedure is based on the edge-following method described in Subsection 3.4.4. The procedure is as follows, with comments in braces ({ }):

1. $n \leftarrow 7$ {number of points already found};
   $m \leftarrow 0$ {number of ambiguous points};
   Let p be the current point (initially $p=j-3$ for upward tracking, and $p=j+3$ for downward tracking).
2. If p is the end of the segment, then stop.
3. Let j be the next point ($j \leftarrow p-1$ or $j \leftarrow p+1$).
   Let $f'(j)$ be the horizontal position predicted by Eq. (9.25) ($f'(j)=aj+b$).
   $e \leftarrow f(j)-f'(j)$ {error of actual position from the estimated one}.
4. If $|e|>\theta_1$ {the point is obviously out of the line}, then stop.

5. If $|e| < \theta_2$ {the point is obviously on the line}, then go to (6);
   otherwise {ambiguous case}, if $m > \theta_m$, then stop;
   otherwise, $m \leftarrow m+1$; go to (8).
6. If $m > 0$, then adjust the line equation with the previous m points which have been determined to be ambiguous;
   $n \leftarrow n+m$; $m \leftarrow 0$.
7. $n \leftarrow n+1$; adjust the line equation by the point j.
8. $p \leftarrow j$; go to (2).

The threshold θ_m for the maximum number of ambiguous points is determined depending on the quality of the input and complexity of objects (typically $\theta_m = 3$).

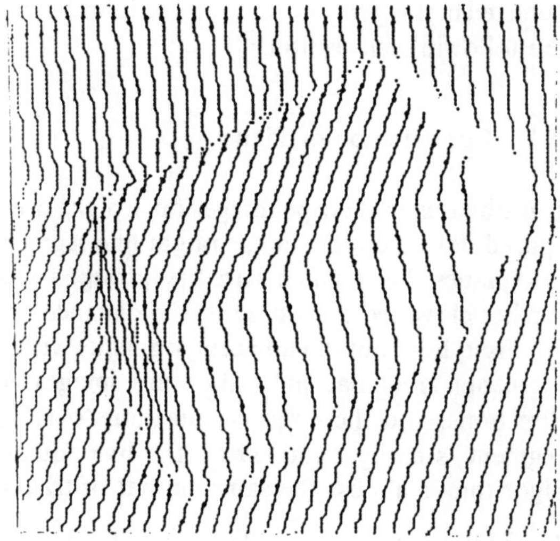

Fig. 9.7. Result of tracking. ◆: starting point

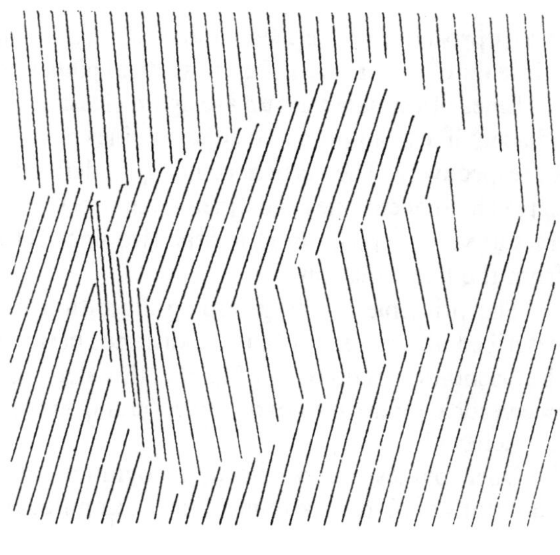

Fig. 9.8. Lines obtained from tracking process

The thresholds θ_1 and θ_2 are monotonically increasing functions of n and m (usually linear functions), and always $\theta_2 < \theta_1$. The line equation is adjusted by fitting it to all points already determined to be on the straight line (line parameters a and b in Eq. (9.25) are updated).

When tracking terminates in both directions, the obtained straight segment is removed from the original continuous segment. The rest of the segment is again searched for a straight part. This process is repeated until no more straight parts are found. Figure 9.7 shows the result of tracking and Fig. 9.8 shows the lines thus obtained.

The tracking method is insensitive to low input noise yet still sensitive to corner edges with small differences in the angle of incident planes. However, it is influenced by the direction of edge lines as described in Sect. 9.2. That is, it is most sensitive to horizontal edges and less sensitive to inclined edges. Although vertical edges are not detected in this process, they may be found in the construction of planes described in the following subsection.

9.4.2 Construction of Planes

It is obvious that stripe images on a plane are approximately parallel and equally spaced. Based on this fact, straight line segments obtained previously are grouped into planes. The segments are first grouped according to orientation, then they are further classified according to the distance between adjacent segments.

First, horizontally adjacent segments with similar orientations are found. Two segments are adjacent if they are images of a stripe projected in successive directions, and their vertical positions overlap each other. The orientation of a segment is easily obtained by the line equation. The principle of the grouping algorithm is almost the same as that of tracking:

1. Find a few successive lines with approximately the same orientation.
2. Compute the average orientation of the successive lines.
3. Find more lines to the right and left of the initial lines.

If this procedure is applied to lines shown in Fig. 9.8, four groups are obtained. (Note that lines on two different vertical planes of the block are in the same group.)

Lines of the same group are again classified according to the distance between adjacent lines. Suppose two adjacent lines have terminal points j_s and j_e, and j_s' and j_e', respectively. The vertical center j_m is defined as $(j_s + j_e + j_s' + j_e')/4$. The distance between adjacent lines is defined as that between intersecting points of horizontal lines at vertical position j_m for the two lines. The intersecting points are obtained from the line equations.

The principle of the grouping algorithm is also similar to that of grouping described above, except that the distance between adjacent lines is used instead of the orientation of lines. For Fig. 9.8, this algorithm can correctly classify lines in the two vertical planes into two corresponding groups. During this stage, vertical edges are detected.

Once planes are obtained, recognition of a simple object is not difficult. Equations of planes are immediately computed from their corresponding groups of lines. Three-dimensional relations between planes are derived from the plane equations. The shape of a plane is derived from the boundaries of planes and the intersecting lines between lines.

9.5 Linking Three-Dimensional Edges

This section describes methods of obtaining edge lines by linking three-dimensional edge points that are detected from range images. Edge linking can be applied to the entire range image in a systematic order or in parallel. Usually, however, it is applied serially in an edge-following procedure. That is, from an edge, similar edges are linked one by one in one direction until the terminal points are found, and then in the other direction.

Three-dimensional edges have much information because, as described in Sect. 9.2, the direction of edges reflects the geometry of surfaces, and edge types are discriminated when edges are detected by edge operators. From range data, five types of edges are discriminated: jump edge, occluding edge, occluded edge, convex edge, and concave edge. Since an edge-linking process usually links only the same type of edges, it may be able to obtain edge lines more reliably even near vertices.

Let us consider a typical edge-linking method which is to be applied to edges detected by two-dimensional edge operators described in Sect. 9.2. Jump edges are first linked because they are the most reliably found.

Let the direction of a jump edge be defined on the image plane. Suppose the direction of a jump edge at (i,j) is $\theta_z(i,j)$. The candidates must be either at the neighbor in the same direction or at the next neighbors in the sense of eight-neighbors. For example, if $\theta_z(i+1,j)$ is 0 (right), then the candidates are either at $(i+1,j)$, $(i+1,j-1)$, or $(i+1,j+1)$ as shown in Fig. 9.9. If more than one candidate is found, the best edge is determined as the one with edge direction nearest to $\theta_z(i,j)$. Figure 9.10 shows the result of jump edge linking.

Secondly, discontinuous edges are linked because they are more reliably detected than corner edges. Occluding edges and occluded edges are separately linked, although the order is arbitrary. The principle of the linking method is just the same as that for jump edges. The direction of a discontinuous edge is also defined on the image plane. The candidate edges and the best edge are similarly selected. Figure 9.11 shows the result of discontinuous edge linking.

Corner edges are linked last because the discrimination between corner edges and points on a smoothly curved surface is subtle. Convex edges and concave edges

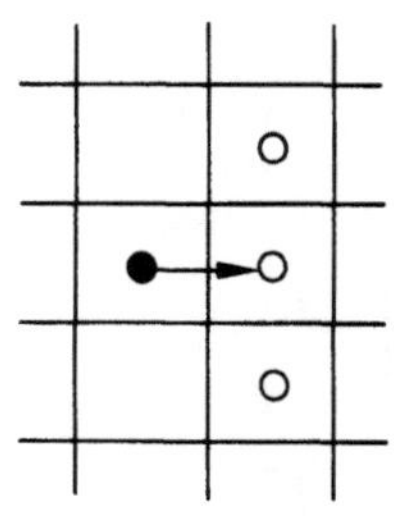

Fig. 9.9. Next candidate edges

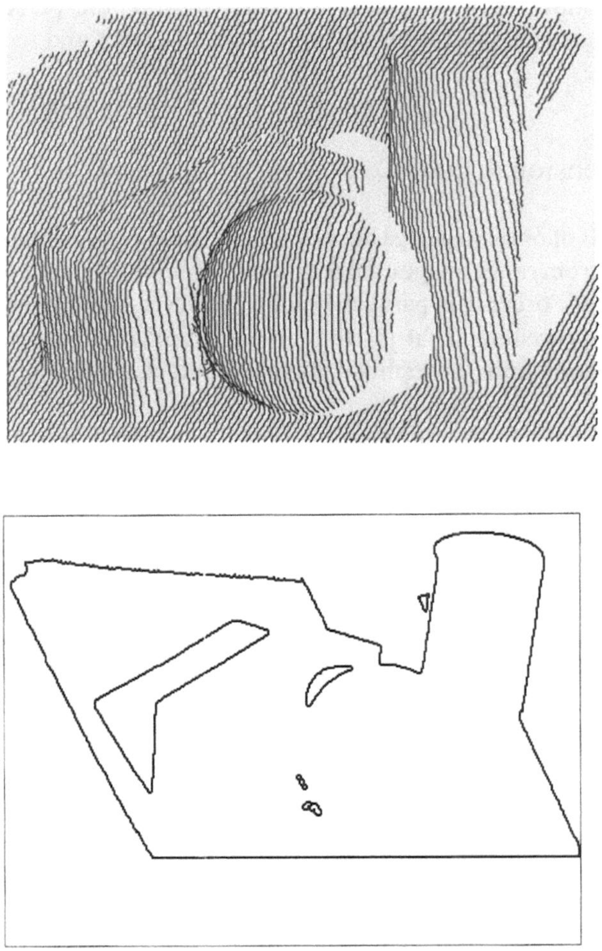

a

b

Fig. 9.10a, b. Example of linking jump edges: (**a**) light-stripe image; (**b**) linked jump edges

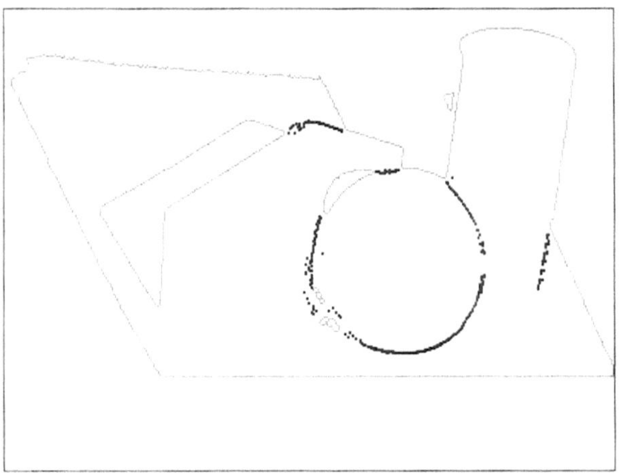

Fig. 9.11. Linked discontinuous edges

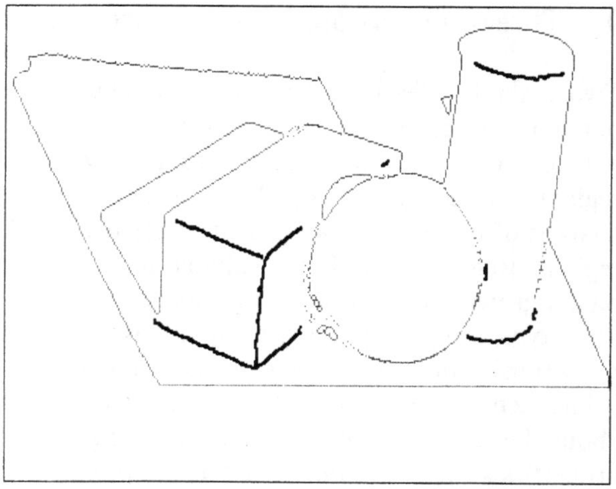

Fig. 9.12. Linked corner edges

should also be discriminated as in the case of occluding and occluded edges. The three-dimensional direction of a corner edge is obtained by operator DD_2 as given by Eq. (9.15). Candidate edges are selected in the same way as for jump edges except that, instead of the direction of $\theta(i,j)$, that of the projection of $\theta(i,j)$ onto the image plane is used. In determining the best edge, not only the difference in edge directions but also the strength of the edge must be considered. One possible criterion for a candidate edge at (i',j') is a combination of the two in the following way:

$$P((i,j),\ (i',j'))=|DD_2(i',j')|\ \cos\{\theta(i',j')-\theta(i,j)\} \tag{9.26}$$

Note that $0 \leq P \leq \pi$ because $0 \leq |DD_2| \leq \pi$ and $|\theta(i',j')-\theta(i,j)| \leq \pi/2$. The best edge is the one that maximizes the criterion. Of course, other criteria may be possible. For example, the following criterion may also be plausible:

$$P'((i,j),\ (i',j'))=\sin\{|DD_2(i',j')|/2\}\ \cos\{\theta(i',j')-\theta(i,j)\} \tag{9.27}$$

Note that P' is normalized such that $0<P'<1$. Figure 9.12 shows the result of corner edge linking.

Instead of applying DD_2, the simplified edge operator DD_1 or DD_1' can be used. Candidate edges are selected in the same way as for jump edges. The criterion for a candidate edge at (i',j') can be defined in the same way as in Eqs. (9.26) and (9.27), except that directions of edges on the image plane are used:

$$P_1((i,j),\ (i',j'))=|DD_1(i',j')|\ \cos\{\theta_z(i',j')-\theta_z(i,j)\} \tag{9.28}$$

$$P_1'((i,j),\ (i',j'))=\sin\{|DD_1(i',j')|/2\}\ \cos\{\theta_z(i',j')-\theta_z(i,j)\} \tag{9.29}$$

9.6 Three-Dimensional Region Growing

Two methods of feature extraction for range images are described above. The first is not uniformly sensitive to edges in different directions. Although the second may be able to detect edges for all directions, it provides no information about the inner regions bounded by the edge lines. Since range images contain rich information, analysis of the interior can provide more detailed knowledge of the shape of the regions. Region methods are suitable for this purpose. This section describes a region-growing method for range images.

A typical region-growing method makes small atomic regions on the basis of properties of an image and then merges similar atomic regions into global regions. While each atomic region of a gray image itself does not contain much information about the scene, that obtained from a range image contains useful geometrical properties such as position and orientation. Therefore, three-dimensional region growing is more reliable than region growing for gray images.

A three-dimensional region-growing method was first proposed by Shirai (1973a), and applied to recognition of polyhedra (Kyura and Shirai, 1973). They used an atomic region which consists of a set of range data points in a small region. The atomic region was called a 'surface element'. Merging the surface elements with similar properties, their program described scenes with a set of plane surfaces. They showed that this approach was effective, even though the scene included complicated polyhedra such as dodecahedra or icosahedra.

The method was extended so that it might be able to deal with curved objects. The intent was to describe a scene including plane surfaced and curved objects in a consistent way without prior knowledge of the objects.

9.6.1 Outline of Region-Growing Method

A conceptual scheme of the region-growing method is depicted in Fig. 9.13. An input range image is represented by $\boldsymbol{x}(i,j)$. Figure 9.13(a) shows a set of points $\boldsymbol{x}(i,j)$ observed from a camera (in the right image). The region-growing process proceeds as follows:

1. Group the points into small surface elements and, assuming each element to be a plane, obtain the equation of the surface elements (Fig. 9.13(b)).
2. Merge the surface elements together into approximately plane regions (elementary regions, Fig. 9.13(c)).
3. Classify the elementary regions into three classes: plane, curved, and undefined (Fig. 9.13(d)).
4. Try to extend the curved regions by merging adjacent curved or undefined regions to produce larger regions (global curved regions) and fit the quadratic surface to them (Fig. 9.13(e)).
5. Finally, describe the scene in terms of properties of regions and relations between regions (Fig. 9.13(f)).

Each stage of the process is described in the following subsections.

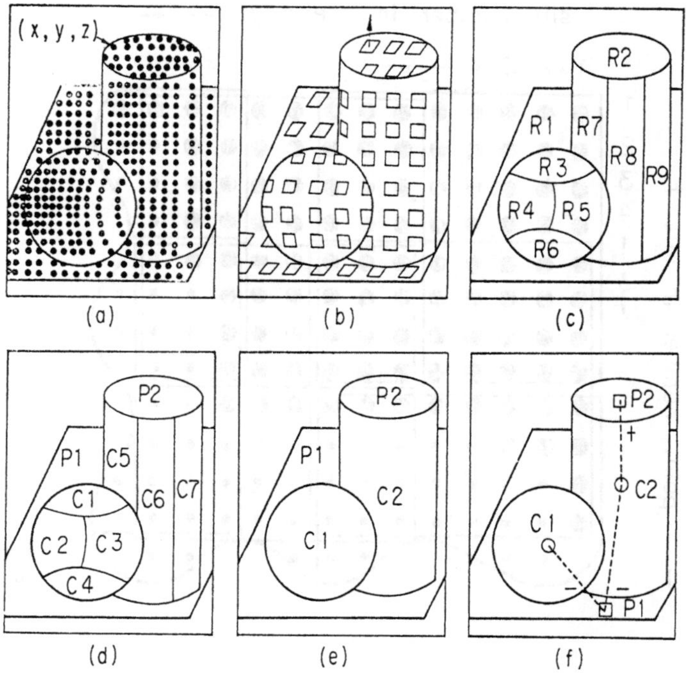

Fig. 9.13a–f. Conceptual scheme of the region-growing process: (**a**) 3D coordinates; (**b**) surface elements; (**c**) elementary regions; (**d**) classified regions; (**e**) global regions; (**f**) description of the scene

9.6.2 Construction of Surface Elements

The points of the range image are grouped into surface elements. Each element consists of adjoining points of a rectangular region in the left image. The size of the rectangle depends on the resolution of the range image and the complexity of the scene. Typically, for a range image that consists of about 400×250 data points, an 8×8 square is selected. Note that some of the data points may be lacking in range data because stripe images are not always completely observed by a camera.

Surface elements are usually overlapped as shown in Fig. 9.14, where three points are shared by horizontal neighbors and four points by vertical ones. Thus the scene is represented by about 80×60 surface elements.

Assuming each element to be a plane, the equation of the plane is fitted to its member points by the least-squares method. A surface element is denoted by the equation:

$$\begin{aligned} f(x, y, z) &= ax + by + cz - d \\ &= 0 \end{aligned} \tag{9.30}$$

Figure 9.15 shows an example of a stripe image and the normal vectors of the surface elements. Of course, equations are not obtained for those elements that are lacking in range data. Even if all member points have range data, some of the surface

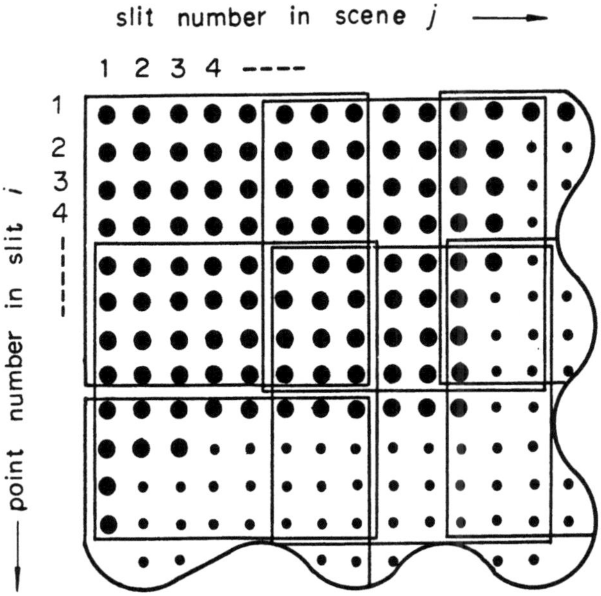

Fig. 9.14. Allocation of surface elements

elements, for example at an edge, are meaningless because they are not considered to be planar. Therefore, the elements with too large a standard deviation, σ, of the least-squares fitting are ignored in the further processing.

9.6.3 Merging Surface Elements

The surface elements are merged into approximately plane regions (elementary regions). The process is divided into two stages: (1) search for a kernel of an elementary region in the scene, and (2) find a region around the kernel by merging surface elements. These stages are iterated.

9.6.3.1 Kernel Finding

The candidates of a kernel are those elements which do not belong to any region already found. In finding a plane surface, it is desirable that the kernel be a part of a smooth surface. The best of the candidates is selected according to the evaluation function, e, which is calculated from the number, n, of the candidates in the eight-neighbors and their mean standard deviation, σ, of the plane fitting:

$$e = w/n + \sigma \tag{9.31}$$

where w is a constant. If e is small, it means that the element has many candidates in its neighbors and constitutes a smooth surface. Therefore, the element with the minimum value of e is chosen as the kernel.

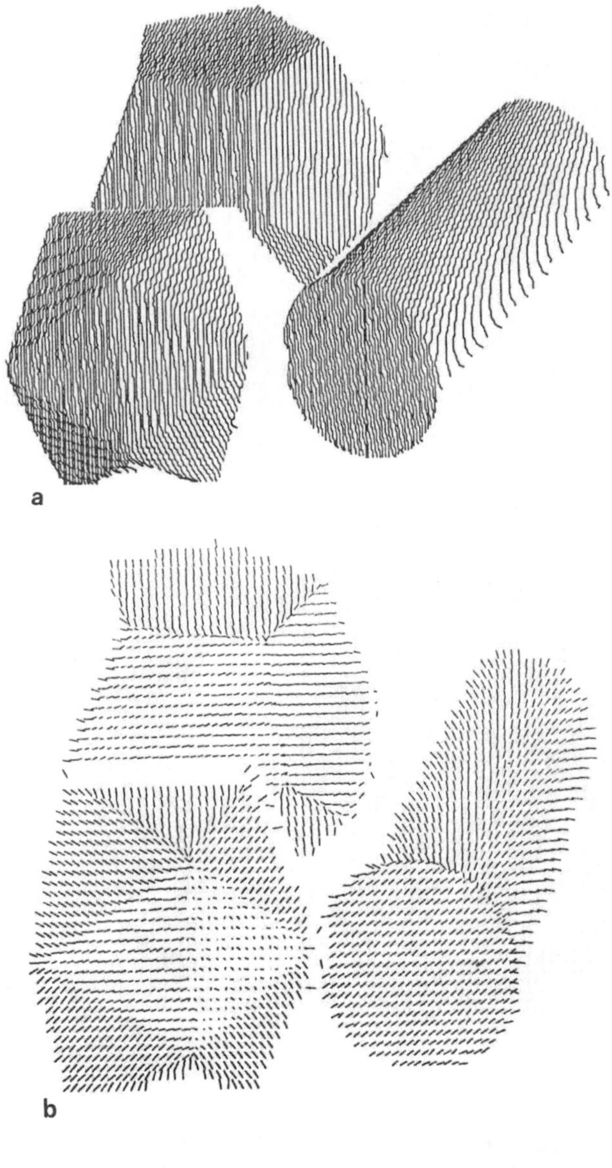

Fig. 9.15a, b. Example of normals of surface elements: (**a**) stripe image displayed every four lines; (**b**) normals of surface elements

9.6.3.2 Region Merging

The program extends a region around the kernel by merging its neighboring elements. The candidate element to be merged must currently be adjacent to the region. If the plane equation of a candidate is similar to that of the region, it is merged into the region. The merging conditions for element k are:

$$p_k^2 = (a_k - a_r)^2 + (b_k - b_r)^2 + (c_k - c_r)^2 < p_t^2 \tag{9.32}$$

$$|d_k - d_r| < d_t \tag{9.33}$$

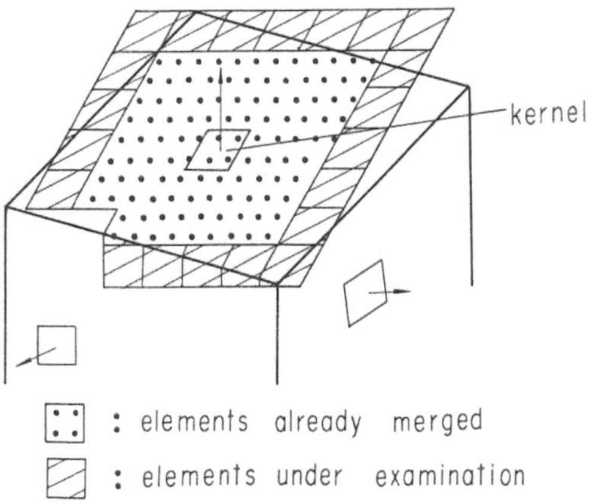

Fig. 9.16. Intermediate state of region-growing process

Fig. 9.17. Elementary regions for Fig. 9.15

where a, b, c, and d correspond to those in Eq. (9.30), 'r' denotes the region, and 't' denotes thresholds. Figure 9.16 depicts the intermediate state of the process, where the dotted elements are already connected to the kernel and a set of marginal elements (hatched in Fig. 9.16) is under examination. Each time a set of marginal elements has been examined and appropriate elements have been merged, the plane equation of the region is updated. The program repeats this process until no extension is possible.

An example of the region map is illustrated in Fig. 9.17 (which corresponds to Fig. 9.15). In Fig. 9.17, a letter corresponds to a surface element, and the character represents the appropriate region label. As shown in the figure, a plane corresponds to an elementary region, but a curved surface corresponds to multiple elementary regions that are approximately planar.

9.6.4 Classification of Elementary Regions

Each elementary region corresponds to a plane surface or a part of a curved surface. During this stage the elementary regions are classified on the basis of their geometries. It is difficult to draw a strict distinction between plane and curved regions on the basis of local criteria. A smooth plane, for example, does not always yield a region with uniformly distributed points due to noise and digitization error.

During this stage, therefore, regions are classified as plane, curved or undefined. The undefined ones are considered later with the benefit of global information.

First, the reliability of each region is examined. During the stage described in Subsection 9.6.2 surface elements with too large a standard deviation, σ, are rejected, mainly to discard meaningless elements around plane edges. Some elements which are left may still be unreliable, especially at the position where stripe images are broad and weak. Such elements have larger values of σ than do reliable elements. Elementary regions which consist of these kinds of elements are not reliable. Therefore, by using the average of the standard deviation, $\bar{\sigma}$, of the member elements, a region with large $\bar{\sigma}$ is classified as undefined.

The rest of the elementary regions are classified on the basis of two parameters. The first parameter, p_m, is the mean variance of the angle of the region, and is given by:

$$p_m = \sum_{k=1}^{n} p_k/n \tag{9.34}$$

where p_k is defined by Eq. (9.32), and n is the number of elements in the region. The second parameter is a so-called ‘effective diameter’ of the region map, which is defined as follows (see Fig. 9.18):

$$\phi_e = \min(\max(\phi_{11}, \ldots, \phi_{1n_1}), \ldots, \max(\phi_{41}, \ldots, \phi_{4n_4})) \tag{9.35}$$

The regions with too small a value of ϕ_e are small or slender. They are classified as undefined. A curved surface with a large curvature has a small value of ϕ_e. The rest

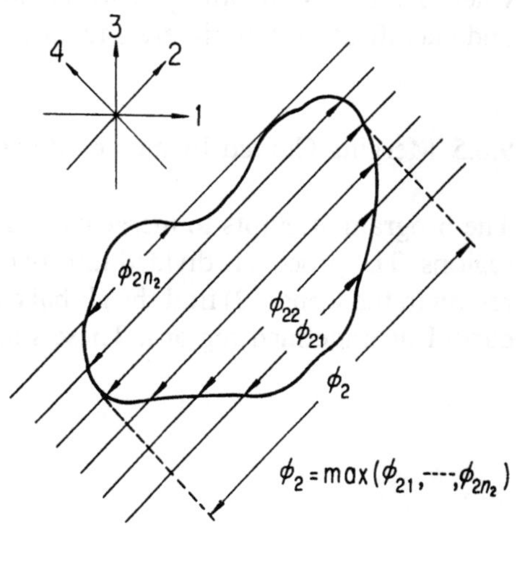

Fig. 9.18. Effective diameter

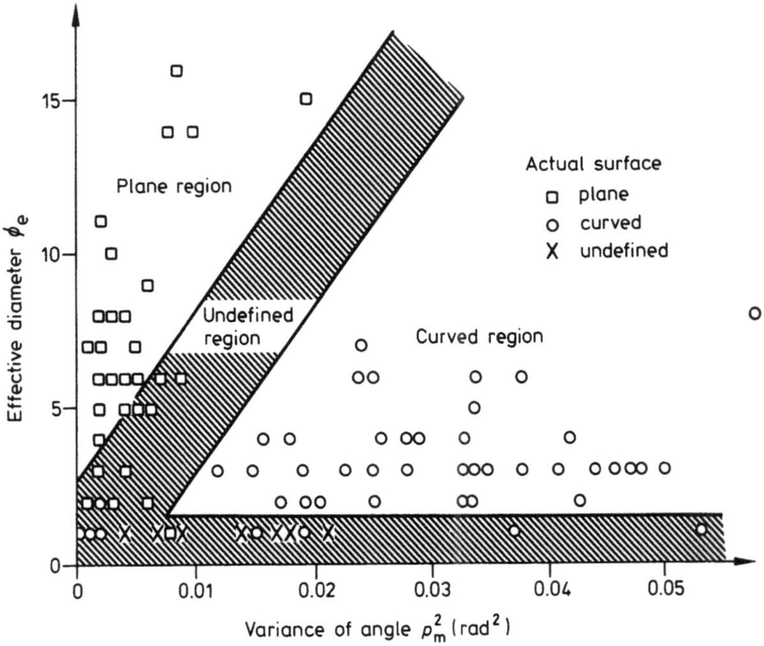

Fig. 9.19. Classification criteria and sample data for elementary regions

of the regions are, therefore, classified according to the classification criteria given by the following equations:

$$q = \alpha p_m^2 - \phi_e \tag{9.36}$$

$$q \begin{cases} < -q_t & \text{plane region} \\ > q_t & \text{curved region} \\ \text{otherwise} & \text{undefined region} \end{cases} \tag{9.37}$$

where α is a constant, and $q_t(>0)$ is a threshold. Data obtained from several scenes and classification criteria are shown in Fig. 9.19.

9.6.5 Merging Curved Elemetary Regions

The program attempts to merge curved and undefined regions into global curved regions. The process is divided into two stages: (1) search for a kernel of a global region in the scene; (2) find the global curved region around it by merging suitable curved or undefined regions. These stages are iterated.

9.6.5.1 Kernel Finding

The candidates for the kernel are elementary curved regions which do not belong to any global region already found. As a larger region is more reliable for a kernel, the evaluation function r for every candidate region is computed by:

$$r = w_{\phi}\phi_e + n \tag{9.38}$$

where n is the number of elements in the region and w_{ϕ} is a constant. A region with large r means that it has a large effective diameter and has many surface elements. The candidate with the maximum value of r is chosen as the kernel.

9.6.5.2 Region Merging

The program extends a global curved region around the kernel by merging its neighboring elementary regions. The candidates to be merged are the curved and undefined elementary regions which are currently adjacent to the global region.

The program proceeds step by step. At first, candidates are only those that are just adjacent to the kernel. An intermediate state of the global region growing is shown in Fig. 9.20. The program checks whether each candidate region can be merged or not to the global region, using the elementary regions called 'touchstones'. The touchstones are those elementary regions which are included in the global region and adjacent to the candidate. Supposing that region 11 is checked as shown in Fig. 9.20, then regions 4 and 5 are the touchstones. If the candidate is determined to be smoothly connected to one of the touchstones, it is merged.

The test is made as follows. Suppose in Fig. 9.21, C_A and C_B are the three-dimensional points corresponding to the centroid of the candidate and that of the touchstone respectively. Planes P_A and P_B are set to be perpendicular to the line segment $C_A C_B$. Two sets of surface elements between two planes (two hatched areas in Fig. 9.21) are each approximated by plane equations. The two regions are determined to be smoothly connected if the angle θ between the normals of the planes satisfies the following condition:

$$\theta < w_{\theta} p_t \tag{9.39}$$

where p_t is the same as in Eq. (9.32) and w_{θ} is a constant. The smoothly curved body (for example, a sphere) may yield different elementary regions by Eq. (9.32), and the

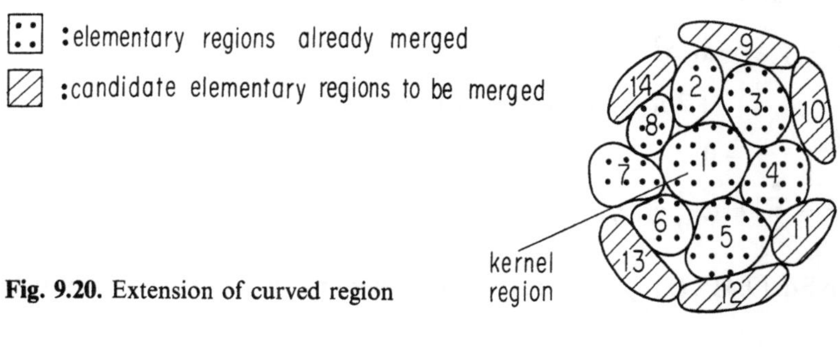

Fig. 9.20. Extension of curved region

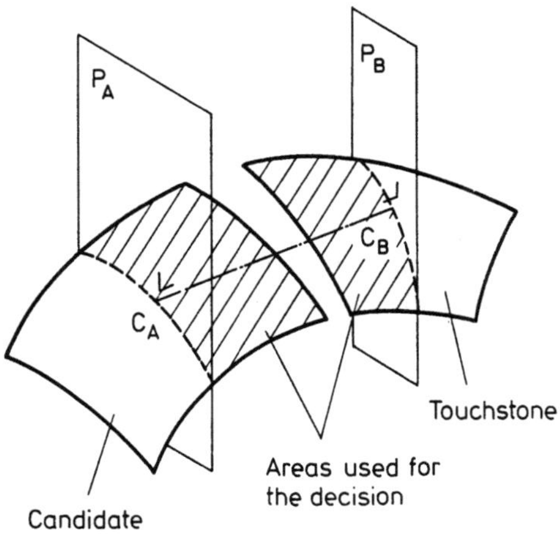

Fig. 9.21. Test of smoothness between candidate region and touchstone

Fig. 9.22. Result of region merging for Fig. 9.17

angle between two neighboring regions is expected to be proportional to p_t. The threshold in Eq. (9.39) is related to p_t so that the same body yields the same global region for various p_ts.

After global curved regions are found, the unassigned surface elements are reconsidered. If the angle between a surface element and its neighboring elementary region is small, the element is merged into the same global region. This time the threshold is greater than that used in Eq. (9.32). Figure 9.22 shows the result of the region-merging operation applied to the side of the cylinder shown in Fig. 9.17.

9.6.6 Making Descriptions

Having found the map of the global regions, the program makes basic descriptions of the scene in terms of properties of regions and relations between regions.

9.6.6.1 Fitting Quadratic Surfaces to Curved Regions

Global curved regions are approximated by quadratic surfaces and they are classified into several types. The quadratic surface is expressed in Eq. (9.40), and the evaluation function s^2 to be minimized in the approximation is given by Eq. (9.41).

$$\begin{aligned} h(x,y,z) = {} & a_{11}x^2 + a_{22}y^2 + a_{33}z^2 \\ & + 2a_{12}xy + 2a_{23}yz + 2a_{31}zx + 2a_1x + 2a_2y + 2a_3z + a_0 \\ = {} & 0 \end{aligned} \tag{9.40}$$

$$s^2 = \sum_{k=1}^{n} h^2(x_k, y_k, z_k) \tag{9.41}$$

In Eq. (9.41), (x_k, y_k, z_k) are the coordinates of the point in the curved global region.

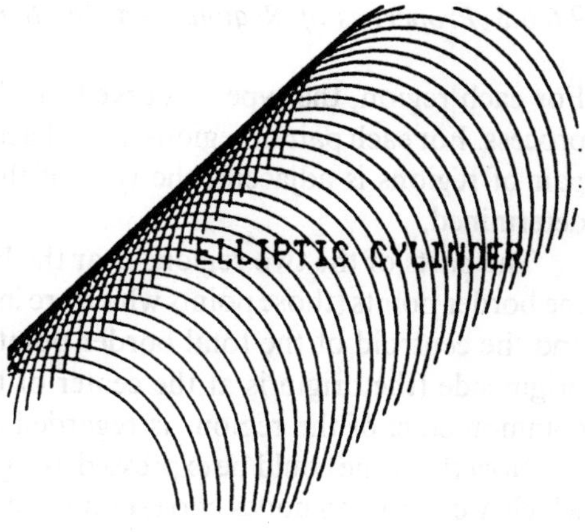

Fig. 9.23. Result of quadratic surface fitting to the region shown in Fig. 9.22

The minimization is solved by a conventional least-squares method. If the mean variance s^2/n is greater than a threshold, the surface is not approximated by a quadratic surface and is classified as undefined. The rest of the regions are classified, using the coefficients in Eq. (9.40), as follows: a parabolic cylinder, an elliptical cylinder, a hyperbolic cylinder, a paraboloid, a cone, an ellipsoid, and a hyperboloid. The classification is executed in the conventional mathematical way except that coefficients are set to zero by thresholding. Figure 9.23 shows the result of quadratic surface fitting to the global region shown in Fig. 9.22.

9.6.6.2 Edges of Regions

The method of finding edges of the global regions depends on the following two cases:

(a) the edges between surfaces which are approximated by equations;
(b) the others.

In case (a), the intersecting line can be derived from the equations of the regions. This method is less sensitive to noise than an edge detection method with local edge operators, because all the points in the incident regions contribute to the determination of the line equation. If more than two plane regions adjoin one another, the corresponding line segments should meet at one vertex. In this case, the coordinates (x_v, y_v, z_v) of the vertex are determined to minimize d, the total sum of the squares of the distances to each plane.

$$d^2 = \sum_{k=1}^{n} f_k^2(x_v, y_v, z_v) \tag{9.42}$$

where n is the number of related planes, k corresponds to each plane, and f is the same as in Eq. (9.30).

In case (b), the edge is described by a series of edge points which are extracted from the region map by using a 3×3 local edge operator.

9.6.6.3 Properties of Regions and Relations Between Them

For each region, the type — curved or plane — has been given in the preceding process. For each pair of regions, the adjacency between them has been checked. If a pair of regions is adjacent, the type of the common edge (convex or concave) is determined.

The parts of the two regions near the border are approximated by planes from the border points (those points which are in the vicinity of the border) of the regions, and the centroid of the total border points is calculated. If the centroid is on the origin side (the origin is at the center of the rotating mirror) of both planes, the common edge of the regions is regarded as concave.

Now the scene could be expressed as a graph whose nodes are the regions, and in which arcs between nodes correspond to connecting relations between them. These properties and relations could be useful in describing the scene.

Figure 9.24 shows an example of the description of the scene (corresponding to Fig. 9.15). In Fig. 9.24, the label of regions is prefixed by 'R' (RB, for example, means region B), and the label of adjacency is prefixed by 'A'; the marks '□' and '○' mean that the regions are plane or curved, respectively; and the dotted lines with the mark '+' mean that the two regions are adjacent and that the common edge between them is convex. Only the two-dimensional picture is shown here (although the three-dimensional one exists in the computer).

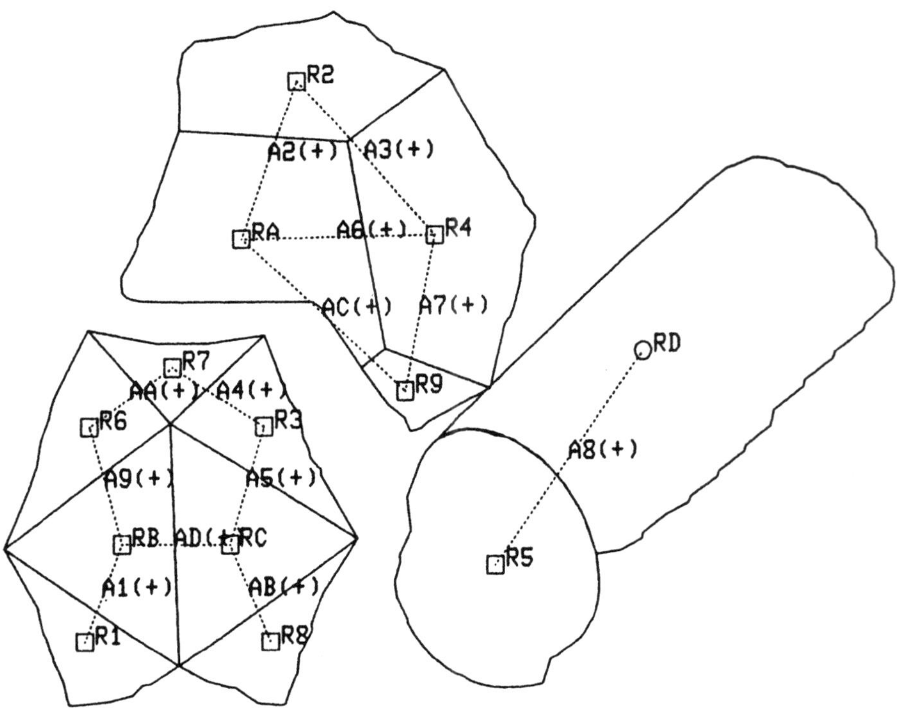

Fig. 9.24. Description of the scene corresponding to Fig. 9.15

10 Three-Dimensional Description and Representation

When we see 3D objects, we describe them in various ways: in terms of edges, surfaces, or volumes. For example, mountains beyond forests may be characterized by the shape of the edge, terrains by the shape of the surface, or buildings by a combination of simple geometric volumes.

For recognition of objects, models of objects are necessary. 3D models may be powerful because they represent objects viewed from various directions. They are represented in the same way as real objects are described. Since representations of models may be generated by humans, it is possible to include information such as shapes of invisible parts or details which cannot be obtained from range data.

In the preceding chapter some basic descriptions of features such as planes and quadratic surfaces are given. Other important 3D descriptions, which may also be used for representing 3D models, are given in this chapter. The first two sections deal with 3D curves and free surfaces. They are useful for initial description of range data as well as for generation of models of man-made objects such as machine parts. The next section describes a method of generating surfaces connecting two serial sections extracted from input images. The subsequent two sections introduce volume descriptions: generalized cylinders which are proposed for describing complex objects like animals, and geometric models which have originally been proposed for mechanical CAD (computer-aided design). Finally, a more abstract representation called 'Extended Gaussian Image' is introduced. This chapter concentrates on descriptions and representations; their use is discussed in Chap. 14.

10.1 Three-Dimensional Curves

When we take range data using a rangefinder based on a light-stripe method, the 3D positions of points are obtained along lines on object surfaces. One way to describe the shape of a surface is to describe first each series of points with a smooth curve. The derivation of the surface shape from those curves is described in the following section.

10.1.1 Three-Dimesional Curve Segments

A line on a surface may be a straight line or an arc depending on whether the surface is a plane or a sphere, respectively. General 3D curves, on the other hand, are usually represented by parametric splines. They are similar to the 2D parametric splines described in Subsection 4.1.3 except that $\boldsymbol{x}(t) = [x(t)\ y(t)\ z(t)]$. The tangent vector is

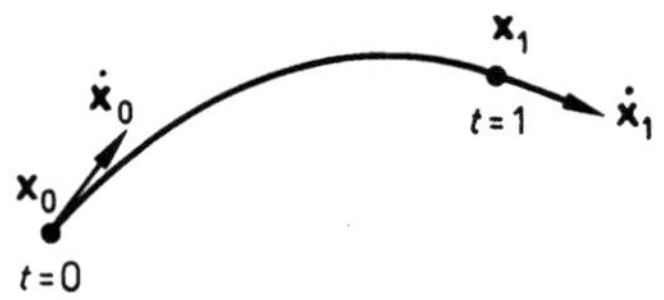

Fig. 10.1. Boundary conditions of a curve

similarly given by $\dot{\boldsymbol{x}}$ ($=\mathrm{d}\boldsymbol{x}/\mathrm{d}t$). The equation of the curve is similarly represented by a 1×3 matrix:

$$\boldsymbol{P}(t)=[x(t)\ y(t)\ z(t)] \tag{10.1}$$

where t ranges from 0 to 1. In order to represent general curves, the order of $\boldsymbol{P}(t)$ is at least three. Let us represent a curve from $\boldsymbol{x}_0$ to $\boldsymbol{x}_1$ by the following polynomial of order three:

$$\boldsymbol{P}(t)=[t^3\ t^2\ t\ 1]M \tag{10.2}$$

where M is a 4×3 matrix. The relations $\boldsymbol{P}(0)=\boldsymbol{x}_0$ and $\boldsymbol{P}(1)=\boldsymbol{x}_1$ hold.

If the curve is further constrained by the relations that the derivatives at $\boldsymbol{x}_0$ and $\boldsymbol{x}_1$ are $\dot{\boldsymbol{x}}_0$ and $\dot{\boldsymbol{x}}_1$, respectively, as shown in Fig. 10.1, the matrix M is uniquely solved as:

$$M=\begin{pmatrix} 2 & -2 & 1 & 1 \\ -3 & 3 & -2 & -2 \\ 0 & 0 & 1 & 0 \\ 1 & 0 & 0 & 0 \end{pmatrix}\begin{pmatrix} \boldsymbol{x}_0 \\ \boldsymbol{x}_1 \\ \dot{\boldsymbol{x}}_0 \\ \dot{\boldsymbol{x}}_1 \end{pmatrix} \tag{10.3}$$

where $\dot{\boldsymbol{x}}_0$ and $\dot{\boldsymbol{x}}_1$ denote the derivatives (tangent vectors) at $\boldsymbol{x}_0$ and $\boldsymbol{x}_1$. Equation (10.2) can be rewritten as:

$$\boldsymbol{P}(t)=H_{0,0}(t)\boldsymbol{x}_0+H_{0,1}(t)\boldsymbol{x}_1+H_{1,0}(t)\dot{\boldsymbol{x}}_0+H_{1,1}(t)\dot{\boldsymbol{x}}_1 \tag{10.4}$$

where

$$\begin{aligned} H_{0,0}(t)&=(t-1)^2(2t+1)\\ H_{0,1}(t)&=t^2(3-2t)\\ H_{1,0}(t)&=(t-1)^2 t\\ H_{1,1}(t)&=(t-1)t^2 \end{aligned} \tag{10.5}$$

This curve is called 'Ferguson's curve'.

It is known that a curve of order $(2k+1)$ is necessary if the derivative of up to kth order is given at the boundaries. For $k=0$, for example, the curve becomes a straight line passing through $\boldsymbol{x}_0$ and $\boldsymbol{x}_1$:

$$\boldsymbol{P}(t)=(1-t)\boldsymbol{x}_0+t\boldsymbol{x}_1 \tag{10.6}$$

If the curvature is specified (i.e., $k=2$), a 5th-order curve is obtained as:

$$\begin{aligned}\boldsymbol{P}(t)=&K_{0,0}(t)\boldsymbol{x}_0+K_{0,1}(t)\boldsymbol{x}_1+K_{1,0}(t)\dot{\boldsymbol{x}}_0+K_{1,1}(t)\dot{\boldsymbol{x}}_1\\&+K_{2,0}(t)\ddot{\boldsymbol{x}}_0+K_{2,1}(t)\ddot{\boldsymbol{x}}_1\end{aligned} \tag{10.7}$$

where $K_{0,0}(t), K_{0,1}(t),\ldots, K_{2,1}(t)$ are 5th-order polynomials.

It is often necessary to fit a smooth curve to a sequence of points. These curves are not convenient to use because the boundary conditions must be explicitly specified. For example, in order to get a curve such that the first derivative may be continuous at each knot, we must specify the derivative at each knot.

10.1.2 Three-Dimensional B-Splines

B-splines are suitable for representing continuous lines specified by a sequence of points. The definition of 2D B-splines described in Subsection 4.1.4 is extended to 3D B-splines where control points are in a 3D space. For example, for a given sequence of 3D points, $\boldsymbol{x}_0, \boldsymbol{x}_1, \ldots, \boldsymbol{x}_n$, the ith cubic polynomial is given by Eq. (4.9) where the $\boldsymbol{B}_i(t)$s are given by Eq. (4.11).

Generally, the B-spline does not pass the control points, just as with the 2D B-spline. 3D B-splines inherit the properties of 2D B-splines.

10.2 Surfaces

10.2.1 Coons Surface Patches

General surfaces are represented by a set of surface patches, each of which is bounded by four curves as shown in Fig. 10.2. A patch is represented by a 1×3 matrix with two parameters, u and v:

$$\boldsymbol{P}(u,v)=[x(u,v)\; y(u,v)\; z(u,v)] \tag{10.8}$$

where $0\leq u, v\leq 1$. One of the difficulties in representing a general curve is how to specify the curve. A well known representation proposed by Coons is called the 'Coons surface patch', which is specified by the bounding curves. Let the bounding curves be represented by $\boldsymbol{x}(u,0)$, $\boldsymbol{x}(u,1)$, $\boldsymbol{x}(0,v)$, and $\boldsymbol{x}(1,v)$, and the four corner

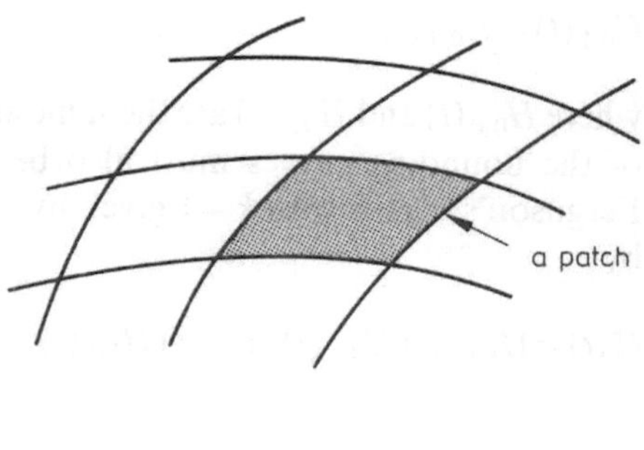

Fig. 10.2. Surface composed of patches

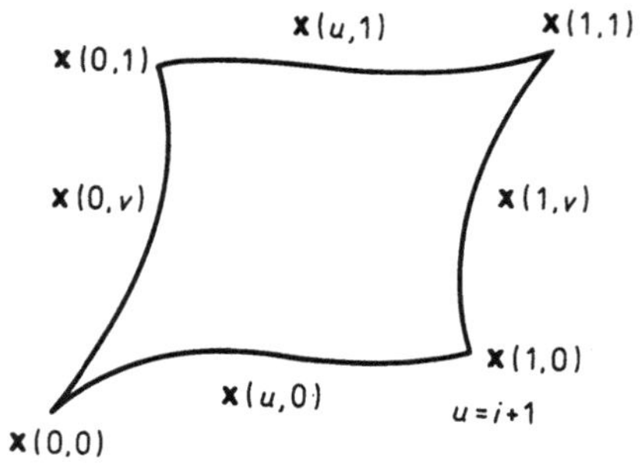

Fig. 10.3. Boundary conditions of a patch

points be represented by $\boldsymbol{x}(0,0)$, $\boldsymbol{x}(0,1)$, $\boldsymbol{x}(1,0)$, and $\boldsymbol{x}(1,1)$ as shown in Fig. 10.3. The equation of the Coons patch is formulated as:

$$\begin{aligned}\boldsymbol{P}(u,v) = {} & [C_{0,0}(u)\,C_{0,1}(u)]\begin{bmatrix}\boldsymbol{x}(0,v)\\ \boldsymbol{x}(1,v)\end{bmatrix} + [C_{0,0}(v)\,C_{0,1}(v)]\begin{bmatrix}\boldsymbol{x}(u,0)\\ \boldsymbol{x}(u,1)\end{bmatrix}\\ & -[C_{0,0}(u)\,C_{0,1}(u)]\begin{bmatrix}\boldsymbol{x}(0,0)\,\boldsymbol{x}(0,1)\\ \boldsymbol{x}(1,0)\,\boldsymbol{x}(1,1)\end{bmatrix}\begin{bmatrix}C_{0,0}(v)\\ C_{0,1}(v)\end{bmatrix}\end{aligned} \tag{10.9}$$

where functions $C_{i,j}(t)$ $(i=0,1,\ j=0,1)$ are called 'blending functions', and are determined from the boundary conditions. The minimum boundary condition is that the surface must coincide with the bounding curves on the boundary. For example, $\boldsymbol{P}(u,0)=\boldsymbol{x}(u,0)$. The blending functions of the least order are:

$$\begin{aligned}C_{0,0}(t) &= 1-t\\ C_{0,1}(t) &= t\end{aligned} \tag{10.10}$$

This patch is continuous on the border, but the derivative is not. The bounding curves are usually Ferguson's curves with $k=0$ given by Eq. (10.6). The patch is a bilinear surface:

$$\boldsymbol{P}(u,v) = [1-u \quad u]\begin{bmatrix}\boldsymbol{x}(0,0) & \boldsymbol{x}(0,1)\\ \boldsymbol{x}(1,0) & \boldsymbol{x}(1,1)\end{bmatrix}\begin{bmatrix}1-v\\ v\end{bmatrix} \tag{10.11}$$

So that the first derivative may be continuous, the following blending functions are used:

$$\begin{aligned}C_{0,0}(t) &= H_{0,0}(t)\\ C_{0,1}(t) &= H_{0,1}(t)\end{aligned} \tag{10.12}$$

where $H_{0,0}(t)$ and $H_{0,1}(t)$ are the same as those defined by Eq. (10.5). The derivative of the bounding curves must also be continuous. The condition is satisfied by Ferguson's curves with $k=1$ given by Eq. (10.4). Let $\boldsymbol{H}(t)$ denote a matrix defined by

$$\boldsymbol{H}(t) = [H_{0,0}(t)\,H_{0,1}(t)\,H_{1,0}(t)\,H_{1,1}(t)] \tag{10.13}$$

Then the patch is represented by:

$$\boldsymbol{P}(u, v)=\boldsymbol{H}(u)\begin{pmatrix} \boldsymbol{x}(0,0) & \boldsymbol{x}(0,1) & \boldsymbol{x}_v(0,0) & \boldsymbol{x}_v(0,1) \\ \boldsymbol{x}(1,0) & \boldsymbol{x}(1,1) & \boldsymbol{x}_v(1,0) & \boldsymbol{x}_v(1,1) \\ \boldsymbol{x}_u(0,0) & \boldsymbol{x}_u(0,1) & 0 & 0 \\ \boldsymbol{x}_u(1,0) & \boldsymbol{x}_u(1,1) & 0 & 0 \end{pmatrix}\boldsymbol{H}(v)^{\mathrm{t}} \tag{10.14}$$

where $\boldsymbol{x}_v$ denotes the differential of $\boldsymbol{x}$ with respect to v, and so forth.

Later, a more general equation of surface patches was proposed by Coons. Let $\boldsymbol{C}(t)$ denote the matrix of the blending functions:

$$\boldsymbol{C}(t)=[C_{0,0}(t)\ C_{0,1}(t)\ C_{1,0}(t)\ C_{1,1}(t)] \tag{10.15}$$

Let $\boldsymbol{M}_x$ denote the following matrix:

$$\boldsymbol{M}_x=\begin{pmatrix} \boldsymbol{x}(0,0) & \boldsymbol{x}(0,1) & \boldsymbol{x}_v(0,0) & \boldsymbol{x}_v(0,1) \\ \boldsymbol{x}(1,0) & \boldsymbol{x}(1,1) & \boldsymbol{x}_v(1,0) & \boldsymbol{x}_v(1,1) \\ \boldsymbol{x}_u(0,0) & \boldsymbol{x}_u(0,1) & \boldsymbol{x}_{uv}(0,0) & \boldsymbol{x}_{uv}(0,1) \\ \boldsymbol{x}_u(1,0) & \boldsymbol{x}_u(1,1) & \boldsymbol{x}_{uv}(1,0) & \boldsymbol{x}_{uv}(1,1) \end{pmatrix} \tag{10.16}$$

The surface patch is given by:

$$\begin{aligned}\boldsymbol{P}(u, v)=&\ \boldsymbol{C}(u)[\boldsymbol{x}(0,v)\,\boldsymbol{x}(1,v)\,\boldsymbol{x}_u(0,v)\,\boldsymbol{x}_u(1,v)] \\ &+\boldsymbol{C}(v)[\boldsymbol{x}(u,0)\,\boldsymbol{x}(u,1)\,\boldsymbol{x}_v(u,0)\,\boldsymbol{x}_v(u,1)]-\boldsymbol{C}(u)\,\boldsymbol{M}_x\,\boldsymbol{C}(v)^{\mathrm{t}}\end{aligned} \tag{10.17}$$

Matrix $\boldsymbol{C}(t)$ is similarly determined by the boundary conditions. In order to make the patch continuous up to the first-order derivative, we can use $\boldsymbol{H}(t)$. The bounding curves must also be continuous up to the first-order derivative. This condition is satisfied by Ferguson's curves with $k=1$ (defined by Eq. (10.4)). Then the Coons patch is represented by the following equation:

$$\boldsymbol{P}(u, v)=\boldsymbol{H}(u)\,\boldsymbol{M}_x\,\boldsymbol{H}(v)^{\mathrm{t}} \tag{10.18}$$

Since the elements of $\boldsymbol{H}$ are cubic polynomials, the patch is called a 'cubic Coons patch'. To fit a smooth surface to a set of points, this surface patch is not convenient because the boundary conditions must be explicitly specified just as for Ferguson's curve described in the previous subsection.

10.2.2 B-Spline Surfaces

B-spline functions are suitable for representing continuous surfaces. Using cubic polynomials for B-splines defined by Eq. (4.9), a cubic B-spline surface patch is defined by the 16 control points as shown in Fig. 10.4. Let $\boldsymbol{B}(t)$ denote the matrix of

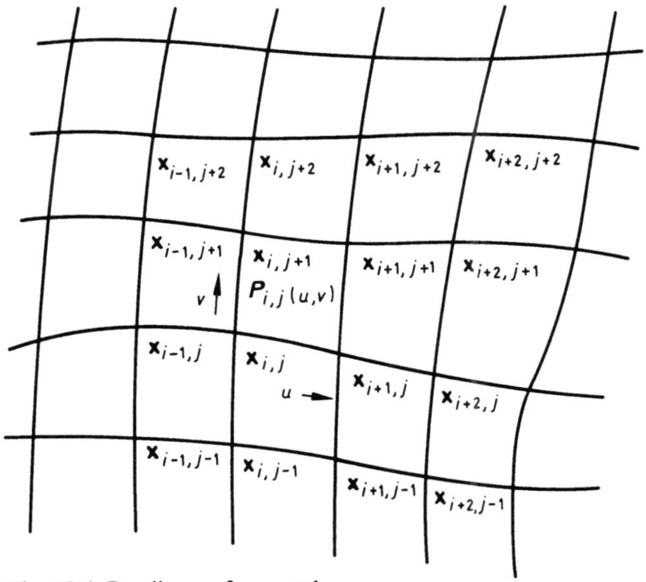

Fig. 10.4. B-spline surface patch

the blending functions:

$$\boldsymbol{B}(t) = [\boldsymbol{B}_{0,0}(t)\, \boldsymbol{B}_{0,1}(t)\, \boldsymbol{B}_{1,0}(t)\, \boldsymbol{B}_{1,1}(t)] \tag{10.19}$$

The equation of the surface patch $\boldsymbol{P}_{i,j}(u, v)$ is:

$$\boldsymbol{P}_{i,j}(u,v) = \boldsymbol{B}(u) \begin{pmatrix} \boldsymbol{x}_{i-1,j-1} & \boldsymbol{x}_{i-1,j} & \boldsymbol{x}_{i-1,j+1} & \boldsymbol{x}_{i-1,j+2} \\ \boldsymbol{x}_{i,j-1} & \boldsymbol{x}_{i,j} & \boldsymbol{x}_{i,j+1} & \boldsymbol{x}_{i,j+2} \\ \boldsymbol{x}_{i+1,j-1} & \boldsymbol{x}_{i+1,j} & \boldsymbol{x}_{i+1,j+1} & \boldsymbol{x}_{i+1,j+2} \\ \boldsymbol{x}_{i+2,j-1} & \boldsymbol{x}_{i+1,j} & \boldsymbol{x}_{i+2,j+1} & \boldsymbol{x}_{i+2,j+2} \end{pmatrix} \boldsymbol{B}(v)^{t} \tag{10.20}$$

Note that the B-spline surface does not pass through the control points, just as for B-spline curves.

The corner points ($\boldsymbol{P}_{i,j}(u, v)$ at $u = 0, 1$ and $v = 0, 1$) are near the control points.

10.3 Interpolation of Serial Sections with Surface Patches

3D positions are often obtained along contours of cross-sections. A typical example is provided by map contours, which correspond to boundaries of cross-sections at different altitudes. In designing mechanical parts, irregular-shaped objects are also described by a series of cross-sections. Other important examples are cross-sections of various parts in X-ray computerized tomography (CT) images. In these cases multiple cross-sections are obtained along an axis. Reconstruction of 3D shapes from serial sections is usually straightforward; however, if the distance between adjacent sections is large and the shapes of the sections are complex, the problem becomes more difficult. Moreover, a sufficient number of data points is not always available along the contour of each section. The reconstruction problem for such cases is interesting.

10.3.1 Description of Problem

Let us consider the problem of finding surfaces which connect two adjacent cross-sections. That is, the surfaces are derived from the two sections, neglecting the others. The contours of sections may be represented by curves or polygons. However, in this section, let us assume that the contour is approximated by a polygon.

Now the problem is formulated as follows. Given two polygons (as shown in Fig. 10.5), find a proper set of triangles which compose a surface between these polygons. The problem is divided into two subproblems. The first is how to find the initial pair of vertices. The second is, given a pair of vertices P_i and Q_i as shown in Fig. 10.6, how to select the next vertex (P_{i+1} or Q_{i+1} in the figure). Since the actual surface is unknown, the meaning of 'proper set of triangles' is ambiguous. However, let us try to find the triangles that seem to be natural to humans.

The following subsections describe a method for reconstruction of 3D surfaces from serial sections extracted from X-ray CT images of a head. Figure 10.7 shows an example of an image and the cerebrospinal fluid region extracted from the image. For simplicity, let us assume that vertically serial horizontal sections are given.

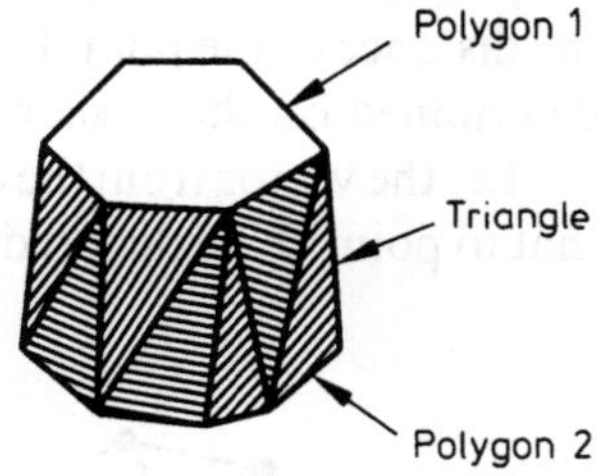

Fig. 10.5. Triangular surface patches between polygons

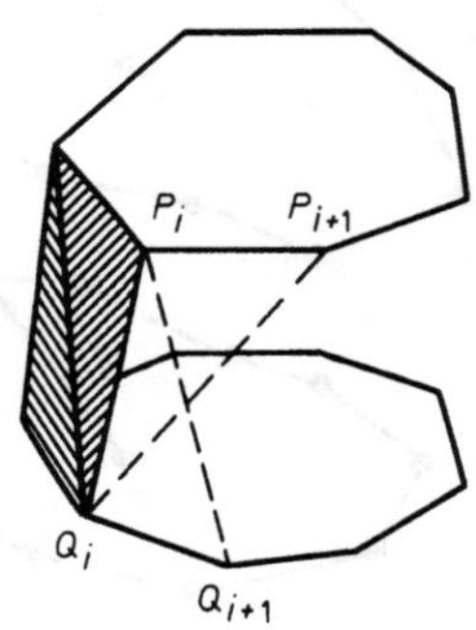

Fig. 10.6 Two candidates for the next vertex

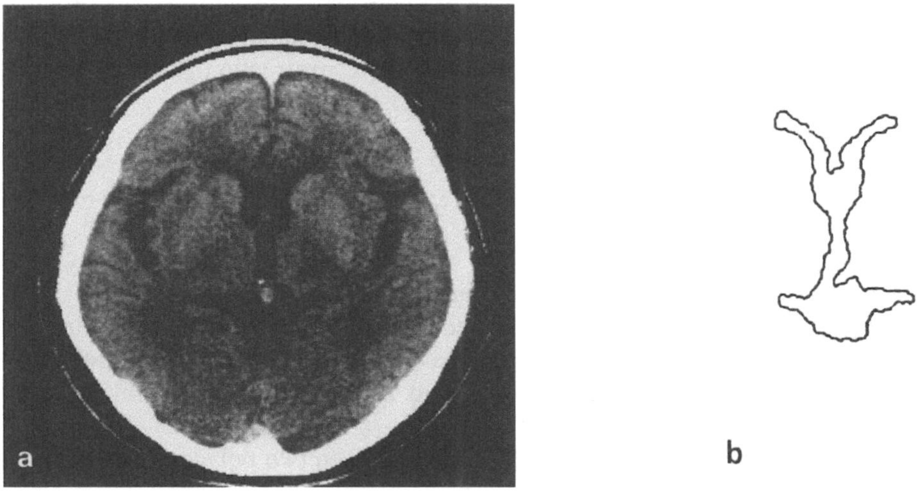

Fig. 10.7. (**a**) X-ray CT image of a head; (**b**) the cerebrospinal fluid region

10.3.2 Determination of Initial Pair

The vertices forming the initial pair should be similar from various points of view. That is, they must exhibit similar features in their respective polygons. For example, if one vertex is a concave point, the other must also be a concave point.

The problem is what kind of features are most important. Candidate features are the position of the vertex, the direction of the edges connecting the vertex and the adjacent vertices, the angle between the two edges, the direction from the centroid to the point, and so on. The direction from the centroid to the point is a stable feature if the distance of the point from the centroid is large. Considering this fact, the pair is determined on the basis of the direction and the distance.

Let the vector from the centroid to point P_i be denoted by $\boldsymbol{U}_i$ in one polygon and that to point Q_j be denoted by $\boldsymbol{V}_j$ in the other (see Fig. 10.8). The initial pair (P_i, Q_j)

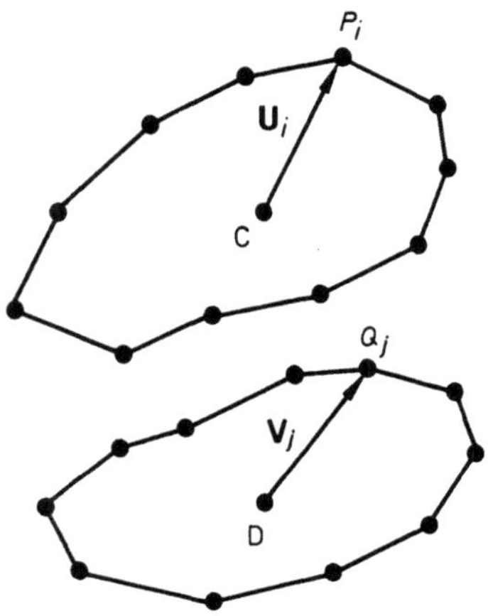

Fig. 10.8. Vectors for determining the initial pair

is selected such that the inner product of the vectors $U_i \cdot V_j$ is a maximum. If two polygons are similar, the farthest pair is selected.

The amount of computation for polygons of m and n vertices is the calculation of $(m+n)$ vectors and at most $m \times n$ comparisons to obtain the maximum pair. We can use better algorithms if something is known about the shape of the sections. For example, if both shapes are approximately similar, we can start from the farthest vertex of one polygon, select the vertex of the other in the same direction, and search only its neighboring vertices to obtain the pair with maximum inner product.

10.3.3 Selection of Next Vertex

Given the previous pair of vertices as shown in Fig. 10.6, either of the two vertices P_{i+1} or Q_{i+1} is selected as the third vertex of the triangle. If P_{i+1} is selected, triangle $P_iQ_iP_{i+1}$ is generated, and the next pair is (P_{i+1}, Q_i).

The criterion for this selection may be the area of the triangle, the length between the next pair, the direction from the centroid, and so on. It is experimentally shown that the criterion is based on the length of the next pair. Usually the next pair is selected as the one with the shorter length. It seems to be natural to connect the nearest points.

The criterion based on length alone, however, is not enough, especially when the horizontal position of vertices is different. Suppose, for example, the current pair is (P_i, Q_i) as shown in Fig. 10.9, where the value of the x coordinate of P_i is larger than that of Q_i. Then $P_{i+1}Q_i$ may be shorter than P_iQ_{i+1}. Humans may select Q_{i+1} because the direction of the edge P_iP_{i+1} is quite different from that of $Q_{i-1}Q_i$. Therefore, the difference in direction is taken into account. Let the difference in direction between P_iP_{i+1} and $Q_{i-1}Q_i$ be denoted by α_i, and that between $P_{i-1}P_i$ and Q_iQ_{i+1} be denoted by β_i. The selection algorithm in the case of $P_{i+1}Q_i < P_iQ_{i+1}$ is as follows:

if $\cos\alpha_i > t$	select P_{i+1}
otherwise, if $\cos\beta_i > t$	select Q_{i+1}
otherwise	select P_{i+1}

where t is a threshold.

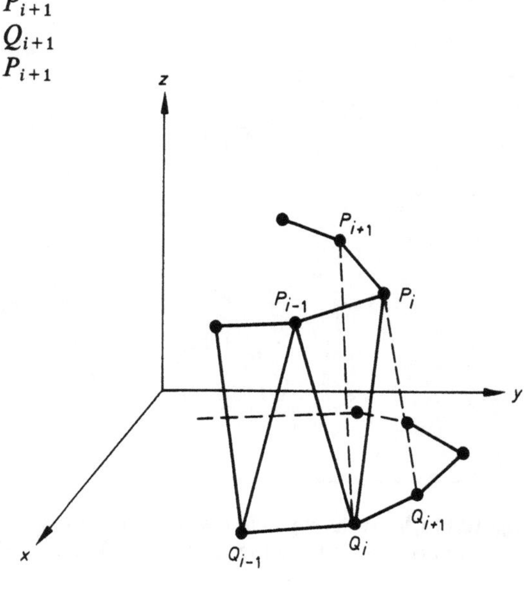

Fig. 10.9. Selection of the next vertex

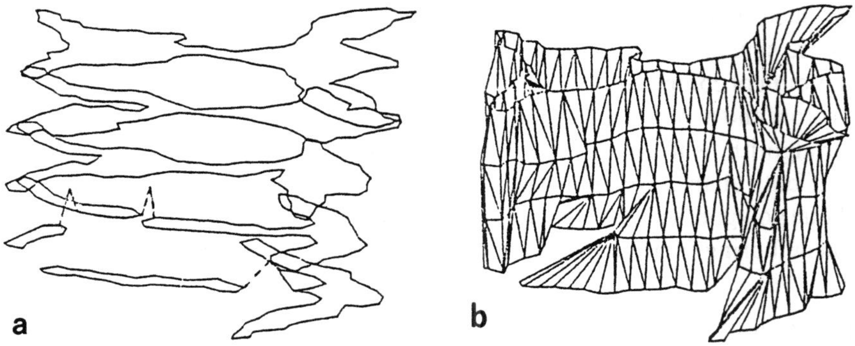

Fig. 10.10a, b. Generated surface patches: (**a**) five sections; (**b**) generated patches

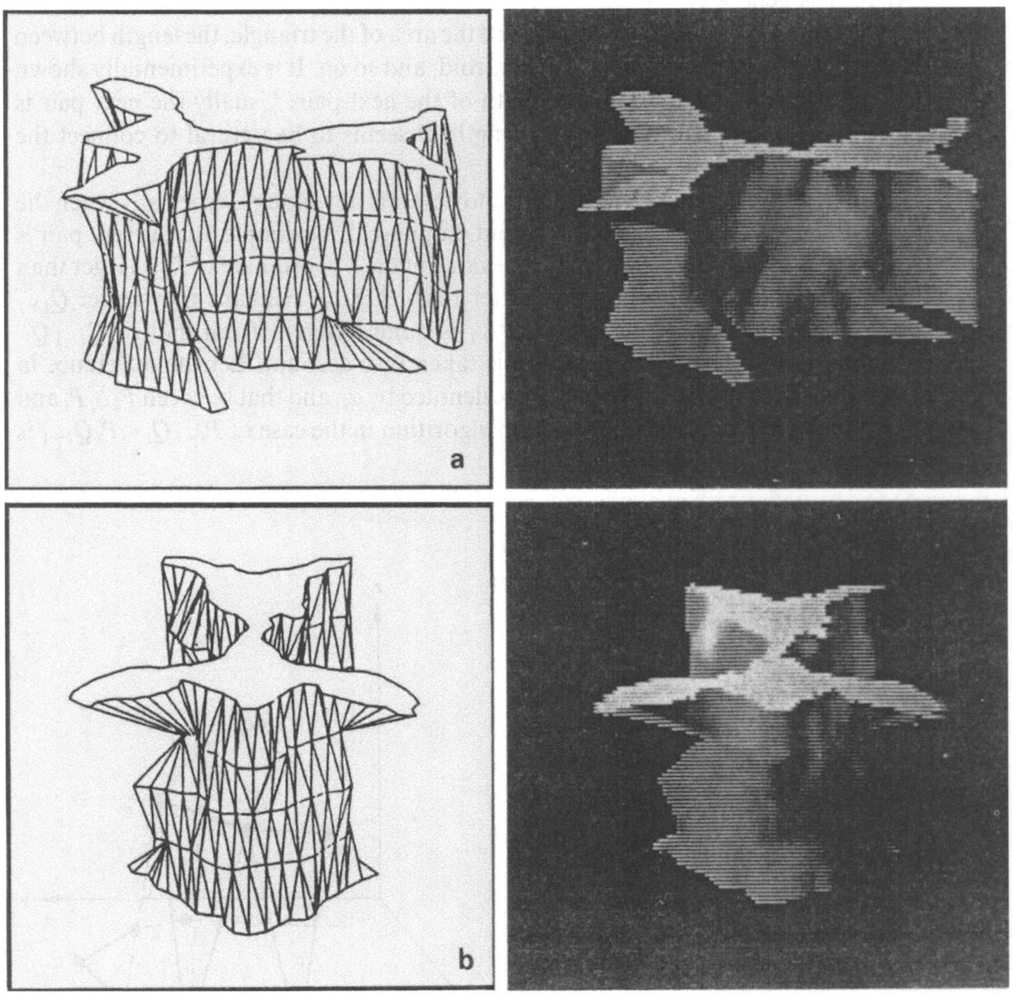

Fig. 10.11a, b. Surface patches with upper horizontal cover and shaded images: (**a**) upper horizontal cover added to Fig. 10.10(b); (**b**) rotated about the z axis

An experimental result is shown in Fig. 10.10. Five serial sections are given in part (a) of the figure. The lowest section consists of two regions and the next section consists of three regions (they are connected by broken lines). The above procedure is applied sequentially for four pairs of sections. The solution is not trivial because the section shape changes considerably between sections. In order to grasp the 3D shape of the reconstructed body, we can synthesize shaded images. For a given direction of illumination, the brightness of each triangle surface patch is computed, and then the whole image is smoothed. Figure 10.11 shows examples for two different orientations of the body.

10.4 Generalized Cylinders

Many objects may be characterized by an axis and cross-sections. Animals, for example, are composed of several principal parts: legs, bodies, and a head. We can define, for each part, an axis and cross-sections. Many such parts may be approximated by cylinders. Generalized cylinders were proposed by Binford (1971) to represent mainly such cylinder-like objects.

The generalized cylinder is a volume description which defines the space taken by an object. Since range data represent only surfaces, the volume description is made by fitting a surface to the range data.

10.4.1 Properties of Generalized Cylinders

Generalized cylinders are a class of objects obtained by extending the definition of a cylinder. An ordinary cylinder is the volume swept out by a circle moving along a straight line axis, with the circle kept normal to the axis.

The definition of a cylinder can be generalized by one or more extensions:

1. The axis may be curved (Fig. 10.12).
2. The radius of the circle may vary as a function of its position along the axis (Fig. 10.13).
3. The cross-section may be some planar shape other than a circle (Fig. 10.14).
4. The cross-section may be held at some nonperpendicular angle to the axis (Fig. 10.15).

Those extensions may be combined (Fig. 10.16).

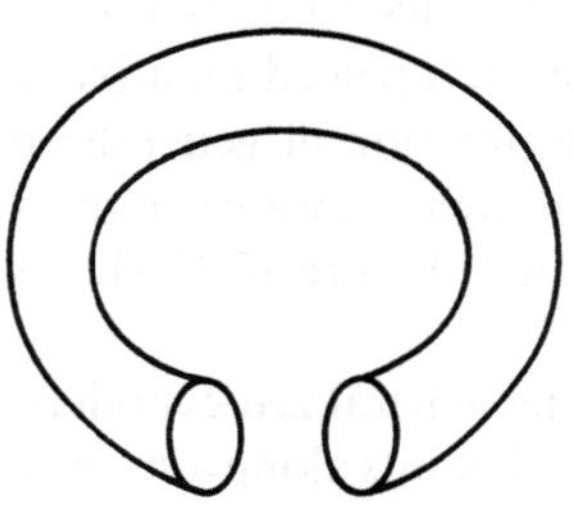

Fig. 10.12. Curved axis generalization of cylinder

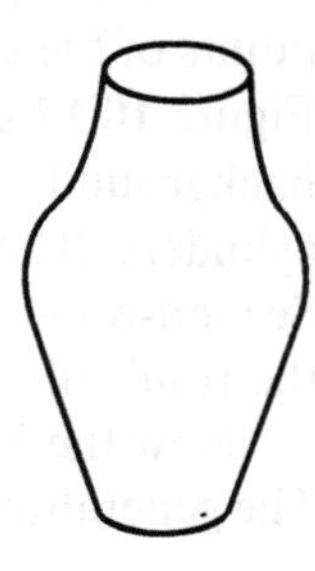

Fig. 10.13. Variable radius generalization of cylinder

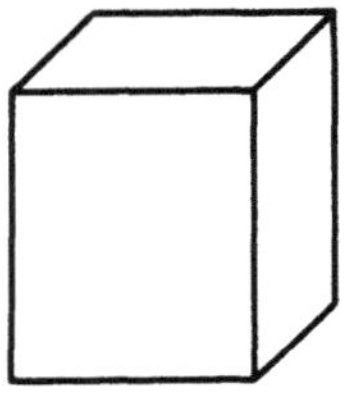

Fig. 10.14. Arbitrary cross-section generalization of a cylinder

Fig. 10.15. Non-normal axis generalization of a cylinder

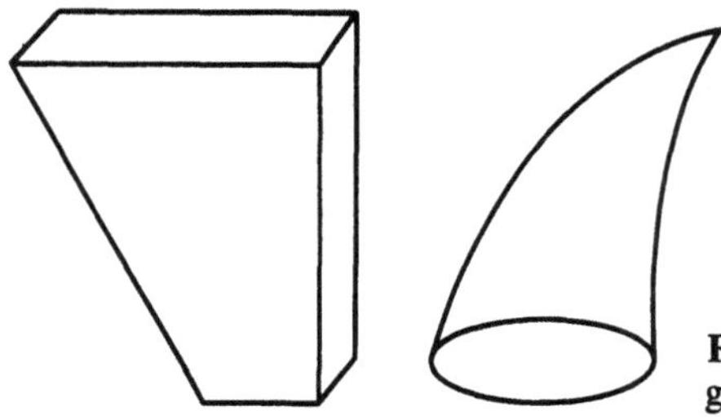

Fig. 10.16. Combination of extensions for generalization of a cylinder

There are infinitely many ways of representing an object by a generalized cylinder. In generating a model of an object, we can choose the best axis and cross-sections. In making a description of range data, however, the choice of the best combination of the axis and the cross-section is not easy. One way to avoid a bad choice is to limit the extensions shown above. For example, the radius of the cross-section may change linearly along the axis.

In object modeling, a complex object is usually represented by a combination of simpler parts. A system for modeling must support such operations as extracting useful geometric properties (e.g., volume, edges, view, etc.) from the model defined by a combination of parts. Currently, such operations can be carried out only on a certain class of shapes. The definition of the generalized cylinder must also be constrained in this respect.

10.4.2 Describing Range Data by Generalized Cylinders

This subsection describes early work on fitting generalized cylinders to real range data (Agin and Binford, 1973; Agin and Binford, 1976). Range data are obtained by a laser ranging system based on a light-stripe method. A scene is scanned by a light plane tilted 45° from a vertical axis, and then scanned again by the light plane tilted 45° to the other side of the vertical axis.

Each image of a light-stripe is thresholded and thinned to obtain the center points of the stripe. Straight lines or second-order curves are fitted to those points. Figure 10.17 shows the result of curve fitting (for a bright doll placed on a black background). These curves are first grouped for initial estimation of generalized cylinders. If adjacent curves are nearly parallel and close enough, they are grouped. Second-order curves are approximated here by straight lines. Figure 10.18 shows the result of grouping.

Now the 3D position of each point is used for extracting generalized cylinders. The generalized cylinder used here is defined as a sequence of points along a smooth

Fig. 10.17. Curves fitted to stripe images from a model of a doll (Agin and Binford, 1976)

Fig. 10.18. Grouping of line segments (Agin and Binford, 1976)

curve (axis), and circular cross-sections with a linear radius function:

$$R(n)=R(0)+kn \tag{10.21}$$

where $R(0)$ and k are parameters, and n means the nth center point along the axis.

The initial estimate of the generalized cylinder is made for each group of curve segments. The midpoints of the segments of Fig. 10.18 are transformed into three dimensions, and used as the estimate of the axis. Figure 10.19(a) illustrates the axis points and straight line segments. This simple example will be used for explaining the following operations. The radius of each cross-section is also estimated from the corresponding 3D curve segment.

The estimate of each generalized cylinder is improved in the following steps:

1. For each point on the axis, determine a cross-section plane normal to the axis direction.
2. For each cross-section plane, find data points in the vicinity of the plane, and obtain an estimate of the diameter of the circle (Fig. 10.19(b) illustrates the initial estimate of the axis and the circles).
3. Fit Eq. (10.21) to the circles.
4. Fit circles of radii determined by the equation to the data points. Center points of the circles are updated (Fig. 10.19(c)).
5. Modify cross-sections if the initial cross-section plane is not perpendicular to the new axis (Fig. 10.19(d)).

When a generalized cylinder is obtained, an attempt is made to extend it until the axis is not extended smoothly or the radius is not represented by Eq. (10.21)

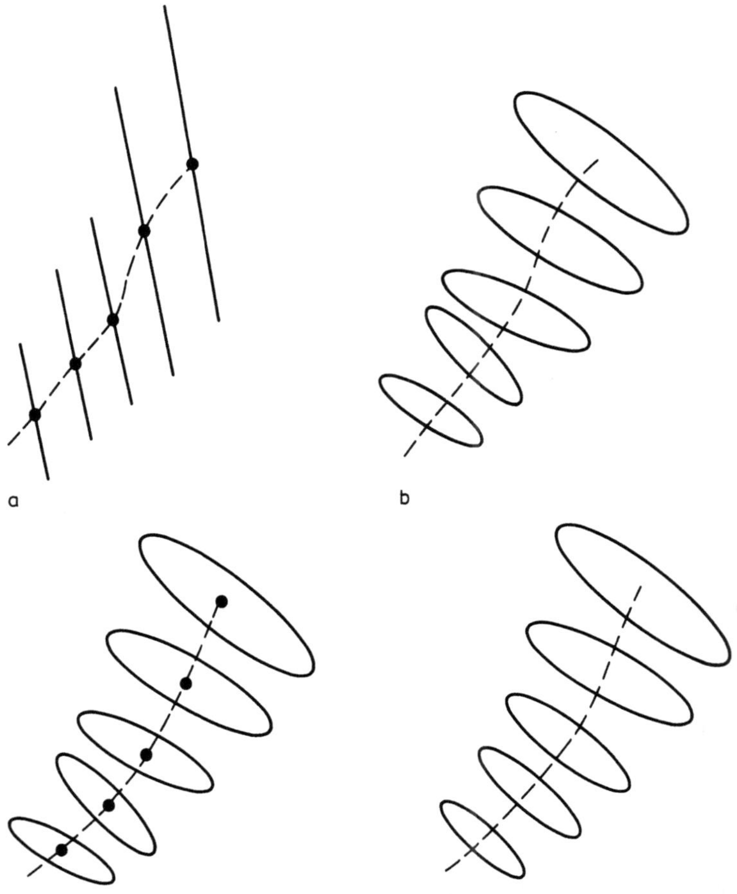

Fig. 10.19a–d. Sequences for obtaining a generalized cylinder: (**a**) initial estimate of axis; (**b**) estimate of circles; (**c**) circles fitted to radius function; (**d**) refined generalized cylinder

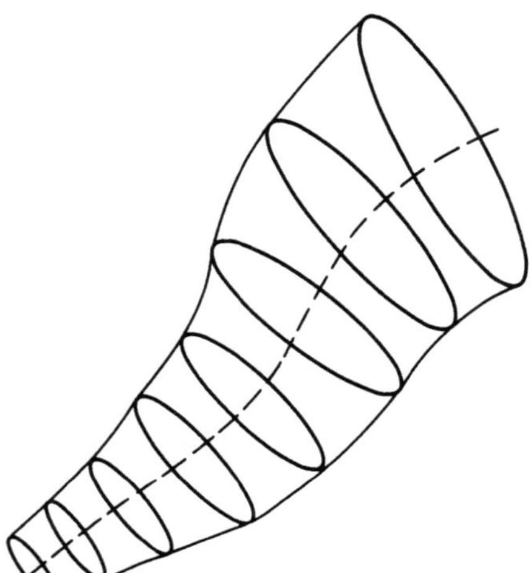

Fig. 10.20. Extended generalized cylinder

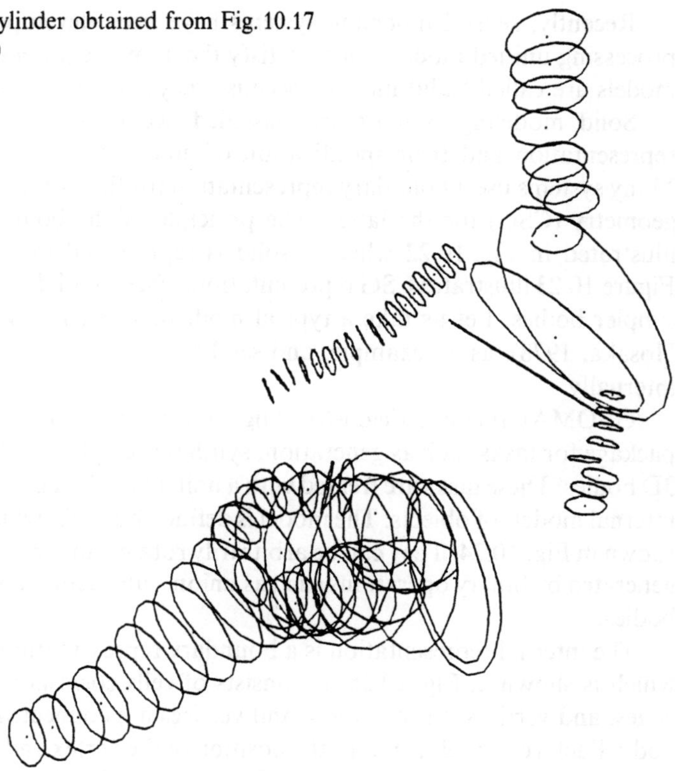

Fig. 10.21. Generalized cylinder obtained from Fig. 10.17 (Agin and Binford, 1976)

(Fig. 10.20). Figure 10.21 shows an example of generalized cylinders obtained by this method.

10.5 Geometric Models

Modeling of 3D objects has been studied in the field of CAD. The goal of modeling is to represent the 3D geometry of objects in a computer. The model must satisfy the following requirements.

1. The geometry of an object is precisely represented so that the object may be created from the model.
2. Various geometrical properties (e.g., volume, centroid, or production drawings) are derived from the model.
3. The model can easily be generated by humans.

The birth of geometric modeling may be traced to the work of Roberts (1963) on recognition of polyhedra as described in Chap. 5. Similar models have been used for computer graphics. Other models have been used for numerical control (NC) programming languages and drawings. Those models, however, did not satisfy the above requirements, since they were made for a single purpose. If we want to use a model for another purpose, we must manually prepare a model in another format.

Recently, several modeling systems have been developed for generating and processing unified models which satisfy the above requirements. These geometric models are called 'solid models' because they unambiguously represent solids.

Solid modeling systems are classified according to their primary internal representation and their specification of input (Requicha and Voelcker, 1982). Many systems use a boundary representation for the former and constructive solid geometry (CSG) for the latter. The principle of the boundary representation is illustrated in Fig. 10.22 where a solid is represented in terms of its boundary. Figure 10.23 illustrates CSG representation, where a solid is represented in terms of simpler bodies. Let us take a typical modeling system, GEOMAP (Kimura and Hosaka, 1978), as an example, and see how objects are defined and represented internally.

GEOMAP (Geometrical Modeling And Processing) is a FORTRAN program package for tasks such as generation, synthesis, display, and kinematic analysis of 3D bodies. These tasks are treated with a unified method of building and processing internal models of objects. The model is defined by CSG, which uses basic bodies as shown in Fig. 10.24. They can be arbitrarily rotated and translated. New bodies are generated by binary operations such as union, subtraction and intersection of basic bodies.

The internal representation is a boundary representation, the data structure of which is shown in Fig. 10.25. It consists of cells corresponding to a body, faces, edges, and vertices. Faces, edges, and vertices are connected by rings through the body. Each vertex cell contains the position of the vertex and a pointer to one of the edges connected to the vertex. Each face cell contains the equation of the face and

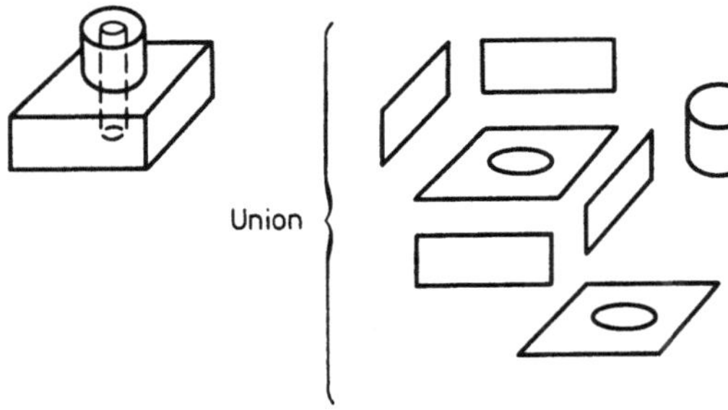

Fig. 10.22. Boundary representation

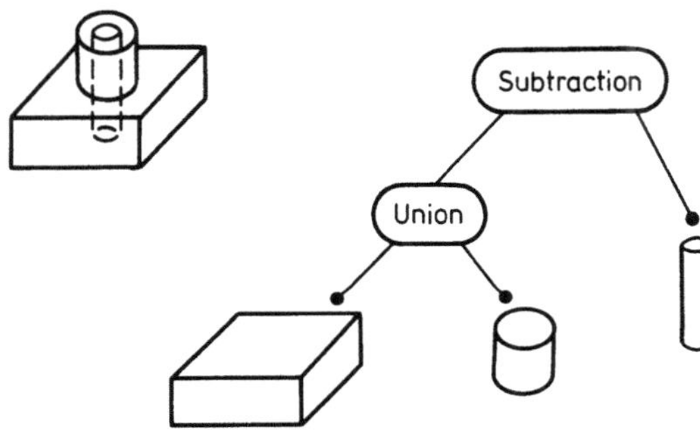

Fig. 10.23. Constructive solid geometry

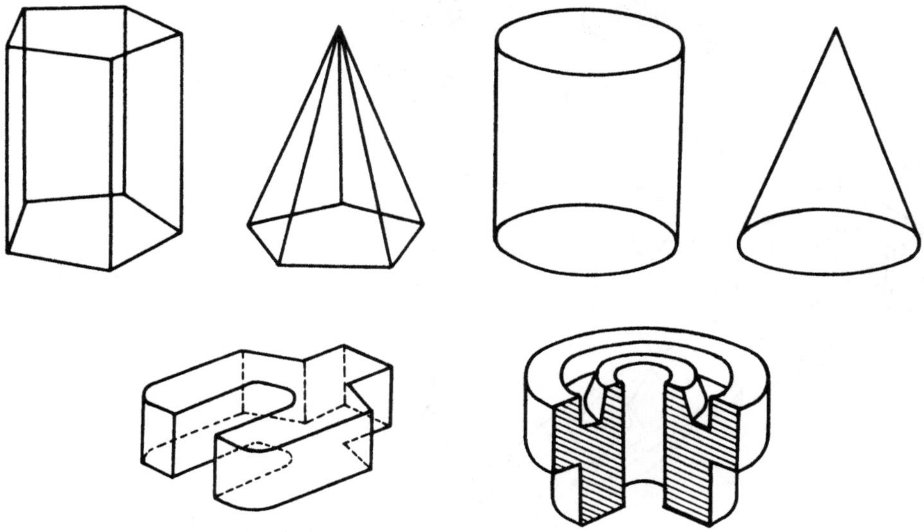

Fig. 10.24. Basic bodies in GEOMAP

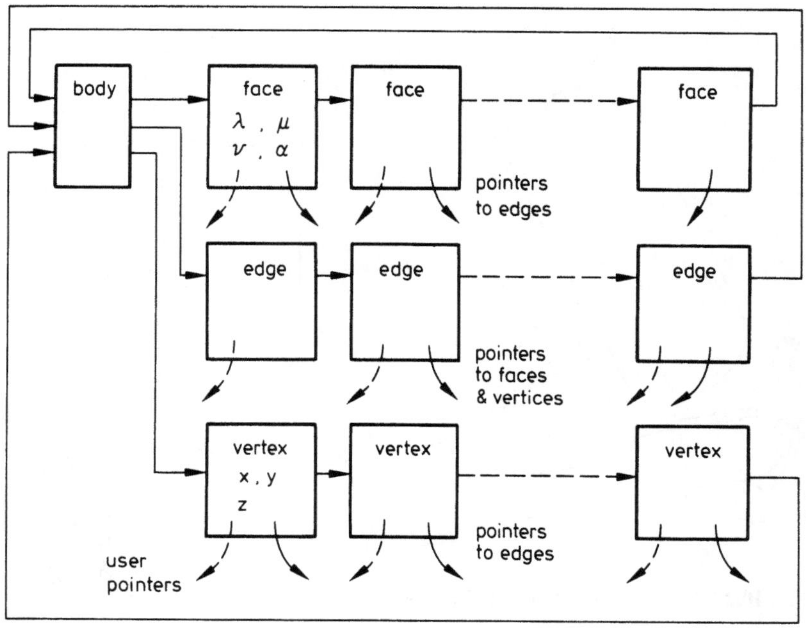

Fig. 10.25. Data structure of GEOMAP

pointers to bounding edges (one edge for a set of bounding edges). Each edge cell contains pointers to vertices in both ends, to faces in both sides, and four adjacent edges which constitute boundaries of the two faces. The body cell contains a transformation matrix between the body coordinate and the space coordinate (common to other bodies).

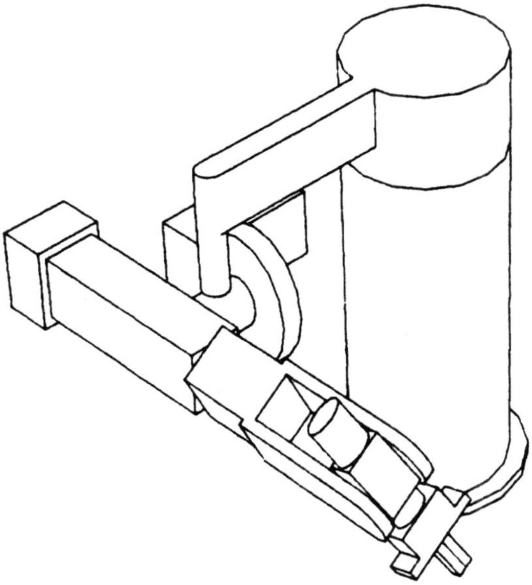

Fig. 10.26. Example of object created by GEOMAP

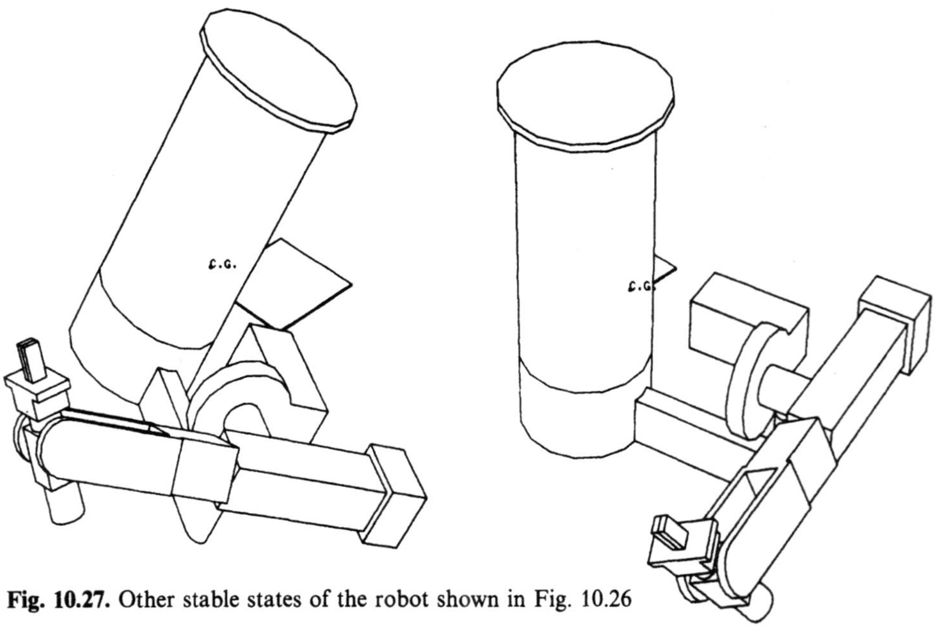

Fig. 10.27. Other stable states of the robot shown in Fig. 10.26

Much useful information about the geometry of an object is accessed by GEOMAP programs. Figure 10.26 shows an example of a perspective drawing of a model of a robot (the model and the drawing are created by GEOMAP). In addition, the user can store in any cell user pointers in order to attach additional information to the cells. For example, areas or perimeters may be stored as properties of faces and used for recognition of the object.

Users can write programs for obtaining geometrical features of objects from models created by GEOMAP. Examples include those for computing moments, strength, or convex hull. Stable states of a polyhedron are easily derived from the convex hull and the center of gravity. Figure 10.27 shows some of the stable states of the robot shown in Fig. 10.26.

10.6 Extended Gaussian Image

Solid models are useful for unambiguously describing objects. In the recognition of objects, however, it is often troublesome to match the scene description to the detail of solid models, especially when models are complex. In such a case, it is desirable to have more simple models which represent objects approximately. An Extended Gaussian Image (EGI) has been proposed as an abstract model of 3D objects (Ikeuchi, 1981b).

The EGI of an object represents the distribution of the surface normals. The surface normal is represented by a well-known 'Gaussian sphere'. A point on the Gaussian sphere corresponds to the surface normal at this point. Figure 10.28 illustrates an example of an EGI, where arrows in (a) show the directions of surface normals, and the length of each arrow in (b) represents the area of surfaces with the same direction (a cylinder is approximated by a prism with many faces). Given a 3D object, the corresponding EGI can easily be generated and used as the model of the object. If the surface normals of an object are obtained, they are described by the EGI (representing only visible surfaces).

The EGI is independent of the position of surfaces. It is known that if objects are convex polyhedra, there is a one-to-one correspondence between the object and the EGI. It is also clear that an EGI may correspond to infinitely many concave objects. Therefore, the EGI is an abstract model which represents a class of objects.

In order to describe the EGI in a computer, we have to tesselate the Gaussian sphere into small cells. The cells should be uniformly distributed and should have the same areas. Since there is no regular polyhedron which has more faces than the

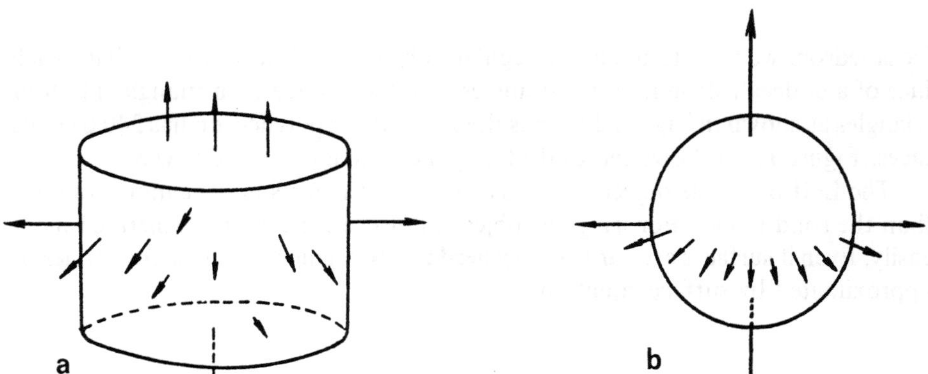

Fig. 10.28a, b. Example of EGI: (**a**) cylinder; (**b**) EGI of cylinder

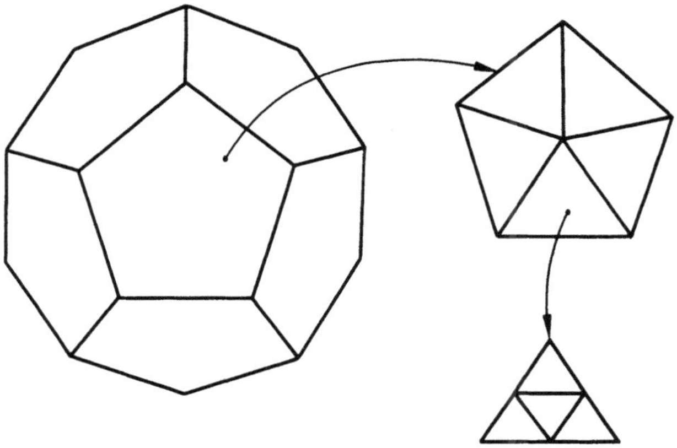

Fig. 10.29. Polyhedral approximation of a sphere

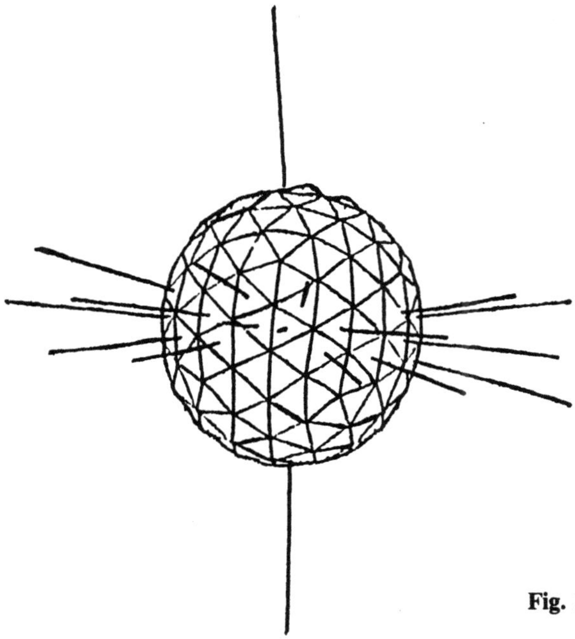

Fig. 10.30. Quantized EGI of a cylinder

icosahedron, we have to use a semiregular polyhedron. One way is to divide each face of a dodecahedron into five triangles, and then divide each triangle into four triangles as shown in Fig. 10.29. Thus the semiregular polyhedron has 240 triangle faces. Figure 10.30 shows the EGI of a cylinder quantized in this way.

The EGI of simple objects such as cylinders or spheres may be more complex than the solid model. For irregular objects, however, the EGI is generated more easily. Even if surfaces are curved, they need not be segmented into simpler ones or approximated by surface equations.

11 Knowledge Representation and Use

Many useful methods for analyzing various images are described above. Although some of those methods are dedicated to particular types of scene, most of them have been developed for various kinds of images. Universal methods, however, are often unsatisfactory for any kind of image. That is, results of image processing do not coincide with what humans expect. For example, results of edge detection may include extra edges caused by noise or shadows but lack many useful edges. Results of edge following are no better than the results of edge detection, and are usually worse because errors in edge detection are amplified by the edge-following process.

It is said that humans use a large amount of knowledge to understand scenes. In computer vision, many efforts have been made to make effective use of knowledge to understand scenes reliably and efficiently.

This chapter surveys types, representation, and utilization of knowledge in computer vision.

11.1 Types of Knowledge

Knowledge is generally classified according to its contents as follows:

Objects:	facts about objects in the world (e.g., prisms have five faces);
Events:	facts about actions and events in the world (e.g., he bought a book);
Performance:	how to do things (e.g., how to ride a bicycle);
Metaknowledge:	knowledge about knowledge (e.g., what knowledge can be used in a certain situation).

In computer vision, two types of knowledge are mainly used currently: objects and metaknowledge, which are also called 'knowledge about scenes' and 'control', respectively.

Knowledge can also be classified according to how it is represented. The simplest way is to describe it in computer programs. More efficient representation methods have been proposed not only in computer vision but also in natural language processing and knowledge engineering. Some typical representation schemes are described below.

11.1.1 Knowledge About Scenes

Knowledge about scenes represents facts about objects in scenes or images. Without other specification, 'knowledge' means this type. The knowledge may be constraints on scenes or, in other words, *a priori* information about scenes.

Knowledge is used at various stages of computer vision. A simple example is interpreting line drawings of polyhedra by matching to object models (knowledge about objects) as described in Chap. 5. This object model is used in the last stage of computer vision. Other examples are given in Chap. 8: knowledge (constraints) is used in extracting 3D information from image features. These constraints are used after image features are extracted. Even in feature extraction, we use implicitly some *a priori* information, such as the knowledge that edges are linear for polyhedral scenes.

In computer vision, knowledge about scenes is often called 'model'. The model can be classified into two types: the 2D model and the 3D model. The 2D model represents properties of images or elements of images (e.g., 'cars are on a road'). The advantage of this 2D model is that it can be matched directly to images or image features. The disadvantage is that 2D models do not represent 3D geometries or 3D relationships between objects. Therefore, 2D models may not be efficient unless a viewpoint or the orientation of objects is fixed.

The 3D model includes properties and relations about 3D positions and shapes of objects in scenes (e.g., 'cars are on a road'). Therefore, 3D models can be used in a variety of conditions. One important problem is how to minimize the effort involved in their generation. Another problem results from the flexibility of 3D models. That is, although 3D models may potentially be effective for various orientations of objects, matching the scene description to models is not easy. These problems will be discussed in later chapters.

11.1.2 Control

In computer vision, it is important to determine which processing step should be performed next. Computer vision usually involves a large amount of complex information processing. In order to carry out processing efficiently with limited computational resources, we must avoid wasteful processing. This issue is called 'control'. Control schemes depend on the goal of the computer vision process and the kinds of knowledge available about scenes.

Vision processing generally consists of various processes as described in Chap. 1. Control of computer vision is characterized by processes that use knowledge. Representative control schemes are described in the following subsections.

11.1.3 Bottom-Up Control

A typical bottom-up control scheme is depicted in Fig. 11.1 (image input is omitted). Since processing depends on input data, it is also called a data-driven process. Knowledge (model) of objects is used only for matching scene descriptions. The lower processes (feature extraction and feature interpretation) are domain independent.

In bottom-up control, raw data are gradually converted into more organized and useful information. The amount of data is compressed as the processing

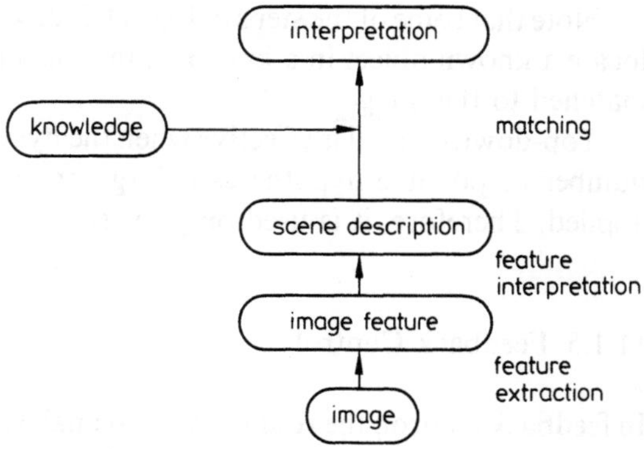

Fig. 11.1. Bottom-up control

proceeds. One of the important advantages of bottom-up control is that objects may easily be changed simply by changing the models of the objects.

On the other hand, the lower processes are not well adjusted to a given particular scene because they are domain independent. Even if some undesirable results are obtained, the vision system does not detect them. The errors may be inherited by the next process, and thus the scene description may involve many errors. In addition, vision processing is inefficient because it is always executed in the same manner regardless of the scene.

11.1.4 Top-Down Control

Top-down control is illustrated in Fig. 11.2. Since processing is controlled by knowledge (model), it is also called a model-driven process. Typically, top-down control is used in a verification vision, which predicts the name or position of objects and verifies the hypothesis. For example, if a white cube is predicted to be on a black desk, the verification vision may extract step type edges near the predicted area to collect enough evidence.

Top-down control is usually very efficient because knowledge about the scene or objects is used in many processes. Only necessary processing is performed by the well-tuned process. Most practical image processing systems use top-down control because of its efficiency.

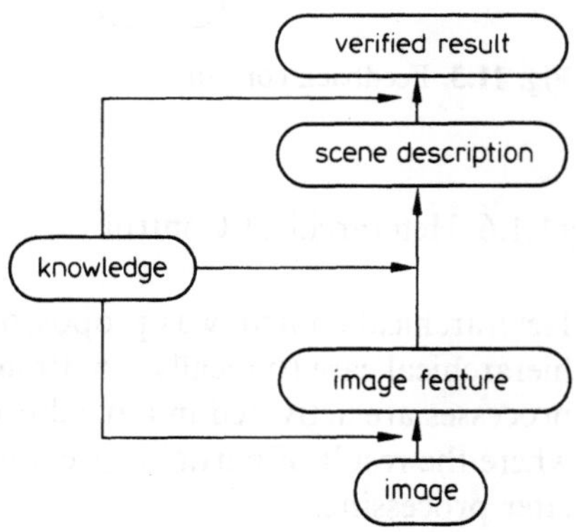

Fig. 11.2. Top-down control

Note that some of the steps in Fig. 11.2 may be skipped. For example, in order to locate a known object in a known plane, the model of the object image is directly matched to the image.

Top-down control is effective when the hypothesis is successfully verified. If the number of possible hypotheses is large or infinite, top-down control cannot be applied. Therefore, it is used only for scenes with strong constraints.

11.1.5 Feedback Control

In feedback control, the result of partial analysis is fed back to lower level processes to improve performance. Figure 11.3 shows an example of this scheme, where the result of feature extraction is fed back to a feature extraction process. In this scheme, *a priori* knowledge about the nature of the features is necessary. The extracted features are examined using that knowledge, and the feature extraction procedure or parameters of feature extraction are improved.

Instead of features, the result of scene description may be fed back to the feature extraction process, or the result of interpretation may be fed back to the interpretation process. In any case, the incomplete result of partial analysis must contain important information to guide the later processing. In such cases, this scheme works effectively even for a noisy input image. Otherwise, feedback information cannot provide much help, and thus wasteful trial-and-error operations may occur between the higher and lower level processes.

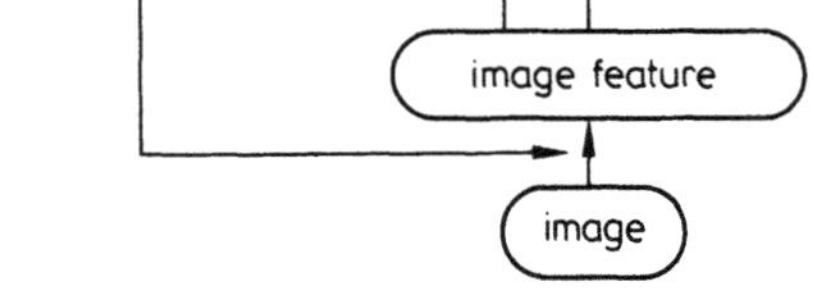

Fig. 11.3. Feedback control

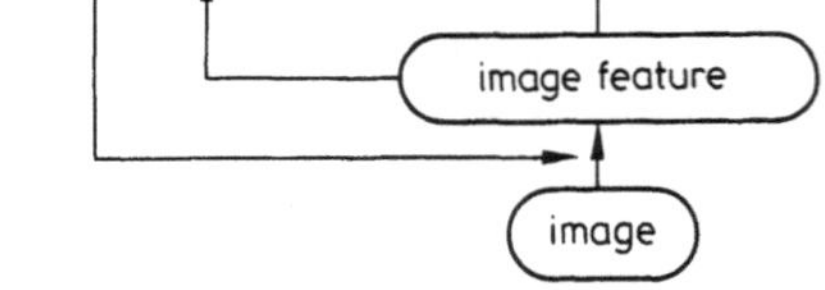

Fig. 11.4. Heterarchical control

11.1.6 Heterarchical Control

Heterarchical control was proposed (Minsky and Papert, 1970) in contrast to the hierarchical case (typically a bottom-up and a top-down control scheme) in which processes are activated in a fixed order. Figure 11.4 depicts heterarchical control, where the result of partial processing at any level is examined and reflected in the later processing.

It is clear that an input image is first processed to a certain extent. But the order of the later processing is not fixed; it rather depends on the input images. Ideally, the most effective processing is performed at any time. This control scheme is most promising for the analysis of complex images.

Heterarchical control can be further classified into two categories according to whether or not knowledge is fed back to the lowest level of image processing. Generally, raw data processing requires much computation. Feedback knowledge is, therefore, very important if wasteful raw data processing can be eliminated by use of the knowledge. However, if higher level processing is activated too early, only poor results are obtained. In that case the feedback knowledge may also be poor and cannot be of much help in the lower level processing.

It is said that lower level processing should work to a certain extent without knowledge of the scene. This is called 'nonpurposive' processing. In a human vision system, a large number of features are extracted by nonpurposive processing in parallel. If various features can be extracted very rapidly, they may be enough for higher level processing. In computer vision, either category is used depending on the situation.

Since heterarchical control is not simple, elegant methods for representing both knowledge about scenes and control are very important. Various knowledge representation schemes have been proposed for heterarchical control. Typical representation schemes are introduced in the following subsection.

11.2 Knowledge Representation

In computer vision, knowledge is represented and used by computers for image analysis. In general, knowledge representation must satisfy the following requirements:

1. A knowledge representation system must be able to handle various kinds of knowledge.
2. It must efficiently store knowledge.
3. It must provide effective access to appropriate knowledge.
4. It must be easily updated by adding, deleting, and changing pieces of knowledge.
5. It must be easily understood by humans.

Some of these requirements are contradictory. For example, in order to satisfy requirement (4), it is desirable to store a set of small pieces of knowledge which are independent of one another. Then, every time knowledge is required, a search is necessary for the piece of knowledge which should be used next; thus requirement (3) is not easily satisfied.

11.2.1 Procedural and Declarative Representations

In the early stages of 3D computer vision research, knowledge was represented in the form of computer programs for image analysis. This is a simple example of procedural representation. Since domain-dependent knowledge is explicitly written as procedures in appropriate places in the program, it is efficiently utilized.

On the other hand, it is not easy to discriminate the parts of the program which represent knowledge. Therefore, it is troublesome for humans to build and update the knowledge. Moreover, distributed knowledge in a program is not readily utilized by other programs.

Procedural representation can have a higher degree of domain independence if it is divided into many modular procedures and each of them is stored in a subprogram. In conventional practice, those subprograms are explicitly called by other programs. Some programming languages for artificial intelligence facilitate automatic calling by patterns of symbol strings. Typical examples are PLANNER (Hewitt, 1972) and CONNIVER (Sussman and McDermott, 1972).

Declarative knowledge, on the other hand, describes static knowledge about objects or relations between them. A simple example is the model of a cube described in Sect. 5.1. It just represents what a cube is. In order to use the representation for recognition of cubes, a matching procedure is necessary. The advantage of the declarative representation is that it can be used for various purposes. When knowledge is organized as a set of declarative representations (it may be called a 'knowledge base'), each representation has greater modularity than in procedural representation. Therefore, the knowledge base can easily be updated.

Declarative representation is often very inefficient. Every time, a vision system must select the best piece of knowledge. Necessary information must be derived from the knowledge base.

There were once disputes about the relative merits of procedural versus declarative representations (Winograd, 1975). If a given task is simple, we may be able to choose the better representation between them. For a complex task, however, neither of them is satisfactory. Recently, mixtures of both representations have been widely investigated. For example, procedural representations have been attached to declarative representations.

The following two subsections introduce declarative representations, and the subsequent three subsections describe useful representations for heterarchical control.

11.2.2 Iconic Models

Iconic models are declarative representations of predicted images. They may be binary images or gray images depending on the input images (input images also depend on scenes). Image processing may be very simple because an input image can be directly matched to the iconic models.

Building iconic models is also easy — we just take images of objects. Therefore, most commerical industrial vision systems utilize iconic models. This scheme is effective only when the number of possible images is small. In 3D computer vision, however, the number of possible images is almost infinite unless the position and orientation of objects are constrained and the illumination condition is fixed.

If an image includes more than one object and their position is not fixed, iconic models of objects may be used. Recognition of objects is carried out first by segmenting an input image into regions which may correspond to objects and then by matching each region to the iconic models (Fischler and Elschlager, 1973). This scheme, however, is effective only when the number of possible objects is small. That is, the orientation of objects must be fixed, no occlusion is allowed, and the illumination condition must not change.

Iconic models are not further described here, since they are not effective for general 3D computer vision.

11.2.3 Graph Models

Graph models represent more abstract properties of objects in images or in 3D scenes. Let us first consider models in images. In graph models, nodes of a graph represent primitives of an image, and arcs represent the relations between primitives. For example, if regions of an image are chosen as primitives, each node may represent properties of the corresponding region, and each arc may represent spatial relations such as inclusion or relative positions.

A typical graph model was used for recognizing isolated curved tabletop objects, such as a cup, a pencil, and spectacles (Barrow and Popplestone, 1971). The primitives in the models are regions. The properties of region A are the following:

1. Compactness: 4π Area (A)/Perimeter (A).
2. Shape: There are six components. These are derived from a Fourier analysis of the ψ–s curve (see Subsection 4.1.2) of the region boundary. The six components are the amplitudes of the first six Fourier components.

The typical relations of region A to region B are the following:

1. Relative area: Area (A)/(Area (A) + Area (B));
2. Adjacency: (Length of boundary between A and B)/Perimeter (A);
3. Distance: (Distance between the centroids)/(Average radius of A);
4. Height: (Vertical distance between the centroids)/(Average radius of A).

Some properties and relations in the model of a cup are shown in Fig. 11.5.

Regions are extracted from an input image by a region method, and the properties and the relations are computed. Since objects are isolated, regions are easily segmented into groups each of which corresponds to an object. The graph representation of objects in a scene is thus created. Each graph is then matched to the graph models.

The graph models are more adaptable than iconic models because they are less sensitive to the illumination condition and small changes in the position and orientation of objects. However, if an object is viewed from different directions, the images may not be represented by the graph model. In Fig. 11.5, for example, the relation between regions A and B may change substantially when the cup is seen from the upper direction.

Graph models of objects in a 3D scene are more flexible because they are independent of the viewer's direction. A model of the cup, for example, may be composed of a bottom, an outside and an inside of a main body, and a handle. Their properties (e.g., shape is conical) and relations (e.g., handle is on outside) are invariant from the viewer's direction.

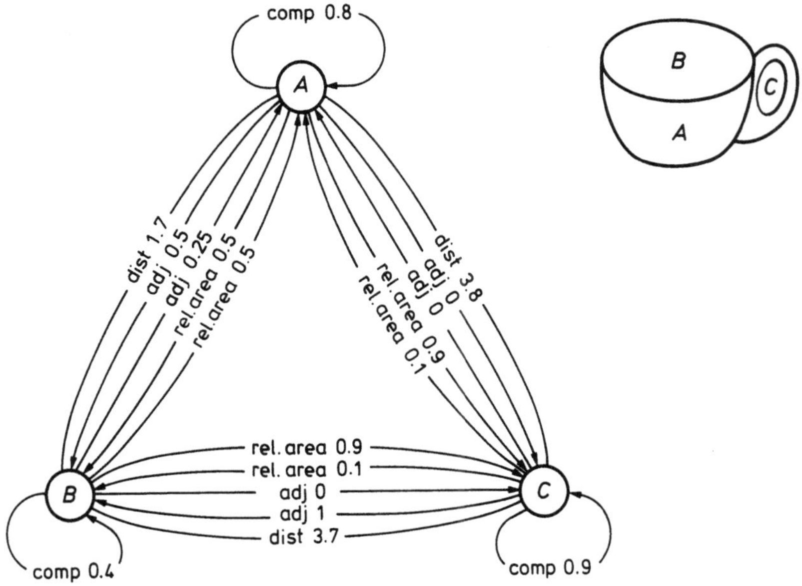

Fig. 11.5. Graph model of a cup (not all the properties and relations are shown in this figure)

On the other hand, those models cannot be directly matched to the features of images. One way to utilize such models is to obtain a scene description from an input image to be matched to the models. Another way is to predict the image of an object on the assumption of the orientation of an object to be matched to the image of the object. Examples of such models are given in other chapters below.

11.2.4 Demons

When knowledge is utilized, items of knowledge are often called by other items. In conventional programs, procedures call other procedures by their names. In some programming languages (e.g., PLANNER), procedures are called by patterns. A procedural representation called a 'demon', on the other hand, is activated by the state of processing (values of variables) which is called the 'global database'. Each demon watches the global database as shown in Fig. 11.6 until a specified condition is satisfied, and then it starts to work. That is, the activation of a demon is not specified in other procedures but in the demon itself.

The notion of the demon is used in various fields. In computer operation systems, for example, the condition of the computer is monitored. When abnormal conditions are detected (abnormality of power, input/output error, etc.), the cause of the abnormality is stored in a specified memory address, and the computer stops. This can be regarded as the work of demons watching the conditions for their activation.

Demons have been used in natural language understanding (Charniak, 1972) for representing common-sense knowledge. For instance, a piece of common sense, 'to

Fig. 11.6. Schematic figure of demons: two demons watch the situation while a third, activated by a specified situation, processes the global database

buy things money is paid', is stored in a demon which is watching input sentences. When it encounters the word 'buy', it suggest that money is paid. Thus the following sentences are understood: 'I bought many books. I now have little money'.

In computer vision, a demon can be used for representing both knowledge about scenes and control. In the interpretation of aerial photographs, for instance, the following knowledge is stored in a demon:

1. The bridge is located after an intersecting road and river is found.
2. The bridge is found by detecting a structure along the road across the river.

The demon watches the process of image analysis, and when an intersecting road and river are found, it starts to work to find a bridge according to procedure 2 specified above.

Demons provide modular representation of knowledge as shown in the above example. If many demons are watching the process, the computational cost may be high. Therefore, it is desirable to control demons (make demons wake and sleep). The concept of the demon is also shared by other knowledge representations such as production systems and blackboards, which are described in the following articles.

11.2.5 Production Systems

Production systems, developed by Newell and Simon (1972) for their models of human cognition, are widely used in the field of AI as a modular knowledge representation scheme. While demons are used in combination with procedures, production systems represent knowledge as a set of demons called 'production rules'.

Each production rule is in the form of a condition–action pair: 'If this condition occurs perform this action'. The condition consists of clauses connected by 'and' conjunctions. An example of a rule is the following:

Rule 1: IF a region is a long stripe region and it is classified as asphalt, THEN the region is a road.

Rule 2: IF a region is a long stripe region and it is classified as water, THEN the region is a river.

Rule 3: IF a region is small region and it is classified as concrete or iron, THEN the region is a man-made structure.

Rule 4: IF a region is at the intersection of a road and a river and it is a man-made structure, THEN it is a bridge.

A set of production rules is a knowledge base. In solving a problem, we need a controller which uses rules in a suitable sequence to obtain a solution. This controller is called an 'inference engine' because it deduces new facts by combining rules.

The inference scheme is roughly divided into forward inference and backward inference. In the above example, the forward inference may first use Rule 1 to Rule 3, and then find a road using Rule 4. The backward inference, on the other hand, first uses Rule 4 to find a road, and then uses Rule 1 to Rule 3 in order to satisfy the condition of Rule 4.

Production systems have been found useful as a clear formalism of representation of declarative and procedural knowledge. They have been used in several application systems called expert systems (Cohen and Feigenbaum, 1982). Examples includes medical diagnosis and diagnosis of machine faults. However, there have been few applications in computer vision; the main reason is that production systems are suitable for handling symbols but not very effective for signal processing. The development of interfaces between symbols and signals is required to make production systems really useful in computer vision.

11.2.6 Blackboards

A blackboard is a data structure which represents states of information processing. It was first proposed for a speech comprehension system called HEARSAY-2 (Lesser and Erman, 1977). Speech comprehension requires a variety of knowledge sources. The knowledge sources (KSs) are viewed as independent modules of expertise. In the HEARSAY model, the independent KSs for phonetics, syntax, semantics and the world were thought of as independent processes that examine the input speech signal and the results of other processes. Hypotheses generated by the phonetic KSs may be examined for feasibility by syntactic and semantic KSs; these, in turn, make suggestions about what words might be expected and post them on the blackboard.

The concept of blackboard is used for computer vision systems such as VISIONS (Hanson and Riseman, 1978) and an aerial photograph analyzer (Nagao, Matsuyama and Ikeda, 1979). The knowledge sources are feature extraction routines, region classification routines and object recognition routines as shown in Fig. 11.7.

When an input image is given, a feature extraction routine segments the image into regions (called elementary regions) that are homogeneous in multispectral properties. In the next stage, regions are classified according to the shape and spectral properties into large homogeneous regions, long stripe regions, vegetation regions and so forth by corresponding region classification routines. Note that a region may have multiple classifications (e.g., a large, homogeneous, vegetation region). The classified regions are called 'feature regions'.

When feature regions are posted on the blackboard, object recognition routines identify objects such as forest, crop field, road, car, house, etc. Some of the routines

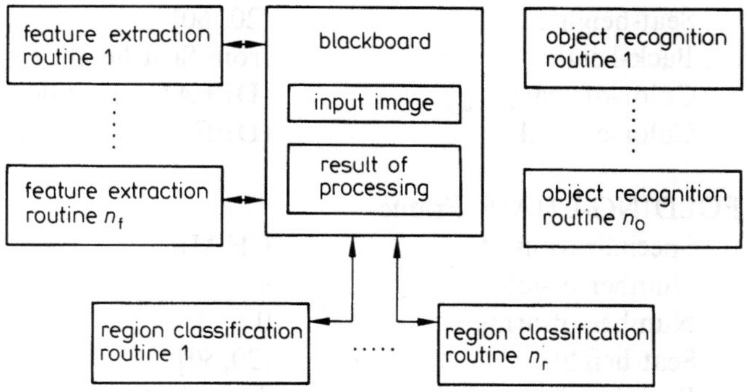

Fig. 11.7. Blackboard for aerial photograph analysis

are activated by the result of other routines. For example, the recognition routine of a car starts when it finds a road region on the blackboard.

Since each KS works independently, an elementary region may be recognized as multiple objects. Such conflicts are resolved on the basis of the confidence values of recognition results. KSs are regarded as production rules which interact with one another interfaced by the blackboard. However, each KS usually contains a larger chunk of knowledge than a production rule.

11.2.7 Frames

Frames were originally proposed by Minsky (1975) as a knowledge representation scheme for computer vision and natural language understanding. A frame is a data structure for representing a stereotyped object or situation, like a certain kind of chair or being in a room. It is said that when one encounters an object or situation, one selects a proper frame from a collection of frames and understands the object or situation according to the frame.

There have been several languages which support frame-like knowledge representation. Typical examples are FRL (Roberts and Goldstein, 1977), KRL (Bobrow and Winograd, 1977), and UNITS (Stefik, 1979). The common features of these languages are as follows. Frames are organized in a hierarchy and a property is inherited from frames at a higher level. For example, a frame of a particular folding chair inherits properties from the FOLDING-CHAIR frame, which also inherits properties from the CHAIR frame.

A piece of knowledge is written in a 'slot' as a slot value. A frame may contain many slots. Simple examples are shown here:

CHAIR Frame

Specialization-of:	FURNITURE
Use:	for sitting
Number-of-legs:	(DEFAULT=4)
Number-of-arms:	0, 1, or 2

Seat-height:	[20, 60]
Back-height:	from Seat-height to [70, 120]
Color-of-seat:	(DEFAULT = GRAY)
Color-of-back:	(DEFAULT = GRAY)
FOLDING-CHAIR Frame	
Specialization-of:	CHAIR
Number-of-legs:	4
Number-of-arms:	0
Seat-height:	[20, 50]
Back-height:	from Seat-height to [70, 100]
FOLDING-CHAIR-1 Frame	
Specialization-of:	FOLDING-CHAIR
Color-of-seat:	BROWN
Color-of-back:	BROWN
Seat-height:	45
Back-height:	from Seat-height to 80

It can be seen that a large amount of knowledge can be efficiently stored in frames by the mechanism of property inheritance.

In the above example, the value of the slot 'Specialization-of' points to another frame. Names of color, 'Gray' and 'Brown', also point to other frames which may represent properties of those colors. The above three frames may provide useful information to find the folding chair in a scene. For example, the back of the chair may be located by finding a brown surface at the specified height. When it is found, the back can be sought just above the seat.

The slot value may be a procedure to compute the value. With the procedure various relations with other slots are represented. Thus frames are able to represent procedural knowledge as well as declarative knowledge.

Frames are often contrasted to production systems. Since a frame stores a larger chunk of knowledge, related facts are retrieved more efficiently. While knowledge is represented in a more rigid structure, frames are less flexible for inferring new facts. For the comprehension of scenes with stereotyped objects, frames seem to be a more promising scheme. Systems have recently been developed which provide features of both frames and production systems.

12 Image Analysis Using Knowledge About Scenes

This chapter deals with methods of heterarchical control in which low level image processing is guided by *a priori* knowledge about scenes and partial results of the scene interpretation. It is clear that if scenes are strongly constrained, that is, knowledge about details of the scenes is available, a very efficient method of scene analysis may be devised. However, it is applicable only to that particular type of scene. We must, therefore, avoid the imposition of an *ad hoc* constraint. In the following sections, only simple constraints are imposed on types of objects and they are effectively used.

12.1 Analysis of Intensity Images Using Knowledge About Polyhedral Objects

At the early stage of computer vision research, scenes with blocks were dealt with because they seemed to be recognized from low resolution images using little computation. This is true if a scene comprises a single block in a uniform background. If a scene includes many objects occluding one another, recognition becomes very difficult.

In most work on recognition of blocks feature points were first found in an entire image, to make a complete line drawing using those feature points, and then the line drawing was interpreted. But it proved very difficult to work out a complete line drawing in this way. If the line drawing had some errors, further analysis on that basis was likely to lead to serious mistakes.

This section describes an attempt to recognize objects without a rigid ordering of processing steps and with fuller use of previous results as analysis proceeds (Shirai, 1973b; Shirai, 1975a). It is assumed that the difference in brightness between objects and background is large, and that objects in scenes are convex trihedral polyhedra without shadows.

12.1.1 General Strategy

The basic strategy is shown in Fig. 12.1. First, the contour lines are extracted on the basis of the *a priori* knowledge that contrast between the objects and the background is high. If more than one contour line is found, as in Fig. 12.2, which has one contour for bodies B1, B2, B3 and another for body B4, then the subsequent processing proceeds independently on the separate groups. Two kinds of global strategy are employed in block 2 in Fig. 12.1.

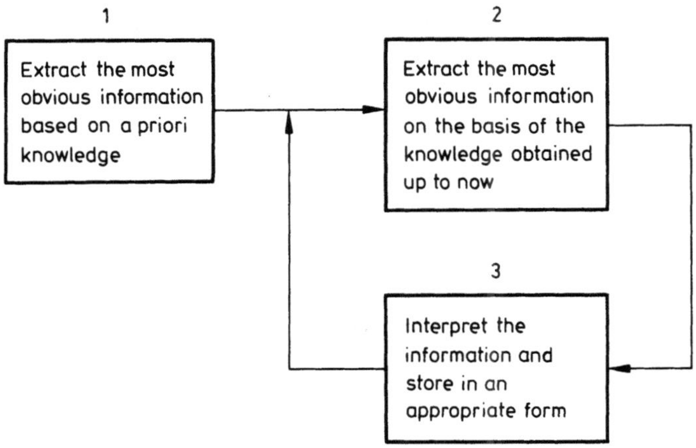

Fig. 12.1. Schematic diagram of the basic strategy

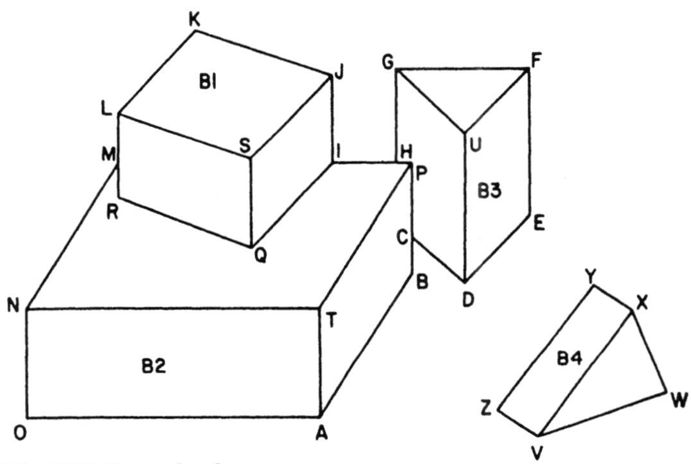

Fig. 12.2. Example of a scene

The first strategy is concerned with the order of line finding. Boundary lines (including cracks) should be found before internal lines, because they are more easily predicted from contour lines and they are often good clues for guessing internal lines. Note that to find boundary lines is to find bodies.

The next strategy is concerned with a search area. In searching for lines, different situations require examination of larger or smaller areas. Higher priority is given to the search of a smaller area. In Fig. 12.2, for instance, to determine the existence of an extension of line BC, it is enough to search a smaller area whose center is on the extension of the line. To find line IQ, however, we should consider all possible directions of a line between IH and IJ. Thus the former search has priority over the latter.

12.1.2 Contour Finding

The input image usually consists of a large number of pixels (say 256 × 256). To speed up the search for contour points, one in every 8 × 8 points is sampled. Thus compressed, the image consists of 1/64 of the number of pixels in the original image. To find a contour, these data are scanned until a contour point is found. Discovery of a contour point is based upon the simple assumption that there is always enough contrast between the background and objects to distinguish them easily. It is then checked whether or not the candidate pixel is a noise point. If the neighboring pixels are also candidates, it is a real contour.

From the contour point, the contour is followed (see Subsect. 4.4.1). In this manner, a set of contour points is found. Then the remainder of the image is again scanned until a new contour point is found. This process is repeated until the entire image has been examined and all the contour points are known.

Now each contour is separately analyzed. The program returns to the original high resolution image. It can approximate the position of a contour point in the original image by supposing it corresponds to the first point found in the sampled image. The precise contour point is sought near this approximation. A set of refined contour points is obtained by following from the precise point in the same way as in the sampled image. A polygon is formed after contour points are connected one by one. To divide the points of this 'curve' into segments, the *k*-curvature is used.

If we sum the curvatures of consecutive points and find the absolute value is greater than some threshold, we can determine the existence of a vertex (see Fig. 12.3). Thus every contour point is classified as being either in the straight part of a line or near a vertex. Using points which belong to the straight part of a line, the equation of the line is calculated. The vertices are obtained as intersections of adjacent lines. Note that determination of vertices based on the curvatures is difficult.

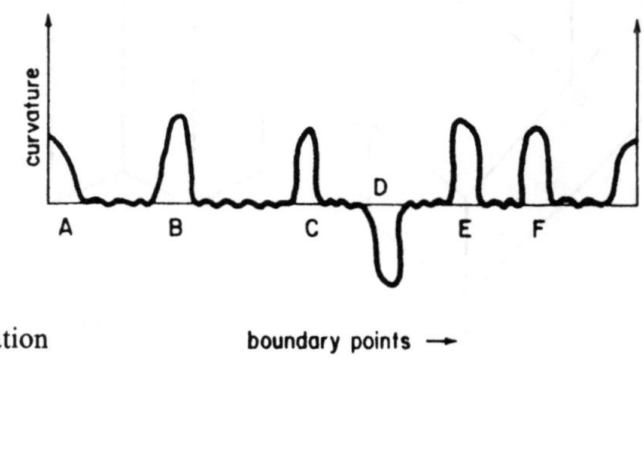

Fig. 12.3. Example of vertex determination

12.1.3 Hypothesizing Lines

Extracting the most obvious information first dictates the following order for the ten heuristic line-proposing steps:

1. If two boundary lines make a concave point (such as the points B in Fig. 12.4), try to find colinear extensions of them. If only one extension is found, follow this line. Most such cases are like the one in Fig. 12.4(b) where one body hides the other. It is easy to see to which body this line belongs.
2. If no extensions of two concave lines are found, try to find another line which starts from the concave point. If one line is found, follow this line. Most of these cases are as in Fig. 12.4(c), where it is not clear locally to which body this line belongs. In Fig. 12.4(c) line BD belongs to the upper body, but this is not always true. That is, the lines AB, BC, BD are not sufficient to form the basis of a decision.
3. If extensions of both lines are found at a concave point, as in Fig. 12.4(d), try to find a third one. If only one new line is found, follow this line.

Whenever line following terminates, an attempt is always made to connect the new line to the other lines already found. If more than one line segment is found in

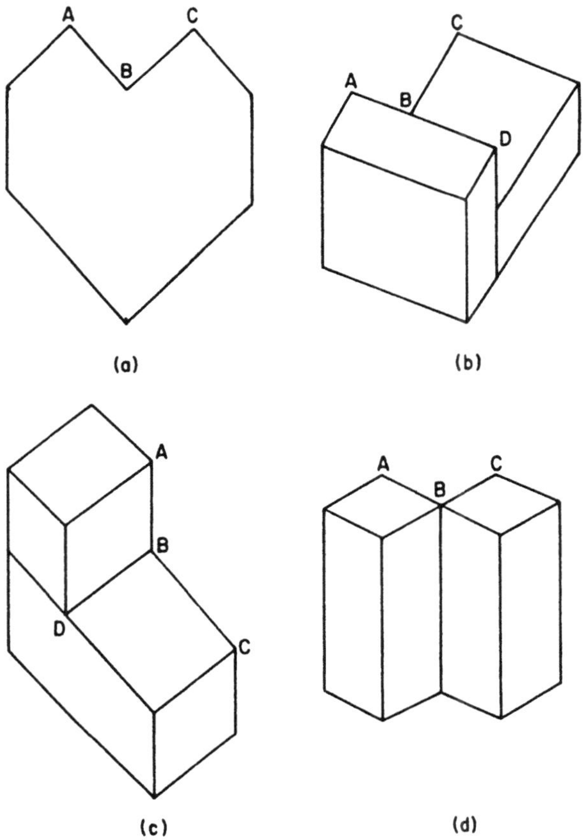

Fig. 12.4. Concave boundary lines

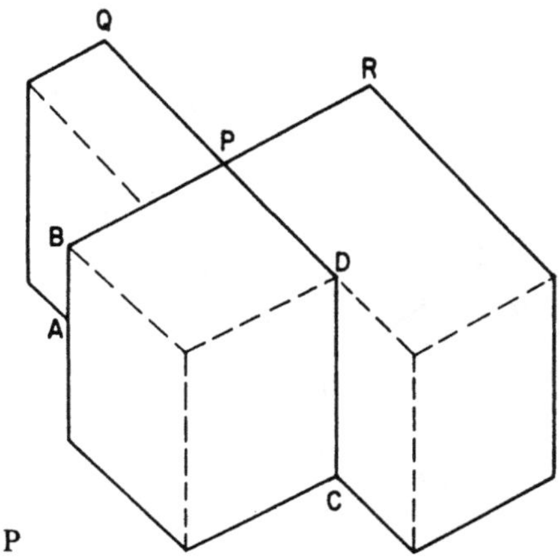

Fig. 12.5. Two extension lines at a concave point P

(1), (2) or (3), the following of all those lines is deferred and it is hoped that the position will be clarified by the results obtained in simpler cases. Figure 12.5 illustrates two extensions found at concave point P. The interpretation of the two lines is deferred in order to treat simpler cases first. That is, one would continue examining the contour, and lines AB and CD might be found next; then, by a circular search (which is explained below) at point B, line BP would be found. At this stage it is easier to interpret lines AB and BP as boundary lines which separate two bodies. Then line DP would be found similarly and interpreted correctly.

4. If an end of a boundary line is left unconnected, as for PQ in Fig. 12.6, try to find the line starting from the end point (Q in this example) by circular search. If multiple lines are found, try to decide which line is the boundary. If a boundary line is determined, follow it. In this figure, the dotted lines are found by circular search and the arrows show the boundary lines to be followed.
5. If no line is found by the circular search, extend the line (PQ in this example) by a certain length and test if the line is connected to other lines. If not, then apply circular search again as in (4). This is necessary because the termination point of the line following is not always precise. Note that this process can be repeated until successful (that is, either the line is connected to other lines or line segments are found by circular search).
6. If the boundary lines of a body are known, select those vertices of the boundary that might have internal lines starting from them. The selection of vertices is based on heuristics such as selecting an upper right vertex rather than a lower right vertex. At each vertex, try to find an internal line which is nearly parallel to other boundary lines. If one line is found, follow it. In Fig. 12.2, internal line JS is parallel to the boundary lines KL and IQ, and QS is parallel to RL and IJ. Line FU is parallel to ED, and XV is parallel to YZ. Thus it is often useful to search for internal lines parallel to boundary lines of the same body. Note that this search for parallels covers only a small area.
7. If no line is found in (6), try to find one by circular search between adjacent boundary lines. When one line is found, track along it. In Fig. 12.7 circular search between BA and BC is necessary to find the internal line BE.

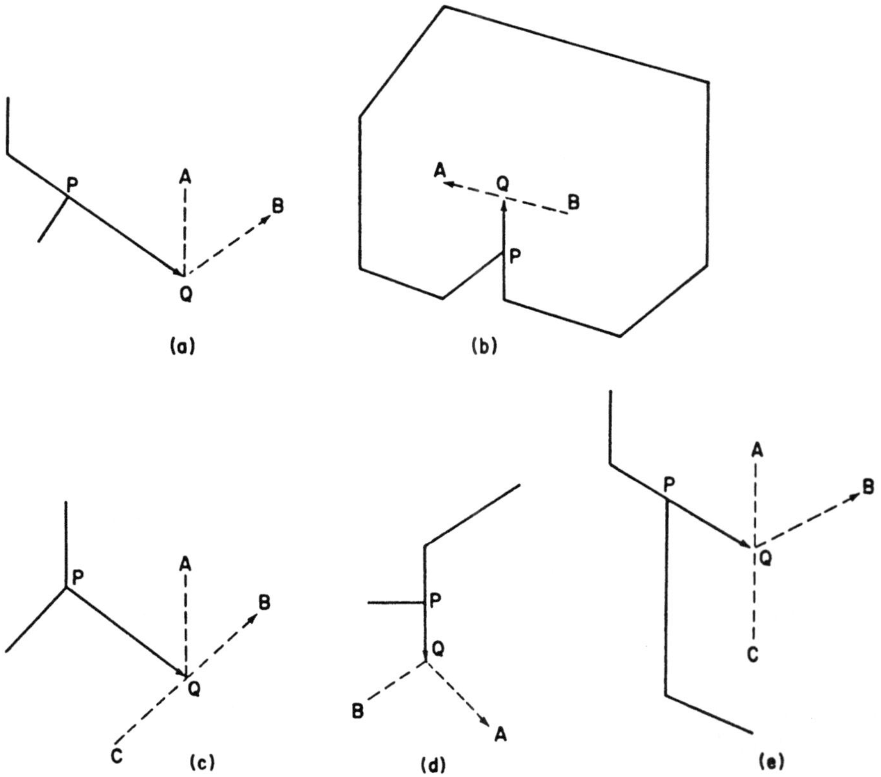

Fig. 12.6. Lines found by circular search

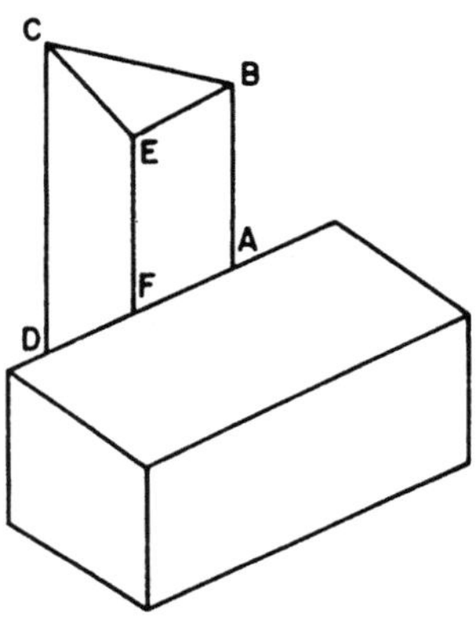

Fig. 12.7. Circular search for internal lines

8. If two internal lines meet at a vertex, try to find another internal line starting at the vertex. This process is useful in two cases. One is where no internal line was found in (7) because of little difference in brightness between adjacent faces. Suppose in Fig. 12.2, that the internal line SJ were not found at vertex J, but that LS and QS were found. Then try to find an internal line starting at S toward J. If there is enough contrast near S, a line segment is found.

The other case is where a body is partly hidden by other bodies. In Fig. 12.7, the triangular prism is partly hidden. After BE and CE are found, EF is sought. Sometimes the direction of the line is predictable and sometimes it is not. If it is predictable, then try that direction. If it is unpredictable or if the predicted direction fails, then apply circular search between the two internal lines. If one line is found, track along it.

9. If an end of an internal line is not connected to any line, try to find lines starting from the end by circular search. If lines are found, follow them one by one.
10. If no line is found in (9), extend the line by a certain length as in (5) and test whether it is connected to other lines. If not connected, try circular search again as in (9). This process can also be repeated until successful. Figure 12.8 illustrates this process. In Fig. 12.8(a) line MN′ is not connected to others at N′, thus step (9) is tried at N′ and fails. The line is extended to P1 and step (9) is again applied. This process is repeated until the line is connected to line KL at N. Figure 12.8(b) shows that line HI is extended by this process to P2 where a new line is found by circular search. Similarly, line CG is extended to P4. This helps to find bodies on obscured edges.

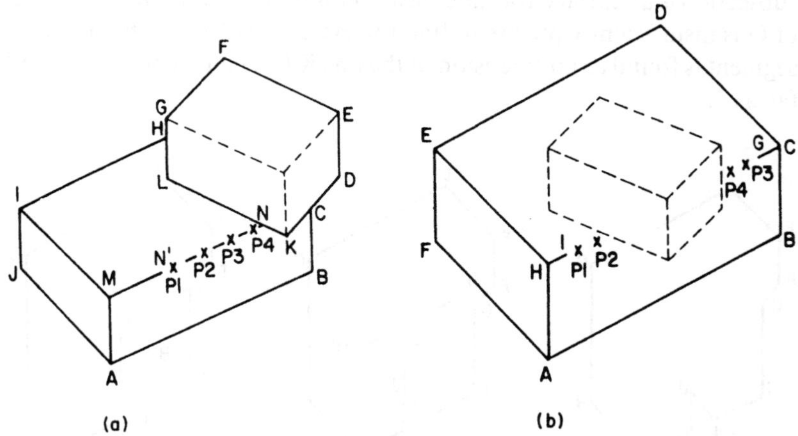

Fig. 12.8. Line verification by circular search. *Dotted lines* are not yet found at this stage

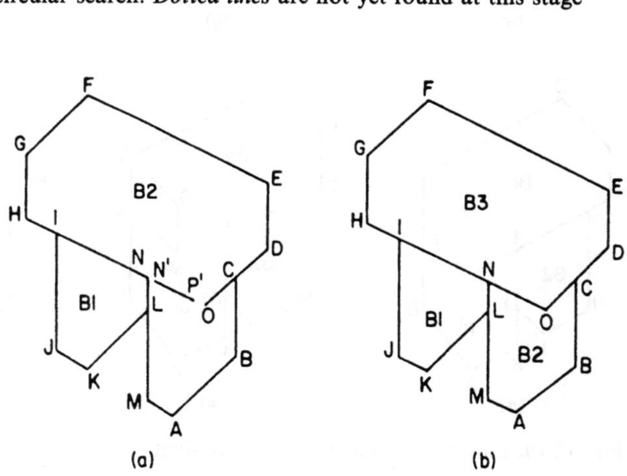

Fig. 12.9. Splitting a body into two new bodies

Whenever one of the above steps is finished, considerable information is stored. It is then available to help guide further search. For instance, if line following terminates, a test is made to see if the line is an extension of other known lines or if the line is connected to a known vertex. If a new boundary line connects two known boundary lines, the body is split into two. In Fig. 12.9(a), line N′P′ is obtained by tracking from point N. This line is interpreted as an extension of HN, and N′P′ are merged into one straight line using the equations of these two lines. It is then connected to CO and Fig. 12.9(b) is obtained. Before the line was connected to CO, there were two bodies B1 and B2 as in Fig. 12.9(a). Now body B2 is split into two bodies, B2 and B3. We can interpret line NO as the boundary of B3 which hides a part of B2. Other properties of lines and vertices are obtained similarly at this stage.

12.1.4 Example of Line-Finding Procedure

The entire line-finding procedure is illustrated with the aid of the example shown in Fig. 12.10. First, the contour lines AB, BC, CD, DE, EF, FG, GH, HI, IJ, JK and KA are obtained as shown in Fig. 12.10(a). Step (1) described in the previous subsection is attempted for the concave points G and J. In this example, the position of G is insufficiently precise to find the extension of FG. On the other hand, a line segment is found as an extension of the line KJ. KJ is extended by edge-following as far as L.

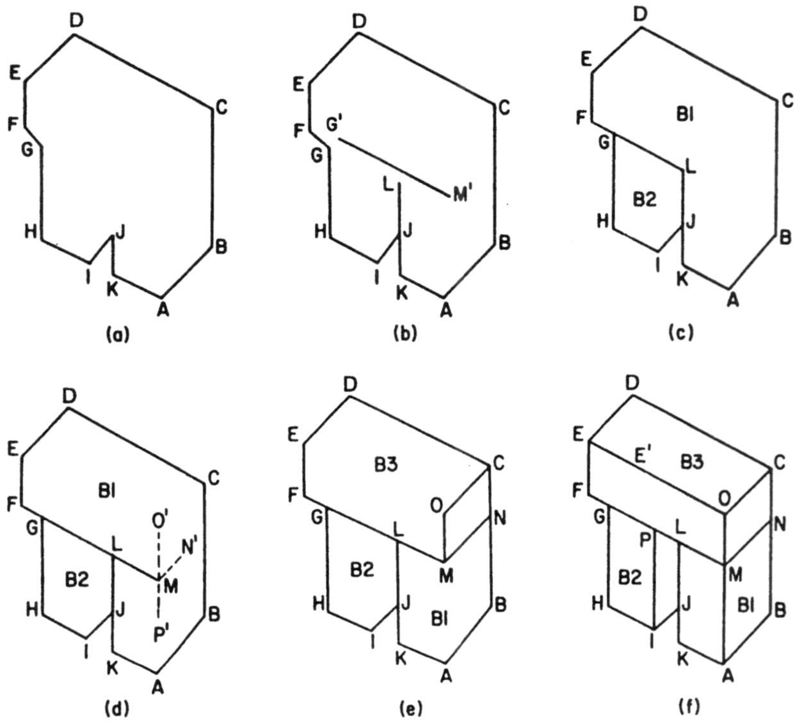

Fig. 12.10. Illustration of steps for line finding

Because there is no other point to which step (1) is applicable, step (2) is attempted for point G. One line segment is found and extended until line following terminates. Thus a line G′M′ is obtained as in Fig. 12.10(b). This line is interpreted as an extension of FG and connected to JL. Then the positions of points, F, G, L are adjusted as shown in Fig. 12.10(c). Now two bodies B1 and B2 are created by the boundary lines GL and JL. It is important to notice this, for it means that step (1) is again applicable at this stage to point L. Thus line FL is extended as far as M in Fig. 12.10(d). (Note that line MN′ has not yet been found.) LM is interpreted as an extension of FL but the end point M is not connected to any other lines. Vertices F, G, L and end point M are adjusted considering the line LM.

Here none of steps (1), (2), or (3) is applicable, so that (4) is now applied to M. Three lines are found by circular search, as in Fig. 12.10(d). MN′ is determined as a boundary line and extended by edge following. When it terminates, the line is connected to boundary line BC at vertex N, as in Fig. 12.10(e). Body B1 splits into bodies B1 and B3. It is known at this stage that B1 is hidden by B3, and B2 is hidden partly by B3 and partly by B1.

Next, step (6) is applied sequentially to each body, selecting first the body for which it is easiest to propose the internal lines. In this example, the order is B3, B1, B2 because B3 hides B1 which hides B2. Internal lines CO and MO are found and connected at vertex O, but no line segment is found using steps (6) and (7) applied to vertex E. This stage is shown in Fig. 12.10(e).

Step (8) is applied to vertex O and a line segment toward E is found. This is extended by edge following as far as E′, as shown in Fig. 12.10(f). Line OE′ fails to be connected to any other line; this failure activates step (10). After a few trials, OE′ is extended to connect to vertex E. Similarly, internal line AM is obtained for body B1, and line IP is obtained for B2. When every step has finished, the three bodies and the relationship between them have been discovered.

We now describe the details of the procedures that are used in the steps stated in Subsect. 12.1.2. Some of them, such as edge following and circular search, are used in more than one step. A procedure used in more than one step may appear in slightly different forms but its essential part is unchanged.

12.1.5 Verifying Hypothetical Line Segments

Testing for a new line usually begins with a given hypothesis about starting point and direction. The procedure described in this subsection takes the given information and explores a small area in order to confirm or refute the presence of the hypothetical line. Confirmation of an initial start leads to edge-following activity described below.

This verification procedure is used for most of the steps described above. The procedure consists of two parts: One is to detect the possible feature points which are to be regarded as elements of the line. The other is to test whether or not the possible feature points do indeed constitute a line segment.

In detecting feature points, we should consider various types of edge as shown in Fig. 3.2. A step type edge is detected by the operator given by Eq. (3.5). The existence of an edge point is determined as described in Subsect. 3.1.6. Note that

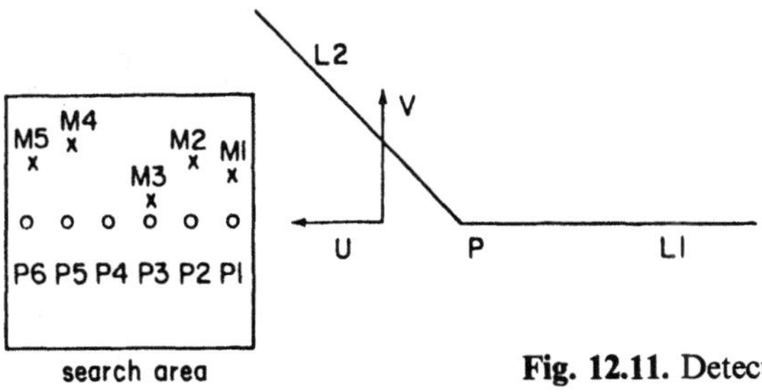

Fig. 12.11. Detection of feature points of a line segment

roof type and edge-effect type edges are detected by combinations of step type edge operators. The threshold for determining those types of edge is lower than that for step type edges.

The other part of the line segment detection is a test of colinearity for the detected feature points. Suppose concave boundary lines L1 and L2 meet at P and suppose the line segment extending L1 is tested as shown in Fig. 12.11. Features are detected in a rectangular search area with given length and width in the direction of L1 at an appropriate place where the detection of feature points is not affected by the edge corresponding to L2. Feature points are sought near the center points P1, P2, ..., P*n* in sequence. If positive peaks M1, M2, ..., M*n* are found, the colinearity of points is determined as follows:

1. The number of feature points must exceed a threshold number T_n.
2. The deviation σ^2 of the points in line fitting with the least-squares method must be less than a threshold T_s.
3. Let θ denote the direction of line L1 and θ' denote that of the line segment obtained by line fitting. Then $|\theta' - \theta|$ must be less than a threshold where $|\theta' - \theta|$ denotes the difference in directions θ' and θ.

Similar tests are made for each of the different types of feature point.

If more than one type of line segment is found, the selection depends on the following criteria:

1. If an edge-effect type is found, then it is selected.
2. For the line segment with σ^2 and θ', let the criterion function be

$$D = \sigma^2 + c|\theta' - \theta|$$

where c is a constant. The line segment selected is the one with the smallest value of D.

12.1.6 Circular Search

Circular search is used to search for lines starting at a given point when the direction of these lines is not known. The range of directions in circular search depends upon the particular case. Suppose two known lines L1 and L2 meet at P as in Fig. 12.12(a) and suppose we wish to search for lines lying between them. The search range, α, is

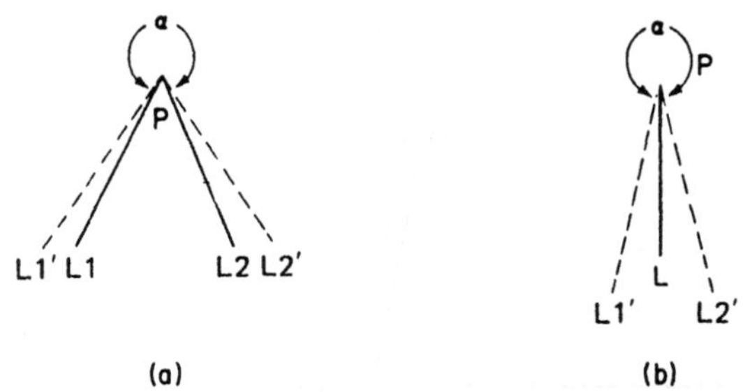

Fig. 12.12. Range of circular search

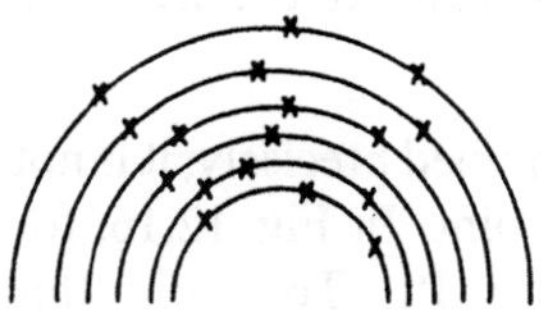

Fig. 12.13. Illustration of a difficulty in finding lines

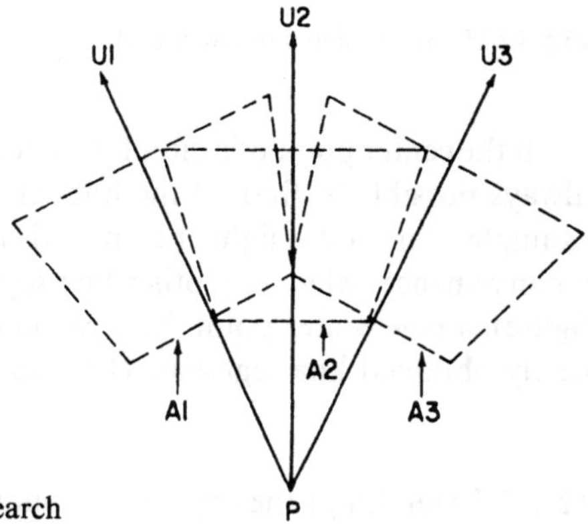

Fig. 12.14. Successive line detection in circular search

between two lines L1′ and L2′ whose directions lie slightly inside L1 and L2 respectively. If lines starting at the end of an unconnected line L are sought, as in Fig. 12.12(b), L1′ and L2′ are similarly set off from L. The center point P of the circular search is not always precisely determined, especially when edge following has terminated at point P as shown in Fig. 12.12(b).

It might be thought natural to try to detect feature points based upon light intensity profiles along arcs around the center. The difficulty with this type of search is the classification of feature points into line segments if there is more than one, as shown in Fig. 12.13. To avoid this difficulty, a simple method is used in this system. Its principle is to apply line segment detection successively in various directions. This is illustrated in Fig. 12.14, where successive line segment detection scans are applied, in several directions.

The size of the direction change between scans, and the search area of each scan, are set so that line segments can be found for any scan near the center point. Thus successive circular search along a line, as shown in Fig. 12.8, can find lines at a point between two adjacent center points (e.g., line L in Fig. 12.15 starting between P1 and P2).

The algorithm for line segment detection is the same as that previously described for verification of initial line segments, differing only with respect to thresholds and search area. Because the search areas for different directions overlap one another, the same line segment may be found in different searches. Each time a line segment is found by line segment detection, a check is made to determine whether it is the same as one obtained by the previous detection.

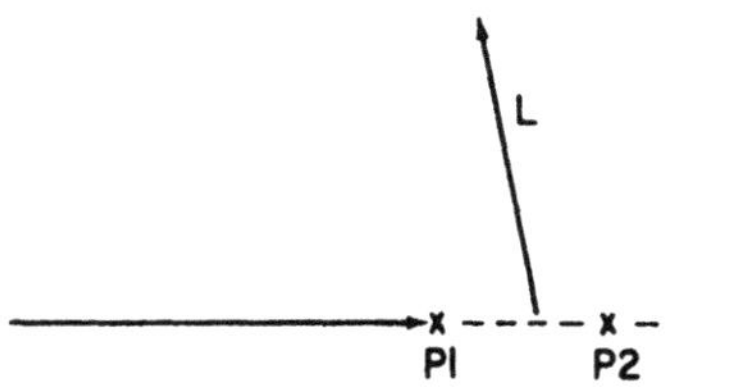

Fig. 12.15. Successive circular search

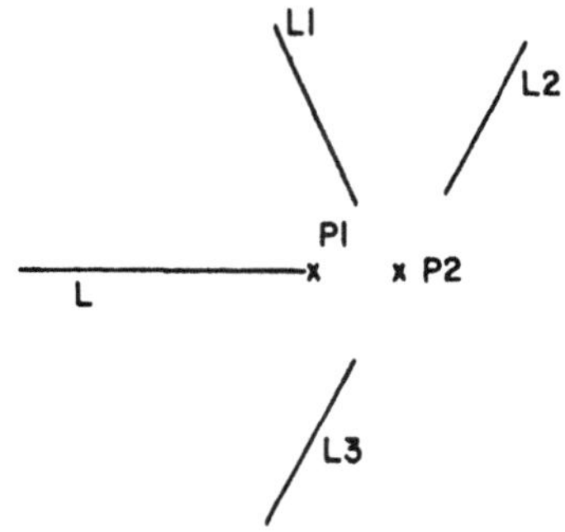

Fig. 12.16. Repeated circular search

If the center point of a circular search has not been determined precisely, it is not always possible to find all the lines starting at the given point. In Fig. 12.16, for example, line L2 might be missed in circular search at P1. To avoid this inconvenience, when any other line segments are found (such as L1 and L3 in the figure), a new center point P2 is calculated on the basis of the known line and the newly obtained line segments (L1 and L3).

12.1.7 Extending Lines by Edge Following

A line is extended from a line segment or an unconnected end of a line by edge following until the end of the line. The basic procedure is described in Sect. 3.4. The starting point is already given, and prediction of the next point is easy because the lines are straight. The result of edge detection is classified into the following four cases:

1. There is no edge point.
2. An edge point is at the predicted position.
3. An edge point is not at the predicted position.
4. It is undecided whether an edge point is at the predicted position or not.

The detection of an edge point is similar to line segment detection except that the type of edge is already known and the thresholds can be adjusted based on the average peak of intensity profiles. The decision among the other three cases is made in a straightforward way, using the distance D between the point and the line fitted to edges traced so far.

If $D < D_1$, then case (2).

If $D > D_2$, then case (3).

If $D_1 < D < D_2$, then case (4),

where D_1 and D_2 are dynamically varying thresholds described below.

As the procedure progresses, confidence in the value of its continuing is determined by two parameters, m and n. The parameter n denotes the number of previous consecutive points classified into (4). Roughly speaking, m is a 'nervousness' parameter: its value increases when a scan yields no feature point and decreases when a feature point is found within the distance D_1 of the progressing line. Recall that D_1 is the threshold which determines if a feature point is in fact on the line. D_1 bears a linear relation to n. They increase in value together when a string of slightly off-line feature points suggests that the line is slightly displaced by some disturbance. Thus, off-line feature points become acceptable if there are enough of them. Both n and D_1 decrease in value as soon as a feature point falls within the widening scope of the threshold D_1 for a string of feature points. Both m and n are initially zero. Edge following stops when the value of m becomes too high, indicating a lack of feature points, or when the sum of m and n becomes too high, indicating a combined insecurity stimulated both by a lack of feature points and by the poor position of those that are present.

According to the result of the edge point search, the following actions are taken.

1. No feature point:

   $m \leftarrow m+1$.

2. Feature point on the line:

   If $m > T_m$, where T_m is a constant, then $m \leftarrow m-1$.

   Otherwise, $m \leftarrow 0$, $n \leftarrow 0$, and reclassify those feature points which have previously been classified in the ambiguous category (4) as belonging to the on-the-line category (2). Adjust the equation of the line with these points and the present feature point.

3. Feature point off the line:

   If $D < T_d$, where T_d is a constant, and $m > T_m$, then $m \leftarrow m-1$.

   Otherwise, no change.

4. Feature point position ambiguous:

   $n \leftarrow n+1$, and if $m > T_m$, then $m \leftarrow m-1$.

The threshold D_1 is represented as $D_1 = c_1 + c_2 n$, where c_1 and c_2 are constants. The other threshold D_2 is a linear function of D_1.

This procedure is repeated and edge following proceeds step by step, extending the line until the termination condition is satisfied. Edge following terminates when either $m > T_1$ or $m+n > T_2$, where T_1 and T_2 are constants. The terminal point is defined as the last point classified as case (2).

Figure 12.17 illustrates how the algorithm works. In Fig. 12.17(a) two lines meet at P. Edge following might finish at some point beyond P (Pm in the figure) which satisfies the termination condition. The termination point of edge following is, however, determined more precisely near P (P1 or P2).

In Fig. 12.17(b), P1, P2, P3, and P4 are classified as belonging to case (4), increasing the value of n, which classifies P5 as case (2). Then the line is adjusted with these points which are now classified as case (2), and edge following proceeds.

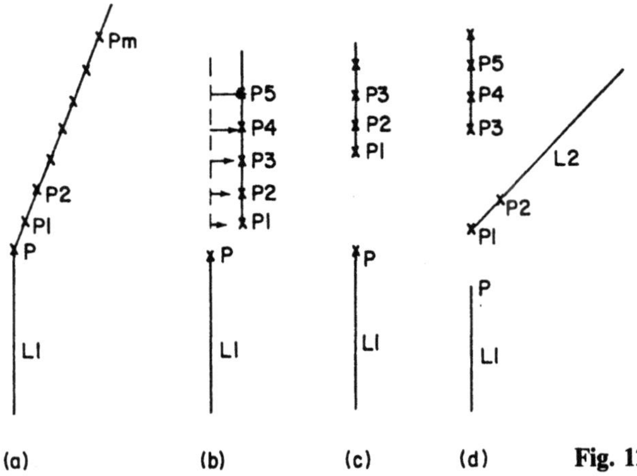

Fig. 12.17. Examples of edge following

Figures 12.17(c) and (d) illustrate that even if a part of the intensity profile is disturbed by noise or other lines, edge following does not terminate here. In Fig. 12.17(d), however, if the light intensity of the right side of L1 changes across L2, the type of feature points might change after crossing L2. Thus feature points P3, P4,... might not be obtained and then edge following might terminate at P1. When edge following terminates, line segment detection is applied at the extension of the line to see if another type of line segment is found. If found, we adjust the line equation, and edge following proceeds. If not found, edge following finally terminates at point P1 and the position of P1 is adjusted with the line equation.

12.1.8 Experimental Results

To test the program, experiments were carried out with scenes including cubes and wedges having relatively uniform white surfaces placed on a black background. Typical experimental images consist of about 400 × 400 pixels. The light intensity is represented by a little less than 100 levels, spanning a range in intensity of about three to one.

The input data for a clear, bright edge on the dark background are blurred due to some optical and electro-optical limitations. If the real intensity change is a step function, there is a transient area in the input data about 10 pixels wide. Thus the resolution of the image can be regarded as 10 pixels. The parameters used in line segment detection and edge following are based upon this resolution.

Some results are shown in Fig. 12.18. The difficulty or processing time of the recognition process depends not only on the complexity of the object but also on the information known at each stage. In Fig. 12.18(a), for example, boundary lines KS and QS are easily proposed as the extension of contour lines. On the other hand, it is not easy to find boundary lines KM or LM in Fig. 12.18(b). That is, after DK and HL are found, circular search is necessary at K and L, respectively. Circular search is less reliable in finding a line segment, and more time consuming. Once all the boundary lines of an object are determined, all the internal lines are proposed in

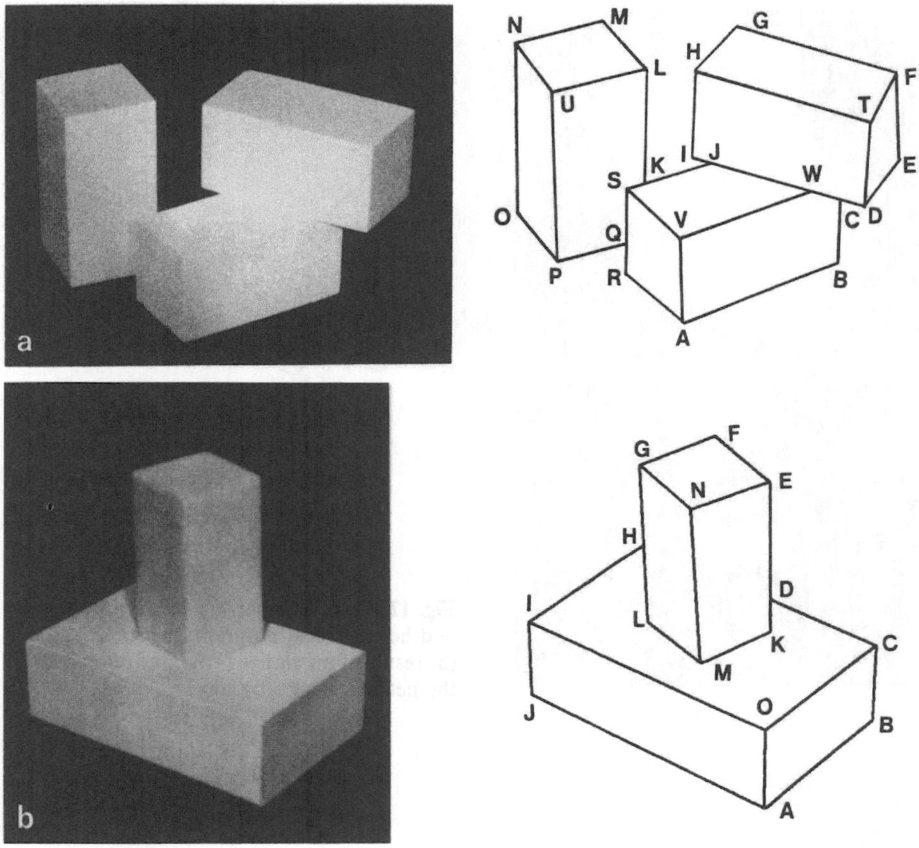

Fig. 12.18. Experimental results

both cases (a) and (b). But edge following along VW in Fig. 12.18(a) and EN in Fig. 12.18(b) terminates in the middle. Then step (10) specified in Subsect. 12.1.3 is applied.

An example of the result of comparison of this program and an earlier bottom-up program is shown in Fig. 12.19. The earlier program looks at the whole scene in a homogeneous way and picks up feature points. Lines are found using those feature points. But it is very difficult to determine *a priori* the various thresholds appropriate for detection of feature points, line fitting, and connection of lines. In the heterarchical program described here, the various thresholds are adjusted in the context of all the information obtained previously. Additionally, the particular edge-following algorithm itself is changed from case to case depending on whether the line is a boundary or an internal type.

The results of experiments with moderately complex scenes are mostly satisfactory. There are, however, some limitations to this program at present, one of which is that bodies may be missed in some cases. Simple examples are shown in Fig. 12.20.

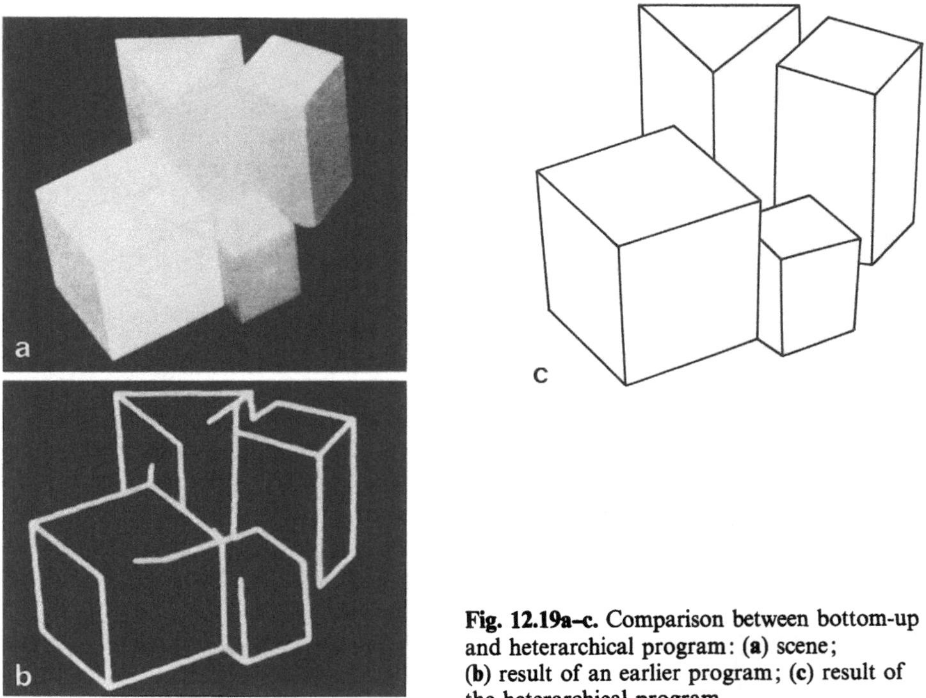

Fig. 12.19a–c. Comparison between bottom-up and heterarchical program: (**a**) scene; (**b**) result of an earlier program; (**c**) result of the heterarchical program

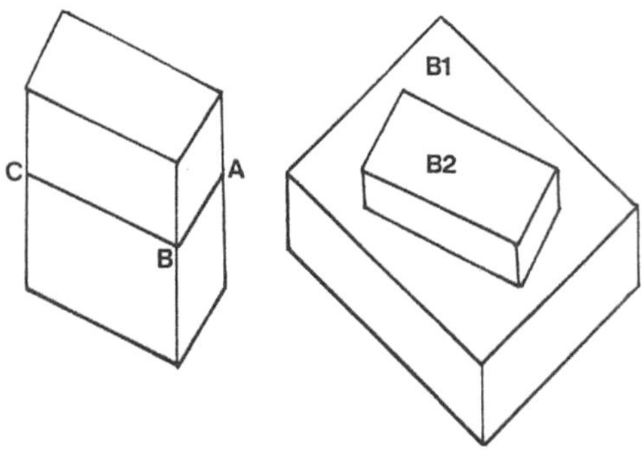

Fig. 12.20a, b. Situations with a lack of cues: (**a**) lines are not proposed; (**b**) body is not proposed

The boundary lines AB and BC in Fig. 12.20(a) are not proposed, though the other contour lines and internal lines are found, because the resulting regions are such that no concave vertices activate step (1). In such a case, when bodies are neatly stacked, it is necessary to search for boundary lines which start from points on the contour line.

In Fig. 12.20(b), body B2 is not proposed. To find a body that is included in a face of another body, it is necessary to search for line segments inside the region.

Though these two kinds of search (search along the boundary line and search in the region) are required to find all the bodies in the scene, they are still more effective than an exhaustive search of the entire scene.

12.2 Analysis of Range Images with the Aid of a Junction Dictionary

This section describes how knowledge about junctions may help the edge-following process in building scene descriptions from range images (Sugihara, 1979). The principle is similar to that described in the previous section. In range data analysis, however, we can obtain more reliable information from an edge detection, as described in Chap. 9. Therefore, instead of heuristics, more systematic knowledge about junctions is available.

The following subsections describe what kind of knowledge is available and how the knowledge is stored in a junction dictionary.

12.2.1 Possible Junctions

We have seen in Sect. 9.5 that 3D edge lines are obtained by edge linking. The edge lines are classified according to their physical properties into four categories: convex, concave, obscuring, and obscured lines. Typical categories are illustrated in Fig. 12.21 which represents a scene with two blocks on a horizontal plane viewed from a camera.

Note that there are two kinds of obscured lines: one viewed from a light source as illustrated in Fig. 12.21 (lines connecting J7, J6, J5, J4, and J10, where junction *i* is denoted by J*i*), and the other viewed from a camera (lines connecting J12, J16, J21, and J20). The peripheral of the range image can be regarded as an obscuring line. Obscuring lines can be distinguished from obscured lines by examining which line oscures the other.

A junction is called a 'shadow-causing junction' when it has a pair of an obscuring line and obscured line. The word 'shadow' means that the obscured line can be regarded as the shadow of the obscuring line. In Fig. 12.21, junctions J2, J10, J12, and J17 are examples of shadow-causing junctions. It will be seen later that shadow-causing junctions are often suggested from an obscuring–obscured line pair.

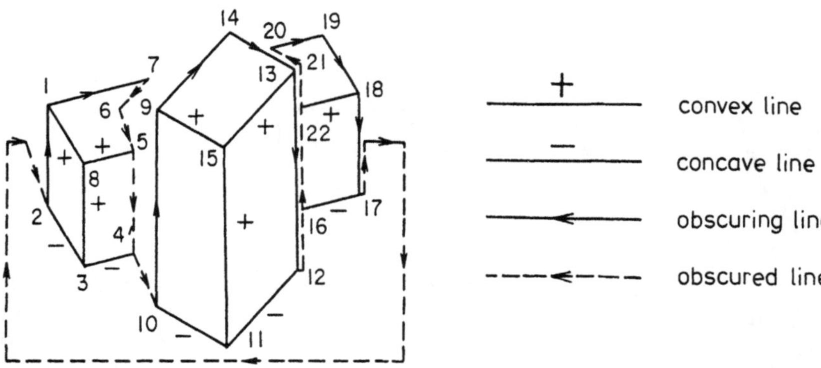

Fig. 12.21. Labeled line drawing

In order to enumerate the possible types of junction, let us first impose the same constraints as those for Huffman's labeling (see Subsection 5.3.1):

(a) Scenes consist of polyhedral objects.
(b) Objects are trihedral.
(c) Objects are in a general position.
(d) Objects are seen from a general position.

In addition, let us assume that the light source is also in a general position.

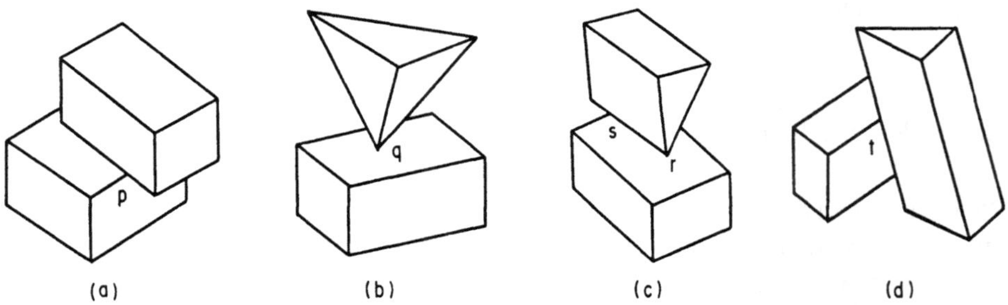

Fig. 12.22. Possible contact relations between two bodies

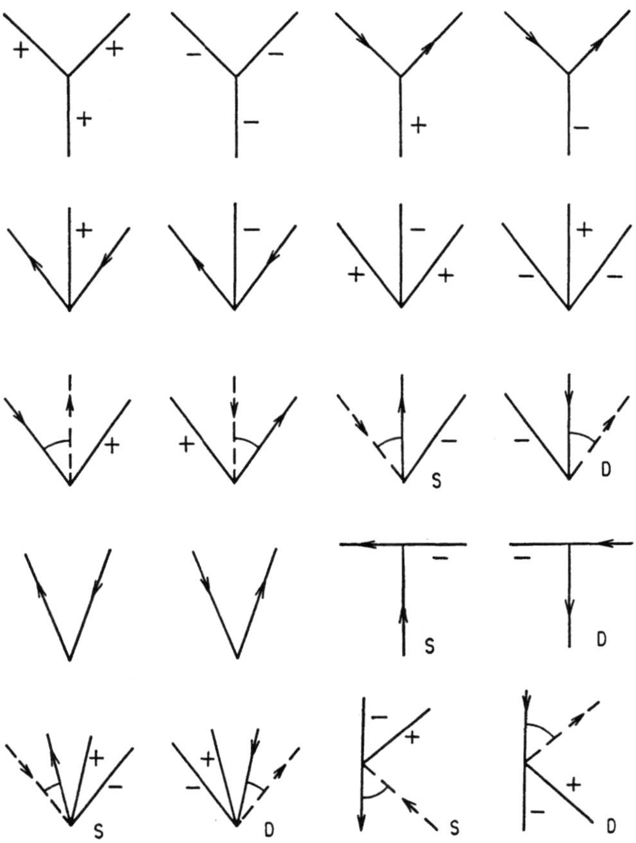

Fig. 12.23. Possible junction types (a pair of obscuring and obscured lines is denoted by an arc connecting them)

The enumeration is performed systematically in the following manner. First, possible trihedral vertices are listed as shown in Fig. 5.9. Then possible relations between two bodies are considered. Since range data are used, we have only to consider junctions generated by contact of two bodies. Possible ways of contact of two bodies are confined by constraint (c) to: (1) face to face, (2) point to face, (3) edge to face, and (4) edge point to edge point, as shown in Fig. 12.22. At each vertex such as q or r, or at each pseudo-vertex such as p, s, or t, the incident planes divide the surrounding space into a finite number of cells. All the possible combinations of directions of the light source and the camera into vacant cells generate the list of possible junctions.

It is, however, convenient to divide a certain class of junction into simpler ones. If a junction has an obscuring line or obscured line with an in-arrow, then it has also a line of the same type with an out-arrow. If a junction has two such pairs, the junction can be partitioned into simpler ones. In Fig. 12.22, for example, the vertex

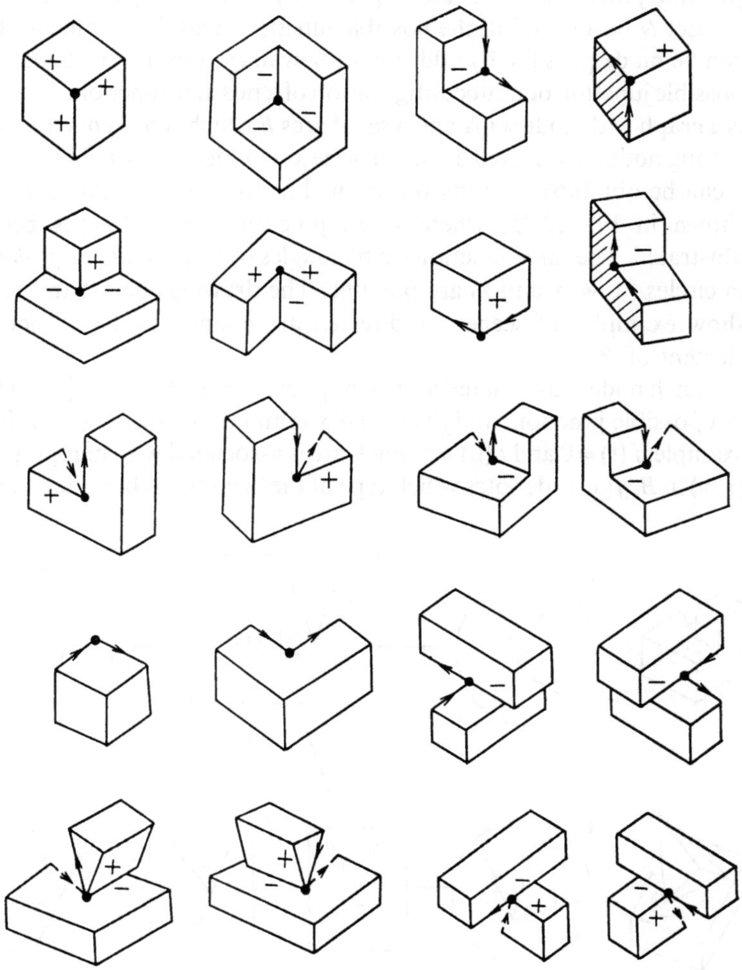

Fig. 12.24. Examples of scenes corresponding to junctions in Fig. 12.23

q and the pseudo-vertex t can be partitioned by a pair of obscuring lines and a pair of obscured lines. The vertex q is partitioned into an arrow type junction and an L type one. When the pseudo-vertex t is partitioned, no junction is generated.

Figure 12.23 is the list of possible junction types, and Fig. 12.24 shows examples of scenes corresponding to those junctions. In the upper two rows, the left three junctions correspond to Huffman's 'Y' shaped and arrow shaped junctions, and those on the right are proper to range images. All of the arrow shaped junctions in the third row and the leftmost two in the next row correspond to Huffman's 'L' shaped junctions. The other junctions are generated from contact of two bodies. Note that they are not partitioned into simpler junctions.

12.2.2 Junction Dictionary

A junction dictionary is used for prediction of missing edges. It contains all the possible junctions and some impossible junctions together with their relations.

Let N be a set of all the possible junctions and those impossible junctions that can be made possible by addition of new lines; that is, an element of N is either a possible junction or a subconfiguration of a possible junction. A junction dictionary is a graph with node set N and a set of arcs $\boldsymbol{B}$ which represents the following relation among nodes: a directed arc from node x to node y (denoted by (x, y)) indicates that y can be obtained by addition of one line to x. Part of the junction dictionary is shown in Fig. 12.25, where seven junctions and relations between them are illustrated. The three junctions in rectangles (t, v and y) are impossible, and the four in circles (u, w, x and z) are possible. The drawings beside the possible junctions show examples of scenes. A directed arc connecting two junctions denotes an element of $\boldsymbol{B}$.

Each node is associated with a mapping f from N to $\{0, 1\}$ such that $f(x) = 1$ if x is a possible junction, and $f(x) = 0$ if x is an impossible junction. In Fig. 12.25, for example, $f(\mathrm{t}) = 0$ and $f(\mathrm{u}) = 1$. Each arc is associated with mappings g and h: for arc (x, y) in $\boldsymbol{B}$, $g(x, y)$ denotes which type of the line should be added to x to reach y, and

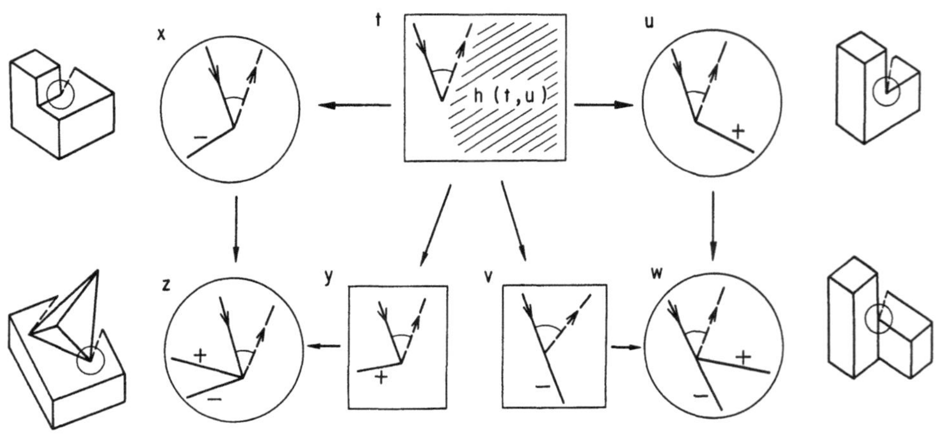

Fig. 12.25. Part of a junction dictionary

$h(x, y)$ denotes the allowable area for the new line. If, for example, we add a convex line in the shaded area of the junction t in Fig. 12.25, we get another junction u. This is formulated as follows:

$f(\mathrm{t})=0$

$f(\mathrm{u})=1$

(t, u) is an element of B

$g(\mathrm{t}, \mathrm{u})=$ convex line

$h(\mathrm{t}, \mathrm{u})=$ shaded area in Fig. 12.25

Adding, furthermore, a concave line to u, we obtain w and get the path (t, u, w) from t to w. When we exchange the order of addition of the two lines, we get another path (t, v, w). These paths suggest the existence of new lines and guide the analysis of the range data. If a junction of type u is found in range data analysis, the dictionary suggests that a concave line 'may' exist at that junction. If, on the other hand, a junction of type v is found, the dictionary suggests that a convex line 'must' exist because v is impossible and w is the only possible junction reached from v.

12.2.3 System Organization

A system for analysis of range data consists of the following main modules: (1) a contour finder, (2) a line-segment finder, (3) an edge follower, (4) a straight-line fitter, (5) a body partitioner, and (6) a vertex-position adjuster. They work cooperatively, guided by the junction dictionary, to make a labeled line drawing of a scene. The function of each module is briefly explained below.

12.2.3.1 Contour Finder

A contour finder extracts obscuring and obscured lines. It scans a range image for a jump edge or a discontinuous edge by applying operator D_2 defined by Eq. (9.9). When an edge is found, an edge of the same type is followed in each direction as far as the ends of the edge line, using an edge-following procedure which is described in Sect. 9.5.

12.2.3.2 Line-Segment Finder

When a junction is given, the line-segment finder consults the dictionary and predicts missing lines emanating from the given junction. Suppose that a junction of type x at (i, j) is given and that multiple junction types are suggested by the dictionary. For each predicted junction type y, a new line of type $g(x, y)$ in area $h(x, y)$ is also given by the dictionary. Then a check is made to determine if there are old lines satisfying the prediction. If old lines are found, the line-segment finder concludes that the prediction is true. Otherwise, new line segments are sought in

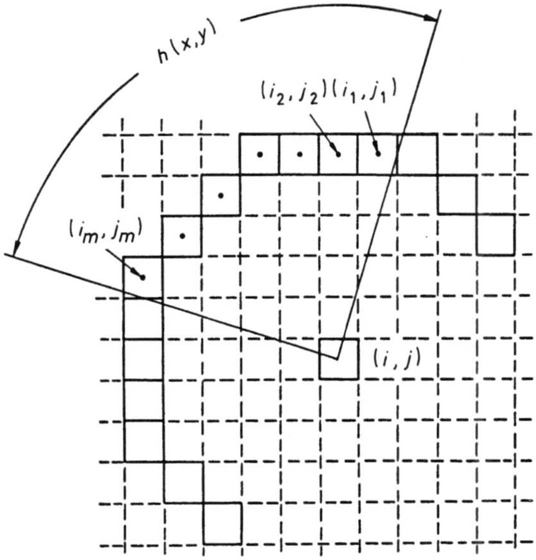

Fig. 12.26. Circular search

$h(x, y)$, the fan-shaped area, along a circular arc as shown in Fig. 12.26. Since the type and the approximate direction of the predicted line segment are known, simple 2D operators $DD(i, j; k\pi/4)$ (for $k=0, 1, 2, 3$) described in Sect. 9.3 are applied at every point as shown in the figure.

The maximum of the absolute values of DD at all points is denoted by $s(i, j; x, y)$, which represents the reliability of the predicted line segment. The reliability is computed for all predicted junction types. The maximum reliability $s(i, j; x)$ among them is defined as:

$$s(i, j; x) = \max_{(x, y) \in B} \{s(i, j; x, y)\} \tag{12.1}$$

It is concluded that the line segment exists if $s(i, j; x)$ is large enough, i.e.:

$$s(i, j; x) > T_1 \tag{12.2}$$

where T_1 is a threshold.

Next, let us consider cases where more than one line is predicted. Each case corresponds in the dictionary to the path from junction x to y through other junctions. That is, there is a path p which consists of arcs (x, z_1), (z_1, z_2), . . ., (z_n, y). Let us limit the paths such that intermediate junctions are all impossible ($f(z_i)=0$) and y is possible ($f(y)=1$). The reliability of the path from x to y is defined as:

$$t(i, j; p) = \min \{s(i, j; x, z_1), s(i, j; z_1, z_2), \ldots, s(i, j; z_n, y)\tag{12.3}$$

The reliability of the path from x is the one which gives the maximum reliability among all the possible paths (denoted by $H(x)$):

$$t(i, j; x) = \max_{p \in H(x)} \{t(i, j; p)\} \tag{12.4}$$

If $t(i,j;x)$ is large, it is concluded that the path exists. The threshold for $t(i,j;x)$ depends on whether or not vertex x is possible:

$$f(x)=1 \quad \text{and} \quad t(i,j;x)>T_2 \tag{12.5}$$

$$f(x)=0 \quad \text{and} \quad t(i,j;x)>T_3 \tag{12.6}$$

where T_2 and T_3 are thresholds ($T_1>T_2>T_3$).

12.2.3.3 Edge Follower

When a new line segment is found by the line-segment finder, an edge follower tries to find the whole of the line. Since the type and the direction of the line are predicted, the same operators as used for line-segment finding are also applied for edge following. The edge following terminates when the line disappears or the type of the edge changes.

12.2.3.4 Straight-Line Fitter

When a string of edge points is extracted by the edge follower, a straight-line fitter approximates it by a straight line. It first finds points with maximal curvatures to divide the strings into substrings of straight parts. This procedure is just the same as that described in Subsect. 10.1.2. An equation of a straight line is fitted to each substring. Joints of two adjacent substrings and the end of the original string are regarded as new junctions.

12.2.3.5 Body Partitioner

Whenever a new line is obtained by the straight-line fitter, a body partitioner checks whether the incident body is partitioned into two smaller ones. The partitioning problem is, however, not solved theoretically. For example, we cannot tell whether or not a concave block is separable at the concave edge. The body partitioner, therefore, is based on the following empirical rules.

Rule 1: If a junction has two pairs of in-arrow and out-arrow lines, partition the surrounding body along the pairs.

An example is shown in Fig. 12.27(a). Note that the list of possible junctions (shown in Fig. 12.23) does not contain junctions which can be partitioned by this rule.

The second rule utilizes the two groups of junctions labeled 'S' and 'D' in the list of possible junctions shown in Fig. 12.23. A junction in the S group or D group has a concave line and an in-arrow out-arrow line pair.

Rule 2: If a chain of concave lines connects an S group junction to a D group junction, or if a chain of concave lines connects an S group junction or D

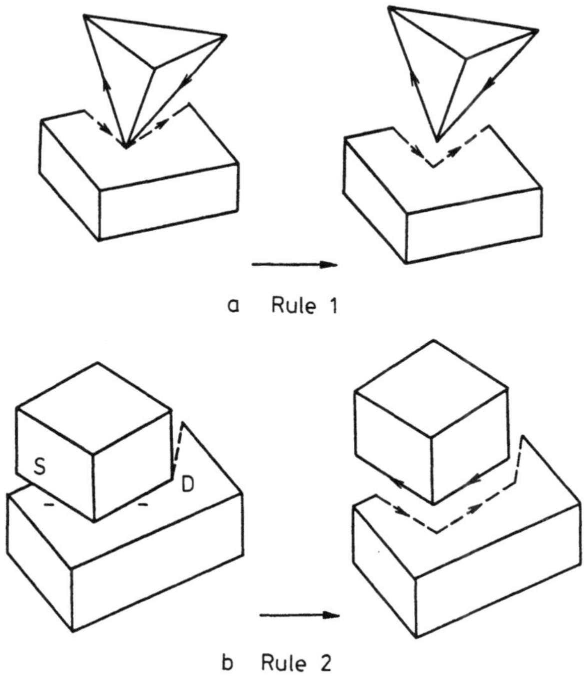

Fig. 12.27a, b. Body partitioning rules: (**a**) rule 1; (**b**) rule 2

group junction to another junction on an obscured line, then partition the body along the concave lines and change the concave lines into pairs of obscuring and obscured lines.

An example is shown in Fig. 12.27(b). Note that the obscuring and the obscured lines can be easily identified by examining the junctions at the ends of the original chain on concave lines.

12.2.3.6 Vertex-Position Adjuster

Whenever a new line is connected to a junction, a vertex-position adjuster updates the position of the junction. The position depends on the lines incident on the junction. If there are only two lines the position is determined as a crossing. If more lines are incident, more than one crossing should be considered. A simple way is to adjust the position as the weighted mean of those crossings, where weights are chosen according to the length of the lines.

12.2.4 Outline of Behavior of System

The system, in the first phase, finds contour lines by activating alternately the contour finder and the straight-line fitter. The range image is generally decomposed into connected regions bounded by the contour lines. The contour lines are classified as obscuring or obscured.

In the next phase, many modules interact with one another to expedite the analysis. The outline of the algorithm is as follows:

1. If there are bodies (connected regions) which have not yet been analyzed, choose one body. Otherwise, stop.
2. If there are junctions unexamined in the current body, choose one junction. Otherwise, go to (5).
3. Find line segments at the current junction (with the line-segment finder). If no lines are found, put the mark 'examined' on the junction and go to (2). If found line segments belong to lines which have already been extracted by edge following, go to (5). Otherwise (new line segments are found), go to (4).
4. Extract lines starting from the new line segments and fit straight lines to them.
5. Connect the found lines to the current junction and adjust the junction position using all the incident lines.
6. Try to partition the current body by examining the improved part of the body. If partitioning succeeds, go to (1). Otherwise, go to (3) (in this case, the type of the current junction has changed).

12.2.5 Experimental Results

Experiments have been carried out with range images originating from real scenes consisting of white polyhedra. The examples in this subsection have been chosen to illustrate and clarify the behavior of the system. Each image consists of 200×240 data points.

Figure 12.28(a) is a range picture (represented by a light-stripe image) of a scene with two blocks, one supporting the other, and Figs. 12.28(b)–(e) show how the system analyzes the scene. The system, in the first phase, extracts contour lines and locates junctions on them.

In the second phase, the system first focuses its attention on junction J1 in Fig. 12.28(b), which is a shadow-causing junction of the type t shown in Fig. 12.25. At this stage, the internal lines J1J2 and J1J3 in Fig. 12.28(b) have not yet been found. The line-segment finder receives a suggestion from the junction dictionary about possible new lines around J1, and finds a concave line segment. The edge follower extracts the whole line, and the straight-line fitter replaces this line with a straight line-segment J1J2. Thus, the new junction J2 and the new line J1J2 are added to the line drawing as shown in Fig. 12.28(b). Now the type of J1 is changed to the type v shown in Fig. 12.25.

The system remains at J1 and searches for other new lines, and finds a convex line J1J3 (this stage is shown in Fig. 12.28(b)). The straight-line fitter fails to fit lines and, therefore, the line J1J3 remains as a string of points. Since J1 is changed to type w in Fig. 12.25 and no further prediction is given, the system turns to another junction.

When junction J4 is examined, it is concluded that the predicted convex line has already been extracted, and the two junctions J3 and J4 are merged into one, which is renamed J3 (Fig. 12.28(c)). In a similar way, a new line J5J6 is extracted when J5 is examined, and the two junctions J2 and J7 are merged into one (which is renamed J2) when J7 is examined.

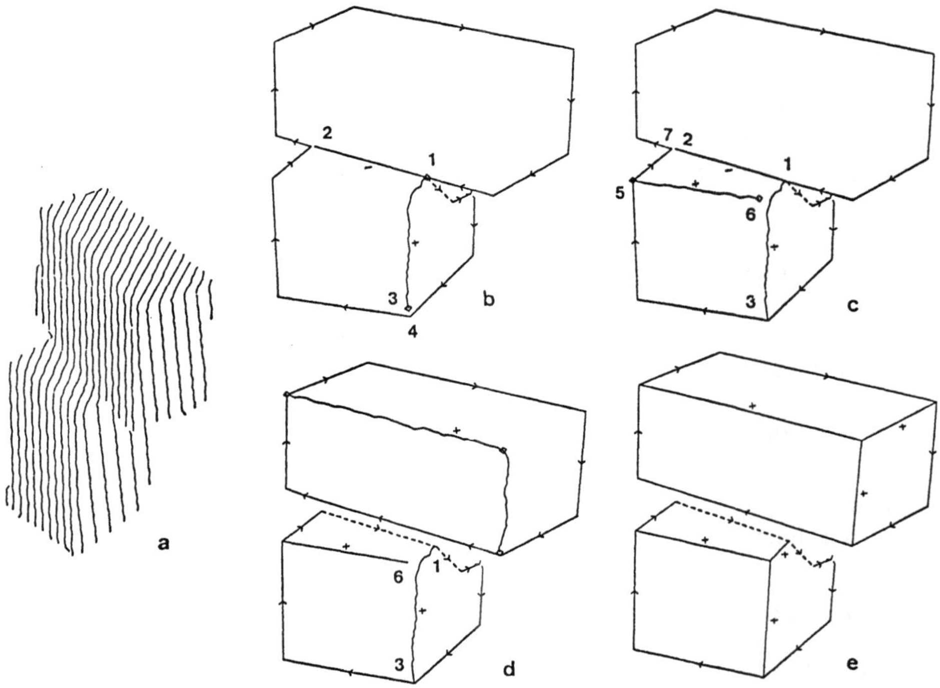

Fig. 12.28. Example of analysis of a range image: one block on top of another

At this stage, the partitioning rule (2) is applicable along the concave line J1J2, because J1 is a D-group junction and J2 is an S-group junction. The body partitioner separates the line drawing into two parts (Fig. 12.28(d)).

The system first chooses the lower body. When J6 is examined, it is connected to the line J1J3, and, consequently, the line J1J3 is divided into the two substrings J1J6 and J6J3. Now the straight-line fitter works for each of them and finds two straight-line segments. The analysis of the lower body has finished.

The other body is similarly analyzed and the final line drawing is obtained as shown in Fig. 12.28(e).

Figure 12.29 shows another example. The scene includes a complicated body with two rectangular prisms, one penetrating the other. Contour lines and junctions thereon are similarly obtained. From junction J1, concave line J1J2 and new junction J3 are found (Fig. 12.29(b)). J2, the end point of the new line, is merged to the neighboring junction and the body is partitioned into two parts along the concave lines. The resulting two bodies are processed separately as shown in Fig. 12.29(c), where the numerals assigned to the junctions show the order in which the new lines are found. The whole line drawings of the two bodies are constructed precisely (Fig. 12.29(d)).

Even if several edges come close to one another in a scene, a perfect line drawing is constructed, because the data processing is supported by appropriate predictions of missing lines and by the powerful edge-detecting operator which is sensitive only to the edges of a particular edge type in a particular direction. Once those labeled line drawings are obtained, recognition of objects, or manipulation of them, will be easy.

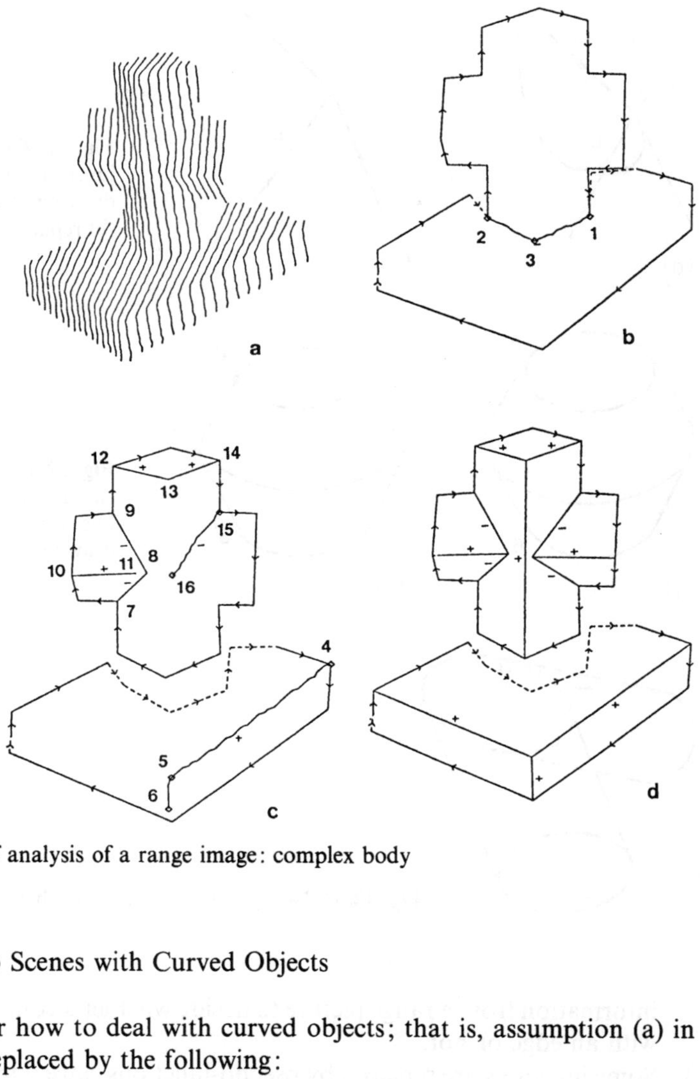

Fig. 12.29. Example of analysis of a range image: complex body

12.2.6 Extension to Scenes with Curved Objects

Now let us consider how to deal with curved objects; that is, assumption (a) in Subsect. 12.2.1 is replaced by the following:

(a′) Objects in the scene are bounded by planar surfaces and/or quadratic surfaces.

The other assumptions, (b), (c) and (d), are unchanged. When a scene contains curved objects, curved lines appear in the associated line drawings. Consequently, a junction dictionary would become tremendously large. In order to limit the dictionary size, three conventions are introduced as follows.

1. Curved lines are replaced by the associated straight lines tangent to them at each junction. For example, junction J in Fig. 12.30(a) is represented as shown in Fig. 12.30(b). This convention is reasonable because it is difficult to distinguish straight lines from curved lines when we see strings of edge points locally.
2. Obscuring lines are also used to represent contour lines of curved surfaces, but they are not always associated with edges of objects (for example, line segments AC and BD in Fig. 12.31(a)). It would be of no use to introduce a new label for contour lines which are not associated with body edges, because we can get no

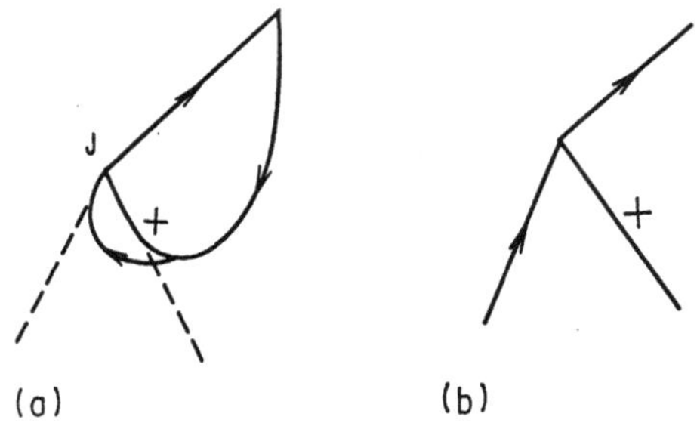

Fig. 12.30a, b. Replacement of junction with curved lines: (a) line drawing of a curved object; (b) replacement of junction J

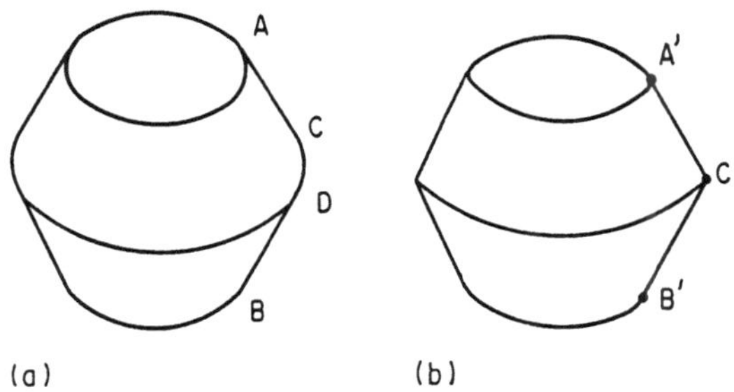

Fig. 12.31a, b. Pseudo-junction caused by curved lines: (a) precise line drawing; (b) practical line drawing

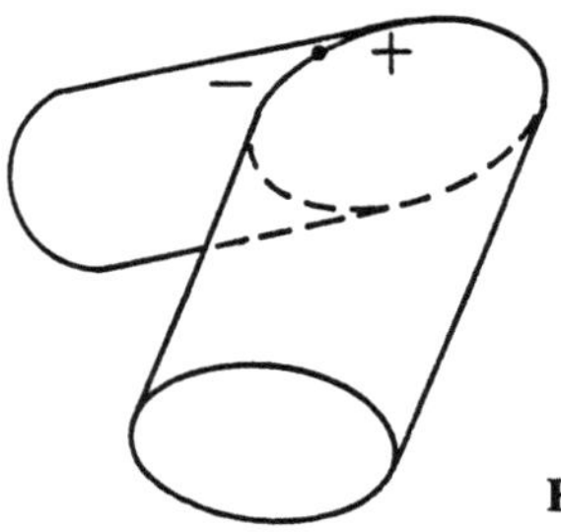

Fig. 12.32. New junction for curved objects

information from a range picture to decide whether a contour line is associated with an edge or not.

3. Some junctions are replaced by pseudo-junctions caused by the limit of picture resolution. A smoothly curved line may often seem to be a corner if the curvature at some point is large. In Fig. 12.31(b), for example, three lines are colinear at point A, and two lines are colinear at point B. But the limited resolution produces corners A′ and B′ shown in Fig. 12.31(b), at which lines are not colinear. Moreover, two closely located junctions are regarded as one junction. Points C and D in Fig. 12.31(a) are so close that they are regarded as only one pseudo-junction, C′.

If planar surfaces are replaced by quadratic surfaces in the scenes we have considered until now, the resulting change of the junction dictionary is very small because of the above conventions. The convention that curved lines are replaced by the associated tangent lines means that we see vertices so locally that we cannot distinguish planar surfaces from curved ones. Therefore, no new junctions occur in line drawings of vertices. New junctions can occur only at the nodes which are not

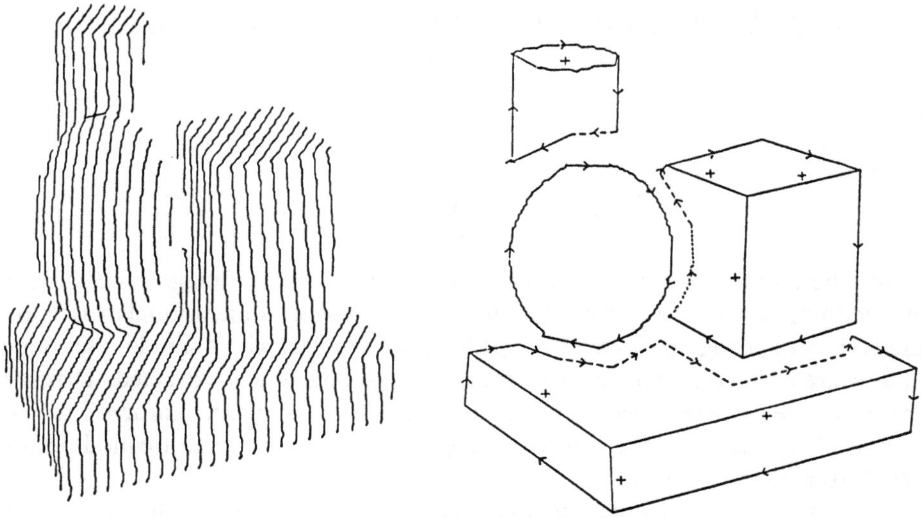

Fig. 12.33. Example of processing for a scene including a curved object

associated with 3D vertices. The junctions A, B, C and D in Fig. 12.31(a) are examples of the new junction candidates; but since they are replaced by the pseudo-junctions, and the types of those pseudo-junctions already exist in the list of possible junctions (Fig. 12.23), those junctions do not cause any change in the dictionary. It can be shown that the only new junction is the one shown in Fig. 12.32, which corresponds to a join of two cylinders. Consequently, the size of a dictionary for curved-object scenes is almost the same as that for polyhedral scenes.

The previous system can analyze curved-object scenes without any modification except a change in the junction dictionary. An example of the input scene and the result of processing using the new dictionary are shown in Fig. 12.33.

13 Image Understanding Using Two-Dimensional Models

While the previous chapter concentrated on how low-level image processing is guided by models of scenes, this chapter describes how two-dimensional models are used for recognizing objects from image features. We start with a simple case where objects are isolated and image features are almost completely extracted. Then we consider cases where objects occlude one another and image features are not completely extracted. In the course of recognizing objects, features are modified or new features are extracted.

The cases are further classified into two categories according to the type of model used: models of images or models of objects. In the former case, segmentation of an image is not a critical problem because the whole image can be matched to models of scenes. In the latter case, however, the whole image cannot be directly matched to models. Therefore, segmentation of the image or image features is very important in order to recognize a part of an image using object models.

13.1 Recognition of Isolated Curved Objects Using a Graph Model

This section describes a method of recognizing a single curved object using the graph model described in Subsection 11.3.3 (Barrow and Popplestone, 1971). The scene includes an object on a table.

13.1.1 Scene Description

The image of the scene consists of 64×64 pixels with 16 levels. Uniform regions are extracted from the image by a region method (see Sect. 3.5). The properties of regions and the relations between them are calculated as described in Subsection 11.3.3. Thus the description of the scene being analyzed and the descriptions of models are similarly represented.

It is convenient to regard the properties of a region in terms of its relation with other identical regions. Then, the properties and the relations are represented in a uniform way. Many relations are calculated for regions either in the scene or in a model. All the relations are represented by numbers as shown in Fig. 11.5.

13.1.2 Evaluation of Matching

Let us denote regions in the scene by S_1, $S_2, \ldots, S_m$ and those in model j by $M_{j,1}, M_{j,2}, \ldots, M_{j,m_j}$, where m is the number of regions in the scene and m_j is the number of regions in model j (generally m is not equal to m_j). Recognition of objects is performed by matching the regions of the scene to those of the models. We need a suitable function for the evaluation of matching. The evaluation is based on the similarities between the relations in the scene and those in the model. Suppose that scene regions $S_1, S_2, \ldots, S_m$ are matched to model regions $M_{j,k_1}, M_{j,k_2}, \ldots, M_{j,k_m}$, respectively, and that the number of the region of the scene is equal to or less than that of the model ($m \leq m_j$). Then the correspondences between the relations in the scene and those in the models are established. Now let us consider how to evaluate the matching between a relation R_S in the scene and the corresponding relation R_M in the model. The principle is that if the difference between the values of the two relations is within a threshold, the two relations are considered to be matched. The threshold is decided experimentally to be $3\sigma_M$, where σ_M is the standard deviation of R_M.

The total evaluation function depends on the number of successive matchings (n_s), the number of relations (n_r), and the number of regions (n_j) in model j. The program tries to minimize the following evaluation function:

$$f = 1 - n_s/n_r + c/n_j \tag{13.1}$$

where a suitable value of the constant c is 0.5.

13.1.3 Matching Strategy

Recognition of objects is now reduced to finding the match that minimizes Eq. (13.1). An exhaustive search, however, is not effective. A better way is to find correspondences one by one on the basis of the evaluation of partial matchings. In the process, when some promising partial matchings are obtained, the next step is to add one pair of regions to the most promising matching. This method is the best kind of first search. The algorithm is as follows:

1. Select an arbitrary region in the scene. Assuming the correspondence of the region to each region in the model, calculate the evaluation function. Store the partial matchings with the function values.
2. Select the best partial match (with the minimum evaluation function value). If all the regions in the scene are matched, then stop (the partial match is the answer).
3. Select one more region in the scene and add to the previously selected set of scene regions. Assuming the correspondence of the region to each of the unassigned regions in the model, calculate the evaluation function for the set of regions. Store the partial matching with the function values. Go to (2).

At an intermediate stage of this process, many partial matchings are stored along with their evaluation function values. Figure 13.1(a) shows an example of partial matchings stored at an intermediate stage (where $M_{j,i}$ is denoted by M_i for convenience). Only the best three matchings are shown, with function values in increasing order. In step (2), the uppermost matching pair in the figure is selected, and in step (3) region S_3 is selected. Suppose the model contains only four regions. Then there are two regions (M_1 and M_4) which may correspond to region S_3.

a		b	
(S_1, S_2) — (M_2, M_3)	0.3	(S_1, S_2, S_3) — (M_2, M_3, M_4)	0.2
(S_1, S_2) — (M_2, M_4)	0.4	(S_1, S_2) — (M_2, M_4)	0.4
(S_1) — (M_1)	0.5	(S_1, S_2, S_3) — (M_2, M_3, M_1)	0.45
⋮		⋮	

Fig. 13.1. Stored partial matchings

Therefore the following two pairs of matchings are possible:

(S_1, S_2, S_3)—(M_2, M_3, M_1)

(S_1, S_2, S_3)—(M_2, M_3, M_4)

The evaluation function values for these matchings are calculated and stored. Figure 13.1(b) depicts this state.

If there are more regions in the scene, the uppermost matching will be expanded in the next step. If there are no more regions, the uppermost matching is the current answer. If the evaluation function value is satisfactory, it is accepted. Otherwise, an attempt is made to expand the next candidate, (S_1, S_2)—(M_2, M_4).

Since this method matches a graph description of a scene to one of models, it is not very sensitive to small changes of shapes of regions, and is, therefore, powerful for recognizing a single object on a uniform background. However, matching is difficult when more than one scene region is extracted for a model region.

13.2 Interpretation of Imperfect Regions Using a Scene Model

This section describes a method of interpreting regions extracted from an image using a 2D model of the scene. At first, the regions do not necessarily correspond to objects. In the course of interpretation, some regions are merged. The following subsections explain how an image of a room scene is interpreted using an approach called interpretation-guided segmentation (Tenenbaum and Barrow, 1977).

13.2.1 Scene Description

An input image is segmented into uniform regions by the region merging method described in Subsection 3.5.1, where the region merging criterion is set to be conservative so that a region may include only one object. Usually the number of regions is larger than the number of objects in the scene.

Each region is given possible interpretations neglecting its relation with other regions. That is, the interpretations are determined only by the properties of the region itself (such as the average light intensity, position, size, etc.). Most of the regions are given multiple interpretations at this stage. If adjacent regions have the same unique interpretation, they are merged.

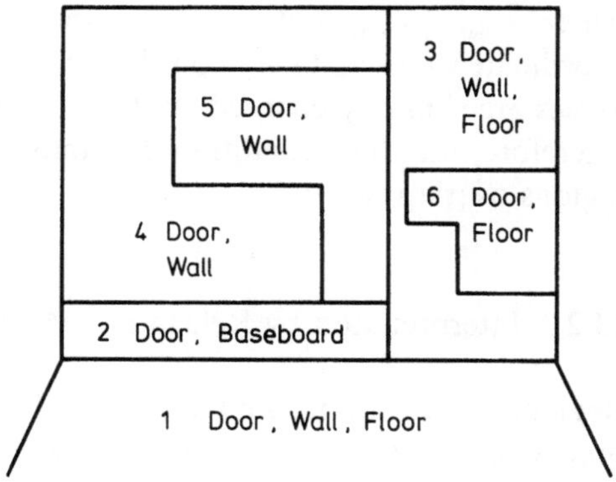

Fig. 13.2. Example of scene description

The description of the scene before using the model consists of imperfect regions with multiple interpretations. Figure 13.2 shows an example of a description of the scene.

13.2.2 Relational Model of Scene

The model of a scene represents spatial relations between objects in the image. In the following discussion, let us consider an example of the interpretation of an image of a room scene. The relations of objects in a room scene are illustrated in Fig. 13.3. The model is described by three predicates: 'inside', 'above', and 'beside'.

Since the predicate 'inside' is a topological relation, the relation is easily defined in the image. The others, 'above' and 'beside', however, are not obvious because two regions are generally neither horizontally nor vertically aligned. One way to define these geometrical relations is to use the relative image coordinates of the regions' centroids and vertices of their bounding rectangles. Region M_1, for example, is defined to be above region M_2 provided that the following conditions hold:

$$y_{1\,\max} > y_{2\,\max}$$

$$y_{1\,\min} > y_{2\,c}$$

$$[x_{1\,\min}, x_{1\,\max}] \cap [x_{2\,\min}, x_{2\,\max}] \neq 0$$

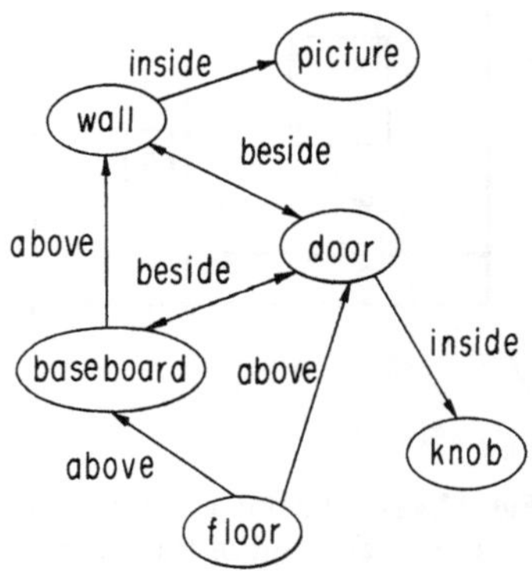

Fig. 13.3. Model of room scene

where $y_{i\max}$, $y_{i\min}$, and y_{ic} denote the highest y coordinate value, the lowest y coordinate value, and the y coordinate value of region M_i's centroid respectively; x values are similarly denoted, and $[x_s, x_e]$ denotes the interval between x_s and x_e. Therefore, the third condition demands that the horizontal intervals of the two regions overlap.

13.2.3 Interpretation by Relaxation Method

Regions and their interpretations are refined here using the relational model. This process is similar to the labeling process by the relaxation method described in Subsect. 5.3.4.

The process is described in this subsection using a simple example, shown in Fig. 13.4. The example involves an image of an empty room that has been correctly segmented into six regions corresponding to the objects Floor (F), Wall (W), Door (D), Baseboard (B), Picture (P), and Knob (K). Initially, every region is assigned possible interpretations as shown in Fig. 13.4(a). In this example, regions 2, 3, and 4 are not allocated interpretations P or K because they are not small enough, and regions 3 and 4 are not allocated interpretation B because they are high.

In the first iteration of the relaxation, the interpretations of every region are filtered by their consistency with the interpretations of the adjacent regions. Region 1 is first examined sequentially against regions 2 and 3. The relation of region 2 to 1 is 'above'. The relation 'above' is found at three places in the model (Fig. 13.3).

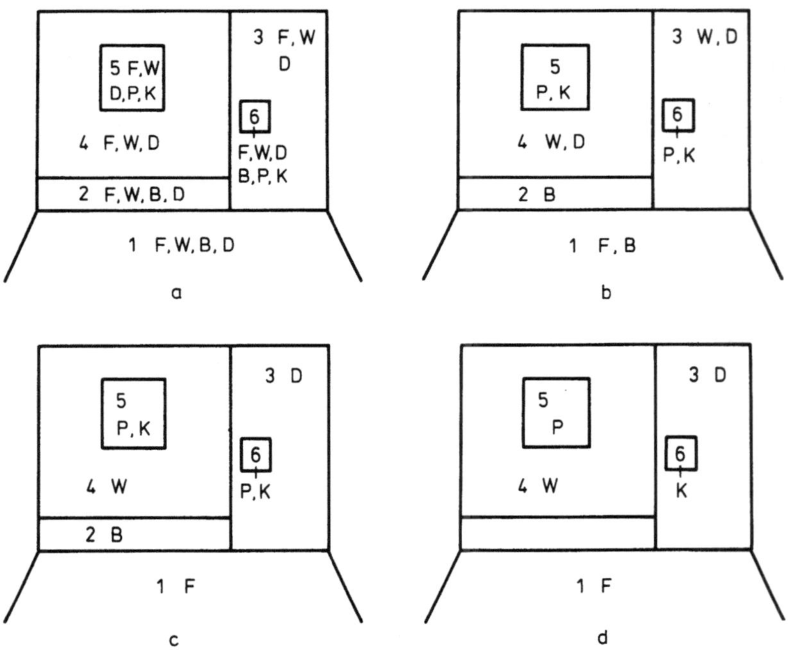

Fig. 13.4a–d. Example of the relaxation process: (**a**) initial interpretations; (**b**) result of the first iteration; (**c**) result of the second iteration; (**d**) final result

Interpretations W and D of region 1 are not consistent with the model because nothing can be above them. Examination of the pair of regions 1 and 3 does not further filter out the interpretations of region 1.

Region 2 is then examined against the adjacent regions 1, 3, and 4. Using the relation 'above' with region 1, interpretation F is removed. Examination of the pair of regions 2 and 4 further filters out interpretations W and D. In this way, the result of the first iteration of the relaxation is obtained as shown in Fig. 13.4(b).

The second iteration proceeds in the same way as the first. Region 3 is now interpreted as D by the relation with region 2, which is already determined as B. The interpretation of region 4 is similarly determined. The result is shown in Fig. 13.4(c).

In the third iteration, small regions 5 and 6 are finally interpreted uniquely as shown in Fig. 13.4(d). Thus the simple relational model of the scene is effectively used to disambiguate interpretations.

13.2.4 Region Merging by Interpretation

In the preceding example, initial regions are assumed to be correctly extracted. In reality, however, they are not correctly obtained without knowledge about scenes. Figure 13.5 shows an example of initial regions and interpretations (where no interpretations are allocated to regions which have all candidate interpretations). In such a case, adjacent regions may have the same interpretation. The scene model shown in Fig. 13.3 is not enough to disambiguate the interpretation of the example (e.g., all the regions may be interpreted as Wall).

Additional constraints are necessary to limit the possible interpretations. First the model is augmented with a new relation, 'contrast'. If the difference of the light intensities of two adjacent regions is large enough, the relation 'contrast' holds between them. In the model the contrast relation holds for the following pairs: Baseboard–Wall, Baseboard–Floor, Door–Knob, Door–Wall, Door–Floor, and

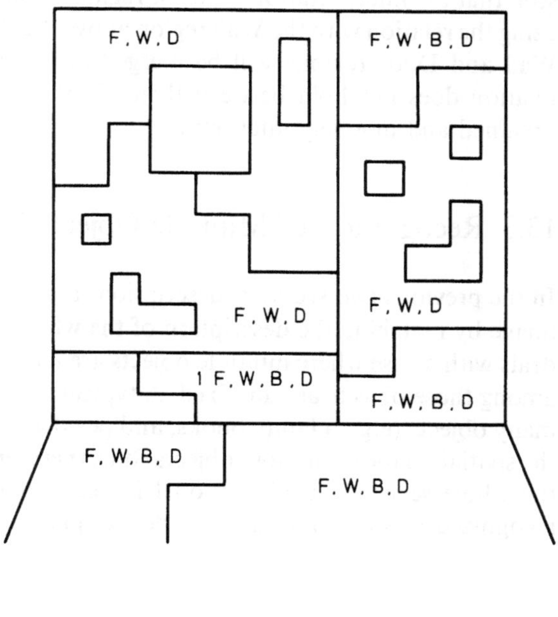

Fig. 13.5. Initial regions and interpretations

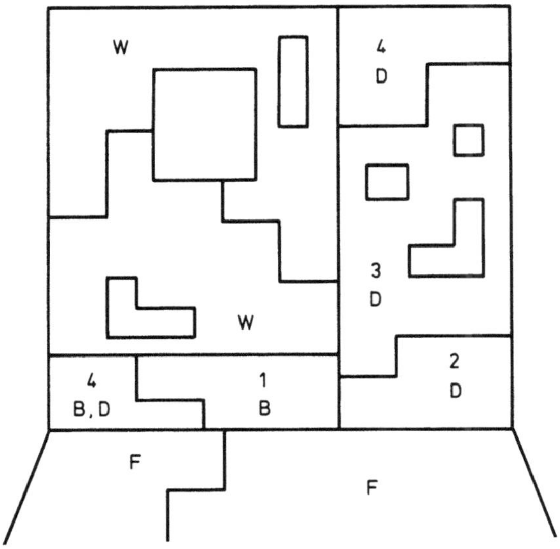

Fig. 13.6. Intermediate state of region merging by interpretation

Wall–Picture. This relation prevents adjacent and strongly contrasting regions from merging.

Second, an arbitrarily chosen pixel within the baseboard area of the image (region 1 in Fig. 13.5) is manually assigned the unique interpretation Baseboard. Although the manual assignment seems to be unrealistic, it may be replaced by some obvious interpretations obtained by computer.

Using the augmented model and initial interpretation Baseboard of region 1, the relaxation process is performed. First, interpretations of regions around region 1 are filtered, and then the constraints propagate all over the image. Figure 13.6 illustrates an intermediate state.

Now, regions 2, 3, and 4 are interpreted uniquely as Door. Therefore, they are now merged to one region. Similarly regions of Floor and Wall are merged. It is also seen that the interpretation Door of region 4 will be removed in the next iteration using the relation with the Wall region above. Furthermore, small regions inside the Wall and Door regions will be merged into the outside regions if the contrast relation does not hold between them. In this way, all the regions are correctly obtained and uniquely interpreted.

13.3 Recognition of Multiple Objects Using 2D Object Models

In the previous two sections, descriptions are given of methods of interpreting an image by matching the description of the whole image to the model. This section deals with a case where multiple objects are included in an image and the relations among those objects are not fixed. A typical example is a scene of a desk on which many objects (e.g., a lamp, books, and pens) are placed. There is no constraint on the spatial relations of those objects. It is, therefore, not effective to use a model of the whole scene. Instead, a model for each object is prepared and objects are recognized by matching those models to parts of the image description.

13.3.1 Control

It is clear that a heterarchical control scheme is necessary to understand an image of a complex scene without strong constraints. In Chap. 12, a description is given of heterarchical controls in which raw data processing is guided by partial results of higher level processing. In this case, however, such a tight control is impossible because there are fewer constraints among parts of the image description.

In the preceding subsection, an incomplete image description (regions) is modified in the interpretation process. The modification, however, is based on the higher level interpretation alone (that is, the raw data are not used). Generally, we do not know how many features should be extracted from an image to understand the scene. A fairly large number of features is necessary for higher level processing to obtain meaningful information. The initial feature set is, however, not always adequate for the purpose of image processing. Without a mechanism to return to the raw data, much computation is required for the initial feature extraction.

A system described in this section first extracts the most prominent features and makes a description of the features. Then, the system tries to recognize objects by using the descriptions. This is the end of the first cycle. If not enough objects are found, the second cycle is performed. That is, less prominent features are extracted and processed in a similar way. These cycles are repeated until enough objects are recognized. After some objects are recognized, the interiors of known objects need not be searched for features. Therefore, raw data processing is accelerated in later cycles.

13.3.2 Edge Finder and Description Maker

This subsection provides a description of feature extraction and description making which are repeatedly executed to recognize many objects in a gray image. Since we cannot use a model of the whole scene, we must select suitable features so that a part of those features may provide a good clue to the identity of an object. Regions, for example, are not suitable features because extraction of closed regions is often very difficult in a complex image. Edges, on the other hand, are better because even incomplete edges may be good clues to the identity of objects.

Edges of planar and curved surfaces are extracted by the method described in Subsect. 3.1.8. In order to find promising edges efficiently, the system uses a reference map. The map represents the approximate contrast of the light intensity at every 4×4 pixels in the image. Let $f(i,j)$ denote the light intensity of the image at (i,j), and $R(i',j')$ represent the approximate contrast in the square region $\{i,j|4i'-3 \leq i \leq 4i', 4j'-3 \leq j \leq 4j'\}$. The map is computed by the following equation.

$$R(i',j') = \max_{\substack{-1<d_i<1 \\ -1<d_j<1}} |f(4i'-1+2d_i, 4j'-1+2d_j) - f(4i'-1, 4j'-1)| \qquad (i',j'=1,2,\ldots) \qquad (13.2)$$

This value is a good approximation of the maximum gradient value in the square region.

The threshold for edge extraction is determined on the basis of the histogram of contrast values in the reference map. The reference map is searched for points such that $R(i'j')$ is above the threshold. Every time a point is found, edge extraction is applied to the corresponding region in the original image. If no edge is found, $R(i',j')$ is updated to the maximum gradient value in the region so that this precise value may be used later.

When an edge point is found, the neighboring region is searched for other edge points. If not enough edge points are found, the edge point is regarded as noise. Otherwise, based on those edges, the edge type, the position and the direction of the edge are determined. Starting from the point, edges of the same type are followed as described in Sect. 3.4.

In this way, edge lines are extracted in the entire image. If not enough edge lines are found, the threshold is lowered and less obvious edges are extracted again. This process is repeated (usually no more than three times) until enough edges are obtained.

After the edge extraction process, an edge is represented as a series of edge points. The direction of an edge is determined such that the left side of the edge is brighter. These edges are then described by combinations of straight lines and elliptic arcs. Each sequence of edge points is first segmented into straight parts and elliptic parts, and then line equations are fitted as described in Chap. 4. According to the result of the segmentation, the series of edge points is also segmented. On the other hand, adjacent edges may be merged if the fitted equations are similar.

13.3.3 Recognizer

A strategy for recognizing an object in a scene depends on how much information is already known. The search can be constrained and directed by the presence of other objects. Assuming that several objects have been recognized, the search for a telephone ought to start within the desk region but outside the book stand region; if the dial, a part of the telephone, has been found, regions adjacent to the dial should be examined for the remainder of the object. The best way to analyze the whole scene is to start from the most obvious object and proceed to the next obvious object making use of the established facts.

Generally, small objects are recognized after larger objects are found. For example, it is not easy to distinguish, by the brightness or the shape of the region alone, a pen from a shadow region caused by a lamp. When a lamp is found, then the shadow region is easily identified.

In this system, the recognition procedure for an object depends on lines and objects already found. It involves the following three stages.

1. Find the main features to obtain clues about the object.
2. Find secondary features to verify the main features and to determine the range of the object.
3. Determine the range and find the other lines that belong to the object.

The recognition procedure proceeds from stage one through three, but it may stop at any stage when it fails.

For recognition of a lamp, for example, the program locates a lampshade in the first stage. The clue to a lampshade is a pair of long, approximately horizontal, parallel lines at a distance within a certain range. When it finds them, it searches for other lines connecting them. There are one or two lines depending on whether or not one side of the lampshade is outside of the image.

If it succeeds in finding the shade, then it proceeds to the second stage, and it searches for the lamp trunk supporting the lampshade. The position of the trunk is precisely predicted if both ends of the lampshade are in the image, and approximately predicted if only one end is obtained. If it finds the trunk, then it searches for a contour of the lamp base supporting the trunk.

If it fails during the search for a certain part, it decides whether the features obtained so far seem really to belong to a lamp or not. Here, recognition of a lamp succeeds when the lampshade and the trunk are found. If recognition succeeds, then a region is determined for the lamp. The region depends on the result of the previous stages. For example, if a lamp base occluded by some object is partly found, the region should not include that object. The lamp region is a good clue to finding the other lines of the lamp which have not been identified (e.g., edges caused by characters or color pattern on smooth surfaces).

Table 13.1 illustrates a hierarchy of features used for recognition. The hierarchy of features for an object is based on two aspects of the features. One is the importance of the feature in implying the presence of the object, and the other is the ease with which it may be found in a scene. Most of the features consist of the edges represented by the equation and the terminal points. Care must be taken in finding a contour of a region because edges of a region do not always constitute a closed line. The properties of a region must be estimated from a part of the boundary. Another problem is that two adjacent edges may not meet at a point. In order to find an edge connected to a certain edge, therefore, the neighbor of the end point must be searched.

For recognition of small objects, a fixed resolution is sometimes inadequate to allow discrimination between similar objects such as a felt pen, a pencil or a ballpoint pen. The system zooms in on an interesting part to take a close-up image,

Table 13.1. Examples of features used for recognition

Object(s)	Main feature	Secondary feature
Lamp	Contour of bright stripe region (lamp shade)	Pair of vertical lines of opposite direction (trunk)
Book stand	Long vertical lines clustered in a rectangular region	Lines connected to main features
Cup	Pairs of vertical edges of opposite directions (sides)	Contours connecting main features (top and bottom)
Telephone	Part of ellipse (dial or a circle of numbers)	Lines surrounding main feature (case)
Small objects (pipe, pen, etc.)	Approximately closed sequence of lines	Size and shape of lines

and examine the shape of the object in detail. The analysis of the new image is easy because the position and the orientation of the object have been predicted.

13.3.4 Total System

This section describes how the system efficiently analyzes a scene to recognize various objects in it. The three modules described in the previous sections work under monitor control as shown in Fig. 13.7. *A priori* knowledge consists of the orientation and direction of the camera as well as the parameters of the camera (zoom, iris, etc.).

First, the map maker makes a reference map as described in Subsection 13.3.2. The monitor sets the threshold of the contrast for edge finding, and determines when edge finding should stop. The stopping condition is based on the number of edges, number of edge points and the threshold of the contrast. This initial setting of these conditions affects the efficiency. If it is too high, not enough edges are obtained; in this case the threshold is lowered and another attempt is made to find edges. Many cycles of this process take much time. On the other hand, if the level is too low, too many edges are collected. The reference map is used to estimate the initial level. Thus, enough edges are usually obtained in one cycle of edge finding.

An edge map in Fig. 13.7 is a 2D array corresponding to the scene containing edge numbers already found. It is used in both edge finding and recognition in order to find edges in a given area. Edge finding uses another map (called a bit map) whose one bit shows the existence of an edge element. The process for edge following checks the bit map to determine if there are other edges crossing the current edge. If other edges are detected, the edge-following processes terminates. Then the edge numbers are found in the edge map, and the relations of the edges with the traced edge are determined according to the position and the direction of the edges. The

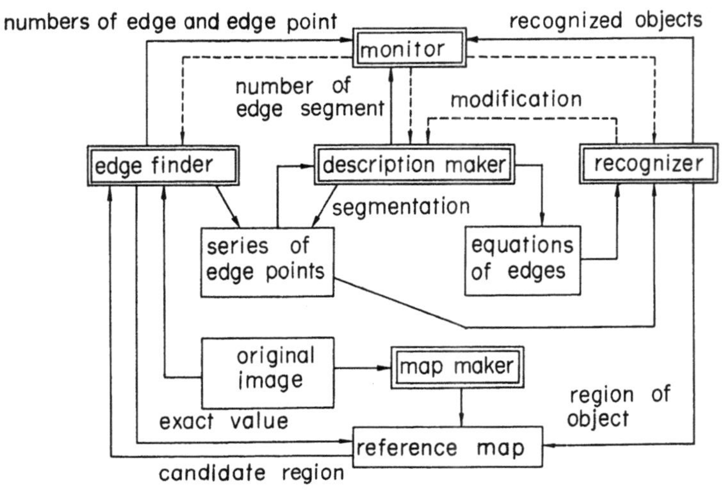

Fig. 13.7. Information flow among main components of the system

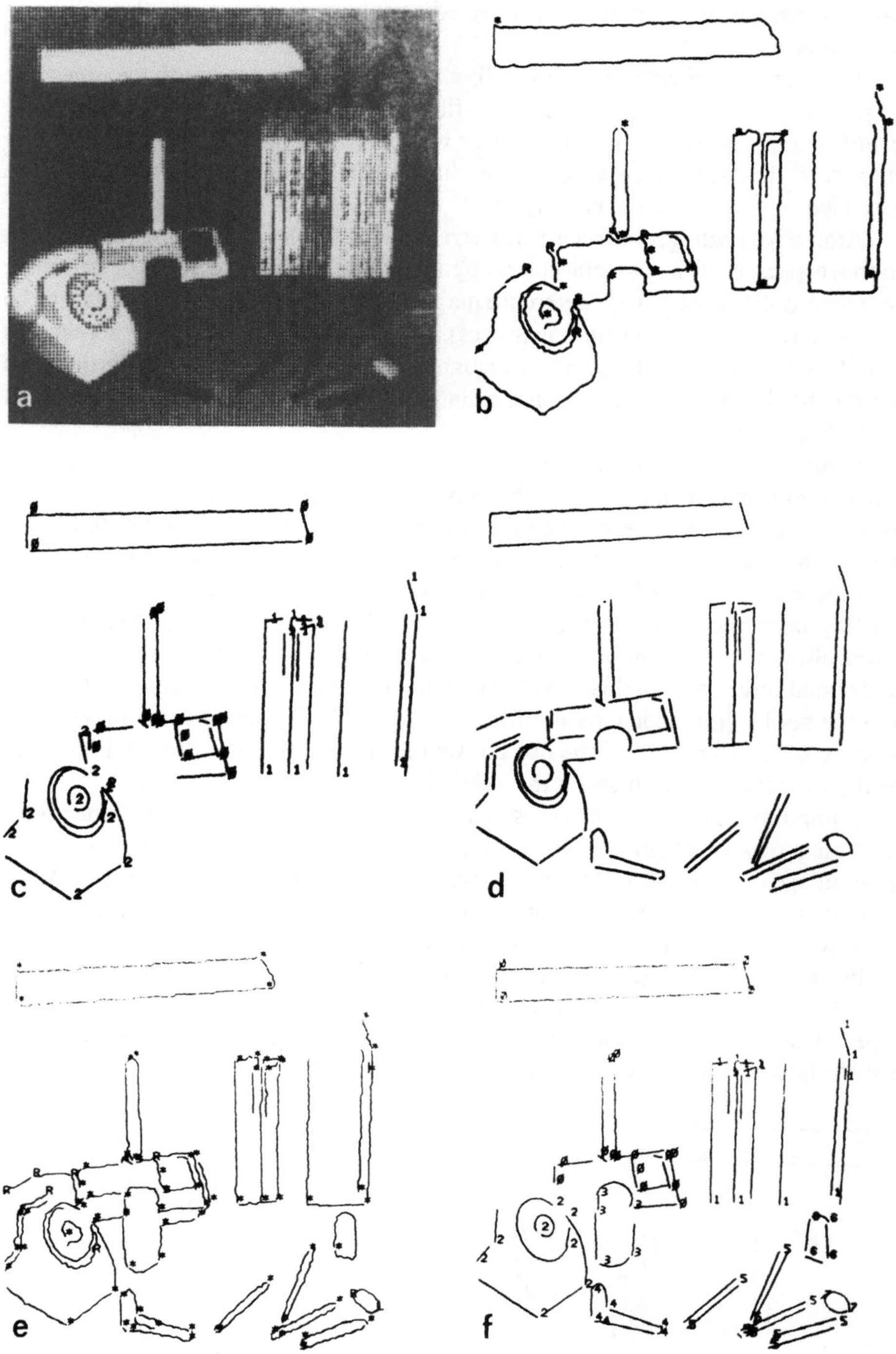

Fig. 13.8a–f. An example of the recognition process: (**a**) original scene; (**b**) edges found in cycle 1; (**c**) recognition (*0*: lamp, *1*: book stand, *2*: telephone); (**d**) description in cycle 2; (**e**) edges found up to cycle 4; (**f**) recognition result (*3*: cup, *4*: pipe, *5*: pen, pencil, ballpoint pen or felt pen, *6*: ink pot, *7*: eraser)

possible relations are 'smoothly connected', 'making a corner', and 'belonging to other objects'.

When enough edges are found, before proceeding to represent those edges, the edge finder tries to extend some edges to fill small gaps between them. The intensity profile of edge points often changes near vertices. The edge-following process may stop near the vertices because of the change of the edge type. Such edges are extended regardless of the edge type.

After edge finding, control is transferred first to the description maker and then to the recognizer. When an object is recognized and the object region is determined, the corresponding part in the reference map is changed so that no edge point may be found there in a later edge-finding process. The descriptions of edges are sometimes modified according to the result of recognition. For example, if two elliptic edges are regarded as parts of the telephone dial, the equation of the ellipse is computed again from both edges.

Figure 13.8 shows an example of the recognition of various objects on a desk. No assumption is made about the brightness of objects compared with that of the desk. All the objects are successfully recognized in four cycles. Edge finding is performed five times with different thresholds (twice in the second cycle).

Figure 13.9 shows edges obtained without feedback from recognition. That is, starting from the same threshold, edges are collected repeatedly, decreasing the threshold until about the same number of edge points is obtained. Edge finding is performed three times in this case. We can observe many edges inside the telephone and the book stand which are not found in Fig. 13.8. This means that more edges must be obtained before all the objects are recognized. It may be more difficult to recognize objects from many unreliable edges.

Computation time depends mostly on the complexity of a scene. For the above example a time of about 3 min was required to recognize all the objects using the input image (6 bit × 256 × 256 points) stored on a disk. Most of the time (80%) was spent on edge finding, while recognition took up the least (5%). If the input image were stored in main memory, computation time might be greatly reduced. Without feedback from the recognition process, edge finding might take much more time for the collection of a greater number of edges. The method has been proved effective by experiments on recognition of various objects on a desk while varying both the distribution and orientation of objects and lighting conditions.

Fig. 13.9. Description of edges found without feedback from the recognizer

14 Image Understanding Using Three-Dimensional Models

It has been observed that three-dimensional models are flexible in that they can potentially be matched to images of objects viewed from various directions. Methods of generating 3D models are described in Chap. 10. This chapter deals with methods for matching 3D models to descriptions of images or scenes.

3D models have recently been used for the verification vision of robots which move in a building and manipulate objects. In verification vision the relationship between the direction of the camera and the orientation of objects is known, so the matching problem is relatively easy because the input image is predicted. If the image of each object does not change, the matching problem is not greatly different from that of a 2D model. This happens when objects are on a plane far from a camera, and 3D rotation is not allowed.

Generally, the matching of 3D models is not easy because the image of an object may change when the object moves or rotates. In such a case, we need some methods for predicting the orientation. Otherwise, matching of a model requires many trials with different orientations.

The difficulty of this problem depends on whether an input scene includes only a single object or multiple objects. In the former case, features of the entire scene can be matched to object models. Recognition of multiple objects occluding one another is more difficult, since we do not know to which object observed image features belong. There are two main approaches to this problem. The first approach is to segment image features into objects and then to recognize objects from segmented features. The second approach is to try to recognize the object before segmentation. The first approach is more simple, because the problem is reduced to recognition of a single object. However, if segmentation is impossible without object models, the second approach is necessary. The following sections describe some of the important methods for these matching problems.

There are still many important problems that will not be dealt with here. One of them is how to recognize flexible objects such as animals or trees. Their shapes are not as well defined as machine parts. Should we develop flexible models, or flexible matching methods? Since solutions to this problem are not yet established, they are left to future reasearch.

14.1 Matching for Verification Vision

Verification vision has various fields of application. In many industrial applications, pattern matching techniques are used for locating objects (Kashioka et al., 1976). Binary images of objects are matched to an object model represented also by a binary image. In most cases, the image is easily predicted because objects are constrained on a plane. This simple matching technique is excluded in this section.

If binary images of objects are not available, more complicated methods are required. One way is to use image features instead of binary images. Edges, lines, corners, and so forth are extracted from an image and matched to the models which are also represented in terms of the same features (Bolles, 1977).

If image features are not easily extracted, gray images must directly be matched to model images. This technique is similar to that for stereo vision described in Chap. 7. Typical matching methods for these two cases are dealt with in the following three subsections.

14.1.1 Matching of Feature Points

Models of objects may be represented in terms of feature points. It is shown in Sect. 5.1 that a model of a block may be represented by the vertices and the edges connecting the vertices. After vertices are extracted from an image, they can be matched to those of models by assuming the model and the corresponding vertices. Remember that the problem is to find a nonlinear transformation matrix H given by Eq. (5.8). Since object types and the position of vertices are not predicted, the matching problem is difficult.

In verification vision, however, the problem can be solved in various ways. One way is to approximate the transformation matrix by a linear matrix. For example, if rotation angles θ, φ, and ψ are predicted as θ_0, φ_0, and ψ_0, respectively, R_x in Eq. (5.4) is reduced to

$$R_x=\begin{pmatrix} 1 & 0 & 0 & 0 \\ 0 & \cos\theta_0-\Delta\theta\sin\theta_0 & -\sin\theta_0-\Delta\theta\cos\theta_0 & 0 \\ 0 & \sin\theta_0+\Delta\theta\cos\theta_0 & \cos\theta_0-\Delta\theta\sin\theta_0 & 0 \\ 0 & 0 & 0 & 1 \end{pmatrix} \tag{14.1}$$

where $\Delta\theta=\theta-\theta_0$. R_y and R_z are similarly represented as linear matrices with respect to $\Delta\varphi$ and $\Delta\psi$, respectively. Note that the higher orders of these variables are neglected. For a pair of corresponding points in the model and in the image, two linear equations with respect to six variables (three for translation, three for rotation) are obtained. Three pairs are enough to obtain the solution. If more pairs are available, a least-squares method can be applied.

Another way of matching is to directly compute nonlinear equations. For a predicted position and orientation of an object (usually represented by six parameters), the positions of the features are predicted in the image. These positions are compared with those of actual features extracted from the input image. If they do not fit well, the parameters are modified. In order to evaluate how well the predicted features fit to the actual ones, we can use the sum of squares of the distance between pairs of corresponding features (similar to Eq. (5.10)). The problem is to find a set of parameters which minimizes a nonlinear function.

It is generally difficult to solve this nonlinear optimization problem. In verification vision, however, the problem is solved by a hill-climbing method

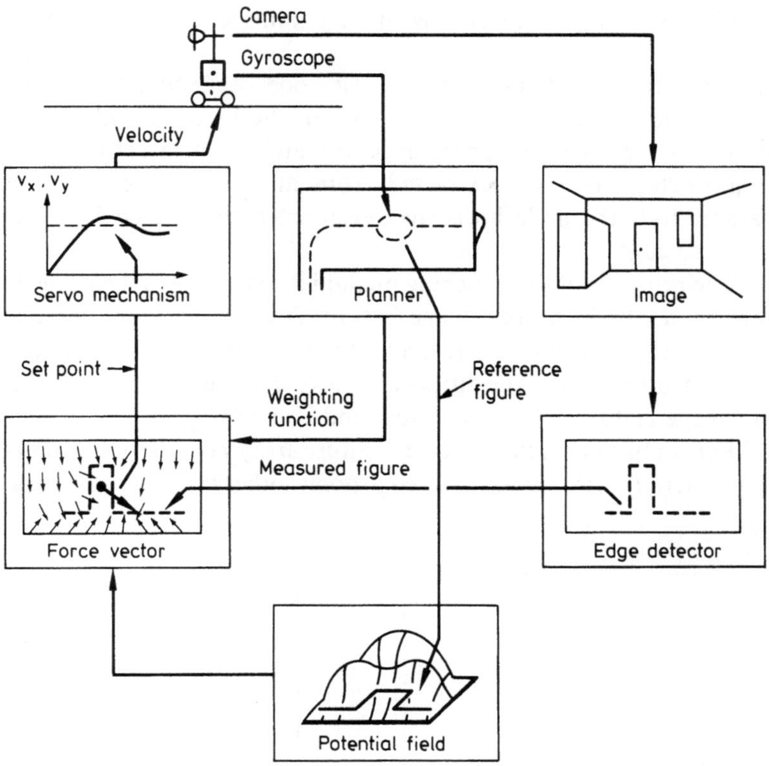

Fig. 14.1. Concept of a visual navigation system

because the initial point is given near the optimum point. Since the same distance array can be used in each iteration, the computation burden is decreased.

Vision systems for mobile robots usually verify their position by frequently looking at their environment. In such cases, features are precisely predicted. The real image can be regarded as just a translation of the predicted image. The parameters are the translations along the horizontal and vertical axes in the image. The optimization problem is more easily solved by the hill-climbing method.

This problem can be solved in another way. Instead of the distance array, an array of 'force' is prepared. Each element of the force array contains a vector pointing toward the nearest feature. Evaluation of matching can be similarly obtained by adding the vectors at predicted feature points. If the magnitude of the total vector is small, the matching is successful. If not, the next prediction is immediately derived from the average vector (the total vector divided by the number of feature points). This is as if the model were attracted by the force.

The force matrix can also be defined as the potential of the 'gravity' caused by model features. The total force is computed by summing the gravity at each image feature. This time, image features are moved by the force. For a mobile robot, the position of the robot is corrected so that the image features extracted by robot vision may move in the direction of the force. Figure 14.1 shows the concept of a visual navigation system based on this method (Kamejima et al., 1984).

14.1.2 Matching of Features Without Finding Correspondence

In verification vision, feature points of a model can be matched without determining corresponding image features. A typical method is explained by using the example shown in Fig. 14.2: the problem is to match a set of feature points in a model (Fig. 14.2(a)) to edges extracted from an input image (Fig. 14.2(b)). If six parameters of the model are correctly estimated, the predicted feature points may lie on those edges.

The principle of the matching method is to assume that each feature of a model corresponds to the nearest image feature. The distance to the nearest feature can be obtained from a distance array, an element of which represents the distance to the nearest feature point. The distance values can be determined in two passes through the image feature array (Rosenfeld and Kak, 1976).

For simplicity, let the size of the feature array $f(i,j)$ be $n \times n$. Initially $f(i,j)=0$ if the point (i,j) corresponds to an edge point; otherwise, $f(i,j)$ is given the maximum

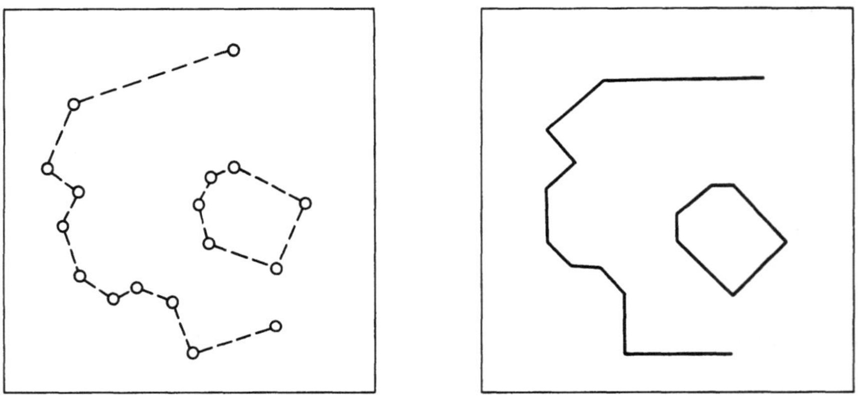

a b

Fig. 14.2a, b. Example of matching problem: (**a**) feature points of a model (edge candidates in broken lines); (**b**) edges extracted from an input image

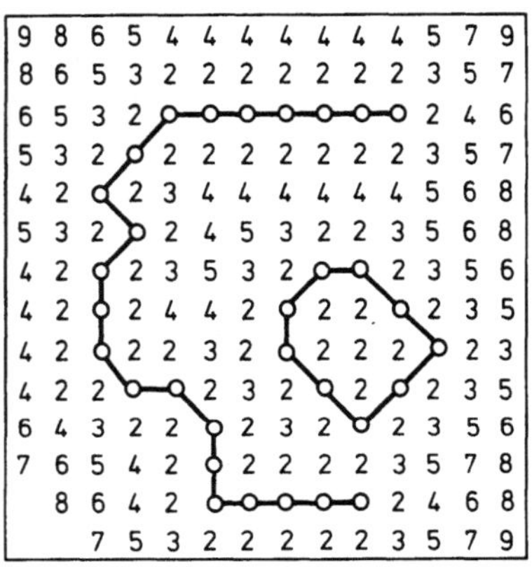

Fig. 14.3. Distance array derived from the feature array shown in Fig. 14.2(b)

possible distance. The first pass modifies the feature array as follows:

for $j=2$ step 1 until n

for $i=2$ step 1 until n

$$f(i,j) \leftarrow \min\{f(i,j), f(i-1,j)+d(i-1,j), f(i-1,j-1)+d(i-1,j-1), f(i,j-1)+d(i,j-1), f(i+1,j-1)+d(i+1,j-1)\};$$

where $d(x,y)$ denotes the distance between (i,j) and (x,y). For example, the distance to the horizontal or vertical neighbor is 2 and the distance to the diagonal neighbor is 3 (Barrow et al., 1977). The second pass further modifies the feature array as follows:

for $j=2$ step 1 until n

for $i=2$ step 1 until n

$$f(i,j) \leftarrow \min\{f(i,j), f(i+1,j)+d(i+1,j), f(i+1,j+1)+d(i+1,j+1), f(i,j+1)+d(i,j+1), f(i-1,j+1)+d(i-1,j+1)\}.$$

Figure 14.3 shows an example of a distance array. The evaluation of the matching can be easily obtained from the values at the predicted feature points. For example, if the evaluation function is the sum of the distances, the value can be computed by stepping through the predicted feature points and simply summing the distance array values of those elements.

The matching problem is reduced to a nonlinear optimization problem just as in the previous subsection. The optimal set of parameters is also obtained by a hill-climbing method.

14.1.3 Matching Gray Images Synthesized from Surface Models

It is not easy to extract reliable features from images with curved surfaces. Edge extraction, for example, is disturbed by sharp brightness changes on curved surfaces. In such cases, gray images may be used for matching. It is, however, inefficient to store all possible models of gray images. In verification vision, models of gray images may be synthesized from 3D models of surfaces. The light intensity of a given surface can be obtained from the condition of illumination and reflectance, as described in Sect. 8.1.

Let us consider the problem of matching a gray image of a terrain taken by a satellite to a map containing the same region (Horn and Backman, 1978). A surface model can be synthesized from contours of the map. We can obtain, by the method described in Sect. 10.3, triangular surface patches connecting adjacent contours.

In order to match an input gray image to the model image, the latter is synthesized with the same illumination condition. The light source is regarded as a point source corresponding to the sun. The illumination direction is then easily obtained from the time and date when the image was taken. If the surface is regarded

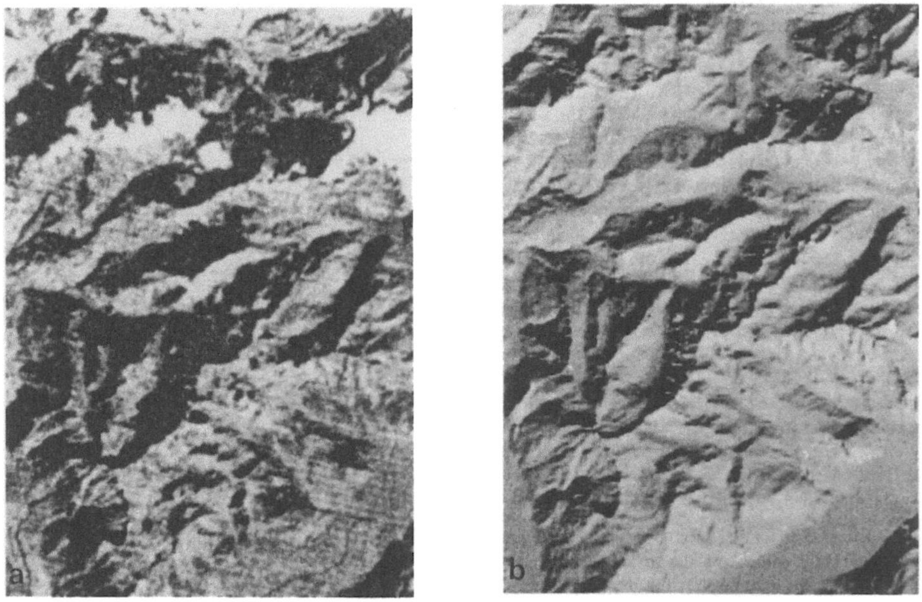

Fig. 14.4. (**a**) Synthetic image of snow-covered terrain; (**b**) real image (Horn and Backman, 1978)

as perfectly diffuse, the light intensity of each triangular surface patch is computed from the direction of the surface normal and that of the illumination.

We can assume that the image is formed by orthographic projection because it is taken at a high altitude. The transformation between the real image and the synthetic image is then represented by Affin transformation and a scale change. Let x and y designate points in the synthetic image and x' and y' points in the real image. The following relation holds:

$$\begin{bmatrix} x' \\ y' \end{bmatrix} = s \begin{bmatrix} \cos\theta & \sin\theta \\ -\cos\theta & \sin\theta \end{bmatrix} \begin{bmatrix} x \\ y \end{bmatrix} + \begin{bmatrix} u \\ v \end{bmatrix} \qquad (14.2)$$

where s is a scale, and u and v are the shift in x' and y', respectively.

Now we can synthesize a gray image for a given set of parameters (θ, s, u, and v). The next problem is how to evaluate the similarity between the real image and the predicted image. Similarity measures are similar to those for stereo vision described in Subsect. 7.2.2. We can use, for example, the correlation of the two images, or some modifications of the correlation. Then the problem is again reduced to finding the optimum parameters for a given evaluation function. This problem is easier than the previous ones because the number of parameters is lower. Figure 14.4 shows an example of a synthetic image and a real image used for an experiment with this method (Horn and Backman, 1978).

14.2 Object Recognition by Predicting Image Features from Models

Some matching techniques for verification vision are described above. Such techniques are applicable only to those cases where the object is known, and the position and orientation of the object are predicted. It is often necessary to recognize objects when only an object is known but the position and orientation are not precisely predicted. For example, in order to locate cars on a highway or to find machine parts on a conveyor, we can approximately predict their shapes and orientation.

It is useful to have a system to deal with such cases in a systematic way. A domain-independent model-based vision system called ACRONYM (Brooks, Greiner, and Binford, 1979) has been developed. Figure 14.5 shows major modules (boxes), the data base of models, and data structures (ellipses) of ACRONYM.

The user interactively generates object models in a graphic display. The system automatically predicts which image features to expect, finds candidate features, and interprets them. The following subsections explain the main functions of the system.

14.2.1 Modeling

The shape of objects is modeled with a combination of generalized cylinders as described in Sect. 10.3. The model can be made flexible by using variables. For example, the length and the radius of a cylinder may be specified by variables which

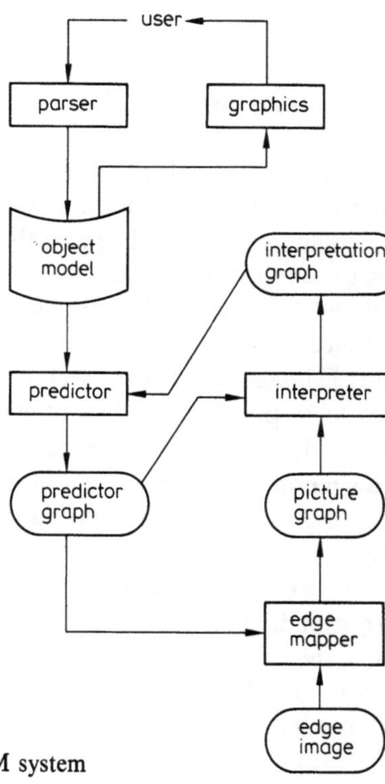

Fig. 14.5. ACRONYM system

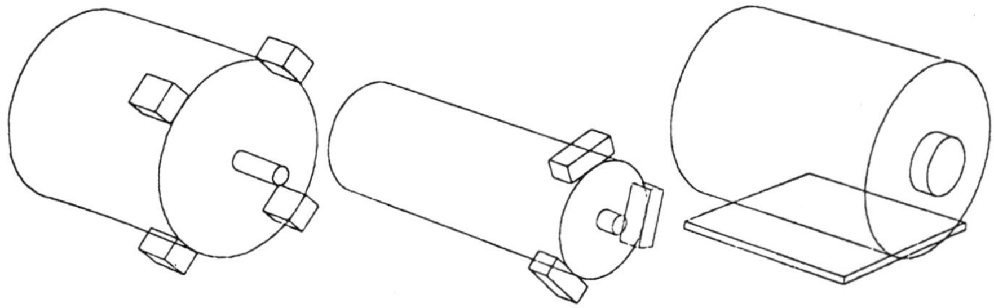

Fig. 14.6. Three specializations of a generic model of a motor (Brooks, 1981a)

are constrained by inequalities such as:

$$6 < \text{LENGTH} < 9$$

$$17 < \text{LENGTH} \times \text{RADIUS} < 21$$

There are two types of models: generic models and specialized models. The former roughly describe a class of objects, and the latter describe each object in detail.

A generic model of a motor, for example, is just an ordinary cylinder with two variables for the length and the radius. A user can specialize the generic class of motors by giving specific numerical values and by attaching subparts such as spindles or flanges. Examples of three specializations are shown in Fig. 14.6 (Brooks, 1981a). The hierarchy of models according to the level of abstraction is useful not only for modeling but also for efficient object recognition, as described below.

14.2.2 Prediction

Given a set of models and their relationships, the system predicts features that are invariant over the modeled range of variations. Remember that the shapes of models are represented by generalized cylinders. Generalized cylinders are assumed here to have a straight axis and circular cross-section. The radius of the cross-section is allowed to change linearly along the axis.

Since the input to the system is composed of edges extracted from gray images, only 2D image features are available. Primitives of the features, therefore, are closed lines corresponding to edges of generalized cylinders. Two types of closed line are predicted: a quadrilateral (called 'ribbon') corresponding to contours of a side view of a generalized cylinder, and an ellipse corresponding to a circular cross-section. These basic features are invariant to the viewer from directions within a certain range.

The axis of a generalized cylinder is observed in the image as the axis of the corresponding ribbon. If axes of generalized cylinders are parallel to the image plane, the angle between them is approximated by the angle of the axes of the two ribbons. The lengths of axes are good clues for relating the size of the object to its distance from the camera. That is, if the size is known, the distance is estimated, and vice versa.

14.2.3 Making Descriptions

The input to the system is a collection of edges extracted from a gray image by a line finder developed by Nevatia and Babu (1979). The line finder is a domain-independent module which works in a bottom-up fashion. Figure 14.7(a) shows the line segments obtained by the line finder.

Ribbon candidates are extracted from pairs of nearly parallel line segments (Brooks, 1979). For each pair of parallel lines, an axis is estimated as the center line. The ends of the ribbon are determined from the projections of the parallel lines onto the axis. The candidates are filtered out by examining the shape, and the relationship between the ribbon and line segments. Fig. 14.7(b) shows the ribbons produced from the edges shown in Fig. 14.7(a).

14.2.4 Interpretation

Interpretation proceeds by combining local matches of shapes into more global matches. Let us consider the problem of finding a class of airplanes in an airport from aerial photographs taken from an altitude in a certain range.

It is not efficient initially to try to match all types of airplane models to features in the picture graph. Instead, the system first uses the most general set of constraints associated with the generic class of airplanes. From the generic model, shapes and sizes of wings and fuselages are predicted. For example, the length of a wing is specified within a certain range, and the ratio to that of the fuselage is constrained by a set of inequalities. The shape and the size of the corresponding ribbons are predicted from the model and the range of the camera altitude. Based on the prediction, candidates of wings and fuselages are found.

For each candidate, the system tries to find adjacent candidates corresponding to other components of the same airplane using the relationships between them. The relationships involve the distance, the angle between the two axes, and the relative size. If at least two components are found from two wings and a fuselage, the existence of the airplane is established. The interpretation graph consists of those interpreted components. Figure 14.8 shows the interpretation graph obtained by matching the generic model to ribbons shown in Fig. 14.7(b).

Once the generic model of an airplane is matched to a set of ribbons, it is easy to check whether it might also be an instance of a subclass. The system checks for the extra constraints associated with the subclass. The check is made on the basis of the ratio of the length of the components or the angle between them. Figure 14.9 shows two instances of subclass models. The airplane in Fig. 14.8 is consistent with the constraints for an L-1011, but not for a Boeing-747.

Once the subclass name is determined, it might be possible to find other components in the picture graph. From Fig. 14.8, for example, the tail of the airplane may be predicted as ribbons, and they may be verified in Fig. 14.7(b). More components might be found back in the edge image (these functions are not yet implemented). In Fig. 14.7(a), for example, two engines may be found in the predicted positions.

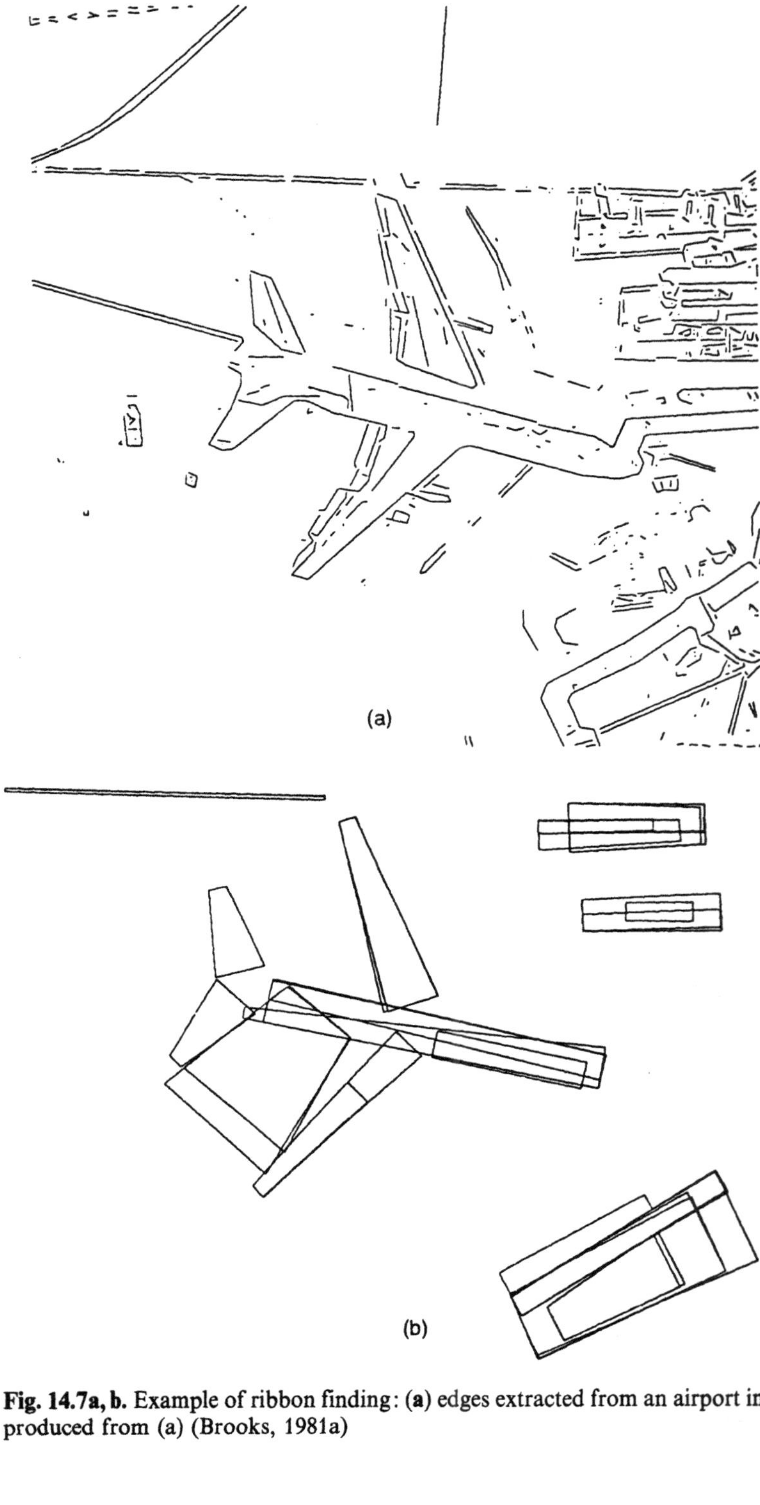

Fig. 14.7a, b. Example of ribbon finding: (**a**) edges extracted from an airport image; (**b**) ribbons produced from (a) (Brooks, 1981a)

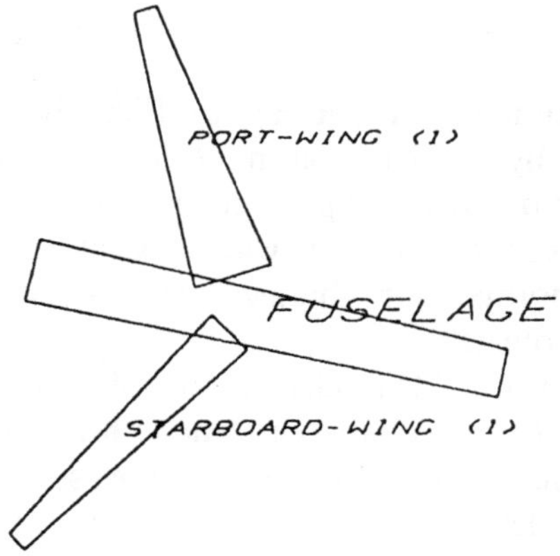

Fig. 14.8. Three components interpreted from Fig. 14.7 (Brooks, 1981b)

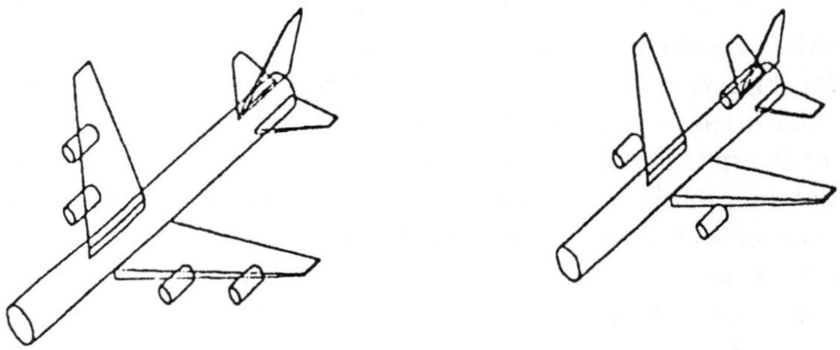

Fig. 14.9. Subclass models of Boeing-747 (*left*) and the Lockheed L-1011 (*right*) (Brooks, 1981b)

ACRONYM efficiently recognizes objects using hierarchical models. Invariant features are easily predicted because objects are constrained on a plane and 3D rotation is not allowed. However, the appearance of objects may generally change greatly and the length of generalized cylinders or the angle between the axes do not correspond to those of the ribbons. The development of an efficient recognition method in such cases is left to future studies.

14.3 Matching Geometric Models to the Description of a Single Object

Recognition of objects is generally difficult because their orientation is not known. If only one object is included on a known background, the recognition becomes much easier. All features found in an image belong to the same object, and each object model can be tested against those features. One of the important problems in such a case is how to find a matching model from many models.

This section describes three methods of hierarchical matching for object recognition. The first and the third methods use the geometric modeling system GEOMAP (described in Sect. 10.5) for generating and manipulating solid models. The second method is for matching in the Extended Gaussian Image, which is used by the third method as a higher level matching.

14.3.1 Recognition of Glossy Objects from Surface Normals

Recognition of glossy objects is difficult because properties of such objects are not obtained by conventional input devices. It is shown in Sect. 8.2 that the surface normal is derived by a polarimetric method. The method, however, provides only normals of those surfaces where specular reflections occur. Typically, only a few surface normals are obtained. This is not enough to recognize many kinds of complex objects.

However, if 3D models of possible objects are available, we can select a set of object models which is consistent with the observed surface normals. We can even find a unique model if a set of observed surface normals is consistent with only one object model. Note that curved surfaces are represented by polygon surfaces in most geometric modeling systems and also by the current version of GEOMAP.

Now recognition of unknown objects is equivalent to matching of observed surface normals to object models. For convenience, the recognition system (Koshikawa and Shirai, 1985) also uses the constraint that objects be placed in a stable orientation on a horizontal plane (a table). Stable orientations of each object are determined *a priori* from the geometric model as described in Sect. 10.5. Note that, in a stable orientation, at least one plane of the convex hull lies on the table. For each stable orientation, one such surface is selected and stored in the model (by using a user pointer). Let us denote such planes by 'base plane'. Use of this constraint is, therefore, equivalent to adding one more surface normal to those observed.

The strategy of matching is to select promising models quickly and then check them in more detail. The following matching process obtains a list of matching models:

1. Select a new model. If no model is left, stop the process.
2. Select a new base plane of the model. If no base plane is left (all base planes are already examined), go to (1).
3. Assuming that the base plane is on the table, find all sets of surfaces which are consistent with the observed surface normals and relative angles between these normals. If no such set is found, go to (2).
4. Select a new set of surfaces found in (3). If no such set is left, go to (2).
5. Place the candidate model on the table so that observed directions of surface normals coincide with those of the model. Find the translation on the horizontal plane so that observed positions of surface normals coincide with those of models in the image. If no such translation is found, go to (4).
6. For the object model in the orientation, check if the observed surface normals are really observable (not hidden by other surfaces). If the check is successful, add the model to the matching model list. Go to (4).

When the process stops, the possible models are stored in the candidate list. In step (3), observed surface normals are given sequential numbers, and surfaces of the model are selected according to the sequence. The first face is selected such that the relative angle to the base plane coincides with that of the first observed surface to the table (the normal is downward). Then the second surface is selected such that both the relative angle to the base plane and that to the first surface coincide with those of the second observed surface, and so on. When a set of surfaces is selected, the system tries to find other sets. For the base plane, all candidate sets are obtained in this step.

In step (5), the translation of the model is generally not easily obtained. Here, the problem is simplified by assuming an orthographic projection in the range of small translations. The method is explained by using the example shown in Fig. 14.10, where S_1, S_2, and S_3 denote the position of the observed surfaces (bottom right corner), and M_1, M_2, and M_3 denote regions of the corresponding model surfaces in the image. Note that the regions in the image are obtained from the model and the camera parameters.

First M_2 and M_3 are translated by vectors S_2S_1 and S_3S_1, respectively. If the intersection of M_1 and the two translated regions is empty, there is no consistent translation. Otherwise, the intersection (the hatched region) corresponds to S_1; that is, the translation is usually determined in a certain range.

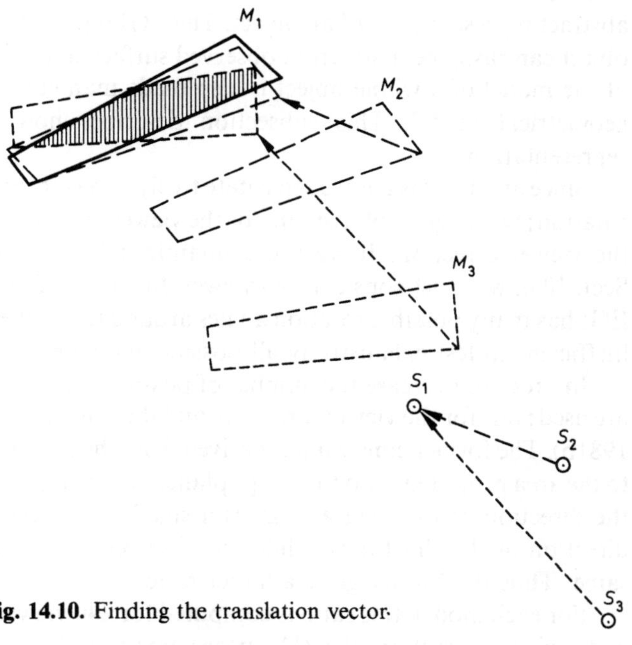

Fig. 14.10. Finding the translation vector

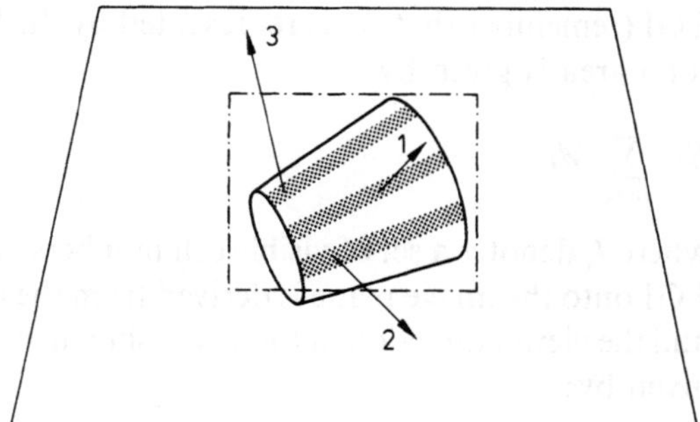

Fig. 14.11. Recognition result

Step (5) needs more computation than step (3). Note, however, that candidates to be examined in step (5) have been filtered out in step (3). In step (6), the check of visibility of a surface requires examination of other surfaces of the model. The amount of computation is still more than that in step (5). Candidates to be checked here have further been filtered out in step (5).

The method employs a hierarchical matching: first in surface normals and then in positions. The first matching is at an abstract level, for it neglects the position of surfaces. This two-stage matching attains an efficient performance. Figure 14.11 shows the experimental result of recognition for observed surface normals indicated by arrows.

14.3.2 Matching in the Extended Gaussian Image

It has been mentioned in Sect. 10.6 that the Extended Gaussian Image (EGI) is an abstract representation of an object. The EGI representation of a visible part of an object can easily be made from observed surface normals. The EGI representation of the model of a whole object is also made manually or automatically from the geometrical model. This subsection describes how to match the two EGI representations.

Since an object is allowed to rotate freely, it has three degrees of freedom for the rotation: two degrees of freedom for the viewer direction and one for rotation about the viewer direction. If we use a quantized EGI with 240 planes as shown in Sect. 10.6, we must consider 240 viewer directions. For each viewer direction, the EGI has many possible rotation angles around the viewer direction. It is, therefore, inefficient to test exhaustively all possible matching pairs.

In order to decrease the number of possible directions, two kinds of constraint are used: one for the viewer direction, and the other for rotation around it (Ikeuchi, 1981b). The former constraint is derived from the ratio of the observed surface area to the area projected onto the image plane. For example, an ellipsoid observed from the direction of the long axis gives a smaller projected area than that from the direction of the short axis, while the observed surface area is approximately the same. Thus the former gives a larger ratio.

For each model, this ratio is computed for 240 viewer directions. Given an EGI and a viewer direction, the 3D surface area is easily computed. The total surface area is the sum of the visible surface areas. Let M_i denote the area of the ith cell in the EGI (remember that M_i is represented by the length of an arrow in the EGI). The total area is given by:

$$S=\sum_{i\in I_v} M_i \tag{14.3}$$

where I_v denotes a set of visible cell numbers. The area projected by each cell in the EGI onto the image plane is derived from the angle (e) between the surface normal and the viewer direction of the cell as shown in Fig. 14.12. The total projected area is given by:

$$S_p=\sum_{i\in I_v} (\cos e_i) M_i \tag{14.4}$$

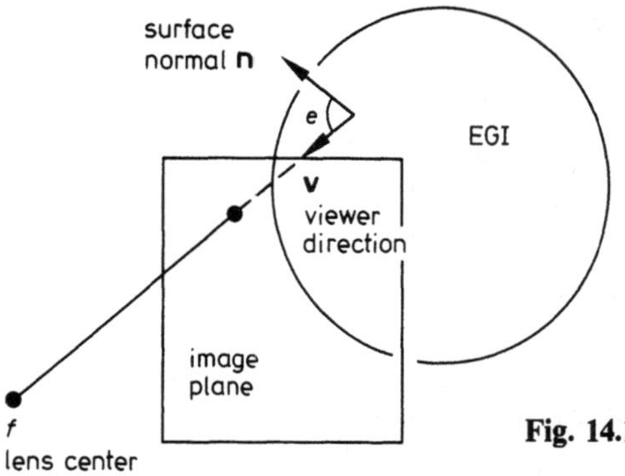

Fig. 14.13. Masses projected from the EGI of a cylinder

Fig. 14.12. Computation of projected area from EGI

The ratio S_p/S is computed for the observed EGI in the same way. This ratio usually constrains the viewer direction to a few candidates.

Another constraint is derived from the projection of the EGI onto the image plane. The area of each visible cell of the EGI is projected onto the image plane as a point with mass proportional to the area. Figure 14.13 illustrates the projection of the EGI of a cylinder. The principal axis of a set of these points can easily be obtained (see Sect. 3.3). For each viewer direction, the model of the EGI is normalized so that the principal axis may be horizontal. The direction of the principal axis limits the candidate rotation angles around a viewer direction.

A few candidates which have passed the constraints described above are matched to the original EGI. Note that, for each candidate, the correspondence of cells of the EGI has already been established. The matching criterion for the candidate model j is based on the areas $M_{j,i}$ of each visible cell and S_i in the corresponding cell of the observed EGI. The criterion function f can be defined as follows:

$$f_j = \sum_{i \in I_v}^{S_i} (S_i - M_{j,i})^2 \tag{14.5}$$

A model is selected which minimizes the above function.

Although the computation of Eq. (14.5) requires much time, it is actually performed only for a few candidates filtered by two constraints. The matching in the EGI is easy because the position of each surface can be neglected. The method may be used for recognition of a certain class of isolated objects. Note, however, that some objects may not be discriminated if their observed EGIs are the same.

14.3.3 Recognition of Objects Using EGIs as Higher Level Models

This subsection describes a system for recognizing objects from the surface normals. The surface normals can be obtained by various methods as described in Chap. 8. A set of surface normals is regarded as a needle map (see Subsect. 8.1.3). The needle map has more information than the EGI because it contains the 2D position of each surface (in the image plane). It is inefficient directly to match the observed needle

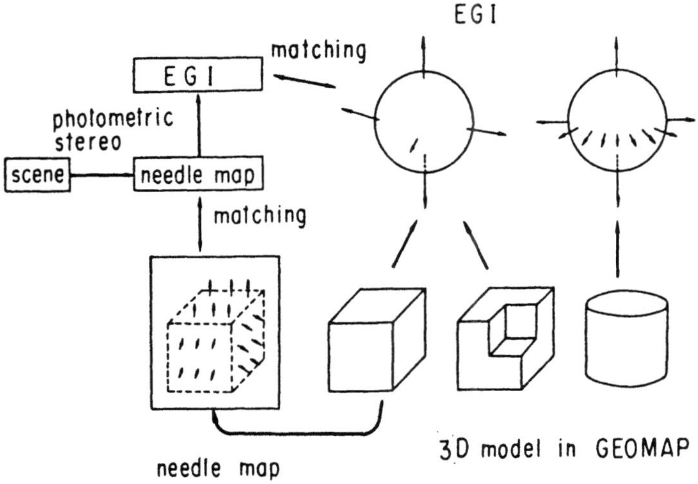

Fig. 14.14. Use of EGI as a higher level model

map to that of models when the viewer direction is not known *a priori*. One better way is a hierarchical matching using the EGI representations as higher level models.

The EGI is easily derived from the needle map. On the other hand, the EGI representation of an object model is also derived from the geometric model represented by GEOMAP. The matching between two EGIs can be executed as described in the previous section. Note that the EGI representation is ambiguous unless objects are convex. Even if a single model is selected by the matching, it may correspond to multiple objects. Figure 14.14 shows an example of multiple correspondences. Typically, a few models may correspond to an EGI representation.

When the best EGI or a few promising EGIs are selected, the corresponding models are examined in the needle map representation. The system synthesizes needle maps of these candidates from the geometric models, then they are matched to the original needle map of the scene. The difference between two needle maps is easily calculated by the following function.

$$g_i = \sum_{i \in I_v} (u_i - v_{i,j})^2 \tag{14.6}$$

where u and v denote the ith surface normal vector of the observed needle map, and that of the jth model, respectively.

Thus efficient object recognition is performed by the hierarchical matching using the EGI representation as a higher level model representation. An experiment has been performed for recognition of polyhedra and a cylinder by this method (Ikeuchi and Shirai, 1982). A few candidates were selected in the first stage, and one correct model was determined in the second stage.

14.4 Recognition of Multiple Objects After Segmentation

Even if multiple objects are included in a scene, recognition of objects from segmented features is just the same as recognition of a single object. Therefore, it is preferred that features be segmented without referring to their context. For example, if only trihedral objects are included in a scene, and the range data are available, then the description of the scene can be segmented into objects as described in Sect. 12.2

Without 3D data, however, the segmentation problem is usually more difficult. 2D images do not contain enough clues for correct segmentation, unless the type of object is strongly constrained. Interpretation of the line drawing described in Sect. 5.3 presents an example which exploits such strong constraints.

If surface normals are available (they are not full 3D data), the problem of segmentation is possible under a certain constraint. Ikeuchi et al. (1983) proposed a smoothness constraint as a clue for segmentation. It is natural to assume that the surface normal changes smoothly over a surface, and that discontinuity of the surface normal implies the existence of an edge there. If every object is bounded by a smooth surface, discontinuity corresponds to the boundary of objects.

Usually, the surface normal is not obtained near occluded regions. For example, a photometric stereo method (see Sect. 8.1) is not able to determine most surface normals near occluded regions because those regions (as shown in Fig. 14.15) are often not illuminated by all light sources. Figure 14.16 shows examples of three images taken with different illumination directions, and Fig. 14.17 shows the needle map derived from them (Ikeuchi et al., 1983).

In this case, the boundary between occluded and occluding objects is easily detected. Segmentation, therefore, becomes much easier. Suppose surface normals are represented by a 2D array whose element (point) at (i,j) stores the surface normal vector in the viewer direction (i,j). Let the surface normal (with unit length) at (i,j) be denoted by $f(i,j)$, and let $f(i,j)$ be 0 if the surface normal is not obtained at (i,j). Then smoothly connected regions are found by a method similar to the labeling method described in Subsect. 4.4.3. In order to find four-connected regions, the first pass in that subsection is slightly modified.

Since the input is not a binary image, a criterion is necessary for deciding if the current point belongs to the same surface as the neighboring point. The decision is

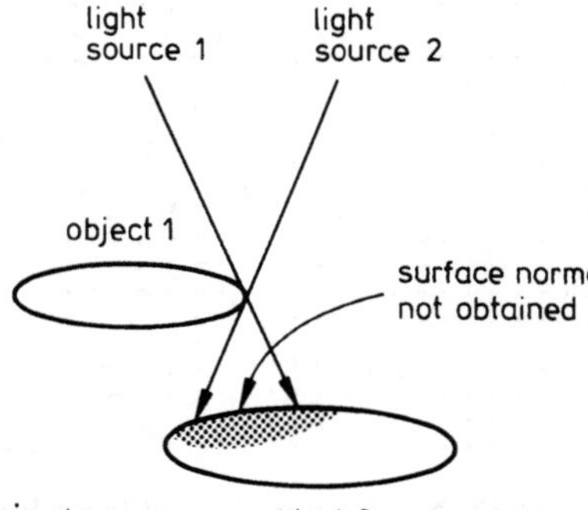

Fig. 14.15. Surface near occluded region in photometric stereo

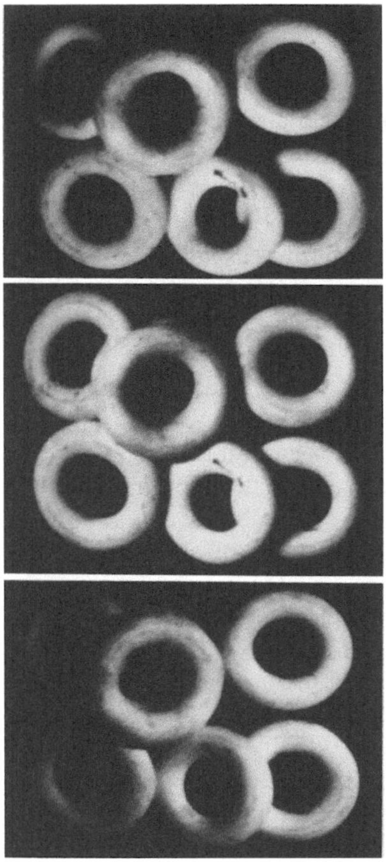

Fig. 14.16. Three input images for a photometric stereo method, taken with different illumination directions (Ikeuchi et al., 1983)

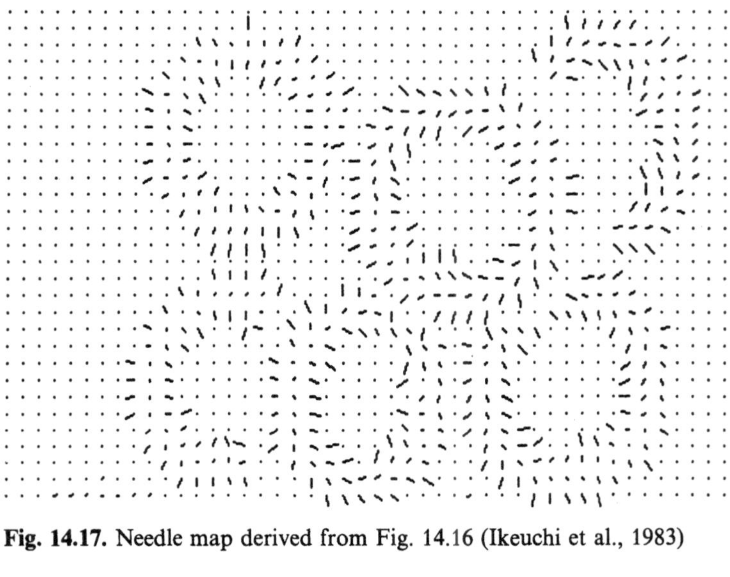

Fig. 14.17. Needle map derived from Fig. 14.16 (Ikeuchi et al., 1983)

based on the surface normals $f(i,j)$ and $f(i',j')$ at the neighbors. We can use the following simple criterion, where d is a threshold:

If $|f(i,j)-f(i',j')|<d$, then the points are in the same surface.
Otherwise, they are in different surfaces.

Let us use the notation $f(i,j)\approx f(i',j')$ to express that the two surfaces satisfy the above condition, and $f(i,j)\not\approx f(i',j')$ otherwise. Note that the threshold, d, is set to be smaller than 1 so that for any non-zero $f(i',j')$, $f(i,j)\not\approx 0$. The labeling procedure is shown as follows:

$k\leftarrow 0$; {k is the number of regions}
for $j=2$ step 1 until $n-1$
for $i=2$ step 1 until $n-1$
  if $f(i,j)=0$, then $g(i,j)\leftarrow 0$; {$g(i,j)$ is an output array}
  else
    if $f(i,j)\not\approx f(i-1,j)$ and $f(i,j)\not\approx f(i,j-1)$,
      then $g(i,j)\leftarrow k$; $k\leftarrow k+1$; {new region found}
    else
      if $f(i,j)\not\approx f(i-1,j)$, then $g(i,j)\leftarrow g(i,j-1)$;
      else if $f(i,j)\not\approx f(i,j-1)$, then $g(i,j)\leftarrow g(i-1,j)$;
        else
          if $g(i-1,j)=g(i,j-1)$, then $g(i,j)\leftarrow g(i,j-1)$;
          else $g(i,j)\leftarrow g(i,j-1)$; {two regions merge here}
            record that $g(i-1,j)$ and $g(i,j-1)$ are in the same class;

After the first pass, as described in Subsect. 4.4.3, the region numbers are updated and labeled again in the second pass. Figure 14.18 shows a binary image representing segmented regions obtained from Fig. 14.17.

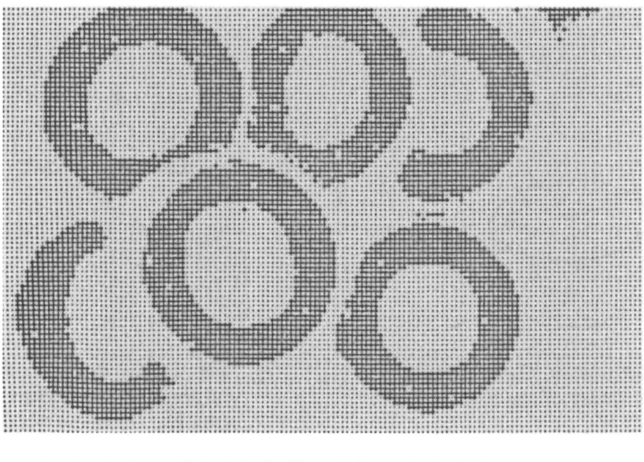

Fig. 14.18. Segmented regions obtained from Fig. 14.17 (Ikeuchi et al., 1983)

Each of the connected regions belongs to a single object. Each connected region is, therefore, matched to object models in the same way as described in Sect. 14.3. It is natural that unoccluded objects can be more reliably recognized than occluded objects. Occluded objects may not be recognized if only a small portion of their surface normals is obtained with a photometric stereo method. For robot vision systems, however, those occluded objects may be recognized after occluding objects are recognized and picked up by a manipulator.

14.5 Recognition Without Segmentation

It is generally difficult to segment features into objects. The discontinuity of surface normals need not correspond to the boundaries of objects. A simple example is a polyhedron where surface normals are not smoothly connected across two adjacent planes.

The problem of segmentation is still difficult even if range data are available. The discontinuity of surfaces does not always correspond to the boundaries of objects. In Fig. 14.19, for example, two surfaces A and B of a cup are observed to be discontinuous.

Moreover, if a scene includes stacked objects, the problem becomes further complicated. Range data are not always discontinuous at boundaries of objects. Figure 14.20 shows a case where segmentation is impossible from range data alone. However, if models of objects are given, segmentation may be possible. In this example, if only models of blocks are given, the scene is interpreted as shown in Fig. 14.20(a). If only a model of an L-shaped prism is given, the interpretation shown in Fig. 14.20(b) is selected. If both models are given, then both interpretations are possible.

In such cases, segmentation is not possible until objects are recognized. It is necessary, therefore, to develop a method for recognizing objects from features before they are segmented. One of the promising methods developed by Oshima and Shirai (1983) is explained in the following subsections.

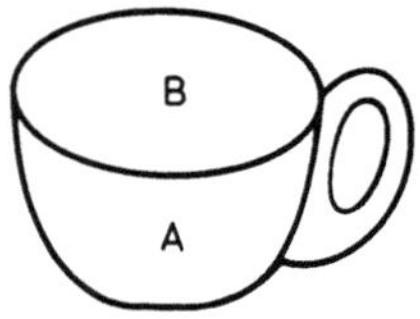

Fig. 14.19. Discontinuous surfaces of the same object

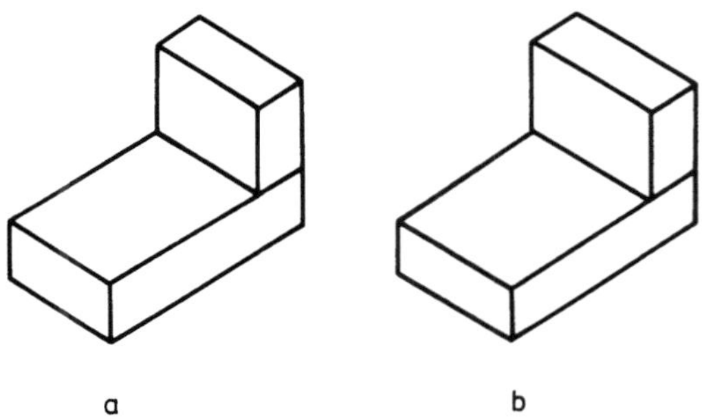

Fig. 14.20a, b. Scene where segmentation is impossible from range data alone: (**a**) two objects; (**b**) one object

14.5.1 Outline of Recognition Process

The system works in two phases: learning and recognition, as shown in Fig. 14.21. In the learning phase, known objects are shown to the system one by one. The description of each object is made by the region method described in Sect. 9.6, and the result is stored as a model of the object. The model thus created is not complete in the sense that the shape of the object can be completely reconstructed from the model. It is, however, invariant to small changes of the viewer direction, because the description includes 3D information. If one view is not enough to describe an object, several typical views are shown and multiple models are generated.

In the recognition phase, the system is shown a scene that includes multiple objects occluding one another. The description of the scene is made in the same way as in the learning phase. The system then tries to find sets of regions corresponding to those of models. Finding such correspondences requires a search. Since a blind search is very time consuming, the following strategy is adopted for efficient matching.

The system first selects from among unknown regions those that seem to be most reliable and useful for recognition. Part of the scene consisting of these regions is called a 'kernel' (see Fig. 14.22).

Models are then selected that include regions corresponding to the kernel (this part is a data-driven process). Once candidate models are chosen, regions neighboring the kernel are sought by a model-driven matching process. Since the search is a model-driven one, the number of trials is expected to be considerably smaller. After an object is found, the rest of the scene regions are processed in the same manner. Further details of description and matching are given in the following subsections.

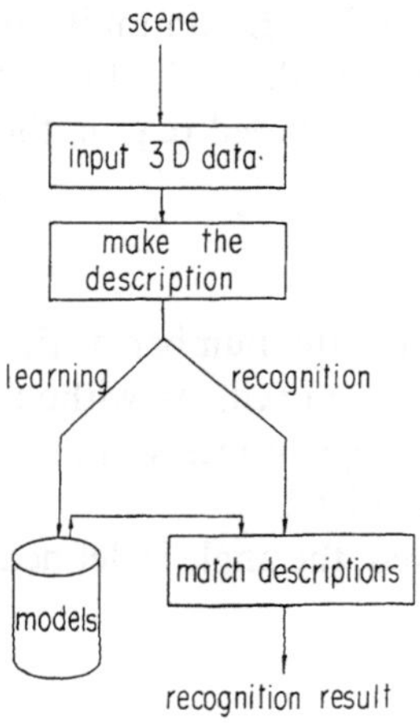

Fig. 14.21. Main control scheme of system for recognizing objects before segmentation

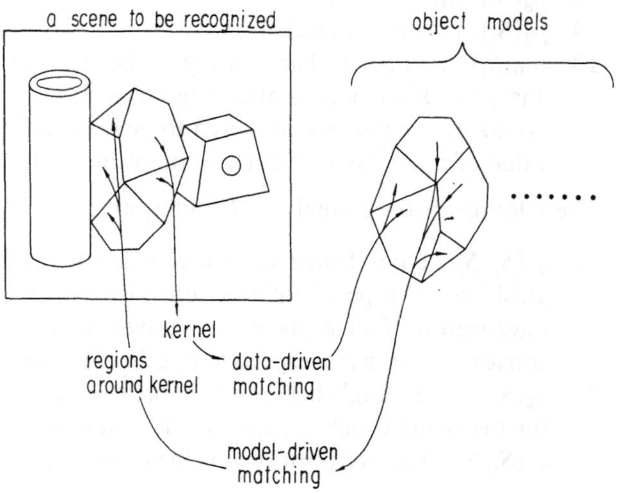

Fig. 14.22. Matching process in recognition phase

14.5.2 Description of Scenes

The description of a scene is first made by the region method in terms of the properties of regions (corresponding to visible surfaces) and the relations between regions as described in Sect. 9.6. In order to recognize objects easily, the system adds some extra properties which are directly derived from the original description.

The properties of each region S_i are as follows:

1. $p_1(S_i)$: surface type fitted to the region S_i. The type is classified as planar, curved or undefined using the mean variance of orientations of surface elements in the region and size of the region. The curved surface is further divided into one of the following: ellipsoid, hyperboloid, cone, paraboloid, cylinder, or other surface. Here $p_1(S_i)$ represents a number for distinguishing type and class so that it can be used in checking the correspondences between regions.
2. $p_2(S_i)$: the number of adjacent regions. Two regions are adjacent if any part of one region is adjacent to another region. Then $p_2(S_i)$ represents the number of regions adjacent to S_i.
3. $p_3(S_i)$: area. A plane equation is fitted to the points in the region, where points are again projected onto the plane. These points constitute a two-dimensional region called the 'silhouette'. Here $p_3(S_i)$ represents the area of the silhouette. The following properties, p_4–p_9, are defined with respect to the silhouette:
4. $p_4(S_i)$: perimeter.
5. $p_5(S_i)$: compactness ($4\pi \times$ area/perimeter^2). Though $p_5(S_i)$ is not independent of p_3 and p_4, it is useful for deciding if the shape is similar to a circle.
6. $p_6(S_i)$: mean radius. The mean distance (radius) from the centroid of the silhouette to each point on its border.
7. $p_7(S_i)$: standard deviation of radii.
8. $p_8(S_i)$: minimum radius.
9. $p_9(S_i)$: maximum radius.
10. $p_{10}(S_i)$: occlusion. The vicinity of border points with 3D discontinuity is analyzed. If there is another region in front of the region along the border points, the region is considered to be occluded. For the occluded region, the value of $p_{10}(S_i)$ is 1; otherwise the value is 0.

The relations between regions S_i and S_j are:

1. $q_1(S_i, S_j)$: type of intersection. Here $q_1(S_i, S_j)$ represents the number distinguishing the type of intersection, i.e., convex, concave, mixed, or without intersection. If all segments are convex or concave, the type of intersection is convex or concave, respectively; otherwise the type is mixed.
2. $q_2(S_i, S_j)$: the angle between regions. If a region is curved, the angle is defined for the plane which is fitted to the points in the region.
3. $q_3(S_i, S_j)$: relative positions of the centroids.

14.5.3 Kernel Selection

A kernel usually consists of two regions, called the ‘principal part’ and the ‘subordinate part’. The system selects the principal part first, and then selects the subordinate part if possible.

14.5.3.1 Selecting the Principal Part of a Kernel

The candidates for the principal part are those regions which have not yet been interpreted as a part of an object and are not occluded by other regions. The principal part of a kernel is selected on the basis of the type of region, its area, and the number of adjacent regions. The observed relative directions of planar surfaces are less sensitive than those of curved surfaces to rotation or partial occlusion. Thus, planar regions are given priority over curved regions.

Candidates with a larger area are also more useful because the properties of larger regions are less sensitive to noise. Regions having many neighbors are also more useful because many relations can be used in matching.

The following function, f_1, is calculated for each candidate, S_j. The region S_k which maximizes the function is selected as the principal part of a kernel:

$$f_1(S_j) = \lambda_1 h(p_1(S_j)) + \lambda_2 p_2(S_j) + \lambda_3 p_3(S_j) \tag{14.7}$$

where

$$h(p_1(S_j)) = \begin{cases} 1 & \text{if } S_j \text{ is curved} \\ 2 & \text{if } S_j \text{ is planar} \end{cases}$$

Here p_1, p_2, p_3 are the region type, number of adjacent regions, and area of the region respectively. In the experiments, the weights λ_1, λ_2, λ_3 are set so that the influence of p_1, p_2, p_3 on f_1 decreases in the order p_1, p_2, p_3. If no candidate exists for the principal part, the matching procedure terminates.

14.5.3.2 Selecting the Subordinate Part of a Kernel

The candidates for the subordinate part are those regions which are adjacent to the principal part and which also satisfy the conditions of a candidate for the principal part. The candidate which maximizes f_1 is selected as the subordinate part. A kernel consists of the principal part and the subordinate part, if there is a candidate for the subordinate part. Otherwise, a kernel consists of the principal part alone.

14.5.4 Model Selection

The system selects probable models which include regions corresponding to the kernel. There are two cases depending on whether the kernel consists of the principal part alone or the principal and the subordinate parts.

14.5.4.1 Kernel Consisting of Only the Principal Part

In this case, those models are selected which have a region corresponding to the principal part. The selection is based on the 'selection' function, which evaluates the dissimilarity in properties between the kernel and the model region. Let $M_{i,r}$ denote the rth region of the ith model. The function compares the properties of S_k and $M_{i,r}$. Let p_j denote the jth property of the region, and let D_j denote an operator which evaluates the difference between the jth property values. Here D_j is defined as follows:

For $j=1$

$$D_j(p_j(S_k),\, p_j(M_{i,r}))=\begin{cases}0 & S_k \text{ and } M_{i,r} \text{ are the same type}\\ 1 & S_k \text{ and } M_{i,r} \text{ are not the same type}\end{cases} \tag{14.8}$$

For $j=5$ or 7

$$D_j(p_j(S_k),\, p_j(M_{i,r}))=p_j(S_k)-p_j(M_{i,r}) \tag{14.9}$$

For other values of j

$$D_j(p_j(S_k),\, p_j(M_{i,r}))=|p_j(S_k)-p_j(M_{i,r})|/p_j(M_{i,r}) \tag{14.10}$$

The selection function is then defined as follows:

$$f_2(S_k, M_{i,r})=\sum_{j=1}^{9} \mu_j D_j(p_j(S_k),\, p_j(M_{i,r})) \tag{14.11}$$

A value of 1 is set on the weights μ_j in the experiment.

Here, f_2 is of small value (ideally zero) if the kernel coincides with the region in the model. The system selects models whose f_2 value is small, and assumes the correspondences. If there is no model whose f_2 value is small, the system decides that the principal part does not coincide with any model region and backs up to make another kernel selection.

14.5.4.2 Kernel Consisting of the Principal Part and the Subordinate Part

In this case, those models are selected which have a pair of regions corresponding to the kernel. The selection is also based on the selection function, which evaluates the dissimilarity in relations, as well as in properties, between the kernel and the model regions. Let $M_{i,r}$ and $M_{i,r'}$ denote the candidate regions in the model which correspond to the principal part S_k and subordinate part $S_{k'}$ respectively (see Fig. 14.23). The selection function compares the properties of S_k to $M_{i,r}$, and compares those of $S_{k'}$ to $M_{i,r'}$. The function also compares the relations between S_k and $S_{k'}$ to those between $M_{i,r}$ and $M_{i,r'}$. The selection function is defined as follows:

$$f_2'(S_k, S_{k'}, M_{i,r}, M_{i,r'})=f_2(S_k, M_{i,r})+f_2(S_{k'}, M_{i,r'}) + \sum_{m=1}^{3} v_m D_m(q_m(S_k, S_{k'}),\, q_m(M_{i,r}, M_{i,r'})) \tag{14.12}$$

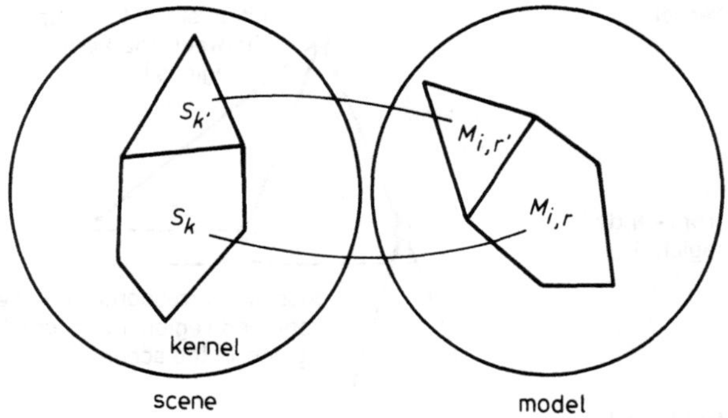

Fig. 14.23. Comparison between the kernel and model regions

where q_1, q_2, q_3 denote the type of the intersection, the angle between regions, and the relative positions of the centroids of the regions respectively. The weights v_m are set so that the influence of q_1, q_2, q_3 on f_2' decreases in the order q_1, q_2, q_3. Note that f_2' is insensitive to the translation or rotation of objects. The system selects models whose f_2' values are small, and assumes the correspondences.

The value of f_2' is not small if the subordinate part does not correspond to the entire model region, or does not correspond to the model. If there is no model whose f_2' value is small, the system decides that the subordinate part is inadequate and backs up to select another subordinate part.

If a single model is selected, the system initiates a further matching process (matching between regions), which is described in the following subsection. Here, the kernel is called the 'kernel with a single model'. If multiple models are selected, the system suspends further matching processes for that kernel until the matching processes for all other kernels with a single model are finished.

14.5.5 Matching Between Regions

The system searches the scene around the kernel for the regions corresponding to those in the model. A depth-first search process is used here. Starting from the model regions corresponding to the kernel, the matching process proceeds region by region. The search tree is illustrated in Fig. 14.24, where each node represents the correspondence between a scene region and a model region. At each step, the system selects a new region called the 'front-end region' among those which are adjacent to known regions in the model (that is, the regions which have been selected and matched in the earlier steps). Here function f_1 defined by Eq. (14.7) is used for the selection. If there is no candidate for a front-end region, the matching process terminates.

Whenever a front-end region is selected from the model regions, the system searches the scene for the corresponding region called the 'matched region'. The candidates for the matched regions are those regions adjacent to known regions in the scene. The search is based on the 'dissimilarity' function for relations as well as properties between the front-end region and the candidate region.

In Fig. 14.25, suppose $M_{i,u}$ and S_n are the front-end region and a candidate for a matched region, respectively. Here p_j and q_m are a property and a relation

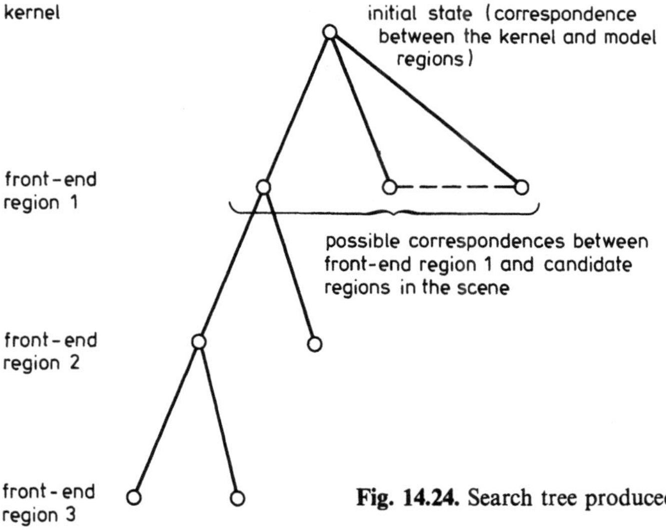

Fig. 14.24. Search tree produced by the matching process

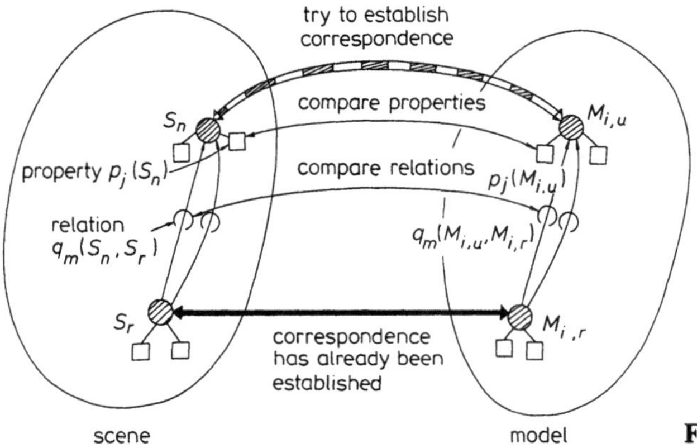

Fig. 14.25. Comparison schema

respectively. Suppose $M_{i,r}$ and S_r represent a known pair of regions. The dissimilarity function compares the properties of the front-end region $p_j(M_{i,u})$ to those of the candidate in the scene $p_j(S_n)$. The function also compares the relations $q_m(M_{i,u}, M_{i,r})$ between the front-end region and the known regions $M_{i,r}$ of the same model to those $q_m(S_n, S_r)$ of the corresponding regions in the scene. Let K denote a set of already known regions. The dissimilarity function is defined as follows:

$$\begin{aligned} f_3(S_n, M_{i,u}) = & \sum_{j=1}^{9} \varrho_j D_j(p_j(S_n), p_j(M_{i,u})) \\ & + \sum_{m=1}^{3} \tau_m \sum_{r \in K} p_3(M_{i,r}) D_m(q_m(S_n, S_r), q_m(M_{i,u}, M_{i,r})) / \sum_{r \in K} p_3(M_{i,r}) \end{aligned} \tag{14.13}$$

where weights ϱ_j and τ_m are set in the same manner as in Eqs. (14.11) and (14.12). The areas p_3 are used as weights so that more reliable regions contribute to a greater extent to f_3. Note that f_3 is insensitive to the translation or rotation of objects.

If the value of f_3 is small (ideally zero) and all terms in Eq. (14.13) are less than thresholds, the match between regions is determined as acceptable. In this case, the system tries again to find another front-end region. If there are multiple matched regions for a front-end region, one of them is selected first and the matching process proceeds. When the subsequent matching process terminates, other matched regions are initiated in the same manner.

Here, f_3 is not small if an object surface is not seen entirely, or the region does not correspond to the assumed model. An attempt is made to match a partially occluded plane to the model region. If no matched region is found and the type of the front-end region is planar, the system tries to find a planar region among the candidates which satisfies the following conditions:

1. The region is occluded.
2. The dissimilarity of the relative direction between the region and the front-end region is small.
3. The 3D position correspondence (q_1, q_2, q_3) is adequate.
4. The area of the region is less than that of the front-end region.

If such a region exists, it is decided that the region corresponds to a portion of the front-end region.

When the process for a kernel terminates, the candidate body is considered to be acceptable if only one candidate model is found. If there are multiple candidates, the system does not accept them until the matching procedure for the whole scene terminates.

14.5.6 Scene Interpretation

When the matching procedure terminates, multiple candidates are examined to filter out the interpretations. Suppose that, for a kernel S_k and a model M_i, a set of

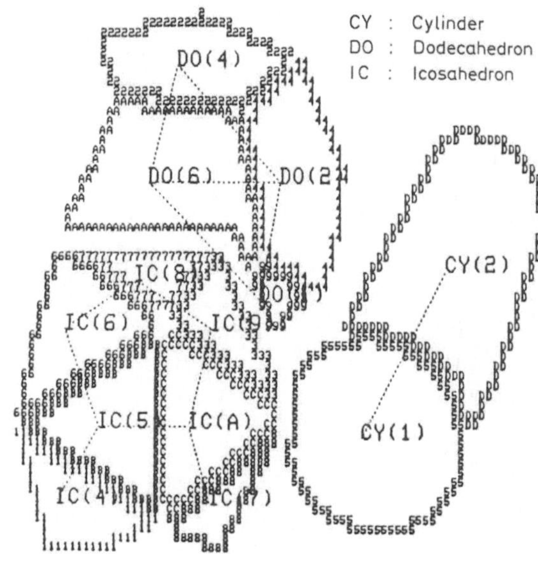

Fig. 14.26. Recognition result for the description shown in Fig. 9.24

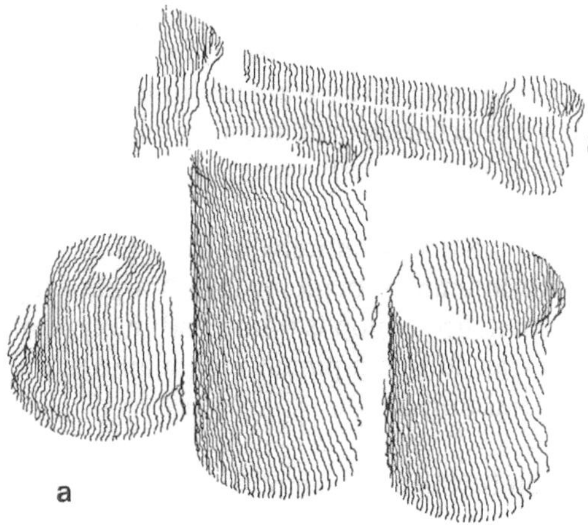

a

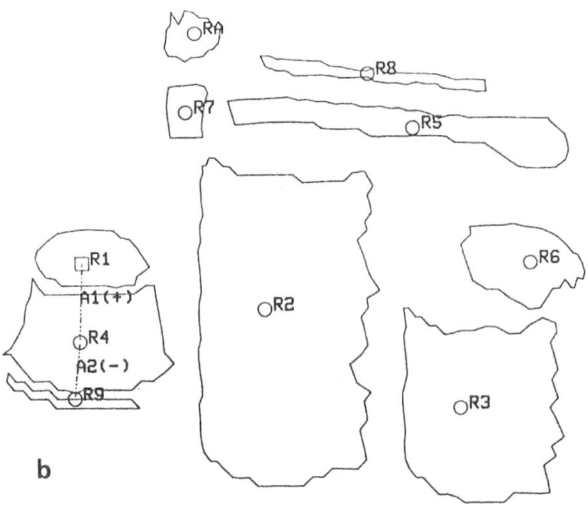

b

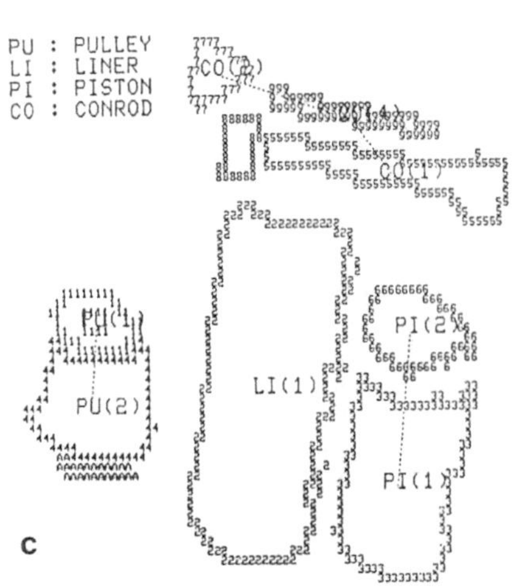

c

Fig. 14.27a–c. Experimental result for a scene containing machine parts: (**a**) stripe image of a scene; (**b**) description; (**c**) recognition result matched regions is obtained. The set of regions is called the 'candidate body' of the model M_i with respect to the kernel S_k, and is denoted by $B(S_k, M_i)$. The candidate body $B(S_k, M_i)$ with respect to a kernel S_k and $B(S_{k'}, M_{i'})$ with respect to another kernel $S_{k'}$ are 'inconsistent' if they have a common element (note that $S_{k'}$ is not included in $B(S_k, M_i)$. Otherwise, they are 'consistent'. For each kernel, S_k, the candidate body $B(S_k, M_i)$ is rejected if it is included in another candidate body, $B(S_k, M_{j'})$ with respect to the same kernel, which is consistent with the other candidate bodies. Among the rest of the candidate bodies, all consistent combinations are adopted. Each combination gives an interpretation of the scene. The positions and orientations of the objects are easily calculated from the correspondences of the regions.

Two kinds of experiment are shown here. In the first experiment, ten kinds of objects with planar and/or quadratic curved surfaces were used. First, about twenty models were built by showing each of them to the system. One of the recognition results is shown in Fig. 14.26 (obtained from the description shown in Fig. 9.24). The first two letters in a region indicate the model, and the character in parentheses indicates the corresponding region in the model.

In the second experiment, machine parts (a pulley, liner, piston, and connecting rod of a car) were built into models. A example of the input image is shown in Fig. 14.27(a). The description of the scene and the final result are shown in Fig. 14.27(b) and (c), respectively.

References

Agin, G.J., Binford, T.O. (1973): Computer Description of Curved Objects. Proc. 3rd IJCAI, Stanford, pp. 629–640

Agin, G.J., Binford, T.O. (1976): Computer Description of Curved Objects. IEEE Trans. *C-25*, No. 4, pp. 439–449

Barnea, D.I., Silverman, H.F. (1972): A Class of Algorithms for Fast Digital Image Registration. IEEE Trans. *C-21*, No. 2, pp. 179–186

Barrow, H.G., Popplestone, R.J. (1971): Relational Description in Picture Processing. Machine Intelligence Vol. 6, pp. 377–396. Meltzer, B., Michie, D. (eds.). Edinburgh University Press, Edinburgh

Barrow, H.G., Tenenbaum, J.M. (1978): Recovering Intrinsic Scene Characteristics from Images, Computer Vision System, pp. 3–26. Hanson, A.R., Riseman, E.M. (eds.). Academic Press, New York

Barrow, H.G., Tenenbaum, J.M., Bolles, R.C., Wolf, H.C. (1977): Parametric Correspondence and Chamfer Matching: Two New Techniques for Image Matching. Proc. 5th IJCAI, Cambridge, pp. 659–663

Binford, T.O. (1971): Visual Perception by a Computer. Proc. IEEE Conf. on Systems and Controls

Bobrow, D.G., Winograd, T. (1977): Experience with KRL-O: One Cycle of a Knowledge Representation Language. Proc. 5th IJCAI, Cambridge, pp. 213–222

Bolles, R.C. (1977): Verification Vision for Programmable Assembly. Proc. 5th IJCAI, Cambridge, pp. 569–575

Brice, C.B., Fennema, C.L. (1970): Scene Analysis Using Regions. Artificial Intelligence *1*, No. 3, pp. 205–226

Brooks, R.A. (1979): Goal-directed Edge Linking and Ribbon Finding. Proc. Image Understanding Workshop, pp. 72–78. Science Application Inc.

Brooks, R.A. (1981a): Symbolic Reasoning Among 3-D Models and 2-D Images. Artificial Intelligence *17*, Nos. 1–3, pp. 285–348

Brooks, R.A. (1981b): Model-based Three-dimensional Interpretations of Two-dimensional Images. Proc. 7th IJCAI, Vancouver, pp. 136–143

Brooks, R.A., Greiner, R., Binford, T.O. (1979): The ACRONYM Model-based Vision System. Proc. 6th IJCAI, Tokyo, pp. 105–113

Charniak, E. (1972): Toward a Model of Children's Story Comprehension, TR-266. AI Laboratory, MIT

Clarke, D. et al. (1971): Polarized Light and Optical Measurement. Pergamon Press, Oxford

Clowes, M.B. (1971): On Seeing Things. Artificial Intelligence *2*, No. 1, pp. 79–116

Cohen, P.R., Feigenbaum, E.A. (eds.) (1982): The Handbook of Artificial Intelligence Vol. 3. Pitman, London

Coleman, E.N., Jr., Jain, R. (1981): Shape From Shading for Surfaces with Texture and Specularity. Proc. 7th IJCAI, Vancouver, Vol. 2, pp. 652–657

DeBoor, C. (1978): A Practical Guide to Splines. Springer, Berlin, Heidelberg, New York

Duda, R.O., Hart, P.E. (1972): Use of Hough Transformation to Detect Lines and Curves in Pictures. Comm. ACM *15*, No. 1, pp. 11–15

ACM	Association for Computing Machinery
IEEE	Institute for Electrical and Electronics Engineers
IJCAI	International Joint Conference on Artificial Intelligence
IJCPR	International Joint Conference on Pattern Recognition

Duda, R.O., Hart, P.E. (1973): Pattern Classification and Scene Analysis. Wiley, New York
Ejiri, M. et al. (1972): A Prototype Intelligent Robot That Assembles Objects from Plan Drawings. IEEE Trans. *C-21*, No. 2, pp. 161–170
ETL (1970): Special Edition: ETL-ROBOT Mk 1. Bull. Electrotechnical Laboratory
Falk, G. (1972): Interpretation of Imperfect Line Data as Three-dimensional Scene. Artificial Intelligence *3*, No. 2, pp. 101–144
Feldman, J.A. et al. (1969): The Stanford Hand-Eye Project. Proc. 1st IJCAI, pp. 521–526a
Fischler, M.A., Elschlager, R.A. (1973): The Representation and Matching of Pictorial Structures. IEEE Trans. *C-22*, No. 1, pp. 67–92
Forsen, G.E. (1968): Processing Visual Data with an Automaton Eye. Pictorial Pattern Recognition, pp. 471–502. Chen, C.G., Ledley, S.R., Pollock, K.D., Rosenfeld, A. (eds.). Thompson, Washington D.C.
Griffith, A.K. (1973): Edge Detection in Simple Scenes Using *a priori* Information. IEEE Trans. *C-22*, No. 4, pp. 371–381
Grimson, W.E.L. (1981): From Images to Surfaces. A Computational Study of the Human Early Visual System. MIT Press, Cambridge, MA
Grimson, W.E.L., Marr, D. (1979): A Computer Implementation of a Theory of Human Stereo Vision. Proc. ARPA Image Understanding Workshop, pp. 41–45. Baumann, L.S. (ed.)
Guzman, A. (1968): Decomposition of a Visual Scene into Three-dimensional Bodies. AFIPS (American Federation of Information Processing Societies) Proc. Fall Joint Computer Conf., Vol. 33, pp. 291–304
Hanson, A.R., Riseman, E.M. (1978): Segmentation of Natural Scenes, Computer Vision Systems, pp. 129–163. Hanson, A.R., Riseman, E.M. (eds.). Academic Press, New York
Hewitt, C. (1972): Description and Theoretical Analysis (Using Schemata) of PLANNER: Language for Proving Theorems and Manipulating Models in a Robot, TR-258. AI Laboratory, MIT
Horn, B.K.P. (1975): Obtaining Shapes from Shading Information. The Psychology of Computer Vision. Winston, P.H. (ed.). McGraw-Hill, New York
Horn, B.K.P. (1977): Understanding Image Intensities. Artificial Intelligence *8*, No. 2, pp. 201–231
Horn, B.K.P., Backman, B.L. (1978): Using Synthetic Images to Register Real Images with Surface Models. Comm. ACM *21*, No. 11, pp. 914–924
Hueckel, A.H. (1971): An Operator Which Locates Edges in Digitized Pictures. J. ACM *18*, No. 1, pp. 113–125
Huffman, D.A. (1971): Impossible Objects as Nonsense Sentences. Machine Intelligence Vol. 6, pp. 295–323. Meltzer, B., Michie, D. (eds.). Edinburgh University Press, Edinburgh
Idesawa, M., Yatagai, T. (1980): 3-D Shape Input and Processing by Moire Technique. Proc. 5th IJCPR, Miami, pp. 1085–1090
Idesawa, M., Yatagai, T., Soma, T. (1976): A Method of Three-dimensional Shape by New Type of Moire Topography. Proc. 3rd IJCPR, Cornado, CA, pp. 708–712
Ikeuchi, K. (1981a): Determining Surface Orientations of Specular Surfaces by Using the Photometric Stereo. IEEE Trans. *PAMI-2*, No. 6, pp. 661–669
Ikeuchi, K. (1981b): Recognition of 3-D Objects Using the Extended Gaussian Image. Proc. 7th IJCAI, Vancouver, pp. 595–600
Ikeuchi, K. (1984): Shape from Regular Patterns. Artificial Intelligence *22*, No. 1, pp. 49–75
Ikeuchi, K., Horn, B.K.P. (1981): Numerical Shape from Shading and Occluding Boundaries. Artificial Intelligence *17*, Nos. 1–3, pp. 141–184
Ikeuchi, K., Shirai, Y. (1982): A Model-based Vision System for Recognition of Machine Parts. Proc. 2nd Annual National Conf. on Artificial Intelligence, Pittsburgh, pp. 18–21
Ikeuchi, K. et al. (1983): Picking Up an Object from a Pile of Objects. Robotics Research: First International Symposium, pp. 139–162. Brady, M., Paul, R. (eds.). MIT Press, Cambridge, MA
Ishii, M., Nagata, T. (1976): Feature Extraction of Three-dimensional Objects and Visual Processing in a Hand–Eye System Using Laser Tracker. Pattern Recognition *8*, No. 4, pp. 229–237
Kamejima, K. et al. (1984): Visual Guidance of a Mobile Robot. Proc. 2nd Conf. of Japan Robotics Society, pp. 225–226 (in Japanese)

Kanade, T. (1980): A Theory of Origami World. Artificial Intelligence *13*, No. 3, pp. 279–311

Kanade, T. (1981): Recovery of the Three-dimensional Shape of an Object from a Single View. Artificial Intelligence *17*, Nos. 1–3, pp. 409–460

Kashioka, S. et al. (1976): A Transistor Wire-bonding System Utilizing Multiple Local Pattern Matching Techniques. IEEE Trans. *SMC-6*, No. 8, pp. 562–570

Kender, J.R. (1979): Shape from Texture. Proc. 6th IJCAI, Toyko, pp. 475–480

Kimura, F., Hosaka, M. (1978): Program Package GEOMAP. Proc. Geometric Model Project Meeting, Saint Louis. CAM-I, Inc.

Koshikawa, K. (1979): A Polarimetric Approach to Shape Understanding of Glossy Objects. Proc. 6th IJCAI, Tokyo, pp. 493–495

Koshikawa, K. (1982): A Method of Finding Surface Orientation by Polarization Analysis of Reflected Light. Trans. SICE *18*, No. 10, pp. 77–79 (in Japanese)

Koshikawa, K., Shirai, Y. (1985): A Model-based Recognition of Glossy Objects Using Their Polarizational Properties. Journal of the Robotics Society of Japan *3*, No. 1, pp. 4–9 (in Japanese)

Kyura, N., Shirai, Y. (1973): Recognition of Three-dimensional Objects Using Region Method. Bull. Electrotechnical Laboratory *37*, No. 11, pp. 996–1012 (in Japanese with English abstract)

Lesser, V.R., Erman, L.D. (1977): A Retrospective View of HEARSAY-II Architecture. Proc. 5th IJCAI, Cambridge, pp. 790–800

Mackworth, A.K. (1973): Interpreting Pictures of Polyhedral Scenes. Artificial Intelligence *4*, No. 2, pp. 121–137

Marr, D. (1982): Vision. Freeman

Marr, D., Hildreth, E. (1980): Theory of Edge Detection. Proc. Roy. Soc. (London) *B 207*, pp. 187–217

Marr, D., Poggio, T. (1979): A Computational Theory of Human Stereo Vision. Proc. Roy. Soc. (London) *B 204*, pp. 301–328

Meadows, D.M., Johnson, W.O., Allen, J.B. (1970): Generation of Surface Contours by Moire Patterns. Applied Optics *9*, No. 4, pp. 942–947

Minsky, M. (1975): A Framework for Representing Knowledge, The Psychology of Computer Vision. Winston, P.H. (ed.). McGraw-Hill, New York

Minsky, M., Papert, S. (1970): 1968–1969 Progress Report, Report AIM-200. AI Laboratory, MIT

Nagao, M., Matsuyama, T., Ikeda, K. (1979): Structural Analysis of Complex Aerial Photographs. Proc. 6th IJCAI, Tokyo, pp. 610–616

Nathan, R. (1968): Picture Enhancement for the Moon, Mars and Man. Pictorial Pattern Recognition, pp. 239–266. Cheng, G.C. et al. (eds.). Thompson

Nevatia, R., Babu, K.R. (1979): Linear Feature Extraction and Description. Proc. 6th IJCAI, Tokyo, pp. 639–641

Newell, A., Simon, H.A. (1972): Human Problem Solving. Prentice-Hall, Englewood Cliffs, NJ

Nilsson, N.J. (1969): A Mobile Automaton: An Application of Artificial Intelligence Techniques. Proc. 1st IJCAI, pp. 509–520

Nitzan, D., Brain, A.E., Duda, R.O. (1977): The Measurement and Use of Registered Reflectance and Range Data in Scene Analysis. Proc. IEEE *65*, pp. 206–220

O'Gorman, F., Clowes, M.B. (1973): Finding Edges through Colinearity of Feature Points. 3rd IJCAI, Stanford, pp. 543–555

Ohlander, R.B. (1975): Analysis of Natural Scenes. Ph.D. Thesis, Computer Science Department, Carnegie-Mellon University

Ohta, Y., Maenobu, K., Sakai, T. (1981): Obtaining Surface Orientation from Texels Under Perspective Projection. Proc. 7th IJCAI, Vancouver, pp. 746–751

Oshima, M., Shirai, Y. (1979): A Scene Description Method Using Three-dimensional Information. Pattern Recognition *11*, No. 1, pp. 9–17

Oshima, M., Shirai, Y. (1983): Object Recognition Using Three-dimensional Information. IEEE Trans. *PAMI-5*, No. 4, pp. 353–361

Oshima, M., Takano, Y. (1973): Special Hardware for the Recognition System of Three-dimensional Objects. Bull. Electrotechnical Laboratory *37*, pp. 493–501 (in Japanese with English abstract)

Otsu, N. (1978): Discriminant and Least Square Threshold Selection. Proc. 4th IJCPR, Tokyo, pp. 592–596

Pavlidis, T., Horowitz, S.L. (1974): Segmentation of Plane Curves. IEEE Trans. *C-23*, No. 8, pp. 860–870

Powell, M.J.D. (1970): Curve Fitting by Splines in One Variable, Numerical Approximation to Functions and Data. Hayes, J.G. (ed.). Athlone Press

Requicha, A.A.G., Voelcker, H.B. (1982): Solid Modeling: A Historical Summary and Contemporary Assessment. Computer Graphics and Application *2*, No. 2, pp. 9–24

Roberts, L.G. (1963): Machine Perception of Three-dimensional Solids, Optical and Electro-Optical Information Processing, pp. 159–197. Tippet, J.T. et al. (eds.). MIT Press, Cambridge, MA

Roberts, R.B., Goldstein, I.P. (1977): The FRL Primer, Report AIM-408. AI Laboratory, MIT

Rosenfeld, A., Hummel, R.A., Zucker, S.W. (1976): Scene Labeling by Relaxation Operations. IEEE Trans. *SMC-6*, No. 6, pp. 420–432

Rosenfeld, A., Kak, A.C. (1976): Digital Picture Processing. Academic Press, New York

Rosenfeld, A., Vanderburg, G.J. (1977): Coarse-Fine Template Matching. IEEE Trans. *SMC-7*, No. 2, pp. 104–107

Shirai, Y. (1972): Recognition of Polyhedra with a Range Finder. Pattern Recognition *4*, No. 3, pp. 243–250

Shirai, Y. (1973a): A Context Sensitive Line Finder for Recognition of Polyhedra. Artificial Intelligence *4*, No. 2, pp. 95–119

Shirai, Y. (1973b): A Step Toward Context-Sensitive Recognition of Irregular Objects. Computer Graphics and Image Processing *2*, pp. 298–307

Shirai, Y. (1975a): Analysing Intensity Arrays Using Knowledge About Scenes. The Psychology of Computer Vision. Winston, P.H. (ed.). McGraw-Hill, New York

Shirai, Y. (1975b): Edge Finding, Segmentation of Edge and Recognition of Complex Objects. Proc. 4th IJCAI

Shirai, Y. (1978): Recognition of Real-world Objects Using Edge Cues, Computer Vision Systems, pp. 353–362. Hanson, A.R., Riseman, E.M. (eds.). Academic Press, New York

Shirai, Y., Inoue, H. (1973): Guiding a Robot by Visual Feedback in Assembling Tasks. Pattern Recognition *5*, No. 2, pp. 99–108

Shirai, Y., Suwa, M. (1971): Recognition of Polyhedrons with a Range Finder. Proc. 2nd IJCAI, London, pp. 80–87

Stefik, M. (1979): An Examination of a Frame-Structured Representation System. Proc. 6th IJCAI, Tokyo, pp. 845–852

Sugihara, K. (1979): Range-Data Analysis Guided by a Junction Dictionary. Artificial Intelligence *12*, No. 1, pp. 41–69

Sugihara, K. (1982): Mathematical Structures of Line Drawings of Polyhedrons; Toward Man-Machine Communication by Means of Line Drawings. IEEE Trans. *PAMI-4*, No. 5, pp. 458–469

Sussman, G.J., McDemott, D.V. (1972): From PLANNER to CONNIVER. Proc. FJCC, pp. 1171–1180

Takasaki, H. (1970): Moire Topography. Applied Optics *9*, No. 6, pp. 1467–1472

Tenenbaum, J.M., Barrow, H.G. (1977): Experiments in Interpretation-guided Segmentation. Artificial Intelligence *8*, No. 3, pp. 241–274

Tomita, F., Shirai, Y., Tsuji, S. (1982): Description of Textures by Structural Analysis. IEEE Trans. *PAMI-4*, No. 2, pp. 183–191

Tomita, F., Yachida, M., Tsuji, S. (1973): Detection of Homogeneous Regions by Structural Analysis. Proc. 3rd IJCAI, Stanford, pp. 572–577

Tsugawa, S., Yatabe, T., Hirose, T., Matsumoto, S. (1979): An Automobile with Artificial Intelligence. Proc. 6th IJCAI, Tokyo, pp. 893–895

Turner, K.J. (1974): Computer Perception of Curved Objects Using a Television Camera. Ph.D. Thesis, School of Artificial Intelligence, Edinburgh University

Waltz, D.L. (1975): Understanding Line Drawings of Scenes with Shadows. The Psychology of Computer Vision, pp. 19–91. Winston, P.H. (ed.). McGraw-Hill, New York

Winograd, T.A. (1975): Frame Representation and the Declarative/Procedural Controversy, Representation and Understanding: Studies in Cognitive Science, pp. 185–210. Bobrow, D.G., Collins, A. (eds.). Academic Press, New York

Winston, P.H. (1972): The MIT Robot. Machine Intelligence Vol. 7, pp. 431–463. Meltzer, B., Michie, D. (eds.). Edinburgh University Press, Edinburgh
Woodham, R.J. (1978): Photometric Stereo: A Reflectance Map Technique for Determining Surface Orientation from Image Intensity. Proc. SPIE (Society of Photo-optical Instrumentation Engineers) 22nd Technical Symposium, Vol. 155, San Diego, pp. 136–143
Yakimovsky, Y., Feldman, J.A. (1973): A Semantics-based Decision Theory Region Analyser. Proc. 3rd IJCAI, Stanford, pp. 580–588
Yasue, T., Shirai, Y. (1973): Binocular Stereoscopic Vision for Object Recognition. Bull. Electrotechnical Laboratory *37*, No. 13, pp. 1101–1119 (in Japanese with English abstract)
Zucker, S.W., Hummel, R.A., Rosenfeld, A. (1977): An Application of Relaxation Labeling to Line and Curve Enhancement. IEEE Trans. *C-26*, No. 4, pp. 394–403

MIX
Papier aus verantwortungsvollen Quellen
Paper from responsible sources
FSC® C105338

If you have any concerns about our products,
you can contact us on
ProductSafety@springernature.com

In case Publisher is established outside the EU,
the EU authorized representative is:
Springer Nature Customer Service Center GmbH
Europaplatz 3, 69115 Heidelberg, Germany

Printed by Libri Plureos GmbH
in Hamburg, Germany